CONSPIRING WITH THE ENEMY

# Conspiring with the Enemy

THE ETHIC OF COOPERATION
IN WARFARE

Yvonne Chiu

Columbia University Press
*New York*

Columbia University Press
*Publishers Since 1893*
New York   Chichester, West Sussex
cup.columbia.edu
Copyright © 2019 Columbia University Press
All rights reserved

Library of Congress Cataloging-in-Publication Data
Names: Chiu, Yvonne, (Political scientist), author.
Title: Conspiring with the enemy : the ethic of cooperation in warfare / Yvonne Chiu.
Other titles: Ethic of cooperation in warfare
Description: New York : Columbia University Press, [2019] |
Includes bibliographical references and index.
Identifiers: LCCN 2018060759| ISBN 9780231182447 (cloth : alk. paper) |
ISBN 9780231182454 (pbk. : alk. paper) | ISBN 9780231544177 (ebook)
Subjects: LCSH: War—Moral and ethical aspects. | Military ethics—History. |
War (International law)—Case studies. | Conflict management—International cooperation. |
Violence—Prevention—International cooperation. | Cooperation—History. | Enemies.
Classification: LCC U22 .C5248 2019 | DDC 172/.42—dc23
LC record available at https://lccn.loc.gov/2018060759

Columbia University Press books are printed on permanent
and durable acid-free paper.
Printed in the United States of America

Cover design: Milenda Nan Ok Lee

Cover art: Wyndham Lewis, *Timon of Athens—The Thebaid, 1912,* private
collection copyright © Christie's Images/Bridgeman Images

# Contents

Preface  vii
Acknowledgments  xv

I   The Horrors of War and the Nature of Cooperation  1

II  Cooperation for a Fair Fight  36

III Cooperation to Minimize Damage to Particular Classes of People  90

IV  Cooperation to End War Quickly  135

V   The Limits of Ethics of Cooperation in Warfare  161

VI  Cooperative Ethics, Just War Theory, and the Structure of Modern Warfare  193

VII Abdication of Judgment, Noncooperative Fights, and the Meaning of War  234

Notes 251
References 301
Index 327

# Preface

Many have questioned the decision to write about cooperation between enemies in warfare, but far from surreptitiously sanitizing the carnage of war or apologizing for its injustices, this project seeks to humanize it. In October 2017, I attended a conference at West Point fêting (and critiquing) Michael Walzer's *Just and Unjust Wars*, on the occasion of its fortieth anniversary. It is a book read not only by philosophers and military ethicists, but also by every cadet in every American military academy. Soldier after soldier got up to recount the seriousness with which they studied this work, and one retired officer who had seen many deployments and battles in his time attested, "This book has been my constant companion for thirty years." It was a humbling moment for those of us in the academy who also aspire to practical import, and in a similar vein, this project strives to both make sense of and contribute to the soldier's experience.

My interest in issues of warfare was first piqued when I read a long newspaper piece about soldiers coming home from the field and having difficulty adjusting to civilian life: they felt out of place in the free-flowing disorder, disgusted at the excesses of commercial society, adrift with purposelessness, and disheartened by the meaninglessness of people's everyday trivialities.

The disconnect between soldier and civilian is part of the inherent tensions in civil/military relations in liberal democracies. These conflicts will never be fully resolved, as successful militaries must always be hierarchical to a certain degree, in a way that contradicts the freedom of liberal democratic life, yet liberal democracies rely on that hierarchy and submission in order to secure those liberties. This often has tragic results for individual soldiers who cannot find their place in society upon returning home. While more can be done for returning fighters, their displacement is all the more heartbreaking because it will always be necessary.

Similarly, the horrifying endeavor that is war will always be with us. No matter how much moral progress we make, the nature of humanity is such that someone will always be willing to use the final trump card of violence to settle a dispute. It is also the case that sometimes, brutality must be used in the service of justice: nonviolence can be highly effective, but only against regimes capable of feeling shame, of which there are but a few. Given that war cannot be eliminated, we must try to contain it, and this book explores some unexpected yet pervasive attempts to do so.

Warfare itself is rife with contradiction, one of the most notable of which is that its utter chaos coexists alongside orderliness and rules. In the same vein, fighters will butcher one another, yet simultaneously cooperate for various purposes with the very people they are trying to kill. These tensions are inevitable yet irreconcilable—but for those who fight and experience wars, all these phenomena exist at once seemingly without dissonance.

These valiant—and sometimes devastating—efforts between enemies to constrain warfare and impose some boundaries, order, and meaning on what is fundamentally a radical, anarchic, and lawless activity are in part analogous to the project of the Leviathan, who attempts to sublimate private justice in favor of public right. For centuries, the global moral order has been struggling to constrain international anarchy, trying to solidify that first stage of instituting a Leviathan to govern over tribal violence and adjudicate questions of justice. Moral philosophy has tackled these problems in a global distributive context, but far more needs to be done in the global retributive context.

In the course of tracing the genealogy of the ethic of cooperation between enemies in warfare, this book takes a different approach than that of the dominant strands of just war theory today. The standard modern approach rests on two major premises: the moral equality between fighters and their acquisition of a collectivized moral status that permits them to do what would otherwise be disallowed, namely, kill people. Since then, an alternative strand has rejected the special status and powers of the state, and sought to overturn this principle of moral equality of combatants by analogizing killing in war to domestic self-defense and connecting it to the philosophical and legal literature on killing innocents (e.g., causal, culpability, or liability approaches). These have been largely or entirely philosophical enterprises.

In contrast, by looking at the genealogy of agreements and contracts in warfare and their accompanying moral demands, by practicing "*e.g.* philosophy" (in the words of Avishai Margalit) in order to integrate historical and theoretical ethical claims, I hope to shed more light on contemporary practices and normative expectations in warfare.

This genealogical exploration is an empirical project (unearthing a moral psychology, military sociology, and military and legal history) as well as a philosophical endeavor establishing what various recurring concepts (such as fairness, responsibility, legitimacy) mean both generally and with respect to war. I then seek to merge the empirical and philosophical by exploring problems with those conceptions and how they might be resolved both in theory and in practice.

## Self-Imposed Constraint

While the international laws of war could be considered yet another form of hegemony imposed by stronger states upon weaker ones, they also make it harder to win, which is why even the more dominant countries and their fighters are constantly trying to break the rules and get away with it. Why would states and soldiers make it harder for themselves to win and end wars?

The rules were created and sustained at least in part by sincere beliefs that there are right and wrong ways to win, and that it matters both practically—e.g., in building good will and reciprocity with opponents, whether they end up as vanquished or conquerors—and morally.

The live-and-let-live system in World War I trenches could be the exception that proves the rule, but in fact, the very structure of modern war itself is a cooperative enterprise. Rather than being nihilistic, anarchic, or unconditional, war can be viewed (as often exemplified by Clausewitz) as a legitimate tool of conflict resolution—a way of reaching sustainable agreement—because violence is often undertaken with broader political goals in mind. As such, decisions about going to war and even war as a whole become collaborative in nature, as wars are a way of determining who is effectively right.

Furthermore, norms of war rely on agreement on the existence and content of the laws of war, especially who they should apply to, who qualifies as a combatant, and so on. These questions have been asked throughout history, for example, which peoples deserve "civilized" warfare (e.g., fellow Greeks, fellow Chinese) and which do not, whether guerrillas or blacks fighting in the American Civil War qualify for protections under the laws of war, and similarly now whether terrorists warrant the same.

The answers to these questions affect the content of other types of cooperation. During the modern period (from the sixteenth century onward), the ethic of cooperation between enemies has become systematized in international laws and institutions, which themselves constitute a kind of cooperation. The development of international laws and its concomitant attempt to enforce them with supranational institutions have broader implications for the future of the nation-state system in international politics.

Systematic cooperation between enemies is taken so much for granted that we hardly notice it: weapons bans, POW regulations, requirements to wear uniforms into combat, and protections for clergy and medics who are national military personnel, among others. These cases are especially interesting because they developed before any widespread discussion of human rights. They are conventional, a practice that has been agreed upon. Why should medics, for example, be treated as neutral (so long as they do not pick up arms) even when they are part of a national military? Their jobs are essential to the war effort, and the very soldiers they heal may return to the battlefield and continue to fight.

These practices have many motivations, but one major goal was to minimize overall damage—although where the line is drawn can be arbitrary. The distinction between soldiers and civilians, for example, is a matter of convention. Historically, no such differentiation was made, even if women and children were spared more often than men, and when members of the civilian population contribute in varying ways to the war effort, as they inevitably do, the boundary between who is and is not a legitimate target (e.g., munitions factory workers can be targeted, but medics cannot) is subjective and a matter of agreement.

At this point, some context is required: (1) Cooperation in warfare is certainly not the norm: historically, and even in contemporary times, it is an anomaly in human history. Guerrilla, or "irregular," warfare—indirect raids, ambushes, sabotage, and short skirmishes—has been and continues to be the dominant mode of combat for over 150 millennia. (2) Cooperation in warfare is not a uniquely modern phenomenon. It has happened all throughout human history, on a variety of levels and in different forms, although the contemporary systematization of this cooperation through international law and institutions is distinctive. And (3) although the rules are not always obeyed—in fact, they are more often deliberately violated—and even if international law looks much less dramatic and interesting than tensely negotiated truces in muddy trenches, the systematization of cooperation at the interstate and international levels and the extent to which individuals do obey those rules in the field are enormously significant. It shows that moral considerations are possible even in the most horrifying of human activities, and between people who have much to gain from not cooperating with one another.

## Secularization of Just War Theory

One challenge for contemporary just war theory is that it uses religiously derived principles—proper authority, just cause, and right intention, which are then constrained by last resort, proportionality, and probability of success—but without their religious foundations. For example, the principle of right intention is meant to reconcile pacifist readings of Christianity with the act of killing, and allows killing only for the purpose of attaining the just cause. It cannot be done with malice, out of revenge or self-interest, or similar motives, which then gets us the Doctrine of Double Effect. But contemporary and secular concerns with justice beg pressing questions about the principle of right intention. For example, if justice is the primary principle, how important is the spirit with which a just action is committed? Does an improper motive make it any less just? It does in classical just war theory, because the conception of justice incorporates motive. In most modern and contemporary interpretations, however, it is the institutional processes or outcomes that matter, and proper personal motivations—while helpful—are not strictly necessary for justice to be done.

Do the classical just war principles that ground contemporary just war theory need to be reestablished with some nonreligious foundations and, if so, what might those be? Such reconceptualization is particularly important as the emergence of a language of rights—especially human rights since World War II—can cause problems for a crudely secularized version of just war theory. For example, one may have a right to not be killed, or a right to not be harmed in certain ways under human rights–based ethics of warfare, but that right may be contravened by accepted traditional/contemporary just war principles. There are several influences at work, feeding into contemporary just war theory, and in order to better understand the ethics of warfare, we have to unravel these influences and the relationships between them. We should recognize and explore where they intersect and where they are inconsistent with one another, because they push military ethics and just war theory in different directions and toward different—and sometimes contradictory—conclusions about acceptable ways and reasons to wage war.

One major operator in military ethics is the ethic of cooperation, which is at once pervasive, overlooked, and taken for granted. Understanding it can both better explain many of the contradictions in military practice and philosophy and offer some alternatives to help resolve those tensions.

The sum of the exceptions to the brutality of war is more than its constituent parts, and they add up to an ethic of cooperation between enemies in warfare. This ethic is all the more surprising given its persistent coexistence with the brutality of war. Sometimes, the ethic of cooperation overlaps with other moral principles invoked in war, sometimes not. Repeated cooperation between enemies in no way diminishes the horrifying barbarism of 99 percent of warfare. Rather, these meaningful exceptions are an attempt to contain and make sense of war's atrocities, even if frequently in vain. For a soldier, there are two ways to wage war. One can turn nihilistic and cold. Said Green Beret commander Colonel Robert Rheault, whose murder and conspiracy scandal during the Vietnam War was a partial inspiration for the character of Kurtz in *Apocalypse Now*: "I was at the top of my game when I was in combat. You don't have the luxury to indulge your fear, because other people's lives depend upon you keeping your head cold. . . . When something goes wrong, they call it emotional numbing.

It's not very good in civilian life, but it's pretty useful in combat—to be able to get absolutely very cold about what needs to be done, and just stick with it."[1]

Or one can try to salvage something from war. There are many different stories that can be told about the history of war, the history of man, the history of rules in warfare. This is but a single story—but one that I think is true, insightful, and helpful.

# Acknowledgments

All first books demand a long list of recognition, and this one all the more so because I unwisely abandoned my graduate school project and started from scratch with a new idea and different methodology, so this process was unnecessarily long and fraught.

I would like to thank several anonymous members of and translators for various militaries and governments who shared their experiences with me in interviews and conversations, as well as Danielle Allen, Edward T. Barrett, Eric Beerbohm, Cristina Beltrán, Elizabeth Popp Berman, James Blaker, Brandice Canes-Wrone, Joseph Chan, Steve Ealy, Didier Fassin, Jeffrey Flynn, Stefan Gosepath, Ian Holliday, David C. Johnston, Loretta Kim, Sharon Krause, Michael Kulikowski, Eliza Lee, Helen Liu, David Luban, Jeff McMahan, Andrew Murphy, Emily Nacol, Vanessa Ogle, Manuela Picq, Noah Salomon, Kim Lane Scheppele, Joan Wallach Scott, Injoo Sohn, Uwe Steinhoff, Ellen Stroud, Robert S. Taylor, Henning Trüper, Michael Walzer, Xiaojun Yan, all the members of the 2013–14 class of the School of Social Science at the Institute for Advanced Study, and participants in workshops at Rutgers University Department of Political Science and Walt Whitman Center for the Culture and Politics of Democracy (2014), Freie Universität Institut für Philosophie (2014), Columbia University Seminar on Social and Political Thought (2014), and World International Studies Committee (WISC) Early Career Researchers Workshop

(Goa University, 2017). I am beholden to two reviewers for their exceedingly careful and thoughtful engagement with the manuscript.

For research assistance, I thank Catherine Cheng, Alexander Chiu, Beata Lee Chiu, Victoria Chiu, Ryan Hsu, Janice Leung, and Ho Yin Yuen.

Institutional and grant support gave me essential time, space, and intellectual camaraderie to finish this project: The University of Hong Kong, University Grants Committee (Hong Kong) General Research Fund, Lord and Lady Sterling of Battersea, AeroOberst HkdC, The Rebellion/Torture Club, Paint Frays Foundation, Q Consortium, and the Institute for Advanced Study (IAS) twice over. This project was slowly deconstructed during my first stint at IAS, then reconstructed afterward, so it was with especial pleasure that I finished the manuscript during the second round there.

My editor Caelyn Cobb, copy editor Robert Demke, and the editorial and production teams at Columbia University Press shepherded this project safely through.

Finally, I have been extremely lucky in my family and friends, especially for my father and my mother, whose endless sacrifices, wit, wisdom, and uncommon iconoclasm paved the way, my indomitable grandparents, each of my siblings, and my chosen family. Everywhere I have lived, I have been blessed to have found amazing and generous friends and family, and reliable comrades-in-arms. I am grateful for their enduring trans-Pacific support during trials and tribulations, even as I and they have moved across oceans and continents. Finally, my longtime piano teacher, the late Robert E. Turner: I was fortunate enough to have been educated, with great patience, in creativity without sacrificing the demands of rigor and precision. This is not the musical ode that he deserves, but one that I hope he would have appreciated.

CHAPTER I

# The Horrors of War and the Nature of Cooperation

> . . . you men of Harfleur,
> Take pity of your town and of your people,
> Whiles yet my soldiers are in my command;
> Whiles yet the cool and temperate wind of grace
> O'erblows the filthy and contagious clouds
> Of heady murder, spoil and villany.
> If not, why, in a moment look to see
> The blind and bloody soldier with foul hand
> Defile the locks of your shrill-shrieking daughters;
> Your fathers taken by the silver beards,
> And their most reverend heads dash'd to the walls,
> Your naked infants spitted upon pikes,
> Whiles the mad mothers with their howls confused
> Do break the clouds, as did the wives of Jewry
> At Herod's bloody-hunting slaughtermen.
> What say you? will you yield, and this avoid,
> Or, guilty in defence, be thus destroy'd?
> —SHAKESPEARE, *HENRY V*, 3.3

Across the ages, war is most often characterized in history and literature as the epitome of conflict, fought over an intractable disagreement that can only be settled by force, a last resort so primal and desperate that people inevitably lose their moral compass as it goes on. Despite the influence of just war theory and constraints of international military law, once fighting begins, it descends into an arena of anger, malice, deceit, subterfuge, and ruthlessness, as endless examples of massacre, rape, torture, and enslavement tell us: victors seize their prizes, and there is little room for rules or civility, much less morality.

Yet, throughout the story of human cruelty also run threads of mercy, kindness, and virtue, as well as, surprisingly, cooperation. Even at its most horrific, there are not only ad hoc and coordinated attempts at moral action in warfare, but also repeated cooperation between enemies. By this, I do not mean alliances of convenience between antagonists against a mutual foe, à la "the enemy of my enemy is my friend" for the moment. Rather, adversaries often cooperate even as they are trying to kill one another.

Cooperation between enemy fighters takes different forms: it manifests in an exchange of prisoners, for example, or by wearing a uniform in order to make oneself a better target and help protect civilians in the process. It can be planned or institutionalized, or it can be a brief emotion, a fleeting moment, as when a sniper does not shoot an unsuspecting target because it seems unfair. The practice of cooperation ebbs and flows, but it can be traced throughout the breadth of warfare. Although many instances of cooperation are random, isolated incidents, they are not merely that.

These are meaningful exceptions to the brutality of war, and their sum total is more than that of its parts: they add up to what constitutes an ethic of cooperation between enemies in warfare, which is the idea that cooperating with the enemy in certain ways within war is the right thing to do and has moral purchase. This belief can rest on different grounds, including a sense of warrior honor, human rights, or efficiency. Not only have instances of cooperation between enemies arisen time and time again, but some of its practices have been institutionalized into the international laws of war and the current Westphalian nation-state system.

There are two commonly held yet contradictory perceptions of war: first, cooperation is so commonplace in some areas that it goes unnoticed and its structures and corresponding behavior are taken for granted, notably in the institutional structure of international law. At the same time, it is also understood that war is so terrible that it cannot sustain morality; this makes it difficult to accept that there can be and is cooperation between enemies in warfare, because that requires some amount of honesty, trust, sincerity, and predictability that would be impossible if moral behavior at all were untenable.

It certainly appears as if mercy, much less ethical consideration, has no place in battle. Siege warfare, for example, hardly makes allowances for the well-being of the women, children, and elderly trapped inside cities. Everyone starved and suffered, and whoever survived after defeat would be hauled off to slavery, as Hector fears for his wife Andromache, in the Trojan War (*The Iliad*, 6.533–55). Despite powerful and clever female gods who shape the course of human events, women on Earth are, then as now, little more than property, spoils of war, loved only by their families. Mortal women can drive martial aspirations, but usually inadvertently, through their seizure and trade—the most famous of all being Helen. Other women suffer the same fate: at first, Agamemnon refuses to ransom Chryses's daughter back to him, declaring, "The girl—I won't give up the girl. Long before that, / old age will overtake her in *my* house, in Argos, / far from her fatherland, slaving back and forth / at the loom, forced to share my bed!" Later, when he is coerced into relinquishing Chryseis, he demands that they "fetch me another prize, and straight off too, / else I alone of the Argives go without my honor," which then sets in motion a series of crucial developments in the rest of the war (1.33–36, 138–39).

Neither are there niceties on the battlefield, whether out of pity or greed. When Adrestus is captured, he begs for his life in exchange for a "priceless ransom." Tempted, Menelaus is about to agree, when Agamemnon intervenes:

> . . . "So soft, dear brother, why?
> Why such concern for enemies? I suppose you got
> such tender loving care at home from the Trojans.
> Ah would to god not one of them could escape
> his sudden plunging death beneath our hands!
> No baby boy still in his mother's belly,
> not even he escape—all Ilium blotted out,
> no tears for their lives, no markers for their graves!"
> And the iron warrior brought his brother round—
> rough justice, fitting too.
> Menelaus shoved Adrestus back with a fist,
> powerful Agamemnon stabbed him in the flank
> and back on his side the fighter went, faceup.
> The son of Atreus dug a heel in his heaving chest
> and wrenched the ash spear out.
>
> (6.63–77)

Although ancient Greece is often taken as the birthplace of Western civilization, at times it can be hard to see how its predecessor—archaic Greece—also held the seeds of the modern warrior and modern warfare, even albeit through a long, circuitous, and inconsistent path. When one remembers, however, that the past century alone has seen the Nanjing

Massacre, the Holocaust, the firebombing of Tokyo, and torture in Abu Ghraib, among other countless horrors, the continuity is a little clearer, and the bloody rage and cruelty of the archaics and ancients now transition seamlessly to more recent atrocities.

Despite the litany of contemporary domestic regulations and international laws, when war begins, it seems that any sense of morality goes too. Soldiers and civilians alike usually have little desire to make room for courtesies when their lives are at stake, and understandably so. The essence of war is captured by images of frenzied, merciless, mutual slaughter between the Aegeans and the Trojans as told in *The Iliad*, rapes depicted in Goya's *The Disasters of War*, torture portrayed in *The Battle of Algiers*, or indiscriminate napalm bombing in Vietnam dramatized in *Apocalypse Now*.

War is a desperate, primal activity, and simultaneously seductive and addictive in the power one can wield to kill or to spare men's lives. Says war correspondent Chris Hedges:

> War breaks down long-established prohibitions against violence, destruction, and murder. And with this often comes the crumbling of sexual, social, and political norms as the domination and brutality of the battlefield is carried into personal life. Rape, mutilation, abuse, and theft are the natural outcome of a world in which force rules, in which human beings are objects. The infection is pervasive. Society in wartime becomes atomized. It rewards personal survival skills and very often leaves those with decency and compassion trampled under the rush.[1]

It seems war is so wretched that, however dressed up in uniforms, protocols, and strategies, the trappings of civilization and adherence to ethical principles are impossible to sustain under such circumstances. It often begins with the simple desire to survive. Says Erich Maria Remarque, through his narrator Paul Bäumer in the fictional but exemplary *All Quiet on the Western Front*:

> We have become wild beasts. We do not fight, we defend ourselves against annihilation. It is not against men that we fling our bombs, what do we know of men in this moment when Death is hunting us down.... No longer do we lie helpless, waiting on the scaffold,

we can destroy and kill, to save ourselves, to save ourselves and to be revenged . . . we run on, overwhelmed by this wave that bears us along, that fills us with ferocity, turns us into thugs, into murderers, into God only knows what devils; this wave that multiplies our strength with fear and madness and greed of life, seeking and fighting for nothing but our deliverance. If your own father came over with them you would not hesitate to fling a bomb at him. . . . We have lost all feeling for one another. . . . We are insensible, dead men, who through some trick, some dreadful magic, are still able to run and to kill.[2]

It seems that blood thirst may naturally overtake man in combat, but it is not necessarily a pleasurable excitement. Most who have seen modern combat abhor it. While many a soldier acclimates to existence in the theater and, after some time there, may find it difficult to live a regular civilian life,[3] it is the rare soldier who has seen modern war's horrific scale of destruction and still genuinely and singularly thrills at the fight.[4] Said US general and later president Dwight D. Eisenhower, "I hate war as only a soldier who has lived it can, only as one who has seen its brutality, its stupidity."[5]

## A Very Brief History of Warfare

For the bulk of human history, warfare has been a savage, scrappy, self-interested, no-holds-barred affair.[6] Despite the implications of the name "conventional warfare," it is in fact guerrilla, or "irregular," warfare—an indirect approach utilizing raids, ambushes, sabotage, and short skirmishes—that has been the norm over 150,000 years of *Homo sapiens* history and the millions of years of hominids before that.[7]

Conventional war became possible only once agricultural societies developed, the first appearing after 10,000 BCE in the Middle East (and several thousand years later elsewhere), when there was finally enough surplus wealth and human population to sustain specialty weapons and fortifications and their skilled operators. Not until nearly seven millennia later, after 3100 BCE, however, do the "first genuine armies—commanded by a strict hierarchy, composed of trained soldiers, disciplined with threats of punishment, divided into different specialties (spearmen, bowmen, charioteers, engineers), deployed in formations, supported by a logistics service"—arise in Egypt and Mesopotamia.[8] Pitched battle is the exception throughout history, even during its heyday in the eighteenth and nineteenth centuries, as "most warfare involved hunting down unarmed enemies, slaughtering the men and raping the women, or perhaps enslaving both men and women. Ambush, pillage, and wanton destruction were the norm,"[9] because they minimize risk and maximize advantage.

### Narrative Biases

Despite the historical rarity of conventional conflicts, however, almost all military histories tell the story of conventional war: its direct confrontation is relatively new and of larger scale, so there is more of a historical record, and conventional warfare also supplies more readily identifiable characters and plot elements. Usually, the history is narrated chronologically, recounting major battles and the decisions of kings and generals, while describing geopolitical intrigues, significant technological breakthroughs and organizational developments, and moments of tactical genius.

Conventional fighting dominates our conception of war also because we desire definitive resolution and because it is seen as the most successful way to wage war, so most countries in the world try to emulate it to some degree.

### Mixed Methods and Probable Paths to Victory

Over time, political entities have varied across warring tribes, kingdoms, empires, city-states, caliphates, and states, among others. Furthermore, each scientific improvement has altered the face of war, e.g., use of metal, domestication of horses, evolution of the longbow, introduction of gunpowder, invention of ammunition belts for semiautomatic and automatic guns, and creation of unmanned aerial vehicles.

What is consistent across all these disparate eras is that people naturally seek military advantage in warfare, whether it is under the cover of night or through the element of surprise. One's life is at stake, after all, and it would be foolish to take unnecessary risks with something so crucial. It is therefore unsurprising that guerrilla warfare has continued long after the advent of conventional warfare, and is still used alongside it. Although Thucydides tells the history of the Peloponnesian War as largely a series of conventional encounters centered between Athens and Sparta, irregular fighting was used throughout—there were only fifty-five major battles in a nearly thirty-year war, while within "the first few years the Athenians alone staged hundreds of low-level attacks on various locations"[10]—and contrary to conventional understanding, combat consisted more of "raiding and killing, not formal war as previously defined by the Greeks."[11] This was not unusual: ancient Greek warfare in general used mixed tactics.[12]

Similar conjunctions occur at other times: Against the better-armed and -trained British (and Hessian) soldiers, the rebellious Americans preferred to seize what advantages they could in the Revolutionary War. General George Washington's army ambushed Hessian mercenaries while they slept (and not because they were inebriated) in the Battle of Trenton, which was a standard approach for Washington. In fact, he did not employ classical massed infantry maneuvers for the bulk of the war—between August 27, 1776 (Battle of Brooklyn, which he lost), and October 19, 1781 (Siege of Yorktown, which he won, outnumbering the enemy two to one)—instead preferring ambushes and strategic retreats.[13] Says historian David McCullough, the Revolutionary War

> wasn't beautiful gentlemen of the 18th century in beautiful 18th-century costume.... Soldiers very often in rags, very often with no shoes.... Legendary stories about leaving bloody footprints in the snow in Trenton and other places were all true. They were hungry, they were starving, and they were down by the end of the year to 3,000."[14]

The French-Indian War (1756–63) that Washington had fought in earlier was mostly "wilderness warfare," far different from the Eastern part of the country where there was little wilderness left:

> He had no experience whatever in fighting . . . pitched, formalized battles of the 18th century. . . . It took him a while to catch on that if he came out and faced these English regulars, professional

troops, who by the way were extremely courageous themselves—and they weren't commanded by aristocratic pinheads . . . another misconception— . . . that you can't fight them that way, and to figure out that the point isn't to protect cities or hold New York or hold New Jersey. The point is to keep the army alive and fighting. And it also took the British a while to figure that out: the way to defeat these rebels was to get the army—forget about taking Philadelphia or New York . . . just go get that army and kill it.[15]

The most compelling reason for the persistent use and staying power of guerrilla warfare is that it is highly effective. It leveled the Mesopotamian and Roman empires, and overwhelmed considerable portions of the Chinese and British empires, among others.[16]

Guerrilla warfare is also always available as a weapon of the weak, as the militarily disadvantaged still have a chance to win if they do not meet their foe head-on. It can inflict enormous damage without having to maintain and manage a large bureaucracy, it has low start-up and shutdown costs, and guerrillas can carry on low-intensity insurgencies for long periods of time. Even today, although conventional fighting looms large in our imagination, guerrilla action is still the dominant mode of warfare in the world.

## Considerations of Morality and Justice

Although it is usually in the context of guerrilla or irregular warfare that the modern citizen thinks of martial chaos, anarchy, and lawlessness, the same moral atrocities abound in conventional warfare as well, perhaps even more so: rape, torture, summary execution of prisoners, enslavement of captives, indiscrimination that does not spare or perhaps even targets civilians, and tortuous killing (e.g., chemical weapons), among others.

The rules and structures of conventional warfare do not immunize one to bloodlust or intoxication by war. People are driven to kill one another for any number of reasons—especially competition, diffidence, and glory, says Thomas Hobbes[17]—and the impulse may quite literally be in our nature. Violence has been prevalent since perhaps the beginning of society, and some evolutionary studies suggest that aggressiveness is an adaptive trait that allows people to successfully compete for limited resources.[18]

## Evolutionary Influences

Interestingly, an inclination for cooperation may have evolved alongside that for warfare.[19] There are evolutionary advantages to trust and altruism between close relatives or those in long-term relationships,[20] and it may also pay off evolutionarily to have faith in and be generous with strangers with whom one is in society, as there is always uncertainty about whether a particular interaction is a one-off.[21] Beyond that, there may even be a tendency toward "strong reciprocity": the willingness to sacrifice resources to reward those who are kind and to punish those who are not, even without prospects of future material rewards for oneself.[22] Ironically, some of this genetic drive to altruism may have been made possible by warfare. In fact, self-sacrifice in favor of group (rather than individual) selection may quickly make population rates plummet, but when there is war, higher levels of altruism and thus the self-sacrifice gene may become more sustainable.[23]

All of this altruism and self-sacrifice is happening within groups, however. Even between nonkin or strangers in these groups, there are still shared traits (e.g., culture, nationality, etc.) that delineate some kind of meaningful boundary for group members, and the benefits are doled out among them. As evidenced by countless wars, it seems that such altruism shown to insiders only intensifies the viciousness that is meted to outsiders.

At the same time, although mortal enemies kill one another much more often than not, there are individual instances of pity and kindness shown to enemy soldiers in the midst of barbarism. I mention just two of many examples here. Decorated World War II Luftwaffe pilot Franz Stigler decided to not shoot down an American B-17 because he saw that the tail gunner had already been killed and the survivors were busy aiding their injured, whereupon he not only spared the crew but also escorted the plane to safer airspace, at great risk to himself.[24] During the Iran-Iraq War in the 1980s, young Iranian soldier Zahed Haftlang encountered injured Iraqi soldier Najah Aboud in a bunker during a battle and reached into the Iraqi's pocket to loot from him, but found a Qur'an and a picture of Aboud's girlfriend and her son. "Because of his family and by that photo, he changed my mind," says Haftlang, "I made a decision to save him." Aboud remembers, "Right away he changed into a human, not an enemy, not a killer."

Haftlang gave the Iraqi painkillers, hid him underneath corpses for three days until the battle ended, and then took him to a military hospital. Recounts Aboud, "I never hear about Iranian soldiers saving Iraqi soldiers during the fighting. I never see him again."[25]

Furthermore, there are strong informal regulations for cooperation between enemies in other violent contexts, for example, mafia codes of conduct such as *omertà*, a kind of "honor among thieves" that frowns upon assisting legal authorities to interfere with even one's rivals and enemies. In the midst of intense conflict and horrendous violence, there are not only pockets of cooperation but moreover whole systems.

### *Iterated Games and Empathy*

> It was not, then, for fear
> that I didn't kill you: it was—not to die myself!
> Not to die in you: you were my twin
> or seemed so in the twinned trench.
> —FAUSTO MARIA MARTINI, "WHY I DIDN'T KILL YOU"

Some of the more amazing stories of cooperation in warfare come from the trenches of World War I. How did its brutal, nonsensical slaughter—which ultimately killed over nine million soldiers across all theaters—yield the Christmas truces in 1914 (and to a lesser extent in 1915), during which not only did one hundred thousand British and German soldiers unofficially stop fighting but also, in some places in Belgium, German soldiers who decorated their trenches with candles and trees and sang carols were met with British soldiers singing in kind? Eventually, the two sides mingled in No Man's Land, exchanging gifts, food, and souvenirs, and even engaging in short, casual football games.[26]

It was not just ad hoc cooperation on a shared holy day: opposing trenches also spontaneously developed systematic cooperation over time with a "live and let live" arrangement. Trench warfare was a significant but not particularly interesting aspect of World War II military tactics—rather, it is noteworthy for what fighting did not happen. The famous timed shellings between some trenches in World War I was part of a system of reciprocal exchange of services that allowed each side to anticipate and avoid attacks and minimize casualties. It took different forms during the war: truces lasted anywhere from a few minutes to several months, and some were explicit agreements between fraternizing soldiers in close quarters, while others were indirect, over long distances, and involved large numbers of people.[27] The existence of these truces is surprising, but, notes J. Glenn Gray, a World War II army officer and later philosophy professor, "It is a great boon of front-line positions that . . . disobedience is frequently possible, since supervision is not very exact where danger of death is present."[28]

Historical evidence for the truces is strong. There were numerous reports and even the occasional photo of people walking openly above trenches and of unrestricted movement in and out of the trenches; of Germans frying sausages and Brits frying bacon in the trenches, despite the fact that smoke from the fires would have attracted gunfire on active fronts; and of "quiet" fronts when there was no shortage of ammunition. In some trenches, soldiers hunted and retrieved small game, harvested vegetables, kept dairy cows for fresh milk, and had pianos and books. The British 33rd Division reportedly sent someone to the village each afternoon to purchase eggs, oats, fresh milk, and fruit,[29] and the British 1st Royal Berkshire Regiment and its opposing German unit delivered newspapers to each other.[30] All this would have been impossible without cease-fires of some kind. Some field reports explicitly referenced truces,[31] as well as other direct declarations, such as a sign on a notice board appealing, "Today is BANK HOLIDAY Tommies. Do not fire—give us a rest,"[32] or soldiers' letters describing the front:

> Without at all "fraternizing"—we refrain from interfering with Brother Bosch seventy yards away, as long as he is kind to us. . . . All patrols—English and German—are much averse to the death and glory principle; so, on running up against one another in the long wet rustling clover, both pretend that they are Levites and the other is a Good Samaritan—and pass by on the other side, no word spoken. For either side to bomb the other would be a useless violation of the unwritten laws that govern the relations of combatants permanently within a hundred yards of each other.[33]

> We suddenly confronted, round some mound or excavation, a German patrol. . . . We were perhaps twenty yards from each other, fully visible. I waved a weary hand, as if to say: what is the use of

killing each other? The German officer seemed to understand, and both parties turned and made their way back to their own trenches. Reprehensible conduct, no doubt.³⁴

The man Mike gave some useful hints on trench work. "It's the Saxons that's across the road," he said, pointing to the enemy lines which were very silent. I had not heard a bullet whistle over since I entered the trench. On the left was an interesting rifle and machine gun fire all the time. "They're quiet fellows, the Saxons, they don't want to fight any more than we do, so there's a kind of understanding between us. Don't fire at us and we'll not fire at you."³⁵

Truces arose where there was general reluctance to fight, usually out of a combination of self-interest and empathy. If fired upon, parties would return fire, but both sides preferred to "let sleeping dogs lie." Eventually, the threat of legal sanctions for explicit truces led to tacit ones.

## *Internal Sanctions*

High command did not look favorably on this inactivity, for obvious reasons, so in the latter half of the war, they exerted more direct control over the trenches, for example by ordering specific raids. Soldiers adapted by ritualizing their aggression and conforming with the letter, but not the spirit, of the commands. They would deliberately aim their rounds high, enemy patrols would pretend to not see or follow routes such that they would not encounter one another, and shooters would fire into No Man's Land instead of into trenches or shell the same place or at the same time every day so that the enemy could avoid that area or schedule to suit. Such ritualized aggression still looked like battle from the outside, and reassuring reports could be sent to high command about the times and duration of the battles and how much ammunition was spent.

The internal struggle between command and the front escalated throughout the war, with high command wanting soldiers to put themselves at risk and soldiers trying to find ways to avoid fighting and dying. The truces were hardly easy to maintain. Penalties for treachery were severe, of course. In addition, high command kept trying to break up the tacit collusion by rotating people off the front more frequently. Within the troops, the artillerymen, who were further back and bore less risk, wanted real battle, so it was difficult for the trenchmen in front to hold on to the truce.[36] In an almost perfect example of an iterated game for survival between predator and prey—although here high command and soldiers were ostensibly on the same team despite their conflicting aims—each side continually sought and found new ways to adapt to and outwit the other's response.

Anywhere from 13 to 40 percent of all trench tours—and overall about 33 percent—practiced some form of "live and let live" at some point.[37] That is a significant percentage of the fronts and an extraordinary number of truces, many of which involved no direct communication between the enemies.

*Deterrence*

This is not to say that serving in the trenches was not a brutal experience and that life there was comfortable or safe—far from it. Even when a truce was in place, it was not all fun and games or cuddly cooperation. Underlying the truce, and holding it together, was always the threat of destruction should someone secede from the agreement. For example, ritualized exchange of fire sometimes took the form of repeatedly "just missing" the target. This did not harm the enemy and maintained the truce, but simultaneously showed him that you had the range and accuracy to kill him should peace break down.[38]

Where "live and let live" arose, its motivations evolved along with its forms. At first, everyone had the same but not shared goal of winning the battle and leaving the trenches alive, but eventually, some started sharing the implicit goal of subverting the system, which was the only way they might survive. The ability to sustain at length such complex and uncoordinated cooperation between warring parties—usually without direct communication, while individuals constantly rotated in and out, and sanctions were imposed both between enemies and within each side—is impressive, to say the least.

"Live and let live" is admittedly fairly unique, and made possible partly because of the structure of trench warfare—this kind of cooperation did not develop in other wars that employed different tactics. Trench warfare just happens to have a structure that makes for relatively clean iterative, cooperative games of this sort. Trench warfare's rigid and transparent structure allowed for easier conspiracy, and the "live and let live" arrangement that evolved shows cooperation in its distilled form. Robert Axelrod's *The Evolution of Cooperation* (1984), which drew from his and evolutionary biologist W. D. Hamilton's 1981 paper, reveals how tit-for-tat games and structures apply to many different scenarios and can shape the development and behavior of the actors within, including soldiers trying—or rather, not trying—to kill one another in the trenches.

It does not mean that fellow feeling or the desire to cooperate does not exist in other circumstances; it is simply more diffuse or on a smaller scale (e.g., not sniping a man when he is taking a cigarette break, or trying to not kill women and children), and more difficult to organize.

### Shared Humanity

Although the warring states stoked their populations' nationalistic passions by dehumanizing the enemy, most trench fighters were conscripts with little at stake in the conflict. Initially moved by rousing propaganda, these "ignorant armies clash by night,"[39] but once they experienced war in its full misery, many found that they preferred to save themselves. And once they recognized the humanity of their enemies across the way, the structure of trench warfare allowed them to collaborate with one another in this Prisoner's Dilemma scenario, and they were willing to spare their opponents for the sake of their own survival.

Fictional German conscript Paul Bäumer understands the necessity of killing the enemy, but at various points feels a certain pity and even empathy for them. He acknowledges the suffering of some Russian POWs and recognizes their cruel twists of fate:

> A word of command has made these silent figures our enemies; a word of command might transform them into our friends. At some table a document is signed by some persons whom none of us knows, and then for years together that very crime on which formerly the world's condemnation and severest penalty fall, becomes our highest aim. But who can draw such a distinction when he looks at these quiet men with their childlike faces and apostles' beards. Any non-commissioned officer is more of an enemy to a recruit, any

schoolmaster to a pupil, than they are to us. And yet we would shoot at them again and they at us if they were free.[40]

Later, trapped in a foxhole with the body of a man he killed, Bäumer regrets his actions:

> Comrade, I did not want to kill you. If you jumped in here again, I would not do it, if you would be sensible too. But you were only an idea to me before, an abstraction that lived in my mind and called forth its appropriate response. It was that abstraction I stabbed. But now, for the first time, I see you are a man like me. I thought of your hand-grenades, of your bayonet, of your rifle; now I see your wife and your face and our fellowship. Forgive me, comrade. We always see it too late. Why do they never tell us that you are poor devils like us, that your mothers are just as anxious as ours, and that we have the same fear of death, and the same dying and the same agony— Forgive me, comrade; how could you be my enemy? If we threw away these rifles and this uniform you could be my brother.[41]

Bäumer never made good on his promise to his dead enemy-turned-comrade in the foxhole, but others did in real life.

The mutual subversion between enemies of "live and let live"—clean and highly structured, in many ways—is unusual and surprising, but not infrequent when comparable circumstances present themselves.

There is similar but less-developed behavior in trenches elsewhere in World War I,[42] as well as precursors some fifty years earlier in the American Civil War—fittingly, as tactics there presaged European trench warfare in many ways—where fraternization between the two sides was not unusual.[43] One example comes, surprisingly, from the ferocious Korean War (1950–53). American military doctor Otto F. Apel recounts the rare sounding of an air raid alarm one day that panicked everyone, because the United States had already gained air superiority early in the war. At first, nothing happened, and then a plane appeared, but it was not a Soviet MIG-17. Instead, it was an open-cockpit biplane with a solo North Korean aviator who twice passed over the tents so closely "we could see his face clearly. He looked back at us just as we looked at him. He tossed something from his cockpit, presumably a hand grenade, and it fell harmlessly to the ground and exploded a safe distance from us." This spawned much discussion that night, of course, and

> an epidemic of Monday morning quarterbacking swept the MASH. If we had just been ready with the quad-50s [antiaircraft weapons] . . . one burst would have chewed that biplane to bits. Whose fault was it that we did not give him a proper welcome? How did we let that commie get away? Next time, just wait till next time!

The incident repeated itself twenty-four hours later, at 4:00 PM the next day, but

> this time he wore a pair of sunglasses and a nice white scarf around his neck. In the breeze, the scarf trailed back from the leather helmet like the tail of a comet, giving him a World War I ace look. . . . Instead of greeting him with quad-50s, we waved our hands and shouted greetings as he went by on his first pass. On his second buzz, he dipped his wings to return our wave. On he went, climbing skyward and tossing his payload from the aircraft. We shook our heads and laughed as we strolled back to the tents. In a moment we heard the explosion way out in the field. We did not even look back.

"Bedcheck Charley,"[44] as 8076th MASH dubbed him, came regularly at 4:00 PM every day until

> as suddenly as he had appeared, his visits ceased. We felt a bit like a friend was gone. It occurred to us that someone had ordered him to bomb the MASH and continue bombing it until it was no longer operational. In a touch of compassion, this lone North Korean refused to carry out the insane orders to bomb a hospital. Perhaps he reported that his mission was accomplished. Perhaps they knew what he was doing and relieved him of the mission. Perhaps even his military superiors recognized that what he was ordered to do was inhumane and they were touched by a sense of humanity. We will never know. He never reappeared.[45]

This ad hoc, mutual self-restraint was far less systematic than "live and let live" in World War I trenches, but its appearance even in the midst of the particularly brutal Korean War is testament to the possibility of the ethic of cooperation in warfare.

Similar phenomena occur at other phases in conflict. "One of the commonest features" of siege warfare negotiations between city-states in Renaissance Italy during the fourteenth and fifteenth centuries was "the idea of a delayed surrender," in which a town under siege would agree to capitulate if help had not arrived within a set period. In the meantime, "the siege would not be pressed [and the attackers] could look forward to avoiding the most dangerous exercise of all—storming a well fortified city," while the besieged hid their belongings in the event that relief never came.[46]

The warring parties were small principalities constrained by a rough parity between them, so realistically, they could not expect to "annihilate their rivals," but rather hope only to "achieve security and predominance within clearly defined spheres of influence." As a result, "battles were calculated risks, fought to gain advantage not overwhelming victory."[47] While the settled terms of delayed surrender were not always later honored, the frequency of these negotiations indicates some dynamics similar to those in the World War I trenches: mutual advantage to be gained from not fighting and some expectation of repeated future interaction.

## Why Cooperate?

一將功成萬骨枯。
*Yi jiang gong cheng wan gu ku.*
One general's honor is 10,000 soldiers' white bones.
—CAO SONG, "JI HAI TWO POEMS" (TANG DYNASTY)
《己亥歲二首僖宗廣明元年》年代:唐。作者:曹松

One major motivation for "live and let live" is, unsurprisingly, ordinary soldiers realizing that they are being condemned to die for no greater purpose than someone else's vainglory or petty feuds. Their memoirs are filled with lengthy treatments of the abuse they suffer at the hands of senior officers. On only the third page of his collected letters, Pvt. William Wheeler, who fought with the Duke of Wellington's armies in the early nineteenth century, describes a superior officer who "delighted in torturing the men, every man in the Corps hated him, when once a soldier came under his lash it was no use for any officer to plead for him"; only a few months later, he recounts unfair punishments meted out by commanders and, separately, reports that "I have at length escaped from the Militia without being flead alive."[48]

A significant portion of World War I Italian officer Emilio Lussu's memoir, *A Soldier on the Southern Front,* is devoted to relating how senior officers frequently sent soldiers on obviously foolhardy and suicidal missions, such as crossing No Man's Land to cut the enemy's barbed wires in broad daylight, because the officers had recently arrived on the front and did not understand the war, or did not care and simply wanted to see something being done under their watch. Says his trench-mate Ottolenghi:

> Our real enemies are not beyond our own trenches. So first, about-face, then onward . . . all the way to Rome. That's where the enemy's general headquarters is. . . . It seems to me that our generals were sent to us by the enemy to destroy us. . . . Where is our enemy? That is the question. The Austrians? Obviously not. No, our natural enemies are our generals. . . . His Excellency General Cadorna . . . is not anywhere near here. And neither is the commander of our army. Even the commander of our army corps is far away, hiding out at the foot of the high plateau.[49]

There are many such moments, in this war and every war, in which ordinary soldiers recognize that they pay the price for the machinations of kings and generals in which they have no stake.[50] In the course of that realization, they may appreciate that they have more in common with their enemy than with their own officers who are fellow countrymen—and so in order to save themselves, they become willing to cooperate with an unknown enemy by "living and letting live." Naked self-interest, once it is realized, can operate at different levels and lead in different directions.

Is cooperation between enemies possible even when it is not clear that self-interest is being served? In the World War I trenches, the anonymity of fighting between large, modern nation-state armies cut both ways: it allowed soldiers to hold pernicious perceptions of strangers and to kill them with hardly a thought for their opponents' humanity, but it also let them acknowledge their shared attributes and interests, in opposition to their own officers. Ironically, limited personal contact with the enemy can compare favorably to the extensive but contentious and often abusive personal interaction with one's officers or troop mates, and that opens some space for such mutual recognition.

In a strange way, modern warfare is not really about killing. Violence, says Carl von Clausewitz, is simply a way of imposing one's will on another person. Like wrestlers:

> Each tries by physical force to compel the other to do his will: his immediate object is to overthrow his adversary and thereby make him incapable of any further resistance. *War is thus an act of force to compel our adversary to do our will.* . . . Force, that is to say, physical force (for no moral force exists apart from the conception of a state and law), is thus the *means*; to impose our will upon the enemy is the *object*. To achieve this object with certainty we must disarm the enemy, and this disarming is by definition the proper aim of military action. It takes the place of the object, and in a certain sense pushes it aside as something not belonging to war itself.[51]

This builds to his famous statement that war is merely the continuation of policy with other tools,[52] just one instrument among many. As violent action is a means to an end, not a good in itself, if the outcome could be achieved without killing a single person, so much the better.

This then leaves room for other dynamics and motivations to operate, even if not always efficiently, in the service of warfare, such as upholding a sense of honor or protecting the weak and innocent. The self-interest of "live and let live" can also emerge in that space, and is just one rationale for conspiring with the enemy. Other collusions include sparing women, children, and other innocents or treating POWs according to some international standard, each of which grows out of its own complex of motives, as we will see.

## What Is Cooperation?

Cooperation is a fraught concept, with different definitions and uses growing out of rich traditions such as evolutionary biology or game theory that can inform one another.[53] In fact, Axelrod begins *The Evolution of Cooperation* with an exploration of World War I trenches' "live and let live." The broader field of conflict theory, started by Thomas Schelling's *The Strategy of Conflict* (1960), looks at war as a form of negotiation involving signaling, communication, coordination, and bargaining, with asymmetric behavior and knowledge.

## The Limits of Game-Theoretic Analysis

Analysis with game theory can be so compelling that in some fields, cooperation in warfare is thought of only in game-theoretic terms. Formalizing cooperation through game theory both gains and loses some insights, however. Its rationalistic approach captures some aspects of cooperation between enemies and certainly enhances our understanding of institutionalized international laws of war agreed upon between states, for example. But it does not necessarily enlighten us on other aspects of collaboration, including cooperating even to one's own detriment and its underlying complex of motivations such as virtue, honor, ideology, morality, and altruism. Game theory can help show that some form of ethic of cooperation exists in warfare, but it cannot encompass or explain the entirety of that moral impulse at the individual or institutional levels.

It behooves us to remember that no matter how rational one's approach,[54] war itself is always grounded in some kind of emotion. Says Clausewitz, who is often mistaken for holding and advocating a purely rational approach to warfare:

> *Conflict between men really consists of two different elements: hostile feeling and hostile intention.* . . . We cannot conceive the most savage, almost instinctive, passion of hatred as existing without hostile intention . . . . *Among savages intentions inspired by emotion prevail; among civilized peoples those prescribed by intelligence. But this difference lies not in the intrinsic nature of savagery and civilization, but in their accompanying circumstances, institutions, and so forth.* . . . Even the most civilized nations can be passionately inflamed against one another. . . . *How far from the truth we should be if we ascribed war among civilized men to a purely rational act of the governments and conceived it as continually freeing itself more and more from all passion, so that at last there was no longer need of the physical existence of armies, but only of the theoretical relations between them—a sort of algebra of action.* Theory was already beginning to move in this

direction when the events of the last war taught us better. *If war is an act of force, the emotions are also necessarily involved in it.* If war does not originate from them, it still more or less reacts upon them, and the degree of this depends not upon the stage of civilization, but upon the importance and duration of the hostile interests. If, therefore, we find that civilized peoples do not put prisoners to death or sack cities and lay countries waste, this is because intelligence plays a greater part in their conduct of war and has taught them more effective ways of applying force than these crude manifestations of instinct.[55]

This complex of emotion, rationality, and interests cuts across different types of societies in various ways to determine how they will pursue their war efforts, but no society or war effort is free of hostile intent.

### *Cooperation as It Is Used*

My purpose is not to propose a final definition of cooperation, but rather to look at counterintuitive forms of cooperation that are noteworthy in the context of warfare, explore their aims and dynamics, and tease out their relationships with one another. To that end, the types of cooperation discussed here cover a range that may not initially appear to constitute cooperation at all or may seem unrelated.

In "cooperation," I include a weak form of intentional cooperation, meaning that if a person thinks of himself as cooperating—however he may understand that, provided he is not insane or otherwise delusional—with the enemy when he engages in certain wartime acts, then I generally take it to be cooperation. In these cases, it is the actor's self-conception that matters.

There is a stronger form of intentional cooperation: working jointly with the intent to achieve an end that is beneficial for somebody (either the actors themselves or a third party) relative to some baseline. This jointness, "with other people," entails some form of communication between the actors, which can be very weak: they do not actually have to talk, write, or otherwise correspond directly with one another, as long as there is interaction that allows a person to infer information. When two men get into a boat, both will row their oars in sync, says David Hume, even without having explicitly discussed an agreement to do so. If a producer of the same product that I make raises his prices at the same time every year, I might be able to infer that he wants me to join in an oligopolistic alliance. If the enemy shells my trench at the same time every day, I might be able to infer that he will do the same tomorrow, and would like me to reciprocate. Conventions and agreements can arise tacitly, "without the interposition of a promise," as Hume describes, simply by "referenc[ing]" the actions of the other and performing on the basis of a "supposition" of the other's performance.[56] Such indirect communication is encompassed within the next requirement, of strategic action.

Jointness also requires strategic, rather than parametric, action. Strategic action involves responsiveness to others' moves and is game-theoretic; in contrast, parametric action is choice-theoretic, more like responding to nature.[57]

Jointness can entail but does not require collective agency or collective planning, however.[58] For example, when a large group of people is trying to get into a tennis stadium in time for the opening serve, the individuals are all cooperating with one another under the constraints presented by others wanting the same thing. In this case, they are working jointly and responding strategically to others' actions, but cannot be said to constitute a collective agent. As Schelling has shown, this kind of coordination can occur even when the parties are in different places and unable to communicate with one another, and when there are any number of equilibrium solutions with similar payoffs for all parties (and therefore no obviously "right" or "better" answer). Under these circumstances, they will tend to choose the most prominent or conspicuous solution, which is "some focal point for each person's expectation of what the other expects him to expect to be expected to do."[59]

Tacit human convention can give rise to explicit rules and institutions, as Hume argues about the origins of justice and property—"it arises gradually, and acquires force by a slow progression, and by our repeated experience of the inconveniences of transgressing it."[60] Even more surprisingly, rules and institutions can be derived from tacit and unspoken coordination even under the high-stakes life-or-death situations of active war, as we shall see with the development of some strong (but never explicitly negotiated) norms of war as well as the legal institutionalization of certain previously tacit rules of war.

In both weaker and stronger senses, cooperation between enemies in warfare does not require direct communication, collective agency or planning, positive sentiment (e.g., altruism, fellow feeling), shared goals (each person could have the same goal), or even mutually beneficial outcomes to the actors themselves. Nor does it preclude selfish motivation—in fact, it is often driven by self-interest.

## The Ethic of Cooperation in Warfare

Despite the antagonistic nature of warfare—in which participants try to kill one another—soldiers, states, and other entities will still *intentionally* cooperate with one another, often in ways that make it harder for them to win.[61] This intent matters even if the actual behavior or outcome is noncooperative, e.g., if the actors are wrong about their actions and effects.

### *How to Cooperate*

Cooperative intent does not have to exist at the level of each individual. Actors such as states or international organizations can behave cooperatively even if the particular individuals that compose them do not always intend that. Cooperation can also be built into institutional structures, such as international law. Enemies can work together by establishing formal and informal practices within war or the rules restricting war. General agreement on the norms of warfare does not necessarily include concurrence on how to justify them, however. Actors can cooperate in a variety of ways and for different reasons, including:

1. *Cooperation for shared goals* (e.g., team-building activities):
This is the cooperation that people most readily think of, when all parties have the same goal and its content applies to each party in the same or compatible way(s). Cooperation itself may be the goal, such as in a company team-building activity to transport a bucket of water using only designated methods. Or people might also cooperate for an external shared goal with either noncompetitive (e.g., playing a Brahms symphony) or competitive ends (e.g., a Tour de France cycling team trying to drive its leader to victory). These take place within definitive structures and constraining rules of action, but there can also be less-defined contexts, such as neighbors building a community garden, random passersby pulling a car out of a ditch, or different military branches (army, navy, air force) engaging in joint-force operations.

2. *Cooperation for the same, but not shared, goals* (e.g., chess game opponents, dueling fencers):

In competitive games with a limited number of winners, each player holds the same, but not shared, goal of winning the match, as that could only be achieved at others' expense. Participants cooperate nonetheless, first, by entering into the competition, as there would be no activity without the requisite number of players; then they play according to rules that restrict how the pieces/players move, specify how and when players may interact (e.g., taking turns), and define how to win. Without players' mutual cooperation in abiding by the rules, there could be no competition as conceived. Any defined competition, mental or athletic, requires such cooperation *in order for* one to beat the others and the competition to yield an outcome. Cooperation in warfare is most frequently of this kind: each side has the same goal of winning, but can only do so at the others' expense (by killing the other), under the constraints of whatever rules or norms have been established.

3. *Cooperation for a variety of goals—some shared, some same, some different—within a shared process/infrastructure* (e.g., a social contract perspective of society):

Here, cooperation *is* the shared process or infrastructure within which people operate. With so many varying and ever-changing goals in a diverse society, the only way people can live together is to mutually abide by specific rules of engagement, from the most fundamental (e.g., whether or not freedom of speech is a principled right) to the most mundane yet practical (e.g., which side of the road to drive on). In warfare, the institution of international law has a similar structure—everyone enters the activity with different, same, conflicting, concurrent, changing goals, but is equally bound by the superstructure of the law.

The peculiar thing about cooperation in warfare is not only that there is cooperation at all—already significant in itself—but that there is beyond that an *ethic* of cooperation in warfare, a belief that it is right to cooperate in war. This ethic is more than mere pursuit of self-interest, for it often cuts against that. Even when cooperation clearly promotes everyone's self-interest,[62] other motivations creep in as well. For example, a veteran of the World War I trenches cajoled his more eager companion: "Come on, let sleeping dogs lie. If we was to throw a bomb you can bet your boots the old Bosche would chuck one back, and Mr. Digby and Mr 'Arris (the soldiers occupying the sap) . . . are both married men. Wouldn't be cricket would it?"[63]

Disturbing the peace would only prove disastrous for soldiers and their families. Still, it is not the only impetus. The appeal to "cricket" entreats the other soldier to also consider the importance of fairness and reciprocity, above and beyond and perhaps against one's own interests—that because the opponent restrains himself, perhaps one should too.

### The Legitimating Effect of Cooperation

Whether or not it is used as such, war is commonly thought of as a last resort after further negotiation and compromise appear impossible. When something seems so important, unjust, or intractable that there is no recourse save violence, it is also natural to deem the enemy so repulsive as to be worth killing. So when there is cooperation, not only are military leaders incensed at the damage to military interests, but the population is also often outraged at the seeming treachery. Soldiers can be court-martialed or executed for simply declining to kill the enemy when given the opportunity, much less colluding with them on or off the battlefield.

For example, the prisoner exchange in May 2014 between the United States and the Taliban—Army PFC Bowe Bergdahl for five Taliban fighters detained at Guantánamo—was controversial amongst both Americans and Taliban across the political spectrum.[64] There were practical fears about whether the exchange served American interests, as the Taliban fighters would be released to Qatar, where they would be allowed to move freely, and no US officials would be involved in their oversight.[65]

Of the other concerns,[66] perhaps the most significant was that although discussions leading to the exchange were limited and unlikely to presage any broader peace talks,[67] many Americans were troubled by the possibility that negotiations and agreements might confer international legitimacy upon the Taliban—something the latter seeks but which the international community has resisted granting.[68] Then US secretary of state Hillary Clinton recounted:

> I was asked if "it would be a surprise and maybe even disturbing" for Americans to hear that we were trying to reconcile with some insurgents even as the President was sending more U.S. troops to

fight the very same Taliban. . . . Could sworn enemies actually come to some kind of understanding that would end a war and rebuild a shattered country? After so many years of fighting, it was hard enough to sit together and talk face-to-face, let alone trust one another. . . . I acknowledged . . . that opening the door to negotiations with the Taliban would be hard to swallow for many Americans after so many years of war. Reintegrating low-level fighters was odious enough; negotiating directly with top commanders was something else entirely.[69]

American officials stated that they could not cite another time in which the United States exchanged prisoners in an unconventional, insurgent conflict.[70] In fact, the United States has negotiated with terrorist groups in the past—including the "arms for hostages" Iran-Contra scandal, which resulted in the release, and then replacement kidnappings, of three hostages[71]—but that was an anomaly, as it usually takes a heavy hand with terrorists and rarely pays ransoms for hostages.[72]

More than a lack of precedent on this matter, however, it was the very idea of doing business—even a self-interested trade—with the enemy that was anathema for many. It is difficult to accept cooperation with someone who has been and is trying to destroy you, and whom you have been and are trying to destroy in turn. Animosity and mistrust, not to mention inevitable villainization of the other, compound over time, making it hard to imagine cooperating even with former enemies to pursue one's self-interest,[73] much less with a current one.

The principle of nonnegotiation with terrorists is meant to not only deter future terroristic acts, but also withhold conferring legitimacy to terrorist groups.[74] It reflects a belief that terrorists, by dint of their unconventional tactics, are untrustworthy—further reason to deny their political legitimacy.

Cooperation unwittingly accords a modicum of respect, trust, and recognition of humanity, which is exactly why cooperating with one's opponent (terrorist or otherwise) *does* lend him a veneer of legitimacy, and why negotiating with terrorist groups is controversial—it appears to confer not just political legitimacy to the organizations, but also moral legitimacy to their military tactics.

Can cooperation occur in isolation without any implications for legitimacy? Several editorials expressed hope that the 2014 US/Taliban prisoner exchange would lead to further dialogue, resulting in a broader reconciliation or larger peace agreement. For example:

> On balance, the exchange made sense. . . . The release is part of a broader effort . . . to engage with the Taliban as the U.S. war effort winds down, and rightly so. . . . If the U.S.'s exit from Afghanistan is not to end in disaster for the people of that country, there must be some kind of accommodation between their government and the Taliban. By releasing the five Taliban commanders, the administration hoped not just to get Bergdahl back, but also to move that larger process along.[75]

> The Bergdahl deal may serve as a prelude to a wider set of talks with the Taliban. . . . Spokesmen for both sides stressed that the deal just made was a prisoner-exchange deal and nothing more—that no further inferences should be made. But American officials from President Obama on down have stressed that a good end to this war can only be a negotiated end, that it must involve an accord with all the factions, and the Taliban are a homegrown faction. Maybe the Bergdahl deal will serve as a prelude to a wider set of talks—in which case this will be looked back upon as a very good day.[76]

But what if this prisoner exchange is just a one-off and does not lead to future negotiation: Would there be something wrong with it? One should always work toward the beginning of the end to the war—as the Obama administration did—but if, ultimately, it was nothing more than a prisoner exchange for the limited purpose of recovering one's soldier, it would be nothing strange or even necessarily incorrect.

Some commentators erroneously claimed that "prisoner exchanges generally come when hostilities have ceased,"[77] but they can be commonplace even in the midst of conflict and do not necessarily indicate any movement toward reconciliation or resolution. During the four-century war between the Arab Caliphate and the Byzantine Empire (629–1050s AD), for example, almost two dozen prisoner exchanges were recorded over nearly two centuries (late eighth through mid-tenth centuries AD). Amid continuous raiding activity, the two empires exchanged prisoners, sometimes by the thousands, by having them simultaneously walk across bridges over the Lamis river on their shared borderland.[78]

In recent times, some countries such as Israel, the United Kingdom, and France have been more willing to exchange hostages,[79] and there is a long history of successful trades, including with terrorist groups. Since its inception in 1948, Israel has frequently traded with its various Arab enemies, releasing over eight thousand prisoners in dozens of exchanges in the past three decades alone for Israeli citizens, amid what could be considered a single, continuous—albeit complicated and ever-changing—quarrel. The myriad bilateral antagonisms in the region (involving Israel, Egypt, Palestine, Syria, Iran, and others) are all part of this complex conflict, with crosscutting interests and shifting microalliances, and the numerous prisoner exchanges involving tens of thousands of people have not been harbingers of any greater resolution.

While most exchanges were with established states (e.g., Syria, Egypt, Lebanon), many were with Palestinian and other Arab political groups it does not recognize or classifies as terrorist, including Fatah, the Democratic Front for the Liberation of Palestine (DFLP), Hamas, and Hezbollah. Recently, in 2011, Hamas released Israeli soldier Gilad Shalit, whom it had captured in 2006, in exchange for 1,027 Palestinian prisoners held by Israel.[80] One has even seen successful hostage exchange involving Boko Haram, a militant Islamic group in Nigeria so extreme it is shunned by many others—here, eighty-two of nearly three hundred kidnapped schoolgirls for some militant commanders.[81]

Clearly, cooperation can take place between enemies—not just between conventional opponents in a structured, iterated game, but also under less organized or stable circumstances—that does not necessarily confer legitimacy. Limited pockets of cooperation can and often do punctuate a longer, sustained conflict, without any contradictions: enemies can negotiate over smaller issues, make agreements in good faith, and keep their word, whether or not the other side is an organized political faction, while simultaneously warring against each other in the broader context.[82]

## Modern Institutionalization of Cooperation and the Rise of International Law

Different forms of cooperation can be arrayed along a spectrum of defined organization and design. At the more structured end, one might find something like redistributive welfare, in which citizens must pay a prescribed percentage of their income and spending in taxes but the particular use of these revenues is left to the vagaries of political negotiations. In the middle of the spectrum, where processes are less constraining, there is, for example, competition between businesses for market share. Beyond the cooperation of obeying laws for product safety, copyright, antiprotectionist or antimonopolist practices, or other commercial restrictions, actors are free to do almost anything else: they might choose to improve on an existing product, create something radically different to do the same thing but better, or something else, so it is also not a zero-sum game. At the more amorphous end of cooperative enterprises would be spontaneous orders, e.g., development of a language or emergence of the use of money.

Usually, cooperative effects without cooperative intent are not particularly significant, as they can be produced quite accidentally,[83] but it is noteworthy when an ethic of cooperation is built in at a higher structural level. The most striking example of such institutionalized cooperation is the establishment and widespread acceptance (at least in name) of international warfare law. Such cooperation, for example, the ban on hollow-point bullets, generates something that looks quite different from individual cooperation to maintain "live and let live" in the World War I trenches: How can they both be considered manifestations of the same phenomenon, an ethic of cooperation in warfare?

In some areas, cooperation is scalable, from the level of the individual actor through intermediary levels to the institution, for example, with expectations for POW treatment.[84] At other times, the form of cooperative ethic is fairly unique, as with "live and let live," and cannot be institutionalized into law. In both cases, cooperation can be considered a good, a positive reason to engage in the action, independent of the other reasons for that action.

Adherence to the law requires the cooperation of all relevant actors (nation-states, soldiers, and everyone in between), not just between adversaries, but also internally, by domestic authorities enforcing the international laws on their own populations. National and international institutions can enable actors' cooperation, or the institutions themselves can be the object of cooperation, such that individuals operating under those laws are primarily rule-following with or without cooperative intent. In the latter case, the intent to cooperate still exists, but not necessarily for each acting individual; the institutions and rules form the cooperative structure and embody cooperative intent.

In between self-interested and intentionally-cooperative conduct lies behavior such as rule-following, and at times, the ethic of cooperation in warfare appears to be merely rule-following. The two can look similar, especially when international law prescribes cooperation as a means or an end such that cooperation in warfare then *entails* rule-following.

But cooperation can contradict the rules or engage where they are silent. "Live and let live" clearly flouted regulations and defied the wishes of high command, for example, while ad hoc decisions to spare someone out of a sense of fairness arise in the absence of established rules or expectations or after all the rules have been obeyed. So there is no clean relationship between cooperation and rule-following.

As with most human action, mixed motivations are the norm in the business of warfare. There are moments when people think that cooperation itself has moral purchase, but the desire to cooperate usually functions alongside and is buttressed by other rationales—foremost among them the self-interested desire to survive—and cooperation can be a means to an end.

It is also sometimes the case that soldiers engaged in cooperative behavior do not necessarily think of it as such, but that does not mean they are not cooperating. For example, says a US Marine deployed in Afghanistan in 2009–10, one of the major strategies was to establish a rapport and broker deals with locals so that they would see it was in their best interests not to fight the Americans: "We thought of it as building relationships, and if they wanted to fight, we'd fight. Sometimes multiple times a day. But if someone wanted to reach out to my extended hand, we'd negotiate, and sometimes we'd do that several times a day. . . . We had a mutual interest in survival. The Marines wanted to go home alive, and they didn't want us to burn their houses down."[85]

Motives evolve as well. The wearing of uniforms in combat is an interesting case of something that started for one reason—the internal objectives of imposing discipline and professionalism on a previously disordered militia and solidifying loyalty to the sovereign from mercenary fighters—that was later superseded by others, including (a) reciprocally and cooperatively protecting civilians, such that soldiers accept the disadvantages of uniforms on the understanding that their opponents do the same, and (b) shielding civilians on the grounds of innocence or human rights.

We are in a period of transition in international ethics, and the justifications for various international laws are in flux. This does not obviate any original cooperative ethic that motivated those laws, and its evolution across a wide range of issues demonstrates its breadth, intensity, and depth.

By "evolution," I do not mean that there has been some kind of natural selection for cooperative behavior such that it is considered more "fit" for or more "right" in warfare—although now there is clearly *institutional* reward via international and national law. Neither do I imply any teleological claim about the development of cooperation over time, as institutionalized cooperation is associated with both more and fewer moral atrocities. The ethic of cooperation in warfare emerges and manifests itself inconsistently, in different ways and in varied settings throughout the history of warfare, and, like evolution, there is nothing teleological about it. It would be difficult to trace a clear progression of increasing cooperation overall, even accounting for halting development and setbacks.

That said, there is, however, something unique about the ethic of cooperation in warfare during the modern period, when it slowly gets systematized in international law and its accompanying institutions. Obviously, there are many ways to fight other than elaborate set pieces à la the Napoleonic era, but modern warfare, which developed in conjunction with the modern nation-state, has many distinctive features. Most visible are massive national armies who, for the first time, expected to die for their national homelands rather than for a god, lord, or paymaster. Along with the swelling size of armies grew the scale of war itself and the industrial production of weaponry, and this required management by a central bureaucracy.[86]

In addition to the military's institutional, organizational, and technological advances, modern warfare is also characterized by the development of governing codes of conduct and international laws that embody and prioritize certain cooperative values, e.g., yielding decisive outcomes.

These explicit international laws and treaties differ from the limiting principles and edicts of warfare previously issued by, for example, kings or religious leaders, in three related ways:

1. *Universalizability*: Adherence to religious edicts hinges on belief in that religion and political orders on loyalty to the king, for example. In contrast, contemporary international laws of warfare are universal in applicability, as modern just war doctrines purport to speak to all states and to all human beings in those states. Compliance with the law is not

grounded in membership in particular states or groups of states or in certain religious beliefs.

2. *Nonreliance on comprehensive doctrines*: Even as religious edicts can persuade only specific audiences, they still make comprehensive claims,[87] whereas contemporary international law does not rely on similarly-comprehensive doctrines and seeks instead to be universalizable. International law could be justified by appeal to certain comprehensive doctrines, but its acceptance does not depend upon holding a particular religious faith or nationalism. Rather, it rests on some overlapping consensus, whatever form that might take, and is universalizable in both justification and application.

3. *Legal specificity*: Finally, these international laws carry with them much more possibility for legal specificity, because their associated courts build up a body of case law through the process of adjudication. How a law applies in particular circumstances is better worked out in a court system than when promulgated by kings and priests, as courts actually hear cases, and from a variety of traditions and religious backgrounds. The ensuing body of case law built by the international judicial structure gives us better understanding of what that law means in specific cases than we had with canon law, e.g., Christian doctrine, which offers less detail for its application and would have pertained only to certain areas (e.g., Europe). In contrast, international law applies to all states and types of regime—whether imperial, anarchic, or other—and provides greater specificity, over a broader range of cases.

The development of established codes of conduct and international laws in the modern period shows that not all morality is lost in warfare. Cooperation is obviously motivated in large part by practical and self-interested considerations, but not entirely. One can interpret the law of armed conflict (LOAC) as yet another tool wielded by the more powerful states to oppress weaker ones; as Thrasymachus explains, "justice is . . . the advantage of the stronger," for "rulers proclaim that what is to their own advantage is just for those who are ruled by them."[88]

It is not so easy to rig the structure in one's favor, however. As Machiavelli counsels the prince: the law alone is insufficient, and he must contest by both law and force, in the way "proper" to man and beast respectively, while simultaneously disguising his actions, "to be a great pretender and dissembler" such that his deception remains hidden and that he continue "to appear merciful, faithful, humane, honest."[89] This is a tall order indeed, one at which most princes fail.

Once established, rules can take on a life of their own and serve as a touchstone. The content and structure of international laws of war do make it harder to win, which is why even stronger countries and their soldiers repeatedly try to break the rules.

The widespread institutionalization of wartime cooperation in international law has not been seen at any other time in history and it may not last, but it is the vehicle for one of the major features of morality in warfare—the ethic of cooperation and reciprocity between both allies and enemies—and it has implications for warfare and for the international political structure. Even in the most appalling of human activities, there is systematic, self-imposed legal restraint, such as banning hollow point bullets (Hague Convention, 1899) or regulating prisoner-of-war treatment (from the Peace of Westphalia of 1648 through the Geneva Conventions of 1949). Most notable is that formalized cooperation has bred normative expectations—and perhaps normative duties—of future collaboration.

## Civilization in War

> If civilization has an opposite, it is war.
> Of these two things, you have either one or the other. Not both.
> —URSULA K. LE GUIN, *THE LEFT HAND OF DARKNESS*

The overwhelmingly dominant influence on contemporary international military ethics is the particular just war tradition that grew out of Augustinian and Thomist thought, which holds that the conduct of warfare should be constrained primarily by the principles of proper authority, just cause, and right intention, and then guided by considerations of last resort, proportionality, and probability of success. It would be difficult to overestimate the role that the secular inspirations from these principles play in the contemporary ethics training of Western militaries and in the content of established international laws. Emphasis on this canon, however, has meant that we have overlooked a significant thread running through different doctrines of military ethics across time and cultures.

Not only do people engage in ad hoc cooperation in war, but they are also influenced by an ethic of cooperation between enemies that has been in play throughout human history. Given the violent, combative nature of war and what is at stake in its pursuit, the existence of this moral principle is surprising, yet simultaneously so commonplace that it defines the idea of modern warfare in largely unnoticed ways. Cooperation between enemies coexists with them trying to kill one another.

This book conducts a genealogical exploration of three different forms that the ethic of cooperation in warfare can take and shows how it has defined the idea of modern warfare in several—contradictory—ways. The three forms I discuss are merely a subset of broader cooperation. There are collaborations in war that I will not study, for example, that which intends to bring harm to a third party (e.g., conspiracies between military, industry, and political interests or the-enemy-of-my-enemy-is-my-friend). This is not because they are less common or important—only that they are unsurprising.

The ethic of cooperation between enemies in warfare is unexpected and perhaps unique in that there can be conscious intent to collaborate for some separate benefit, even while trying to impose the ultimate harm by killing the other. That is why the ethics of cooperation in warfare that are most interesting and counterintuitive draw from a common conception of cooperation as understood by most who engage in it, even if the practitioners themselves would not describe it that way. Understanding the ethic of cooperation in warfare is essential because various forms of this ethos have made their way into the practice of warfare and just war theory unspoken and unseen, so it is critical to recognize when militaries and soldiers act in terms of and are motivated by a cooperative ethic.

There are different ways to categorize cooperation in warfare, including by level (e.g., individuals, battalion units, states) or method (e.g., ad hoc negotiations, institutionalized rules, international law). Here, I look at cooperation by its purpose, and in particular three types (which are not exhaustive): (1) to set up a "fair fight," as soldiers commonly understand it, (2) to minimize damage to particular classes of individuals, and (3) to end the war quickly and/or definitively in order to minimize overall damage.

Studying it in this way reveals important tensions within the practice of war, between warfare and the ethic of cooperation, and between the different types of this ethic, and I then explore the limits of cooperation and its inconsistencies. Finally, I delve into the role that cooperation plays in the broader superstructure of warfare itself, in particular the relationship between war and politics, the international law's focus on *jus in bello* and relative silence on *jus ad bellum*, and determinations about legitimacy in war, the last of which helps to explain some of modern nation-states' inability to engage favorably with noncooperative forms of warfare.

Attempts to place constraints on war can be seen in light of the broad contexts of pacification, civilization, and humanitarianism. In addressing the "logic of violence," cognitive psychologist Steven Pinker turns to evolution:

> Nature does not consist of one big bloody melee. . . . If you attack one of your own kind, your adversary may be as strong and pugnacious as you are, and armed with the same weapons and defenses. The likelihood that, in attacking a member of your own species, you will get hurt is a powerful selection pressure that disfavors indiscriminate pouncing or lashing out. It also rules out the hydraulic metaphor and most folk theories of violence, such as thirst for blood, a death wish, a killer instinct, and other destructive . . . impulses. When a tendency toward violence evolves, it is always *strategic*. Organisms are selected to deploy violence only in circumstances where the expected benefits outweigh the expected costs.[90]

There are limits to analogizing from animal fighting to human warfare, especially when large-scale modern warfare seems to have thrown off any evolutionary constraints. At the same time, although contemporary war is an unusually bloody melee, one finds evidence of intelligent constraint. This book is about some of those different forms of intelligent constraint, which is as much a part of the story of war as its savagery.

CHAPTER II

## Cooperation for a Fair Fight

There are two approaches to waging war, asymmetric and stupid.
—CONRAD CRANE, MILITARY HISTORIAN

Sniping, as far as I know, is recognized as a legitimate means of warfare. And yet there is something sneaking about it that outrages the American sense of fairness.
—ERNIE PYLE, *BRAVE MEN*

The desire to "fight fair" in war flies in the face of rationality, but it is not an uncommon instinct, and is one major manifestation of the ethic of cooperation between enemies in warfare. Most surprisingly, it even appears when there are no rules to guide or enforce such behavior. In his seminal *Just and Unjust Wars* (1977), Michael Walzer gives five examples of soldiers in the two world wars who refrain from shooting: British soldier Wilfred Owen peeked over the top of the trench to see "a solitary German, haring along toward us. . . . Nobody offered to shoot him, he looked too funny"; another Brit, Robert Graves, spotted a German taking a bath, but "disliked the idea of shooting a naked man," so he instructed his sergeant to do it; Italian officer Emilio Lussu was fascinated by his Austrian enemies across the trench "showing themselves to us as they really were, men and soldiers like us, in uniform like us, moving about, talking, and drinking coffee, just as our own comrades behind us were doing at the moment"; and British soldier Raleigh Trevelyan saw a German "wander like a sleep-walker across our line of fire. It was clear that for the moment he had forgotten war and—as we had been doing—was reveling in the promise of warmth and spring," and he merely scared him away instead of shooting him.[1] Walzer's own favorite comes from George Orwell's memoirs of fighting in the Spanish Civil War, when he looks across to the opposite trench:

> At this moment a man, presumably carrying a message to an officer, jumped out of the trench and ran along the top of the parapet in full view. He was half-dressed and was holding up his trousers with both hands as he ran. I refrained from shooting at him. It is true that I am a poor shot and unlikely to hit a running man at a hundred yards and also that I was thinking chiefly about getting back to our trench while the Fascists had their attention fixed on the aeroplanes. Still, I did not shoot partly because of that detail about the trousers. I had come here to shoot at "Fascists"; but a man who is holding up his trousers isn't a "Fascist," he is visibly a fellow-creature, similar to yourself, and you don't feel like shooting at him.[2]

In each case, the prospective shooters were in positions to take easy shots, and they would each have been entirely justified in killing the enemy soldiers under those circumstances, according to the norms of war. They felt ambivalent, however, because what they observed across the lines humanized the enemy, and they held back in that moment.

Different explanations can account for this behavior. Walzer argues that even if the decision was more impassioned "than principled," the restraint is "rooted in a moral recognition" of shared humanity—that, like oneself, the enemy turns out to be not entirely or merely a soldier.[3] One study of World War II behavior by US Brig. Gen. S. L. A. Marshall claimed that 75 percent of American frontline soldiers, and even 25 percent of "well-trained and campaign-seasoned troops," never fired their weapons "under average conditions of combat," especially because of their inadequate training in overcoming a cultural aversion to belligerence.[4] He explains the puzzling ratio-of-fire by the fact that the "average, normal" American

> comes from a civilization in which aggression, connected with the taking of life, is prohibited and unacceptable. The teaching and the ideals of that civilization are against killing, against taking advantage. The fear of aggression has been expressed to him so strongly and absorbed by him so deeply and pervadingly—practically with his mother's milk—that it is part of the normal man's emotional make-up. This is his great handicap when he enters combat. It stays his trigger finger even though he is hardly conscious that it is a restraint upon him. Because it is an emotional and not an intellectual handicap, it is

not removable by intellectual reasoning, such as "Kill or be killed." . . . Fear of killing, rather than fear of being killed, was the most common cause of battle failure in the individual, and . . . fear of failure ran a strong second.[5]

Despite its enormous influence in military thinking,[6] Marshall's work is controversial, as his methodology and lack of evidence of systematic data collection in his field notes or statistical analyses in his papers call into question the veracity and validity of his claims.[7] Even if Marshall were wrong about the ratio by an order of magnitude, however, his explanation for the reluctance to fire warrants some attention.[8]

Contra Walzer, Marshall points to a "*self*-directed 'relief' from not having to kill, rather than an *other*-directed recognition of a 'fellow-creature' who has become too 'careless' to be a proper 'target,'" says philosopher Nolen Gertz, and this difference in orientation is critical. Taking a cue from Marshall, Gertz argues that soldiers seek "existential" recognition from others in order to "maintain the distinction between being identified by others as a soldier and being identified as a *killer*." Killing enemy combatants in and of itself is not a problem, and what restraint is exercised is driven not by the desire to save a life, but rather by the need for his peers to see him as a professional doing his job in a practiced manner and not, for example, as a "grotesque" monster with questionable virtues, morals, or psychology.[9] Why is that important, what might that job entail, and what are its risks or conditions?

## Fairness, Parity, and "Sporting" Behavior

There is another way to interpret these behaviors, and that is with the ethic of cooperation for a fair fight in war, which is consistent with and can encompass or supplement many aspects of the others. Warriors throughout history and across cultures have valued not just winning, but winning in a particular way—namely, fairly. To unpack this notion of a "fair fight," I look at definitions of fairness where they overlap with cooperation in warfare. Then, because the concept of a "fair fight" has developed in part through practice, I study representative examples of self-imposed restraint in warfare and the constitutive cooperation that has since been codified in military traditions, to such an extent that it constitutes a significant ethic in military practice. This chapter then explores influences (such as professional ethics and virtue ethics) that have shaped, promoted, and reinforced this impetus for a fair fight, as well as its problems, internal inconsistencies, and contradictions. Finally, I take a sobering look at how such rules of fair play that are born of the best of intentions can inadvertently make things worse.

Not all restraint is alike, but the most striking cases rest on a principle that is similar to a distinction often drawn when trying to determine who among civilians contributing to the war effort is an acceptable military target in large-scale modern warfare. Military personnel and ethicists alike still struggle over this question, and one popular approach says that those who assist by providing goods and services that would be required in everyday life (e.g., food) are off-limits, while those participating more directly (e.g., workers at military munitions factories) can be targeted.[10]

In refraining from shooting an easy target such as in the sniper stories, the reasoning is similar: certain activities—such as bathing, drinking coffee, smoking, and struggling with one's trousers—are simply human, not wartime, activities, even if in the service of a war, and it can seem inappropriate to kill a soldier under those circumstances.

But why? The distinction is utterly artificial, and the reluctant shooters are the first to recognize that. Said the Italian Lussu of an Austrian officer smoking with his morning coffee: "That cigarette suddenly created a relationship between us. As soon as I saw his puff of smoke I felt the need to smoke. That desire of mine reminded me that I had some cigarettes too. In an instant, my act of taking aim, which had been automatic, became deliberate. I became aware that I was aiming, and that I was aiming at someone. My index finger, pressing on the trigger, eased off. I was thinking. I had been forced to think."[11]

Lussu had "no doubt; it was my duty to shoot," and yet, he was "not going to be the one to kill a man like this!... one man alone."[12] Why not? After all, asks Walzer, "What else... does a sniper do?"[13] Certainly many snipers have fired in similar situations, and such hesitation irrationally contradicts other aspects of warfare. Aristotle, for example, analogizes war to hunting for prey:

> If therefore nature makes nothing without purpose or in vain, it follows that nature has made all the animals for the sake of men. Hence even the art of war will by nature be in a manner an art of

acquisition (for the art of hunting is a part of it) that is properly employed both against wild animals and against such of mankind as though designed by nature for subjection refuse to submit to it, inasmuch as this warfare is by nature just.[14]

Similarly, until that moment, Lussu had likened war to "big-game hunting of men" and "my conscience as a man and as a citizen was not in conflict with my duty as a soldier"; in fact, he "did not see a man there. All I saw was the enemy." Then Lussu explicitly contrasts what he thought would be an acceptable act of war and the circumstances he then faced:

> To lead a hundred, even a thousand, men against another hundred, or thousand, was one thing. Taking a man, separating him from the rest of the men, and then saying, 'There, stand still, I'm going to shoot you, I'm going to kill you,' is another. . . . Fighting a war is one thing, killing a man is something else. To kill a man, like that, is to murder him.[15]

Walzer sees this as a moral consideration, and he is right about that—but it is not *merely* a reflection upon the other's proper categorization as a soldier liable to attack. It is more broadly an assessment of what makes for a fair fight in a war, insofar as you can have one. Part of that comes from recognizing shared humanity, of course, as that is the basis for a fair fight, and it is why one owes fairness to a fellow man and not to a beast.

Contrast, for example, the climactic confrontation between Achilles and Hector, when they finally meet at the end of *The Iliad*. Hector tries to coax Achilles into an agreement:

> . . . I swear
> I will never mutilate you—merciless as you are—
> if Zeus allows me to last it out and tear your life away.
> But once I've stripped your glorious armor, Achilles,
> I will give your body back to your loyal comrades.
> Swear you'll do the same.

Achilles explodes in anger at the very suggestion:

> You unforgivable, you . . . don't talk to me of pacts.
> There are no binding oaths between men and lions—

wolves and lambs can enjoy no meeting of the minds—
they are all bent on hating each other to the death.
So with you and me. No love between us. No truce
till one or the other falls and gluts with blood
Ares who hacks at men behind his rawhide shield.

(20.302–15)

Achilles does not recognize Hector as an equal, a peer, a fellow man, a being of the same species. Therefore, he is neither due any courtesies nor even capable of giving or receiving any.

In the contemporary examples of restraint, the snipers suddenly see their targets as *men*—neither incomprehensible beasts nor degraded enemy—and it is implied that men are owed certain considerations in war, the most important of which is an opportunity to act, to fight back, to defend himself, to maybe survive.

Lussu acknowledges that he would have automatically and happily shot at the officer had he been lying prone on the ground as on other nights, rather than on his knees in a fresh ditch shielded by a bush. His unfamiliar circumstances forced him to start thinking, and he soon realized that he had complete control over the situation:

> Behind that bush, down in the ditch, I was not threatened by any danger. I couldn't have been more relaxed in a room in my own house, in my hometown. Maybe it was that complete calm that drove off my war-fighting spirit. In front of me was an officer, young, unconscious of the looming danger. I couldn't miss. I could have taken a thousand shots at that distance without missing even one. All I had to do was pull the trigger and he would collapse to the ground. This certainty that his life depended on my will made me hesitant. I had a man in front of me. A man! I could make out his eyes and the features of his face.... To shoot like this, from a few steps away, at a man ... like shooting a wild boar![16]

What lurks in the backs of the minds of these snipers is that these circumstances do not seem to constitute warfare—or at least its spirit—and that the enemy might not receive his due, which is a genuine chance of defending himself.

Why does that matter? In some sense, the reluctant shooters are positing a category mistake. War is not an activity in which equal opportunity between combatants has any place, and the snipers themselves are obviously aware of this—yet, they hesitated and ultimately did not fire. It could be out of moral consideration for what the other person is owed as a human being (à la Walzer), or the desire to remain a soldier rather than become a murderer on the basis of how one kills (per Gertz). In either case, it is clear that, sometimes, soldiers feel that certain ways of killing in war are unacceptable—regardless of any inconsistencies between their feelings from one moment to the next, with other acceptable actions in war, or with the enterprise of warfare in general—because there is something about the other person being unaware of his imminent death and therefore unable to defend himself.

It is largely about whether the fight is "fair"—but what does that mean? Once a soldier enters into war, he expects that he could be killed at any time, on patrol, at a rear operating base, during a supply convoy run, while sleeping, or in any other circumstance outside of actual fighting. Fairness does not make much sense in this context, so why has this ethic made its way into war?

### Fairness and Cooperation

The concept of cooperation often overlaps with that of fairness, and it takes particular forms in the practice and morality of warfare. The OED defines *fair*, adj. and n., as

14. a. (a) Of conduct, actions, methods, arguments, etc.: free from bias, fraud, or injustice; equitable, legitimate, valid, sound.
    (b) Of a person: characterized by equitable or lawful conduct; honest, just; reasonable.
   b. Of conditions, circumstances, etc.: providing an equal chance of success to all; not unduly favourable or adverse to anyone.
   c. Of remuneration, reward, or recompense: that adequately reflects the work done, service rendered, or injury received. Also of punishment: commensurate with the crime, injury, etc., in question.
   d. That may be legitimately aimed at or pursued; that is considered a reasonable target for criticism, attack, etc.

e. *Sport* and *Games*. Allowed by the rules; made or done according to the rules; permissible, legitimate; *spec.* not incurring a penalty, the loss of a point, etc. Cf. foul adj. 14a.

It is primarily through two usages of fairness—as equal chance of success not unduly unfavorable to anyone (14.b.) and as sport and games (14.e.)—that we see the overlap between cooperation and "fair fights" in warfare. For the game to be played fairly (i.e., by the rules), players must work jointly to achieve the completion of a well-played game. In the context of sports and games, a necessary—if insufficient—condition for a well-played game is that all the rules (including those for violations of the rules) have been obeyed. In these circumstances, cooperation and fairness overlap completely: to cooperate is to play fairly, and vice versa.

In warfare, cooperation and fair fights can similarly overlap if the rules of engagement provide an equal chance to all (14.b.). (Here, it would be more of a Hobbesian natural equality.) For example, one of the many purposes of wearing uniforms is to make all soldiers equally identifiable and therefore equally vulnerable. There is a connection between 14.e. and other conceptions of fairness, especially 14.a. and 14.b., in which fairness is conceptualized as "free from bias," "equitable," or "of conditions, circumstances . . . providing an equal chance of success to all; not unduly favourable or adverse to anyone."

The more that fairness approaches pure procedural justice (in which there is no criterion for a just outcome beyond the procedure itself), the closer fairness and cooperation get to overlapping, as cooperation from all parties (in adhering to established rules) is necessary for the procedure to work properly. Cooperation and fairness do *not* overlap when there is an independent criterion for a just outcome, either perfect or imperfect procedural justice (e.g., when justice is determined by divine command, meritocracy, natural law, or anything else outside of the procedure itself), or when justice is defined procedurally but that procedure does not entail equity or unbiased decision-rules (e.g., when laws are determined by vote, but there is not universal suffrage). When cooperation and fairness come apart, tensions can arise within the practice and theory of warfare.

To better understand what "fair" killing in war means, it helps to look at athletic competitions. Soldiers and military commentators themselves make these analogies, as they are sometimes guided by similar moral considerations.[17] War has long been highly influential on sports, probably further back than the ancient Olympics, which began circa 776 BCE as a religious festival in honor of Zeus. The original events were stylized versions of fighting actions: footraces, boxing, wrestling, pankration (a martial art combining wrestling and boxing), discus throw, jumping, javelin throw, and chariot races.[18] Further back, in *The Iliad*'s recounting of the Trojan War (c. 1200 BCE), Patroclus's funeral games included chariot racing, boxing, wrestling, a footrace, sparring, iron throw, archery, and spear-throwing.

As in much of war, in sports there are rules, as well as a certain spirit with which they should be conducted. One is often warned against placing excessive importance upon winning: "The most important thing in life is not the triumph, but the fight; / the essential thing is not to have won, but to have fought well," says the modern Olympic creed (adopted in the twentieth century), which is reflected in another common adage, "It's not that you won or lost but how you played the game."[19]

### Competitiveness and Parity

Of course, one always wants to win, but the disposition with which victory is achieved matters, and that is the difference between the spirit and the letter of the law. Sometimes, an action is technically allowed, but one refuses to do it or it is frowned upon by others, because it seems to violate the *spirit* of the law, even if not the letter. This distinction can be found in some uses of the word *sporting*, an adjective that refers to behaving in a "sportsmanlike," "fair," or "generous" manner, or providing "good sport," which includes, among other things, providing a challenge. Giving another a "sporting chance" has come to mean giving him a "reasonable but not certain chance [or] a fair opportunity."[20]

It is not uncommon for athletes to prefer to play "well," not just in a rule-abiding way, but in the "right" way, when the victory and sportsmanship come into conflict. For example, Mountain View High School (Tucson, AZ) soccer coach Brian Ronan had his team play a slow, no-scoring offense once it was clear they would win handily, even though they needed a bigger score differential in order to advance to the 2012 tournament's semifinals. In forfeiting his team's chance to move forward, he said: "It could have been all about putting the ball in the back of the net.... This was a coaching moment, a chance to teach a life lesson. . . . We left the tournament more mature, and together as a team. I think it was the right thing to do. I have no regrets and neither does our team."[21] Advancement was not worth the cost of meting out humiliation, decided the coach.

In the storied 1987 cricket World Cup match between West Indies and Pakistan, West Indies' Courtney Walsh refused during the last over to run off the batter who had backed up too far outside the crease. Instead, he stopped, warned the batter about his position, and bowled again, and it cost West Indies the runs it needed to advance to the semifinals.[22]

What is perceived as sporting is culturally specific (to both the sport and the broader societal context), but adhering to established norms even to one's own disadvantage is a virtue valued across sports and across societies. Sports history is replete with similar stories about competitors who could have "run up" the score and won by even larger margins, whether for its own sake or to advance to the next stage, but refrained from doing so. Said one sports writer:

> The concept of poor sportsmanship shouldn't be difficult to explain. And yet its definition eludes simple words. Poor sportsmanship is commonly one of those 'I know it when I see it' things. . . . When in the 161–2 blowout does someone say enough is enough? Does that come at a 40-point lead? A 60-point lead? The truth is, no one wins with a score this lopsided.[23]

He calls sportsmanship "a matter of common sense, and common decency," implying that everyone knows what is required to behave morally and respectably, making it unnecessary to define or justify what it entails. That is unlikely, but common themes do arise. Of course, winning is often paramount, and it is more common to try to win—and win big—at any cost. For every one of these stories of supererogatory self-imposed restraint, there are many multiples of the opposite. But that such restraint happens at all—and not infrequently—is telling.

Why does running up a large lead sometimes seem improper, when everyone understands that it breaks no rules? Declining to maximize score differentials, or more dramatically refusing to press entirely legal advantages even at the cost of victory, demonstrates an underlying purpose for contestation—that it should be reasonably close, otherwise it is not a contest.

In any competition, leads can be accumulated and built upon, and become insurmountable—even farcical—but it is clearly important to many players and coaches to maintain some semblance of reasonable parity throughout. Sporting events try to generate parity in different ways, e.g., by dividing teams into leagues of different levels, using various kinds of tournaments to try to match the most equal opponents for the final rounds, or implementing particular rules of play to give competitors more opportunities. When these procedures prove inadequate in particular circumstances, the illusion must somehow be maintained by the players themselves and rely on their supererogatory actions of self-restraint. It seems surprising that competitors might do this, but in many cases, both competitors and their audiences want the contest to showcase some parity of skill, or at least not emphasize the overly disparate competencies between opponents.

Furthermore, some norms have developed to try to keep things "competitive." In football/soccer, for example, when a player falls injured, the opposing team is expected to stop play by kicking the ball out of bounds so that the player can be attended to, and then when the ball is put back into play, the injured player's team returns it to the opposing team rather than keep possession as it is entitled to under the rules. This custom is more or less sustained even at the World Cup level, where stakes are high, or even if the opponent thinks that the player is faking his injury (which is unfortunately common in soccer).[24]

It is noteworthy how much restraint is exercised even when it hinders one's ability to win. In the case of this soccer/football norm, the courtesies afforded are for injury, yet so long as they are not deliberately inflicted, injuries are a part of playing sport and also often related to fitness, which is a relevant competitive factor. Insofar as the goal of the sporting event is to find the best athlete/team, it is counterproductive to hold back in those circumstances.

A more extreme example comes from Tour de France professional road racing, where there is an unwritten rule that if the race leader suffers a mishap, the riders themselves will neutralize the race among one another.[25] For example, in 2001, Jan Ullrich led the race when he crashed on a descent in the Pyrenees, but his main rival, Lance Armstrong, slowed and waited for him instead of racing ahead.[26] Two years later, Ullrich returned the favor when a spectator's bag strap caught Armstrong's handlebar and threw him off his bike. This norm is also illustrated by its violations, for example, in an incident in 2010 that either hysterically or mockingly became known as "chaingate": during Stage 15, current race leader Andy Schleck launched an attack in the Pyrenees, but his chain popped off and close rival Alberto Contador (along with two others) rode past him instead of waiting. The commentary that exploded in response was so furious that Contador later apologized for seizing the lead.[27]

This is not to say that cycling is a sport comprised entirely of honor—as demonstrated by rampant doping, glass shards strewn across the road, and spiked drinks, among other blatant cheating—but this "gentlemen's agreement" nonetheless provokes strong reactions. Says cycling journalist and former amateur rider Phil Liggett:

> I don't know when it evolved. It's been a gradual thing, this so-called unwritten code. But now it is understood. You don't attack a fallen man. I can't think of a time, in my 31 years, when a rider attacked someone who had crashed. I know that today, in the German press, it's been written that Ullrich pulled a stupid maneuver by not attacking Lance when he went down. But the attitude in cycling is: You want to win a race? You want to beat someone, not take advantage.[28]

Ullrich himself said, "I have never in my life attacked someone who has crashed. That's not the way I race."[29] It is a curious distinction, between winning and not taking advantage—as if the ideal were two racers in black boxes with no interaction between them—yet one that instinctively resonates. At the same time, the parameters of the norm are a matter of judgment and still controversial in their applications. Moreover, not all misfortunes are created equal.

## The Essence of Warfare

### TYPES OF MISFORTUNE

There are at least three different types of bad luck:

- *Genuine accidents extraneous to the competition*, e.g., the spectator's bag strap catching Armstrong's handlebar: If the intention of the norm is to make sure that the outcome is not influenced by irrelevant external factors, then here, it seems to promote "fairness" in a straightforward manner.

- *Mechanical problems* are ambiguous: Sometimes, they are random unluckiness, e.g., a punctured tire or broken spoke on cobblestones; no one waits for the leader then, perhaps because the cobblestones' randomness is considered part of the race. Other times, mechanical problems reflect the team's quality, which includes technicians, and could be traced to a loose screw, shoddy cleaning, or poorly chosen equipment.[30] Road cycling is a team sport and instruments are as much a part of the game as the athlete's body, so should some of these problems be left unadjusted, in order to reflect the team's work? In some cases, mechanical problems result from poor decision-making or bad performance: many argued that Schleck's chain popped off because he changed gears at the wrong time, and as gear-changing is an important part of bike-handling, it was not an accident and he was fair game.

- *Solo crashes*: e.g., in 2001, Ullrich misjudged and overshot a turn, entirely of his own doing, without weather or road conditions to blame. Even to "purists," crashes on one's own are indicative of skill, both physical and tactical. A cyclist constantly assesses his capacity to ride safely and effectively at any given speed, and testing his descending skill is part of the sport. He can choose to ride slower, and in this case, Ullrich's decision to not slow down further was incorrect. Waiting for a lead cyclist who has crashed of his own accord would be unjustified on the grounds of eliminating irrelevant competitive factors.[31] This is actually a legitimate opportunity to build a lead, because those who did not crash under the same circumstances showed superior skill.[32]

The purpose of making these distinctions is to speak to the question, *What is essential to the activity and what is extraneous?* This is necessary in order to determine what constitutes a "fair" contest. On one hand, an athletic competition is a self-enclosed system, so anything permitted by the rules is "fair," and voluntary restraint simply squanders legitimate opportunity. On the other hand, athletic competition is fundamentally a test of skill between people, and it is important to maintain a certain parity so that the result is as unadulterated by extraneous circumstances as possible. To that end, only some kinds of differences should matter, which is why it is necessary to consider what is essential and what is extraneous to the essence of the sport. These norms of "fairness" are in part an attempt to answer that question—even if those norms are sometimes arbitrary, contradictory, irrational, or even wrong.

## PARITY OF RISK AND OPPORTUNITY

How is this related to warfare? War is an important paradigm through which we view sports, but the influence runs the other way as well. In antebellum United States, the West Point tradition of training taught soldiers to view war as a match or game,[33] and Maj. Gen. George B. McClellan, for example, "learned to think of warfare as a kind of chess match, to be played by professionals in bloodless and honourable competition. His proudest moments were those when 'by pure military skill' as he put it, he won apparent victory with a 'trifling' loss of life."[34]

Something similar happens when the rules are not set up in a way to promote "fairness" yet soldiers take it upon themselves to establish those conditions. To make sense of this phenomenon, we must ask here, too: *What is essential to the activity of war, and what is extraneous?* If the essence of war is "pure military skill," then other factors such as relative material resources, weather, and the vagaries of chance are presumably unwelcome interferences.

In the prelude to the Indo-Pakistani War of 1965, ground troops from both sides had entered the Rann of Kutch before the air forces had done so, and in March 1965, Pakistani Air Marshal Asghar Khan called his Indian counterpart, Air Marshal Arjan Singh, to suggest that the two air forces not operate across their borders in the disputed area at that time.[35] The proposal was taken to the Indian defense minister and prime minister, who condoned it but did not give any explicit guarantees; enough was said, however, that Pakistan was confident enough to convey to its own army that "Indian armed aircraft [were] unlikely to operate in the area."[36] Such (non)agreement was made possible in part because both marshals already knew each other and were former colleagues, having served together in the pre-partition Royal Indian Air Force.[37]

While such restraint was partly due to a lack of military capabilities on both sides, especially the Pakistani,[38] it is still notable for both its process and its motivation. First, it was initiated military-to-military, not by politicians or other civilians. Second, refraining from the use of air power meant the opposing side's civilians, in addition to one's own, would also be safe from air raids and errant bombs; for the Indian air force, which had superior capability, that meant giving up a clear advantage. Finally, deploying air power did not sit well with the commanding officers given the terrain and circumstances. Recounted a Pakistani official of the discussions between the opposing air marshals, "Killing each other's troops in a salt flat without a blade of grass for cover struck them both as none too sporting."[39]

Use of the word *sporting* here is indicative. While restraint saved their respective ground troops' lives for the moment, the motive was not wholly self-interested. There is also unease about *how* one kills, and dropping bombs from miles up in the air on completely exposed troops with nowhere to hide seemed unbecoming of a warfighter.

Running up too high a score differential or taking advantage of an opponent's mishaps means that the other team would no longer have a "reasonable but not certain chance [or] a fair opportunity" to win, and this is part of what people intend when they say something provides "good sport" or gives another a "sporting chance." It is also what the Indian and Pakistani air marshals meant when they discussed withholding their forces from the Rann of Kutch.[40]

## Parity as Equal Opportunity

This principle might be best illustrated by the duel, in which two opponents arrange to meet in regulated combat, with matched, similar, or agreed-upon weapons.[41] In some ways, the duel is a distillation of the concept of equal opportunity in warfare.[42] Structurally, it resembles a sporting match, but with higher stakes—not just a flesh wound, but usually death in defense of one's besmirched honor. While norms varied and were not always strictly obeyed, they were codified in various writings.[43]

Although modern Western duels were often fought by private individuals over honor, in many cases, duels had military import and could affect the war's outcome, for example, the confrontation between Hector and Achilles in the Trojan War, battlefield duels in the Hindu and Bushido tradition, or aerial dogfights in World War I.[44] At the beginning of that war, planes merely conducted reconnaissance and opposing pilots waved at each other in the passing. Before long, one tried to kill the other, and then they were off to the races. Later, planes acquired direct combat function, to stop bombers from reaching their targets, but even then, there were sometimes choreographic elements to the battles. Famed German fighter pilot Capt. Manfred von Richthofen referred to his opponent in a 1916 kill as his "English waltzing partner," in the middle of the serious, extended, and deadly encounter. "The impertinent fellow was full of cheek," he recalled, "and when we had got down to about 3,000 feet he merrily waved to me as if he would say, 'Well, how do you do?'"[45]

In the battlefield context, parity means equal opportunity to fight and win. In the world of Sir Thomas Malory's *Le Morte d'Arthur* (1485), an honorable knight who managed to knock his opponent off his horse should dismount from his own horse and continue fighting on the ground, in order to not take unfair advantage, and both Marhaus and Lancelot do so in separate battles with Gawain. This applies not just to formal contests,[46] but also in real conflicts: Marhaus chooses to fight the giant Taulurd, who had been terrorizing the land, on foot because "there may no horse bear him" due to his size; and Lancelot offers to handicap himself in a trial by battle against Meleagant by binding his left hand and wearing only part of his armor.[47]

These images exemplify an entire age of chivalry, which demanded that knights protect the weak and bring honor to themselves by upholding certain moral virtues and adhering to a strict code of conduct. This epoch has captured the imagination of many, generating visions of handsome knights courageous in the face of danger, noble in the face of adversity, and charismatic in their courtship of charming maidens in stately dress.

The glories of the chivalric age were very much a fantasy—even if it were all true, it would still be a grossly incomplete picture of warfare during the medieval period[48]—but this imagery is embedded in the picture of warfare and is telling of the kinds of norms and behaviors that are idealized.

This is not unique to the West: for example, strict guidelines for dueling battles that basically provide for equal opportunity can be found in legal, religious, and literary Sanskrit texts. Through legends and written legal edicts, various works within the *Dharmaśāstra* convey regulations on fighting, including decrees that battles occur only between sunrise and sunset and then pause so that people may attend to casualties from the day's fighting,[49] and that warriors may duel only if they carry the same weapons.[50] There are prohibitions against striking an opponent below the waist;[51]

using concealed, barbed, or poisoned weapons; striking someone who is sleeping, has lost his weapons or armor, or is engaged in a fight with another person; or continuing to fight if the opponent's topknot comes loose.[52] One must wait until the opponent is ready, which includes first issuing a challenge rather than launching a surprise attack and allowing him time to gather his lost weapon, for example. Warriors who surrender, hide, or retreat are to be spared, as are noncombatants.[53] Although most of the admonitions are broken at some point by various lords and warriors, the epic poems *Rāmāyana* and *Mahābhārata* considered these conditions necessary for righteous war (*dharmayuddha*), so much so that dying while fighting is considered preferable to unfair victory.[54]

Chinese military practices had similar norms. Elaborate, formal, "mannered," and "code-governed" set pieces already existed during the Eastern Chou period (770–403 BCE).[55] Warfare could be highly ritualized, and especially in the seventh and sixth centuries BCE, the dominant warrior aristocracy fought according to detailed, established parameters. Ceremonial offers of meat to the adversary "established bonds between them as fellow nobles," and then formal agreement set the date and place of battle before everyone began preparations for combat. This, along with many other elaborate religious, hierarchical, and preparatory rituals, helped to secure both the fighters' honor and the battle's legitimacy, for "true" combat was considered distinct from that which had been improperly organized.[56]

As combat was frequently seen as a "ceremonial trial of strength," enemies should be fairly evenly matched, and the idea that "one ought not to take advantage of an adversary in distress"—one aspect of a fair fight—was "deep-rooted." This included not invading while a state was in mourning for a deceased lord,[57] or calling off an invasion if there was no resistance.[58] In 614 BCE, when a battle between 秦 (Qin) and 晉 (Jin) paused for the evening, a Qin messenger arrived to notify Jin that the fight would continue in the morning, and Jin admonished, "While the dead and the wounded are not gathered in, to abandon them is not kind. Not to wait for the stipulated time but to attack men while they are in a perilous position, is not brave." As a result, Qin withdrew that night and resumed the fight from a different location.[59] Anyone who has heard the pleas of wounded and dying men and animals on the battlefield would understand how this disadvantages a fighting force—and this consideration carries over to modern-day protections for the wounded, as we will see chapter 3.

Ritualization of the "fair fight" reaches absurd heights at various points in the *Zuo-zhuan* 左傳. In 520 BCE, Hua Pao (華豹) is about to press his advantage by taking a second arrow shot before Prince Ch'eng (公子城) of Sung can fire even once, but the prince admonishes that "not to take turns is pusillanimous," whereupon Hua Pao stays his hand and is promptly killed.[60] In 637 BCE, Duke Xiang of Song (宋襄公) famously had his troops arranged in formation at the Hung River first, but waited until the opposing Ch'u finished crossing the river and lining up, instead of pressing his advantage, whereupon his troops were soundly defeated and he himself wounded. Despite recriminations, he justified his decision: "The superior man [nobleman] does not inflict a second wound nor does he take prisoner anyone whose hair is gray. When the men of old made war, they would not attack an enemy who was in a defile. I am but the heir of a lost dynasty, yet I would not sound the drums [to attack a foe] whose lines were unformed."[61]

Given how common it was to attack an army while it was still midstream, the Duke of Song is nearly a caricature, says Kierman,[62] and he is a controversial figure in Chinese literature.[63] Although Sun Tzu's (孫子) advocacy of the use of deception in *The Art of War* in the sixth century BCE was radical in many ways, showing mercy for an enemy's hardships in military situations was frowned upon, even at the time,[64] and over two thousand years later, Mao Tse-tung (毛泽东) scornfully proclaimed, "我们不是宋襄公，不要那种蠢猪式的仁义道德。"[65]—"We are not Duke Xiang of Song, and have no use for a stupid pig's benevolent justice and morality."

Similarly, although Japanese warrior code (commonly called "Bushido") frowns upon fighting weaker opponents and demands that "combat between equals be fought in an entirely straightforward fashion, [for a] true samurai always challenged his enemy openly[, and] stealth was considered beneath contempt," they still employed deceptive methods such as assassination and bribery.[66] Subterfuge was allowed under some circumstances, especially with someone who is not a peer, as suggested by the opening sequence of Akira Kurosawa's *The Seven Samurai* (七人の侍, 1954), set in the sixteenth century of the Sengoku period, which sees lead samurai Kambei Shimada masquerade as a priest in order to rescue a child taken hostage. Like European chivalric code, the significance of the Duke of Song example and the Bushido protocol may be exaggerated in their contexts, but their purpose is to make a moral point and to tender a certain ideal of military action.

The ritualistic elements of aerial and other duels and of highly formalized fighting are a stylized reflection of the importance of parity. This is not just a projection of misguided or idealized notions of Arthurian chivalry, but also a recurring impulse across multiple cultures. Obviously, circumstances between opponents can never be completely equal, but conditions do not have to be as strict as those in a preset duel in order to provide some kind of "equal opportunity" or "sporting chance"—it could simply be the individual sniper's ad hoc restraint. As with "live and let live," sometimes it is what does not happen that is significant.

This idea of a "fair fight" has even made its way into international law. The Geneva Conventions, for example, require combatants to distinguish themselves from civilians by wearing uniforms or by some other recognizable identifying mark when engaged in or preparing for attack but excepts "situations in armed conflicts where, owing to the nature of the hostilities, an armed combatant cannot so distinguish himself," and extends combatant protections to the nonuniformed so long as they carry arms openly in combat.[67] It does not address the circumstances qualifying for this exception, but the most common scenario (and the one that prompted this exception) is when one party is very resource-poor or lacks legitimate or recognized political authority, such as an insurgent political subgroup. In these cases, a combatant is not required to mark himself in any way in order to retain all the rights and privileges of lawful combatants, provided that he "carries his arms openly" while engaged in or deploying for an attack; he is then exempted from charges of perfidy under Article 37.1.c for "feigning . . . civilian, non-combatant status."[68]

But if the uniform exemption is meant to compensate for disadvantages to the resource-poor, especially groups fighting righteous wars of self-determination, then why dissipate some of that advantage by requiring a nonuniformed combatant to carry his weapon "openly" or don alternative displays of military status?

There is still uncertainty about which side is in the right and one should not assume that it is the weaker, so this hedges one's bets by limiting the compensating privileges. Furthermore, even if the disadvantaged side is in the right, civilians must still be protected to some extent, so one still cannot use any means necessary in order to win. Open-carry when not uniformed is one way of balancing those competing interests.[69]

As a provision for "fair fights," it is debatable whether allowing soldiers to fight incognito is enough of or instead too much of a counterbalancing advantage. It would be impossible to engineer a perfectly level playing field through a complex set of compensations and handicaps, even in enclosed conditions such as an athletic contest, much less in the amorphous and fluid situation of war. In combination with long-standing and cross-cultural unease in military ethics with pervasive stealth tactics, this leads to a compromise solution—no uniforms required, but must open-carry—that reflects concerns with both *jus ad bellum* and competitive parity.

### *Ambushes, Surprise Attacks, and Deception*

War has traditionally stood outside of legal sanction and is wholly consistent with and persistently employs surprise and deception; that the use of some such tactics would be simultaneously disdained in certain ways is difficult to square with the very essence of war.

The history of warfare is primarily that of irregular fighting based on subterfuge such as sabotage and ambush, which are sanctioned in both Western and Eastern just war traditions. Classical Chinese military thinking *promotes* using deception first (e.g., court intrigue, spying, sabotage) not only because it is the nature of war—"all warfare is based on deception," says Sun Tzu[70] and some classic Chinese novels such as *Outlaws of the Marsh* (水滸傳) recount one guerrilla attack after another—but also because it minimizes resort to physical violence. Deception should actually be *preferable* because it can preemptively reduce harm and save lives.

In a different tradition, certain Bible passages seem to forbid ambushes in war,[71] but Augustine prioritizes legitimate authority and right cause, for, "provided the war be just, it is no concern of justice whether it be carried on openly or by ambushes," and cites God's command to Joshua to ambush the city of Hai.[72] Aquinas follows Augustine and, citing different biblical passages (e.g., Matthew 7:6), declares that ambushes "may be lawfully employed in a just war," "nor can these ambushes be properly called deceptions," for they are not contrary to the justice of a well-ordered will.[73] From a tactical standpoint, meeting one's enemy openly and head-on does not make much sense—on this, military strategists and Christian theologians can agree—which is why the mutual full-frontal assault[74] popularly associated with the Napoleonic era is largely an anomaly in the history of warfare.[75]

Nonetheless, discomfort with ambushes and surprise attacks has ancient roots. Accounts of classical Greek hoplite warfare indicate an unspoken understanding among the *poleis* that these tactics were unacceptable. This did not apply to fighting non-Greeks or non-*poleis* Greeks, but *apate* (deception) between hoplites, at least, was frowned upon by "self-respecting" city-states, so much so that "when they finally draw close to the other city some agreement, tacit or explicit, determines when and where the two forces will engage."[76] Even at the end of the classical period, Alexander of Macedon reportedly rejected his general Parmenion's counsel that "surprise was better than open battle, [for] in the dead of the night the foe could be overwhelmed," declaring:

> The craft which you recommend to me is that of petty robbers and thieves; for their sole desire is to deceive. I will not suffer my glory always to be impaired by the absence of Darius, or by confined places, or by deceit by night. I am determined to attack openly by daylight; I prefer to regret my fortune rather than be ashamed of my victory.[77]

He adds prudential reasoning, that the "barbarians" have sentries keeping watch, so deception is not possible anyway. Perhaps, too, Alexander was so confident of his own superiority and impending victory that it was easy for him to prioritize his honor, but the substantial precedent of hoplite battle lends his condemnation of surprise attacks more sincerity.

Soon after, Polybius's *The Histories* refers to pitched battles as "just" (*díkaios*, δικαίως) or "noble" (*gennaios*, γενναίως), and ambushes as the opposite (*ádikos*, ἀδίκως; *agennaios*, ἀγενναίως).[78] Two millennia later, the influential General Orders No. 100, aka Lieber Code (1863),[79] mandates: "Outposts, sentinels, or pickets are not to be fired upon, except to drive them in, or when a positive order, special or general, has been issued to that effect" (§69). Says Walzer:

> In the nineteenth century, an effort was made to protect one type of "naked soldier": the man on guard duty outside his post or at the edge of his lines. . . . "No other term than murder," wrote an English student of war, "expresses the killing of a lone sentry by a pot shot at long range. It [is] like shooting a partridge sitting."[80]

From the perspective of winning a war, this prohibition makes little sense, as one of the best advantages is the element of surprise, and killing a lookout before he can warn his people of the dangers of one's approach is critical;

driving him in merely serves to alert the enemy of one's presence. It is unclear what qualifies an unsuspecting sentry for "nakedness," except his own unawareness of the enemy's presence, and this could be attributable to either his incompetence or the enemy's skill—in either case, that is what war is testing.

## *Declarations of War*

Contempt for ambushes and surprise attacks extends up a level to the traditional expectation for declarations of war, even as official announcements seem increasingly rare nowadays. Formal declarations of war—and offers of peace if the opposition submits to the demands—are found in the ancient Sumerian epic *Gilgamesh and Aga*, as well as in the Old Testament, in which Yahweh orders the Hebrews, "When thou comest nigh unto a city to fight against it, then proclaim peace unto it."[81] When Thebes attacked Plataea by surprise, which ultimately kicked off the Peloponnesian War, the Plataeans called it a "crime" (Thucydides: 2.5).

Although undeclared wars occurred, delivering a herald to proclaim war to the enemy was fairly common, and classical Greeks frequently engaged in drawn battles only after formal challenges were issued and accepted.[82] For example, Xenophon tells of the third or fourth day of Epameinondas's invasion of Sparta in 370 BCE: "The horsemen advanced to the race-course in the sanctuary of Poseidon Gaeaochus by divisions, the Thebans in full force, the Eleans, and all the horsemen who were there of the Phocians, Thessalians, or Locrians. And the horsemen of the Lacedaemonians, seemingly very few in number, were formed in line against them" (*Hell.* 6.5.30–31). Adds historian and epigraphist W. Kendrick Pritchett, "The picture is almost that of a dress parade. Both sides, although one was at a disadvantage, were prepared to commit their troops, and they chose, as if by common agreement, a space of level ground used for equestrian contests. The Lakedaimonians won the battle."[83]

The Roman love of legalistic ritual applied to warfare as well, to the extent that the content and form of justice were closely connected.[84] Early in Roman history, a college of priests, *fetiales*, held special responsibility for deliberations of war, including its declaration. If it was decided that justice was owed, *fetiales* dressed in special robes would journey to the offending city, formally make their demands with elaborate ritual, and, if satisfaction was not given by a specified time, pronounce the war by throwing "a magical spear, dipped in blood or pointed with iron, into the enemy's territory."[85]

As with modern declarations of war, this somewhat mysterious ritual simultaneously serves multiple functions. Formal announcement helps establish legitimate authority for waging war. It had an internal audience, to inform the Roman people that hard times were coming,[86] and the elaborate process of deliberation and heraldry may have served to fulfill one's own "last resort" requirements by giving the enemy one more chance to avoid coercion.[87] So too could it meet "fair fight" demands by making all aware of the impending state of conflict. Said Cicero, "No war is just, unless it is waged after a formal demand for restoration, or unless it has been formally announced and declared beforehand" (*De Officiis* [44 BCE], 1.36). As with the classical Chinese prebattle rituals between enemies (as discussed earlier), only a properly declared war is deemed legitimate. Here, fairness is folded into justice, and justice requires transparency, which means giving one's opponent the opportunity to avoid or prepare for the fight.[88]

This expectation gets codified in international law about two millennia later. To start the Russo-Japanese War of 1904, Japan issued a declaration but attacked before it was received by the Russian government; although Japan was certainly not the first to do so, this contributed to the Hague Convention (III) relative to the Opening of Hostilities (1907), which demands that "in order to ensure the maintenance of pacific relations," "hostilities . . . must not commence without previous and explicit warning" to both warring and neutral parties, "giving reasons or . . . an ultimatum with conditional declaration of war." Taken together, the general responses to surprise attacks, the Lieber Code ban on ambushes and shooting sentries, and the significant ritual element of and international law requirements for declarations of war constitute a systemic manifestation of, among other things, the ethic of cooperation for a fair fight.

*Perfidy, Bad Faith, and Institutional Stability*

Beyond surprise, discomfort with other kinds of deception in warfare also finds broader instantiation in the law. Despite existing bans on the use of false flags, in 1818 during a campaign against the Seminoles (First Seminole War), then Major General of the Tennessee militia (and future US president) Andrew Jackson used false flags (the British Union Jack) to lure two key Seminole leaders aboard what they thought were British cruisers. Once Francis the Prophet and Homathlemico boarded the American ships, they were seized, and then executed by hanging. Not long after, Jackson captured a Scottish trader and a former British army officer he suspected of working with the Creek Indians. He charged both with incitement, aiding and abetting the enemy, and spying, among other indictments; despite a tribunal judgment, Jackson intervened to impose death sentences and executed them forthwith.

The following year, during a congressional debate over Jackson's execution of the Brits, Speaker of the House Henry Clay gave a thunderous speech that condemned the execution of the Seminoles, whose capture was not in line with "fair and open and honorable war," and urged that Americans not forget "our principles, our religion, our clemency, and our humanity."[89] Georgia representative Thomas Cobb referenced Vattel's *The Law of Nations*, declared the situation "nauseous," and bemoaned such treachery:

> In one day has the fair character of this nation been blasted! That character for justice and mercy in which we had thought ourselves pre-eminent, and of which we had so proudly boasted to the other nations of the earth, is now prostrated as low as theirs. They can now say to us, boast no more—you are not less cruel than other nations.[90]

Popular condemnation did not end the fraudulent use of truce flags, of course. This tactic was repeatedly employed in later conflicts against the Seminoles, especially from 1837 to 1838, which Indian leaders protested as an "unprecedented violation of that sacred rule which has ever been recognized by every nation, civilized or uncivilized." Many Americans, too, were horrified by "another breach of national honor."[91]

This disapproval gets written into the Lieber Code, which forbids not only "cruelty and bad faith concerning engagements concluded with the enemy during the war, but also the breaking of stipulations solemnly contracted by the belligerents in the time of peace" (§11), and devotes three sections to procedures for using truce and safe conduct flags (§§111–13), which are "so [necessarily] sacred" that "its abuse is an especially heinous offence" and violators may be considered spies (§114).

The sacrament of the truce flag is part of long-standing cross-cultural tradition that warriors only kill in certain ways. This idea gets folded into the Geneva Conventions, which restrict certain types of "perfidy" but still permit "ruses":[92]

> Protocol I (1977): Art. 37. Prohibition of perfidy
> 1. It is prohibited to kill, injure or capture an adversary by resort to perfidy. Acts inviting the confidence of an adversary to lead him to believe that he is entitled to, or is obliged to accord, protection under the rules of international law applicable in armed conflict, with intent to betray that confidence, shall constitute perfidy. The following acts are examples of perfidy:
>     a. the feigning of an intent to negotiate under a flag of truce or of a surrender;
>     b. the feigning of an incapacitation by wounds or sickness;
>     c. the feigning of civilian, non-combatant status; and
>     d. the feigning of protected status by the use of signs, emblems or uniforms of the United Nations or of neutral or other States not Parties to the conflict.
> 2. *Ruses of war are not prohibited.* Such ruses are acts which are intended to mislead an adversary or to induce him to act recklessly but which infringe no rule of international law applicable in armed conflict and which *are not perfidious because they do not invite the confidence of an adversary with respect to protection under that law.* The following are examples of such ruses: the use of camouflage, decoys, mock operations and misinformation. (emphasis added)

As the ICRC Commentary on Additional Protocol I (1977) notes, "perfidy is injurious to the social order which it betrays" (§1499)—but that applies to all perfidy, so why prohibit only some and permit others?

This regulation expresses an ethic of cooperation at two levels. The first is a bounded idea about fairness at the microlevel, that opponents should enter the arena openly and roughly equally. To that end, "ruses"—*including the uniform exception (Art. 44.3)*—are both expected and permitted, in the service of the principle of fairness. In order to equalize the fight between the militarily mighty and the resource-poor, "the ruse is very often the only course open to a weak combatant, and the law of armed conflict, if it is to be respected, should ensure that the combatants have equal chances" (§1514). There is almost no clearer statement of the importance of an ethic of cooperation for a "fair fight," so much so that the Geneva Conventions consider their own legitimacy to be dependent on it.[93]

To promote this kind of fairness, however, it is necessary to permit some deception in exchange for broader adherence to the cooperative ethic at an institutional level, which specifically targets only the deception that could engender "breaking of faith" in the international law itself. It recognizes that "ruses" are part of the social order of warfare, that war "is no stranger to cunning, skill, ingenuity, stratagems and artifices" (§1512), that deceit is expected. What is unacceptable according to the Conventions is when "the ruse of war . . . serve[s] as a pretext for pure and simple violations of the rules in the force" (§1512).

This is, however, a somewhat arbitrary distinction. The international law is taking itself as given and assuming itself as part of the firmament, which it is not. The very existence of international law is a cooperative—and malleable—enterprise. "A ruse can never legitimize an act which is not lawful" (§1515), says the commentary, but as the law itself defines what is and is not lawful, that begs the question.

In fact, this tautology is intentional. International laws are conventions and can be changed, so in order for this complex and fragile cooperative enterprise to protect its own sustainability, it cannot tolerate deceit implicating the institution itself.

He who uses the international law as a cover "destroys the faith that the combatants are entitled to have in the rules of armed conflict [and] shows a lack of the *minimum respect which even enemies should have for one another*" (§1500, emphasis added). The perfidious acts forbidden by Art. 37 are those that would undermine fealty to the system of international law—by permitting other deception in exchange, it seeks to reinforce the cooperation embedded in the international legal system.

### *Weapons Bans*

> When he fights with his foes in battle, let him not strike with weapons concealed (in wood), nor with (such as are) barbed, poisoned, or the points of which are blazing with fire.
> —MANUSMRTI

Throughout history, there has been consistent bias against weapons that put greater distance between oneself and one's opponents, as they can violate both the "parity" and "awareness" (no surprise attacks) requirements, although distance alone has not been enough to motivate a ban on a weapon. Rather, it is often a weapon's indiscriminate nature that drives its exclusion, for example, the ban on "asphyxiating or deleterious," "poisonous, or other gases." This was first instituted by the Hague Conventions (1899 and 1907),[94] again in the Treaty of Versailles (1919) and the Geneva Protocol (1925) due to gross violations in World War I, and then supplemented by the Biological Weapons Convention (1972) and the Chemical Weapons Convention (1993/1997). Gas, chemical, and biological weapons are so horrifying to soldiers in the way they kill—which their continued use makes very clear to everyone—that it has led some to declare that "the world set a red line"[95] against these "malignant" weapons.[96] They have been controversial from the beginning, as writings from World War I demonstrate:

- Said Captain Thomas of the new "funny accessory" they are about to employ, "It's damnable. *It's not soldiering to use stuff like that*, even though the Germans did start it. It's dirty, and it'll bring us bad luck. We're sure to bungle it" (emphasis added).[97]
- Wrote the presidents of the Royal Colleges of Surgeons of England, Edinburgh, and Ireland, and of the Royal Colleges of Physicians of London, Glasgow, and Ireland; and two medical professors from the Universities of Cambridge and of Oxford:
"The use of gas is self-condemned for the following reasons:
"It is an uncontrollable weapon, whose effects cannot be limited to combatants.
"It is an 'unclean' weapon, condemning its victims to death by long-drawn-out torture.
"It opens the door to infinite possibilities of causing suffering and death, for its further development may well lead to the devising of an agent which will blot out towns, and even nations."[98]
- Using gas is "a cynical and barbarous disregard of the well-known usages of civilised war," said Sir John French, a British Expeditionary Force commander. It is "a cowardly form of warfare," said British Lt. Gen. Charles Ferguson. On the other side, German Third Army commander Gen. Karl von Einem wrote, "I fear it will produce a tremendous scandal in the world. . . . War has nothing to do with chivalry any more. The higher civilisation rises, the viler man becomes."[99]
- Lamented Harvey Cushing, a Harvard neurosurgeon, about treating chlorine gas victims on the French lines: It is "a terrible business—one

man, blue as a sailor's serge, simply pouring out with every cough a thick albuminous secretion, and too busy fighting for air to bother much about anything else—a most horrible form of death for a strong man."[100]

The recurring theme is clear: there is something dishonourable and un-"soldierly" about killing other soldiers en masse rather than one or a few at a time, with poison that they often could not see and against which they could not genuinely fight back. It was how one killed rats and insects, and it was unbecoming of a soldier—or any person—to die that way.[101]

Surprisingly, gas was not used in the European theaters in World War II, even though all sides possessed and had improved on it since the previous war. That was undoubtedly due in large part to self-interested considerations of efficacy and fears of retaliation, but there is some speculation that even Hitler, who had experienced gassing in World War I,[102] was reluctant to utilize it in the field of combat, although he obviously happily used it elsewhere. In a contemporary echo, special adviser to the Foundation for Strategic Research in Paris François Heisbourg said about chemical weapons use by the Syrian government in 2013, "You just have to watch the videos from Syria from Aug. 21. This is killing people like cockroaches and using the same chemicals to do it."[103]

These international bans have been repeatedly violated, partly because chemical weapons are effective stop-gaps when a military faces manpower shortages,[104] but abhorrence to certain types of killing as fundamentally unfair continues to arise especially in response to technology that enables ever-larger-scale massacres. Technological advancements always outpace moral adjustments. As then UK prime minister Winston S. Churchill said of World War II, "The latest refinements of science are linked with the cruelties of the Stone Age."[105]

## Cooperation Without Reciprocity?

Can there be cooperation for a fair fight in cases where there is no reciprocity? Even when opponents start by fighting "fairly," it usually does not last. For example, the Mexican-American War (1846–47) began with careful mutual observance of the "laws and customs of war among civilized nations," including both sides communicating through truce flags, entering formal surrender agreements, adhering to laws on POW treatment, and exchanging prisoners and paroling soldiers. As the war progressed, however, some gangs of American volunteers marauded, pillaged, and indulged in "deeds of wanton violence and cruelty," and Mexican bandits took advantage of their domestic political instability. Although the Mexican military fought pitched battles at first, after a year of persistent losses, their commanders "abandoned the set-piece battles in which they had been so badly overmatched and adopted . . . irregular tactics." They took inspiration from Spanish resistance to Napoleon earlier in the century, and the ensuing guerrilla warfare led to a reciprocal response from American volunteers.[106]

Some "fair fight" actions discussed here are clearly unilateral, such as the ad hoc restraint shown by the snipers or others. When there is no direct or immediate reciprocity, is this not rather just one-sided morality?

It may still be said that there is cooperation. The game is being played not just between two parties or even two sides: it involves observers and potential future participants as well, because one's actions signal to everyone else the expected behavioral norms, their value and relevant circumstances, and the intent behind them, and this influences long-term expectations for future reciprocity.

In the wake of rampant violations of the laws of war, the US Army's commanding general in Mexico, Maj. Gen. Winfield Scott, disciplined his side with special military tribunals. The trials of 303 Americans for "atrocious crimes"[107] were deemed successful in controlling his soldiers, and this "became part of an American national mythology of chivalry," praised as "a blessing to humanity" for "no war, in any age or country, was ever waged upon principles so humane, so civilized," and credited with helping to develop "an integral portion of the international law of the world."[108] Restraining the kind of violence allowed, even if it was not immediately reciprocated, had an audience (and participants) beyond the immediate opponents.

## Sources of the Ethic of Cooperation for a Fair Fight

Obviously, not every soldier desires a fair fight—and definitely not most of the time—but the norm has been strong enough to influence both action and legal code governing legitimate battle. There are multiple sources for the ethic of cooperation for a fair fight, and here I discuss three: professionalism (including mutual respect, murdering versus soldiering, battle function, and professional ethics), philosophical principles, and virtue ethics; then I address concerns with moral injury.

## *Professionalism*

### MUTUAL RESPECT

A warrior has labored to develop specialized skills through intensive training, and has a professional desire to utilize and demonstrate those skills and to do his job well. He knows the same is often true of his opponents, so he admires and appreciates their bravery and prowess for their own sake by putting himself at equal risk—for that is the only fair test of their respective hard-won abilities—and is reluctant to kill opponents he deems to be highly worthy, whether peers or superiors, as it is always a shame to destroy fine specimens of warriors.

Fictional works show this phenomenon of mutual respect quite clearly: after a fatal battle, the Romulan commander tells Federation Capt. James T. Kirk, "I regret that we meet in this way. You and I are of a kind. In a different reality, I could have called you friend."[109] When Inigo Montoya is bested in a duel in *The Princess Bride* (1987) and asks the masked man in black to kill him "quickly," the latter says, "I would as soon destroy a stained-glass window as an artist like yourself. However, since I can't have you following me either [knocks him unconscious]. . . . Please understand I hold you in the highest respect." In Rudyard Kipling's *The Ballad of East and West* (1889), the border chieftain Kamal, who has stolen a horse, and the colonel's son chasing him ultimately admire each other so greatly that Kamal spares the latter's life: "'No talk shall be of dogs,' said he, 'when wolf and grey wolf meet.'"[110] The colonel's son offers his pistol and the horse to Kamal: "Take up the mare for my father's gift,—by god, she has carried a man!" In return, Kamal sends his only son to serve the colonel's son and join the Guides. The poem begins and ends with this stanza:

> Oh, East is East and West is West, and never the twain shall meet,
> Till Earth and Sky stand presently at God's great Judgement Seat;

> But there is neither East nor West, Border, nor Breed, nor Birth,
> When two strong men stand face to face, tho' they come from the ends of the earth!

More metaphorically, in Ernest Hemingway's *The Old Man and the Sea* (1952), the old man pities the defiant, "wonderful and strange" marlin, who is "not as intelligent as we who kill them, although more noble and more able." "Joined together" in an epic struggle far off the shores, he starts to identify with the fish, telling himself, "I'll kill him . . . in all his greatness and his glory," "although it is unjust." By the end of the second day, he thinks of the fish as a "friend" and "true brother": "How many people will [the fish] feed," the old man wonders, "But are they worthy to eat him? No, of course not. There is no one worthy of eating him from the manner of his behavior and his great dignity." In defying him for so long, in such a fashion, the fish becomes his equal, and the old man concedes, "You are killing me, fish . . . but you have a right to. Never have I seen a greater, or more beautiful, or a calmer or more noble thing than you, brother. Come on and kill me. I do not care who kills who."

In *Patton* (1970), the title character is full of esteem for the opponent, at times grudging, at others openly admiring. At one point, Gen. George S. Patton wryly agrees to a toast with a Russian commander, "one sonuvabitch to another," and during a battle in which he thought Generalfeldmarschall Erwin Rommel was opposite, he exclaims, "Rommel, you magnificent bastard, I read your book!," and later muses:

> Rommel is out there some place, waiting for me. . . . I want to fight the champ. If you lose, you've lost to the champ and it's no disgrace. If you win, you're the new champ. . . . If I had my way I'd send that genius sonuvabitch an engraved invitation in iambic pentameter—a challenge in two stanzas to meet me alone out in the desert. . . . Rommel in his tank and me in mine. We'd stop at twenty paces, climb out of the turrets and shake hands. Then we'd button up and do battle—just the two of us. And that battle would decide the outcome of the war.

This recalls McClellan's longing for "pure military skill," and while this admiration might seem far-fetched or impossible across more disparate cultures and ideologies, in real life Patton's esteem for Rommel was genuine and reciprocated.

Sometimes, respect is only that. At the end of the Civil War, Union Gen. Joshua L. Chamberlain ordered his soldiers to salute the surrendering Confederate troops at Appomattox, as they passed.[111]

Allied admiration for German fighter pilot Richthofen was so great that No. 3 Squadron Australian Flying Corps gave him a full military funeral in Bertangles, near Amiens, when he was killed in combat in northern France in 1918. Captains served as pallbearers, he was given a guard of honor, and other units sent memorial wreaths.[112]

During France's Algerian War, infamous for its atrocities, multiple sources assert that captured FLN leader Mohammed Larbi Ben M'hidi was respected by even the notorious Col. Marcel Bigeard, who surprisingly refused to torture him. Although there are conflicting claims about whether he was ultimately hung or shot, he was saluted by the men who executed him in 1957.[113] Recounts Gen. Paul Aussaresses when he ordered Ben M'hidi brought to him in preparation for execution:

> — Présentez, armes! a commandé Allaire au moment où Ben M'Hidi, qu'on venait de réveiller, est sorti du bâtiment. Alors, à ma grande surprise, le groupe de parachutistes du 3e RPC a rendu les derniers honneurs au chef vaincu du FLN. C'était l'hommage de Bigeard à celui qui était devenu son ami. Ce geste spectaculaire et quelque peu démagogique ne me facilitait pas la tâche. Je l'ai même trouvé très déplacé. C'est bien entendu à ce moment-là que Ben M'Hidi a compris ce qui l'attendait.[114]

Differing on the method of execution, French Army Lt. Col. Roger Trinquier similarly claims:

> I know that all of you think we tortured him to death, but we did not. . . . We shot him, but we gave him a guard of honor before we shot him. . . . Because M. Ben M'Hidi was a leader. . . . I didn't want to shoot him. I had never met anyone like that. I would have liked to see him as *le président de la France*. So, once I was ordered to shoot him, I gave him a guard of honor first.[115]

According the enemy rituals of honor before or especially after his death can only be meant sincerely, as it comforts oneself for the loss of an esteemed opponent. Obviously, respect does not always lead to "fair fights," but sometimes it does. During the American Revolutionary War, Scottish marksman Maj. Patrick Ferguson and his riflemen lay at the edge of the woods, when he spied two rebel officers passing by on horseback:

> *I ordered three good shots to steal near to them, and fire at them; but the idea disgusted me. I recalled the order.* The Hussar on returning, made a circuit, but the other passed again within a hundred yards of us, upon which I advanced from the wood towards him. On my calling, he stopped; but, after looking at me proceeded. I again drew his attention, and made signs to him to stop, leveling my piece at him, but he slowly continued his way. *As I was within that distance at which, in the quickest firing, I could have lodged half a dozen of balls in or about him before he was out of my reach, I had only to determine; but it was not pleasant to fire at the back of an unoffending individual, who was acquitting himself very coolly of his duty; so I let him alone.* The day after I had been telling this story . . . one of our surgeons . . . came in and told us they had been informing him, *that General Washington was all the morning with the light troops* . . . dressed and mounted in every point as above described. *I am not sorry that I did not know at the time who it was.*[116]

While it is of historical import that the lucky officer was likely to have been future American president George Washington, what is important here is Ferguson's reasoning. It is rare to get such an explicit statement of "fairness" in war, but this is one: Ferguson was loathe to shoot someone in the back who was not an immediate threat to him. There is recognition that in this nasty business of war each person is only doing his duty, and thus there is a certain lack of grudging against the enemy because the harm done is not personal.

As we have seen, such professional respect is frequently tinged with regret and a sense of tragedy, for the "fair fight" ethic indirectly takes into account one of the most problematic issues in warfare: involuntariness or unwillingness. It recognizes that the enemy, for all his skillfulness, may not want to be there, fighting—and perhaps neither does oneself—and tries to find a way to give the opponent his due under the circumstances.

### MURDERING VS. SOLDIERING

As professionals, warfighters want to be seen as "soldiers," not as "murderers" or depraved killers. Some have argued that this "common morality" is less innate and more born of a fear of external sanction, but it matters less exactly whether they desire a fair fight because it is owed to the other person under natural law or because they want to be perceived as the kind of person who is fair. Internal or external sanction, self-oriented or other-oriented, the result is the same: wait for another opportunity to kill, when the odds are closer to even. S. L. A. Marshall encountered similar sentiments among soldiers when the opposing enemy made the fight too easy:

> I well recall that in World War I the great sense of relief that came to troops when they were passed to a quiet sector such as the old Toul front was not due so much to the realization that things were safer there as to the blessed knowledge that for a time they were not under the compulsion to take life. "Let 'em go; we'll get 'em some other time," was the remark frequently made *when the enemy grew careless and offered himself as a target.*[117]

The barbarism and brutality of war coexist alongside its moral principles, formal and informal rules, and sense of honor. The ethic of cooperation for a fair fight in warfare is actually quite developed, often highly ritualized, and buttressed by strong norms, but part of the challenge, of course, is its inconsistent invocation and application. It is difficult to claim that an ethic exists when it is (1) highly contradictory to other simultaneously held principles and practices of warfare, and (2) so erratically applied. Yet, when it is invoked, it is felt very strongly.

Hesitation motivated in part by "fair fight" considerations occurs in groups as well, not just for an individual sniper looking through his scope at another man. Back in the World War I trenches, Lussu recounts yet another ill-fated assault: upon reaching the opposing trench, the soldiers were supposed to spread across a nearly three-hundred-meter front, but the terrain pushed the few remaining soldiers into a fifty-meter patch directly in front of the enemy line, where they presented a compact target at "point blank" range, when:

> Suddenly, the Austrians stopped shooting. I saw the ones who were in front of us, their eyes thrust open with a terrified look, almost as though it were they and not us who were under fire. One of them, who didn't have a rifle, cried out in Italian, "*Basta! Basta!*"
> "*Basta!*" the others repeated from the parapets.
> The one who was unarmed looked like a chaplain.
> "Enough, brave soldiers, don't get yourselves killed like this!"
> We came to a halt for an instant. We weren't shooting, they weren't shooting. The one who seemed to be a chaplain was leaning out so close to us that if I reached out my arm I could have touched him.

After a mere moment of confusion, the Italian general urged his men forward, and the action continued with quick, close encounters—but for the rest of the assault, the Austrians "kept shooting, but their aim was high. We were safe."[118]

Even to Lussu, who experienced it, this episode was surreal. The Austrians finally had the enemy not just in their sights, but trapped as sure kills. Yet, after all those months of repeated killing, planning, and more fighting, the Austrians stopped right at the moment they were waiting for. Why did they waste their efforts, and endanger themselves in the process? The stoppage was not driven merely by a chaplain's religiously inspired pacifism, for the Austrians were certainly not too delicate to kill Italian soldiers in other, even less "sporting" circumstances. (The danger of Loophole 14 is a recurring motif in the memoir, as the Austrians kept a mounted rifle constantly trained on it and, at any sight of movement there, killed more than one hapless soldier/officer with shots to the head.)

One can only speculate about the collective temporary lacuna and the ensuing "battle" in which soldiers aimed high to allow their enemy to escape, but Lussu's description suggests that the Austrians felt squeamish about killing an enemy unwittingly trapped at point-blank range and certain to die. While not many groups of soldiers would have held back under similar circumstances—and the same troops might have reacted differently in the same situation on a different day—this time, at least, and apparently at other times,[119] they preferred to let their enemy escape rather than kill them like ill-fated animals in a pen.

### BATTLE FUNCTION

Wars are won by killing enough people to make the other side surrender, so what accounts for restraint that defeats that very purpose? Some wartime deaths seem more like murder than legitimate killing. But if the process of war involves continuing to kill people until the opponent surrenders, then what is the difference? Can one "murder" an opposing soldier when there is a known and ongoing state of hostility between the two sides, and soldiers are permitted to kill one another at any time and under almost all circumstances during a war?

There are ways of killing that may not advance the *process* of war, for example, torturing someone to death for retribution rather than to extract information. Along those lines, the Lieber Code mandates that intentional infliction of additional injury or killing an enemy "already wholly disabled" be punishable by death (Art. 71). Such killing serves no battle function, as the "wholly disabled" are incapable of further fighting and effectively removed from the field. This prohibition promotes the idea that wartime killing must serve the purpose of inducing surrender, which occurs when one lacks the resources (including labor) to continue fighting, so additional pain is unnecessary and disallowed. Although enemies can be legitimately killed in all sorts of other, more gruesome ways in war, this is deemed more akin to murder.

In fact, the Lieber Code explicitly describes some killing as murder when it forbids assassinations on the grounds of outlawry:

> The law of war does not allow proclaiming either an individual belonging to the hostile army, or a citizen, or a subject of the hostile government, an outlaw, who may be slain without trial by any captor, any more than the modern law of peace allows such intentional outlawry; on the contrary, it abhors such outrage. The sternest retaliation should follow the *murder* committed in consequence of such proclamation, made by whatever authority. Civilized nations look with horror upon offers of rewards for the assassination of enemies as relapses into barbarism.[120]

Considering this to be illegitimate "murder" during a war is curious when it presumably was perfectly acceptable to kill the individuals in question on the field in the course of a battle. As with sentries, only under certain circumstances was it permitted to kill. If the form of killing is the same (e.g., gunshot to a vital organ) and within the context of ongoing hostilities, why is it a legitimate kill in one situation, yet slaughter in another? After all, asked Charles Sumner, "What is war but organized murder?" Yet, the idea that there is a difference between murder and legitimate wartime killing persists, and is one reason why soldiers are sometimes instinctively driven to ideas about "fair fights" in war.

## PROFESSIONAL ETHICS

Most modern nation-state soldiers are professionals just like any other, albeit with better uniforms, and their killing too must be done in a professional manner. That requires not just technical expertise but also conducting one's business with a certain detachment, with neither personal animosity nor personal enjoyment, or *sine ira et studio*,[121] as well as adherence to appropriate guidelines.

Many professions have codes of ethical practice that set standards for and govern the use of practitioners' specialist knowledge—their purpose is to protect the clients and the public, as well as the professionals themselves. The best-known code belongs to the medical field, whose Hippocratic Oath vows to strive to provide the best possible care; to share knowledge without an eye to reward; to refrain from lying, doing harm, or falling into conflicts of interest; and to keep the patient's confidentiality. While there is no obligation to swear the Oath, most medical students across the world affirm some modern version of it before entering into practice. All versions include proper behavior as well as character ideals—e.g., "to comport myself and use my knowledge in a godly manner"—some of which are detailed in expanded codes of ethics.[122]

Like other professionals, warfighters, too, have codes of ethics, ones that can generate mutual respect and distinguish between murdering and soldiering in warfare. Details differ across militaries, traditions, and eras, but they commonly cover the essentials of international law, such as not intentionally killing civilians and not engaging in torture. For example:

## US Army—The Soldier's Creed

> I am an American Soldier. I am a Warrior and a member of a team. I serve the people of the United States and live the Army Values. I will always place the mission first. I will never accept defeat. I will never quit. I will never leave a fallen comrade. *I am disciplined, physically and mentally tough, trained and proficient in my warrior tasks and drills. I always maintain my arms, my equipment, and myself. I am an expert and I am a professional.* I stand ready to deploy, engage, and destroy the enemies of the United States of America in close combat.[123]

There are reminders of and appeals to the long history of the profession and one's responsibilities toward fellow fighters, pledges to compromise neither integrity nor "moral courage," and explicit ties between professionalism and virtue. "No one is more professional than I," they say, and "I will not use my grade or position to attain profit or safety. Competence is my watchword."[124] The US Marine NCO's Creed declares:

> I am the backbone of the United States Marine Corps. . . . I serve as part of the vital link between my commander (and all officers) and enlisted Marines. I will never forget who I am or what I represent. I will challenge myself to the limit and be ever attentive to duty. I am now, more than ever, committed to excellence in all that I do, so that I can set the proper example for other Marines. I will demand of myself all the energy, knowledge and skills I possess, so that I can instill confidence in those I teach. I will constantly strive to perfect my own skills and to become a good leader. *Above all I will be truthful in all I say or do. My integrity shall be impeccable as my appearance. I will be honest with myself, with those under my charge and with my superiors. I pledge to do my best to incorporate all the leadership traits into my character. For such is the heritage I have received from that long, illustrious line of professionals who have worn the bloodstripe so proudly before me. I must give the very best I have for my Marines, my Corps and my Country for though today I instruct and supervise in peace, tomorrow, I may lead in war* (emphasis added).

The aforementioned honesty is included as an abiding principle in most professional codes of ethics. Truthfulness corresponds to transparency and forthrightness, and it is not much of a stretch to envision how the appeal to honesty combines with mutual respect for another's expertise—which is more peculiar to those engaged in necessarily adversarial professions—to manifest itself in the realm of warfare as the ideal of a fair fight.

Although these statements of virtue and professionalism are not without contradictions—for example, the US Army Soldier's Creed says within a few sentences, "I will always place the mission first. . . . I will never leave a fallen comrade"[125]—certain character ideals are clearly considered essential in helping warfighters remain professional, and are embedded in the professional's self-conception. Both legally imposed discipline and ad hoc restraint are buttressed by the fact that even those who kill for a living can and do think of themselves as professionals.

### Virtue Ethics and Philosophical Principles

The idea of a "fair fight" is part of a larger system of beliefs that says there are right and wrong—virtuous and unvirtuous—ways to live a warrior life and to esteem, fight, and kill one's enemy. Professionalism is inseparable from the possession and exercise of certain virtues, including loyalty, selflessness, respectfulness, discipline, tenacity, physical and moral courage, honesty, integrity, fairness, and honorableness. The US Army separately lists its core values, and its Commissioned Officer's Creed, for example, places great emphasis on the connection between personal and professional virtue:

### Army Values

*Loyalty*—Bear true faith and allegiance to the Constitution, the Army, your unit, and other Soldiers.
*Duty*—Fulfill your obligations.
*Respect*—Treat people with dignity as they should be treated.
*Selfless Service*—Put the welfare of the nation, the Army, and your subordinates before your own.
*Honor*—Live up to all the Army Values.
*Integrity*—Do what's right, legally and morally.
*Personal Courage (Physical or Moral)*—Face fear, danger, or adversity.

## US Army—Commissioned Officer's Creed

I will not only seek continually to improve my knowledge and practice of my profession, but also I will exercise the authority entrusted to me by the President and the Congress with fairness, justice, patience, and restraint, respecting the dignity and human rights of others and devoting myself to the welfare of those placed under my command. In justifying and fulfilling the trust placed in me, I will conduct my private life as well as my public service so as to be free both from impropriety and the appearance of impropriety, acting with candor and integrity to earn the unquestioning trust of my fellow soldiers—juniors, seniors, and associates—and employing my rank and position not to serve myself but to serve my country and my unit. By practicing physical and moral courage I will endeavor to inspire these qualities in others by my example.

The deep connection between the personal and the professional extends across military cultures. One influential interpretation of Japanese Bushido code (武士道) admonishes the warrior to constantly be mindful of death and to handle his own in an appropriate manner (§1); to pursue learning (§3); to be devoted, even to negligent parents (§4); to treat his wife, subordinates, and servants appropriately (§§32, 38, 50); to protect farmers, craftsmen, and merchants (§34); and to "keep a respectful distance from the administration of financial affairs" (§36).[126]

While the martial virtues mentioned here are internally oriented (toward one's country, military institution, fellow fighters, community, and self), there is also a tradition of externally oriented virtues, directed toward one's opponents. Cicero argues that promises made to enemies even under duress should be kept, invoking Regulus's promise to return to captivity under the Carthaginians after being released to arrange a captive exchange during the First Punic War, among other examples. Cicero warns that even if one might get away on a technicality, one must render justice by adhering to the spirit rather than merely the letter of the law, for "in the matter of a promise one must always consider the meaning and not the mere words."[127] This virtue reemerges from time to time even in contemporary war, for example, when British captain Robert Campbell, held as a POW in Magdeburg,

Germany, during World War I, was granted a two-week leave in 1916 to see his dying mother, provided he voluntarily return to captivity afterward, which he did.[128]

Other-oriented virtues include respect for privacy: in the wake of new national cryptographic efforts, for example, US secretary of state Henry Stimson purportedly said in 1929, "Gentlemen do not read each other's mail."[129] While there certainly has been and continues to be many such invasions of privacy, this sentiment persists, even if only out of decorum: in the wake of the WikiLeaks revelations in 2015 that the US National Security Agency (NSA) was spying on its German ally's government officials and media, there was outrage at its unseemliness, although spying is widespread and mutual.

While most warfighters in large, modern, nation-state militaries will not come close to approximating the virtues that are demanded of them, the ideal is still there.

One important virtue that is often overlooked but mentioned in the US *Army Leadership* manual is empathy:[130]

### Empathy

3–17. *Army leaders show empathy when they genuinely relate to another person's situation, motives, and feelings.* Empathy does not necessarily mean sympathy for another, but identification that leads to a deeper understanding. Empathy allows the leader to anticipate what others are experiencing and to try to envision how decisions or actions affect them. *Leaders with a strong tendency for empathy can apply it to understand Army Civilians, Soldiers and their Families, local populations, and enemy combatants.* The ability to see something from another person's point of view, to identify with, and enter into another person's feelings and emotions, enables the Army leader to better interact with others. . . .

3–20. The requirement for leader empathy extends beyond Army Civilians, Soldiers, and their Families. *Within the operational environment, leader empathy is helpful when dealing with local populations, victims of natural disasters, and prisoners of war.* Essentially, empathy produces better cultural understanding of people, missions, and operations and how they connect.[131]

The manual itself extends the application of empathy beyond the realm of one's own soldiers and societies to foreign populations, prisoners of war, and enemy combatants, and it does not require too much stretching to connect this directive to a "fair fight" ethic.

It is difficult to disentangle the cause and effect between virtue and the cooperative ethic, because, historically, it has run both ways. Preexisting beliefs about warrior virtues contributed to the development of norms of open warfare in the Western world.[132] The ancient Homeric ideal of champions squaring off against each other, one-on-one, in a displayed test of their abilities and to determine the fate of armies is a powerful vision, and one that Western soldiers have long aspired to. It manifests in the medieval and chivalric duel, and again during the modern era of exposed "infantry square" battle, including in officers' letters that often praised the manliness of standing and taking fire bravely.

Influence flows the other direction as well, of practice on virtue. In this period, for example, wearing a uniform becomes one of the practices of a virtuous modern soldier. It is a way of demonstrating his bravery, his willingness to sacrifice himself on the behalf of others, and his honorableness, which gets redefined in terms of his willingness to stand for open, equitable combat. It is buttressed by a certain vision of warfare in the modern Western imagination—of soldiers lined up across an open field from one another, in broad daylight, playing by the rules, and settling their disputes like gentlemen.

Why do we fixate on this, when thinking about warfare? It is not just because it is more narratively appealing. This image has come to dominate our modern martial ideal precisely because it is so unusual, and because it gives rise to the possibility of systematic cooperation between warring enemies in the modern era, in a way that is unique in the history of warfare. Warrior virtues influence the ethic of cooperation for a fair fight, which in turn shapes beliefs about the proper virtues, and therefore behaviors, of the warrior.

Morality, character, and the range of virtues are as essential to warriors as their technical skills, for that is what separates them from mere murderers. Virtue also makes them better warriors: this "function argument" holds that the unique nature of military work requires a certain general uprightness in order for warfighters to properly perform their jobs—they must be selfless, sacrificing, courageous, loyal, and trustworthy to one another at the most dangerous of times.[133] There are several concerns with the function argument, but one compelling defense is that "the code is a kind of moral and psychological armor that protects the warrior from becoming a monster in his or her own eyes."[134]

In order to protect the warfighter, it is, in fact, of "clinical importance" that he respect his enemy, says psychiatrist Jonathan Shay from his work with Vietnam War veterans, because

> Restoring honor to the enemy is an essential step in recovery from combat PTSD. While other things are obviously needed as well, the veteran's self-respect never fully recovers so long as he is unable to see the enemy as worthy. In the words of one of our patients, a war against subhuman vermin "has no honor." This is true even in victory; in defeat, the dishonoring absence of human *thémis* linking enemy to enemy is unendurable.[135]

Giving honor to one's enemy helps a warrior be a warrior, rather than just a killer, and reduces the "moral injury" done to the soldier, which can have far-reaching consequences for not just the soldier, but also the state.

## The Problem of Moral Injury

Unsurprisingly, it is difficult to maintain adherence to the rules of war, not only because they are often disadvantageous to one's prospects of victory, but also because the very activity of war is dangerous to one's sense of morality. Even for "good men," says Augustine, "the real evils in war are love of violence, vengeful cruelty, fierce and implacable enmity, wild resistance, and the lust of power, and such like."[136]

Moral corruption is inevitable, for "the employment of organized violence means one must, in fact, abandon fixed and established values," argues war correspondent Chris Hedges. "This is a truth made apparent in *Troilus and Cressida*. It is a truth *Henry V* ignores. Once war, and especially the total war that marked both the ancient and modern way of battle, erupts, all is sacrificed before it."[137]

This is a fact of human nature, and the serious potential for moral injury is one reason the extensive moral code governs both personal and professional lives of warfighters.

Furthermore, virtues can cut both ways. Every society has some concept of "brave" as opposed to "pusillanimous," for example, or "honorable" in contrast to "dishonorable" fighting—but bravery and honor are double-edged swords.[138] Courageous defense of one's honor can contribute to restraints on the type of fighting permitted, but has also commonly led to war.

Honor can also be developed as an independent ethic, or it can be tribally oriented. The close camaraderie between fellow fighting men facing danger and death together does not always lead them to appreciate their enemies—instead, it can reinforce bonds between comrades at the expense of their opponents. For example, members of the elite US Navy SEAL teams have allegedly taken part in revenge killings, unjustified killings, torture, mutilations of corpses for revenge or "sport," the taking of battlefield trophies, embezzlement, and knowingly treating civilians as combatants, many of which rise to the level of war crimes. While a small number of SEALs committed these crimes, the rest overwhelmingly did not report them up the chain of command, and the teams as a whole preferred to handle discipline internally.[139] Said one former SEAL Team 6 leader, "You can't win an investigation on us. You don't whistleblow on the teams . . . and when you win on the battlefield, you don't lose investigations." The strong cultural norms of protecting one's teammates trumped other considerations, and Vice Admiral William McRaven, a Navy SEAL and commander of the Joint Special Operations Command (2008–11), reportedly "said that SEAL Team 6 had effectively made lying to protect a teammate an honorable course of action."[140] Clearly, battlefield honor can manifest in different ways, and not always in forms that accord respect to one's opponents and seek to cooperate with him.

One of the biggest dangers is that moral corruption is often accompanied by some genuine merit (e.g., tribally oriented honor), which fools others into believing that the display of virtue is correct and authentic.[141] This only makes it harder to identify vice, corruption, and moral injury in oneself or in others.[142]

Given the strength of tribal impulses and its impact on how honor is conceived, it is all the more important, then, to instill an *independent* conception of honor that draws on ideas of cooperation, respect, and warrior virtues. No less a philosopher than Immanuel Kant denounced the use of assassins (*percussores*) and poisons (*venefici*),[143] as well as entrapment through false capitulation, as "dishonorable stratagems."[144] To have a stable peace afterward, "some trust in the enemy's way of thinking must still remain even in the midst of war," in order to restrain mutual animosity from degenerating into a "war of extermination (*bellum internecinum*)" and bringing about perpetual peace "only in the vast graveyard of the human race." The Geneva Conventions echo this, saying that he who indulges in perfidy

> *destroys the faith that the combatants are entitled to have in the rules of armed conflict*, shows a lack of the minimum respect which even enemies should have for one another, and damages the dignity of those who bear arms. *As a result of these consequences, perfidy destroys the necessary basis for reestablishing peace.*[145]

Long-term peace is not the only consideration. Along with other "infernal arts, being mean in themselves," such as spying and possibly sniping, these actions corrupt one's morality in all areas of life, beyond warfare, and leave their perpetrators unsuited for republican citizenship.[146] Prior to Kant, Emerich de Vattel asked

> whether we may lawfully employ all sorts of means to take away an enemy's life? whether we be justifiable in procuring his death by assassination or poison? Some writers have asserted, that, where we have a right to take away life, the manner is indifferent. A strange maxim! but happily exploded by the bare ideas of honour, confused and indefinite as they are.

Like Kant, he concludes that "assassination and poisoning are . . . contrary to the laws of war, and equally condemned by the law of nature and the consent of all civilized nations." Vattel then refers to what are apparently self-evident conceptions of honor, in whatever form, and argues that assassination is not synonymous with "surprise," but rather amounts to "treacherous murder," while poisoning is "still more odious."[147]

Hypocritical or not, this distaste for "cowardly tactics" has been shared even by those who favored a fair amount of leeway in the acts of war,[148] and the later Lieber Code declares that "military necessity does not admit of . . . the use of poison in any way," as it is "out of the pale of the law and usages of war."[149]

Contemporary military training sometimes explicitly ties this back to honor. For example, the US Department of Defense's Law of War Manual says that honor "demands a certain amount of fairness in offense and defense and a certain mutual respect between opposing military forces" (§2.6) and it "forbids resort to means, expedients, or conduct that would constitute a breach of trust with the enemy" (§2.6.2). As one of the crucial values in warfare, honor is considered of equal importance to other core principles of *jus in bello* (military necessity, humanity, proportionality, and distinction).[150]

## Inconsistencies in the Concept of Parity

There are some notable inconsistencies within the concept of parity as manifested in war, for some things deemed "fair" and others "unfair" do not seem to differ in ways that are significant to the distinction. Military asymmetries are nothing new. For as long as people have fought one another, there have been glaring gaps in their capacities for war. The Battle of Agincourt (1415) is often cited as one of the major developments in the history of military technology. Henry V's brilliant leadership was aided by horrible tactics from the French, but the English's ability to defeat a force more than four times its size had perhaps more to do with their use of the longbow, which had a much greater range than its predecessors,[151] to defeat a superior French force,[152] which was hardly lacking in absolute terms: about twenty-five thousand strong and comprising largely well-equipped and heavily armored men-at-arms, including some cavalry.

Other obvious examples of battlefield asymmetry come from the introduction of firepower. The Ottoman use of siege artillery (including cannons and mortars that fired 155 to 180 shots per day) greatly contributed to their victories in the siege of Modon in 1500 and in a battle at Mohacs in 1526 against Luis II of Hungary's cavalry. When Aztecs and Incas were first confronted with firepower by Spaniards in the same century, they fared worse than their European counterparts had against the Ottomans.

Technological disparities are not limited to innovations in firepower: in the fifteenth and sixteenth centuries, the Portuguese navy enjoyed many advantages—their ships' hull construction and lateen and square rigging, as well as navigational tools and knowledge—that translated into military benefits whether or not those ships carried cannon. This is not dissimilar to the benefits afforded to modern air forces that possess stealth fighters, vertical-landing jets, and Predator drones. Superior firepower accounts for only part of the technological gap.[153]

## Distance and Anonymity

Strong feelings about "fair fights" are simultaneously accompanied by inconsistent judgments about what is fair. Generally, the greater the distance and the more impersonal (or massive) the method of killing, the more likely it is to be seen as unfair. Spartans, for example, considered it a test of one's "innate valour" to "withstand [in an] orderly array" an onslaught by "barbarians" to whom "flight and attack . . . are equally honourable," as General Brasidas exhorted his troops.[154] Spartans were said to use short swords specifically in order "that we may get close to the enemy," and when one was mortally wounded by an arrow, he purportedly lamented, "I am not troubled because I must die, but because my death comes at the hands of a womanish archer."[155]

Distance is highly influential but not entirely determining, however, and in practice, which weapons will be deemed fair or unfair is a little unpredictable. Beliefs, sentiments, and reasonable judgments about the "unfairness" of particular weapons change over time,[156] and in ways that expose inconsistencies in categorization.

For example, fully automatic machine guns were once held suspect, but are now generally acceptable, yet they still kill indiscriminately. Perhaps it is because someone must at least nominally aim the bursts of individual bullets in order to kill, whereas gas and virus spread on their own once released. The concepts of agency and individuality are essential to an honorable soldier and, as with uniform regulations and exceptions, the norms seem to privilege a vision of one-on-one, face-to-face combat that is entered into cooperatively. Perhaps, too, the recent spread of cheap-yet-robust automatic machine guns such as the AK-47 (Kalashnikov) is now seen as one way to level the playing field and bring more parity of a different kind, and so automatic weapons are no longer scorned in the same way. The content of the warrior virtues is not immutable: they change with the times.

Furthermore, even within the Western world, the Form of the warfighter varies enormously, much less across civilizations. To the modern reader, the ancient Greeks are familiar yet alien. In a modern age strongly shaped by chivalric values, gods like Zeus, Hera, and company engage in surprisingly human disputes, arguments, and trysts, and heroes like Achilles and Ajax are exotic. Magnetic, strong, and courageous though they are—all things we value in modern-day idols—they are also angry, sulking, petty, vengeful, and vain. Western civilization grows from these origins, but the ancient Greek godlike ways seem distant to those living in a world heavily influenced by Christian morality.

No major technological development goes unmatched indefinitely,[157] but every such advancement provokes a sense of unfairness. The introduction of guns produced a seismic shift in a martial world once dominated by close-range or man-projected weapons. This is poignantly depicted in *The Seven Samurai*, for although the samurai (ronin) prevail against gun-wielding bandits in this instance, the film points to the impending end of the samurai's way of life and battle. When master swordsman Kyūzō is fatally shot with a bullet by the bandit chief hiding in a hut, he manages to stagger up from the mud and hurl his sword, perhaps at the unseen enemy, perhaps in disgust. For all his prowess and honor, and the deeply personal nature of samurai ethics, Kyūzō was felled by an anonymous injury, delivered from afar, in a way that no samurai should die.

An analogous ethical shift is now underway with the development and increasing use of unmanned aerial vehicles (UAV), also called remotely piloted aircraft (RPA) or drones. Reports indicate that US military RPA operators are often uneasy about their work. Contrary to a common belief that their video game–like experience desensitizes them (a concern of both military leadership and the wider civilian population), they can feel it viscerally because they see their targets' faces clearly, track them for days as they go about normal life activities, and essentially get to know them before killing them, in a way that a fighter pilot dropping a bomb from miles up in the air does not.[158]

*Reciprocal Risk, Exposure to Endangerment*

An intramural conflict over the status of RPA pilots in the US military was actually an indirect expression of concern over "fair fights." In early 2013, outgoing secretary of defense Leon Panetta announced a new medal for extraordinary achievements not requiring "acts of valor," thus including those outside of traditional combat, with the intention of awarding it to RPA pilots or military personnel working on cyber warfare, among others. This attempted to recognize the changing nature of warfare and crucial accompanying technological developments, but public and veteran outcry was immediate, and sharply critical of the Distinguished

Warfare Medal's placement above the Purple Heart and Bronze Star in the hierarchy of commendation. One popular online petition argued:

> Bronze Stars are commonly awarded with a Valor device in recognition of a soldier's service in the heat of combat while on the ground in the theater of operation. *Under no circumstance should a medal that is designed to honor a pilot, that is controlling a drone via remote control, thousands of miles away from the theater of operation, rank above a medal that involves a soldier being in the line of fire on the ground. This is an injustice to those who have served and risked their lives* and this should not be allowed to move forward as planned.[159]

The reaction was so strong that incoming secretary Chuck Hagel ultimately abandoned this medal, opting instead for adding a "remote impacts" device to be affixed to decorations, for those participating in combat operations via remote technology.[160]

This was an internecine dispute in which different personnel within the same military staked their claims about the relative value and virtue of their respective work, but it revealed quite a bit about what is perceived to count as "warfare," including putting oneself at physical risk. It does not take much empathy or imagination to extend these views to one's enemies and to see how contempt or even mere disregard for remote warfare on one's own side could lead to an appreciation of valor by and promotion of "fair" fighting with the other side.

In fact, this very phenomenon is found in the ambivalent attitudes toward snipers discussed earlier. That a person can be stalked for months without knowing it and then killed in an instant with the push of a button from someone sitting in a safe, air-conditioned compound seven thousand miles away—which is just sniping on an exponentially larger scale—strikes many as unfair.[161] Not only do unmanned fighters put even more distance between themselves and their opponents than sniping, but some view it as qualitatively different because the RPA pilots' distance from the field makes it essentially "risk-free" to them, and "when the level of life-threatening risk incurred between the warring parties becomes so imbalanced that we cross a symmetry threshold," it renders the fight "intrinsically unjust."[162] Contemporary news articles show that this sentiment is readily reflected in the broader population.

Even after other criteria for just war—especially just cause, proportionality, and probability of success—have been satisfied and even if there is no "parity," strictly speaking, there is a sense that for things to be fair, all fighters at a minimum have to be endangered—in this case, physically present in the battlefield and vulnerable to attack.[163]

In the context of how war has been waged since the beginning of human history, however, it is crazy to talk about reciprocal risk in warfare: the history of technological development in warfighting is the history of trying to put distance between oneself and one's opponents.[164] This sense of fairness, which is rooted in a specific notion of reciprocal cooperation, persists, however, and drives many of the questions being asked right now about the ethics of drone warfare.

## *Modes of Suffering*

The ban on poisonous gases presents an interesting comparison with permissible weapons. From the start, gas was perceived as "dirty," "grotesque," and "unsoldierly."[165] Widespread condemnation of chemical warfare in World War I led the League of Nations to commission a study (1920) on the wartime use of poisonous gas, which reported:

Resolution VIII

I. Asphyxiating Gases
   Opinion of the Commission.
   1. The employment of gases is a fundamentally cruel method of carrying on war; though not more so than certain other methods commonly employed, provided that they are only employed against combatants. Their employment against non-combatants, however, must be regarded as barbarous and inexcusable.
   2. It would be useless to seek to restrict the use of gases in war time by prohibiting or limiting their manufacture in peace time.[166]

The Geneva Protocol (1925), which then banned the use of poisonous gases to uneven effect, loftily declared that gas "has been justly condemned by the general opinion of the civilised world." Some users did not resist the injunction because gas had not lived up to expectations: it could not be accurately targeted and had turned out to be relatively ineffective as a weapon.[167]

The moral revulsion was foremost and sincere, however—but even in World War I there were those who argued gas was no worse than other weapons. "I cannot see the difference between killing a man with a chemical substance and rending him to pieces with high explosives. The first-named form of death, as a matter of fact, is the most merciful," wrote Dr. J. F. Elliott to his local paper in 1915.[168]

Why does killing fewer with weapons such as poisonous gas lead to a ban in international law, while killing larger numbers with some conventional weapons does not raise more condemnation?[169] Distinctions between armaments can be a little mysterious and raise questions about whether it is anything more than chance and taste that make a weapon "conventional."

Other terrible weapons used at the same time as gas raised no hackles. For example, the flamethrower appears on the Western Front in 1915, two months before gas, and was used to flush people out of the trenches: those who could run from the searing conflagration, often themselves on fire, were then picked off with machine guns.[170] The machine gun, too, was honed to new levels of murderous perfection, and the biggest killer of all was artillery.

Were those better than death by gassing? Decades later, a US Army lieutenant and embedded combat adviser to Afghan National Security Forces in 2008, who was pinned down with his unit at a mountain pass base under a massive twenty-minute artillery barrage by an unseen enemy, during which no assistance was forthcoming by either land or air, once exclaimed, "Artillery is not fair. You can hear it coming in, like a freight train. There's nothing you can do, you just hope you can survive it."[171] What does it mean, for a weapon to be "unfair," even if it is said only in frustration and fear?

Of course, parity in war or peace is always artificial, but that is generally understood: the desire is usually simply for some kind of parity within a range—an attachment to the spirit of the law rather than the letter, as it were. The particular parity pursued in each situation does not always make sense, and furthermore, despite expectations, there is no reason to make oneself equally vulnerable to one's opponent and thus eschew surprise attacks. In fact, there is nothing traditional at all about trying to engineer parity in warfare, as evidenced by millennia of warfare practices. The norm is actually the opposite, and the same books that lament the "unfairness" of sniping are filled with stories of successful and unrepentant snipers.

Yet, it does not matter that particular types of parity put forth sometimes do not make sense in the context of war or that some conceptions of parity are irrational, misguided, or contradictory. Whatever the parity sought, the principle espoused is enough to constitute at least a weak—but often stronger—norm in military ethics, and has shaped the practice of war, sometimes even becoming codified in its laws.

### Politicizing the Ethic of Cooperation for a "Fair Fight"—Who Qualifies for "Fair" Treatment?

Despite the noble intentions behind the ethic of cooperation for a "fair fight," it can be harnessed for reprehensible purposes, notably in restricting who qualifies for fair/cooperative treatment. Obedience to certain laws of war has long been couched in terms of a society's self-conception as "civilized," as opposed to "barbarian," stretching as far back as the ancient Greeks and classical Chinese,[172] but this is a double-edged sword. It can apply internal pressures to hold one's own military to higher standards of warfare, but it can simultaneously exclude the "uncivilized." Customs and practices for warfare between Greek hoplites and their *poleis* were not applicable to fights with "barbarians," for example.[173] Distinguishing between the civilized and the barbarous in order to hold the former to certain standards is dangerous, as its inverse vindicates the idea that only some peoples deserve to be treated according to the rules of war.[174]

When Andrew Jackson used false flags to lure and hang the two Seminole leaders and executed two British he suspected of aiding and abetting the Creek, he controversially justified it by claiming—erroneously—that it was "an established principle of the laws of nations that any individual of a nation making war against the citizens of another nation, they being at peace, forfeits his allegiance, and becomes an outlaw and a pirate," and that, furthermore, "the laws of war did not apply to conflicts with savages."[175] His supporters considered the Seminoles to be "vagrant savages" and argued that their race was "sufficient evidence" for their execution.[176] Two decades later, another war with the Seminoles in Florida erupted during now President Jackson's second term, and the military followed their commander-in-chief's lead:

> Under Major General Thomas Sidney Jesup, the U.S. Army issued orders reinstituting the medieval and early modern practice of booty and plunder, authorizing individual soldiers to keep hostile Indian property for their own account. In 1837 and 1838, American forces under Jesup repeatedly violated some of the most venerable rules of the laws of war by using flags of truce to lure in and capture the Seminole leadership. Indian leaders protested Jesup's actions as an "unprecedented violation of that sacred rule which has ever been recognized by every nation, civilized or uncivilized." Dismayed American observers cringed at what they called "another breach of national honor."[177]

And once the Seminoles realized that the United States was issuing false flags, this intensified their resistance, and helped prolong the brutal war for another two decades.

It is worth noting, however, that even the forceful ripostes against Jackson mentioned earlier spoke of the Indians in disparaging terms. Henry Clay, who in 1819 excoriated Jackson for his savage treachery and so passionately and eloquently defended respectful treatment of the Indians even if they did not reciprocate, nonetheless considered them ignorant "monsters."[178] Extending laws of war to them, for him and many others, was grounded in custom, habit, and self-interest, not out of a universal principle, and this shows both the strength of the ethic of cooperation (as opposed to human rights motivations) as well as its tenuous foundations.

---

We have seen how ideas of parity in risk and opportunity and "sporting" competitiveness influence the ethic of cooperation for a "fair fight." The "fair play" component of warrior honor leads to voluntary restraint and to restrictions on various uses of surprise, deception, and certain types of weapons, even without immediate reciprocity. In doing so, however, it may unintentionally prolong a war by making it harder to win, and kill more people along the way. This potential conflict between battle function (discussed earlier) and *war* function is a deeply troubling concern that will be revisited in chapter 5.

The valiant quest for fairness is born of professionalism and virtue ethics, but nonetheless can generate internal conceptual inconsistencies and uneven application. The irony of the contrast between the attempts to codify the laws of war during the American Civil War (and many of the "gentlemanly" courtesies also mentioned) and the simultaneous horrific treatment of American Indians should not be lost on anyone. As will be seen even more clearly in the next chapter, the codification of the laws of war also necessarily creates boundaries that can be used to exclude certain people from such treatment and to both justify and perhaps unintentionally worsen their situation—although even then, it is not clear that it would be better to have no rules at all.

CHAPTER III

Cooperation to Minimize Damage to Particular Classes of People

> Viewed in the unclouded light of Truth, what is War, but organized murder,—murder of malice aforethought,—in cold blood,—under sanctions of impious law,—through the operation of an extensive machinery of crime,—with innumerable hands,—at incalculable cost of money,—by subtle contrivances of cunning and skill,—or amidst the fiendish atrocities of the savage, brutal assault?
> —CHARLES SUMNER, "THE TRUE GRANDEUR OF NATIONS," JULY 4, 1845

> Humanitarian action is more than simple generosity, simple charity. It aims to build spaces of normalcy in the midst of what is abnormal.
> —JAMES ORBINSKI, MÉDECINS SANS FRONTIÈRES—NOBEL LECTURE, OSLO, DECEMBER 10, 1999

War without limits—unconstrained by political considerations, unmoderated by moral impulses, isolated from history—is absolute war, which Clausewitz believed was an indulgent "logical fantasy."[1] He theorized for the modern world comprised of nation-states that are considered normatively equal in much the same way that Hobbesian individuals are, and that are driven more by their political pursuits than anything else. Despite the essential role of the passions, war is ultimately bounded by political factors, he thought. But people have always pushed war to the edges of their imagination, and have often defied those boundaries in reality.

Destruction has its purposes, but it is sometimes also pursued for its own sake. Sieges—highly indiscriminate in who they kill—have been used since the earliest records of warfare, from Thutmosis III and the Egyptian Empire's seven-month siege of the Canaanite city of Megiddo (c. 1460 BCE) to a variety of cities in Syria through 2018.[2] Sieges persist not out of necessity—because it is possible to at least roughly discriminate between different types of people—but because indiscrimination is precisely the goal. Says historian and legal scholar John Fabian Witt of General Sherman's siege of Atlanta in the American Civil War: "Sherman marveled at the capacity of his fantastic modern guns to single out particular homes from a mile away, but the Union fire was often indiscriminate anyway. He urged his commanders to concentrate their fire at night (one Union shell killed a father and his daughter while they slept). His aim, he told Major General Oliver Otis Howard, was to 'destroy Atlanta and make it a desolation.'"[3]

Attacking without regard for civilian status has taken ever more technologically sophisticated forms, such as aerial bombings of cities in the twentieth century, but the old-fashioned siege is still a popular choice.

The German siege of Leningrad lasted over two years (872 days, from September 1941 to January 1944) and killed over one million people, about one-third of the population. Early on, a secret order from German chief of naval staff (Staff Ia No; 1501/41, 29.IX.1941) indicated that

> The Führer has decided to erase from the face of the earth St. Petersburg. The existence of this large city will have no further interest after Soviet Russia is destroyed. Finland has also said that the existence of this city on her new border is not desirable from her point of view. The original request of the Navy that docks, harbor, etc. necessary for the fleet be preserved—is known to the Supreme Commander of the Military Forces, but the basic principles of carrying out operations against St. Petersburg do not make it possible to satisfy this request. . . . The problem of the life of the population and the provisioning of them is a problem which cannot and must not be decided by us. In this war . . . we are not interested in preserving even a part of the population of this large city.[4]

The government of Leningrad then decided to preemptively destroy its own infrastructure (factories, bridges, railroads, ports, and so on) in order to deny the enemy its use if the city were captured, a move that the population resented.[5] Starvation struck everyone, and created poignant relationships with food. Said one inhabitant of the siege:

> People are accustomed to think that bread is simply bread and that one gets the same satisfaction from 125 grams. That is not true. Bread can be eaten in different ways, and each person must find the most "satisfactory" method for himself. One can eat it by biting off a piece, or by breaking off crumbs. Others cut it: some into thin, transparent

slices, some into thick squares. All agree that the crust is the most filling. The thoughtless ones eat the bread before they have even left the bakery; the others—they are in the minority—divide the ration into three parts: for breakfast, lunch, and dinner. To know that one can eat one's own piece of bread right away, and to stop oneself from doing it, is an act of heroism.[6]

Many people simply lay down and died wherever they were: on the streets, at work in factories and offices, to or from errands, at home, in the canteen or yards or hospitals or ration lines, and while trying to bury dead family members. Those who died at home alone might not be discovered for days. Workers "ate grease from the guns and oil from the machines," and there were persistent reports of cannibalism, mostly of corpses lying in the streets or stored in morgues, as well as of parents eating their children and the other way around.[7] Says Leon Gouré, whose explosive *The Siege of Leningrad* (1962) was one of the first to publicly reveal the toll of indiscrimination and unearth many revelations about decision-making on both sides:

> Usually death came as no surprise. There was so much of it all around that it seemed to have become a part of the daily routine. The struggle for survival was so harsh that there was little time or energy left for violent grief; often even pity called for more emotion than many could summon up. Sometimes death was almost welcome because it meant one less mouth to feed, or one extra ration card. There was often nothing parents could do but watch in silent despair as their children cried from hunger and slowly wasted away.[8]

Even Party members, who had extra privileges, died in great numbers—about seventeen thousand during the siege, mostly due to disease and starvation.[9]

Centuries earlier, similarly far-reaching destruction reportedly left even Roman commander Scipio Aemilianus in tears after he finally subdued a recalcitrant Carthage following a two-year siege that ended when most of the remaining nine hundred or so survivors immolated themselves in a temple (c. 149–46 BCE).[10]

Sieges are so common that specialized siege and countersiege weapons were developed, e.g., battering rams, siege towers, and catapults, and counterweapons, such as the spiked *ye cha lei* (夜叉擂, malevolent wood) and *lang ya pai* (狼牙拍, wolf teeth striker). The siege is only the most dramatic example, but this tactic's longevity illustrates that throughout human history, most of warfare has been utterly indiscriminate.

It is hard to overestimate how much general attitudes toward discrimination in warfare have evolved in recent centuries, and contemporary efforts to minimize the destruction inevitably wrought on whole populations are remarkable for their exceptionality in human history.

One way to suppress the many intentional atrocities and horrific number of people killed is to cooperate with the enemy in order to protect particular groups. Prominent examples of this ethic of cooperation from international law include requiring soldiers to wear uniforms or to carry their arms openly into combat (in order to distinguish themselves from civilians), providing immunity for medical and religious military personnel, banning the use of certain weapons that more often harm civilians than soldiers, regulating POW treatment and their return after cessation of hostilities, and protecting private property during war.

This chapter explores a number of these protections, their historical development and instantiation in international law, and their moral justifications. These restrictions developed in different ways—for example, uniforms in the West originated for internal reasons, to maintain order, discipline, and loyalty among the troops—but now are justified at least in part by their function in protecting particular classes of people, whether it be civilians, property owners, or soldiers just doing their jobs and making no political claims beyond the fact of their membership in a national military.

As with "fair fights," this well-meaning cooperative ethic to protect groups of people may be used to exclude. It may also inadvertently cause more damage by prolonging the war and killing more people in the long run. In some cases, it might protect the wrong people: this chapter also interrogates protections for political leaders, and whether pressing questions of responsibility and accountability for war are properly addressed.

## Civilian Immunity: A Functional Fiction

One hallmark of modern warfare ethics is tactically distinguishing between soldiers and civilians, which stands in stark contrast to most of the history of warfare, where few if any qualms have been exhibited about laying siege to entire cities, sometimes for years on end, and enslaving women and children whenever possible. The historically little distinctions have heretofore been largely ad hoc or applicable only to coreligionists or "tribe" members broadly speaking.

According to the International Committee of the Red Cross (ICRC), the first rule of customary international law is civilian distinction:

Rule 1. The Principle of Distinction between Civilians and Combatants

The parties to the conflict must at all times distinguish between civilians and combatants. Attacks may only be directed against combatants. Attacks must not be directed against civilians.[11]

International acceptance of this principle did not come easily, and despite the wealth of contemporary international law on this matter, it is difficult to maintain; see, for example, the city of Aleppo, Syria, which was recently besieged by the government for years. There was a precursor in the Fourth Geneva Convention (1958), which provided protection for certain classes of civilians (primarily foreign nationals or those without nationality) in a belligerent state or occupied territory.[12] Only in 1977, nearly twenty years later, is the principle of civilian immunity laid out in the way most familiar to us now, in the Geneva Convention's Additional Protocol I. There is an enormous philosophical and legal literature on who exactly is liable to attack, which cannot be treated here, but the development of this distinction and its widespread acceptance are a major moral innovation—even as they violate it, most states and militaries find it important to acknowledge.

Legally, at least, everyone who is not officially enrolled in a military is considered a civilian (Protocol I, Art. 50), and civilians cannot be expressly targeted or subject to indiscriminate attacks such as area or carpet bombing that do not attempt to distinguish them from military members. (Protocol I, Art. 51).[13] Recognizing the siege's enduring appeal as a military tactic, the Geneva Convention expressly forbids intentional starvation of civilians, which includes attacking their means of sustenance (Protocol I, Art. 54; Protocol II, Art. 14). Furthermore, agricultural projects and other utilities installations necessary for civilian livelihood are protected, as are important historical, religious, and cultural objects/places (Protocol I, Arts. 52–56), and in *non*-international conflicts as well (Protocol II, Arts. 13–18).

### *Civilian Economic and Military Involvement*

Military personnel and ethicists alike struggle over which *people* are acceptable military targets, especially noncombatants contributing to the war effort. This moral question arose prominently in World War II, which saw not only massive bombing campaigns that either targeted or disregarded civilians[14] but also detonation of two nuclear bombs whose very purpose was to kill civilians. As mentioned in chapter 2, one approach "draw[s] a line between those who have lost their rights because of their warlike activities and those who have not," says Walzer:

> An army, to be sure, has an enormous belly, and it must be fed if it is to fight but it is not its belly but its arms that make it an army. Those men and women who supply its belly are doing nothing peculiarly warlike. Hence their immunity from attack: they are assimilated to the rest of the civilian population. We call them *innocent* people, a term of art which means that they have done nothing, and are doing nothing, that entails the loss of their rights.[15]

That certain deeds are simply human acts—even in war—is effectively the distinction made by the Convention addenda of 1977.

In modern societies and modern economies, this strict civilian/soldier distinction is highly artificial, hence the need for a term of art. With a few exceptions (e.g., small children and the very elderly or infirm), most civilians do in fact contribute in some way—directly or indirectly, willingly or unwillingly—to the complex of things that allow a military to go to war, long before it is deployed, and there is no clean line between soldiers and nonsoldiers.

In the case of many noncombatants, their livelihoods depend on a military that consumes a variety of resources, so who qualifies as an acceptable military target, especially in large-scale modern warfare, is highly controversial. As Walzer acknowledges, "this line may be too finely drawn," but "it is drawn under pressure"—judgments must be made.[16]

## Civilian Responsibility for Political Decisions

The distinction is further muddied on political grounds, especially in democracies in which civilians either directly or indirectly authorize the government's and military's actions. In having participated in and been legitimately represented in the process to go to war, it can be argued that democratic citizens are then liable to harm. Said Osama bin Laden after the 9/11 attacks:

> It is a fundamental principle of any democracy that the people choose their leaders, and as such, approve and are party to the actions of their elected leaders. . . . By electing these leaders, the American people have given their consent to the incarceration of the Palestinian people, the demolition of Palestinian homes and the slaughter of the children of Iraq. This is why the American people are not innocent. The American people are active members in all these crimes.[17]

> The American people should remember that they pay taxes to their government, they elect their president, their government manufactures arms and gives them to Israel and Israel uses them to massacre Palestinians. The American Congress endorses all government measures and this proves that the entire America is responsible for the atrocities perpetrated against Muslims. The entire America, because they elect the Congress.[18]

His argument for the civilian responsibility inherent in democratic participation is actually quite similar to many of those in the Western analytic philosophy literature about the democratic citizen's liability therein, as well as their subsequent questions about the principle of noncombatant immunity.[19]

Whatever validity these arguments have will not change the dominant legal and moral verdict on this matter any time soon, however.[20] Though their material, rhetorical, or political contributions mean that the firm division between soldier and civilian is contrived, this distinction is essential in order to shield large swathes of the population, and many norms and practices have developed to attempt the complicated task of protecting civilians in war, including the Geneva Conventions' targeting rules that prohibit sieges, carpet bombing, and attacking objects or installations essential for civilian survival.

Designating civilians as "innocent" and therefore immune from attack is a useful fiction that grew out of a complex of developments during the early modern period, especially the birth of the nation-state and its professional soldier (both mercenary and national), and other differentiations in societal roles and accompanying moral considerations. Just war thinking evolved alongside this: Francisco de Vitoria and Hugo Grotius, for example, rejected holy war's destruction in the name of God. With relentless secularization came acknowledgment that it is difficult, if not impossible, to determine with certainty which side, if any, has just cause.

This generates what is now the traditional "moral equality of combatants," which concedes that right is doubtful, and attempts to constrain what can be done in pursuit of an uncertain justice. If one cannot determine which soldiers are in the right, much less can one pass similar judgment on civilians. This idea was part of the long march toward protecting civilians by assuming them to be innocent and declaring them off-limits.

Few adult civilians are, of course, wholly innocent in the sense of having contributed nothing to the war effort, but this fiction is now broadly accepted, and imposes a moral requirement for discrimination, as codified in the international law. In recent decades, this moral imperative has been buttressed by the growth of human rights discourse. These human rights claims, though compelling, are nonetheless still premised on a conventional distinction between soldiers and civilians and a second artifice of civilians as effectively innocent.

This is not to pass philosophical judgment on the correctness of this designation of civilian innocence and what harm they are liable to, but rather to show that this categorization is the locus of a significant and enormously difficult collaboration between enemies in warfare.

### *Privileges and Responsibilities of Wartime Killing*

Beyond that, there are questions about absorbing supererogatory risk: Is it enough to warn civilians to leave a potential battle area (such that those who choose to stay gamble with being caught in the crossfire),[21] or must soldiers subject themselves to additional jeopardy in order to protect civilians?[22] Expectations have risen over time, and now militaries are criticized if they do not actively and repeatedly take measures to not fight around civilians (e.g., go door to door to clear civilians of a suspect building before bombing it) or if they do not first assume that an approaching person is innocent even in threatening situations.

Two different stories simultaneously illustrate both the force and the fragility of this belief in civilian immunity. In 1968, American forces were intentionally and systematically massacring civilians in the hamlet of My Lai, South Vietnam, when the supporting helicopter crew (pilot Hugh Thompson, Jr., crew chief Glenn Andreotta, and door gunner Lawrence Colburn) recognized what was happening and landed, confronted the troops, and threatened to shoot anyone who interfered with their rescue of the surviving villagers. Despite attempts to bury this incident, it ultimately came to light, but only one of perpetrators involved in the massacre/cover-up was actually charged and convicted (commanding officer Lt. William Calley), and even then, his life sentence was gradually commuted, and he received a limited presidential pardon and ultimately served only three years of house arrest.

The norm of presuming civilians to be innocent was constantly challenged during the war by guerrilla fighters blending in with civilians, but was nonetheless strong enough for the helicopter crew to turn their weapons on their fellow soldiers and their backs toward strangers they could not be sure were harmless. It takes a lot to supersede the hard-wearing bonds of solidarity with one's military compatriots. For these three men, however, the default presumption of civilian innocence and corresponding immunity was even stronger, and they acted extraordinarily courageously. (This case is now commonly taught in ethics classes at US military academies.) When the trio returned to the base and reported what had happened, "They said I was screaming quite loud," recalled Thompson, "I threatened never to fly again. I didn't want to be a part of that. It wasn't war."[23] Colburn later quoted from US general Douglas MacArthur's judgment of Japanese general Tomoyuki Yamashita's World War II crimes:

> The soldier, be he friend or foe, is charged with the protection of the weak and unarmed. It is the very essence and reason for his being. When he violates this sacred trust, he not only profanes his entire cult but threatens the very fabric of international society. The traditions of fighting men are long and honorable. They are based upon the noblest of human traits,—sacrifice. This officer, of proven field

merit, entrusted with high command involving authority adequate to responsibility, has failed this irrevocable standard; has failed his duty to his troops, to his country, to his enemy, to mankind; has failed utterly his soldier faith. The transgressions resulting therefrom as revealed by the trial are a blot upon the military profession, a stain upon civilization and constitute a memory of shame and dishonor that can never be forgotten. . . . No new or retroactive principles of law, either national or international, are involved. The case is founded upon basic fundamentals and practices as immutable and as standardized as the most matured and irrefragible of social codes.[24]

Noble as MacArthur's statement is, it is not exactly correct. The "very essence and reason" for a soldier is not, in fact, "protection of the weak and unarmed"—it is to fight for his country. And the principles of civilian innocence and immunity have hardly been eternal or immutable in practice: American forces also struggled with staying on the correct side of those lines during the very same war.

The point is clear, however. The soldier's greater powers—namely, the weapons at his disposal and his government's permission to kill in its name—come with certain critical responsibilities to be mindful of and care for the effectively innocent: this is the exchange that they make for their greater privileges.[25] MacArthur was trying to redefine—or at least augment the definition of—the warfighter, and it is an aspect of soldiering that many take seriously, even at great risk to themselves, as evidenced by the supporting helicopter crew's valor at My Lai.

Protecting civilians requires not only one's unilateral decisions but also cooperative adherence from one's opponents. In Helmand, Afghanistan, one day in 2012, US special forces and Taliban were positioned on opposite rooftops, engaged in a firefight in a fortified area, lobbing grenades at each other over a house that sat between the opposing buildings. Two girls inside the house were wounded by a grenade exploding over it, and when the radio cracked with that news, "everyone stopped." Eventually a car came and drove the girls away to medical help, and the fighting resumed.

In retrospect, the incident was "very strange," recounted a US special forces member. The lull was a highly opportune time to attack the enemy— especially one that was "very comfortable pretending to be civilians and harming civilians," such as shooting and then running into civilian-inhabited buildings, traveling with civilians as cover, or posing as farmers

COOPERATION TO MINIMIZE DAMAGE [ 99 ]

while setting IED's in civilian areas—"so why were we holding back? [But] no one talked about why," because it was so ingrained in them that a soldier must go to extra lengths to protect civilians from harm.[26]

These two stories from My Lai, Vietnam, and Helmand, Afghanistan—different wars, different times, different places—illustrate any number of things, but here, notably (1) the strength of soldiers' belief in the principle of civilian immunity, (2) the extent of self-policing in adherence to that norm, and (3) the need for further cooperation in order to effectively promote a still tenuously held value.

## Protecting Civilians Through Uniforming

Effectively guarding civilian immunity requires not just ad hoc decisions by individuals or reciprocity between agents known to each other (short- or long-term, one-off or repeated interactions), but also systemization beyond personal interfaces, such as wearing uniforms.

### HISTORICAL EVOLUTION OF UNIFORMS

The stereotypical image of eighteenth- and nineteenth-century European warfare is soldiers in brightly colored, unmistakable uniforms, lined up in rows essentially waiting to be shot, while firing in unison at the opposing army who was similarly aligned. It is obviously a gross oversimplification of this era,[27] and infantries did not array themselves this way entirely out of a misguided sense of battlefield honor or manliness.[28] Having soldiers fire in concentrated volleys boosted troop morale and was more effective militarily. Coordinated attacks were also safer, as inaccurate weaponry and battlefield chaos meant that soldiers were as likely to shoot their surrounding compatriots as their enemies, and holding formation better withstood against cavalry charges.[29] Uniforms also made it easier for commanding officers to see their own troops.

The uniform convention is an excellent example of something that started for one reason (internal cohesion), continued out of expedient cooperation, and then later took on an *ethical* salience in its own right to limit the destruction of war in certain areas. The modern convention of wearing uniforms into combat has undergone a complicated evolution. Members of warrior classes all over the world have long worn distinctive armor and markings (e.g., crests, coats of arms, and other heraldry). Japanese shogunates were probably the first to clothe their armies in official uniform, requiring their samurai to wear the *mon* of their shogun lords as far back as the eleventh century; meanwhile, European knights wore their individual coats of arms or that of their religious orders into battle. The purpose of these distinctions was for the fighters themselves to be able to distinguish ally from enemy.[30]

The practice of national militias wearing coordinated garb in the Western world is not particularly old. Oliver Cromwell was one of the first to clothe his militia in uniform, in the mid-seventeenth century, and the ensuing trend reaches its height with Frederick the Great's elaborate regalia in the mid- to late eighteenth century. Successful European generals during this period paid painstaking attention to detail, including recruitment and training, and the uniform's visual symbol buttressed the professionalization of the military and enforcement of discipline. Uniforms represented standardization as well as sovereign control. Despite impracticalities for movement, combat, or efficiency, such as with certain versions of the British "redcoat" or some wildly extravagant and expensive Napoleonic uniforms, these shortcomings were trumped by the importance of creating cohesion in the military and projecting an image of state power. Unsurprisingly, systematic uniforming coincided with the nation-state's development, and has since become standard practice as well as synonymous with legitimate authority in warfare.

### LEGAL CODIFICATION

This practice extends beyond the European sphere and is now codified in international military law, which is reasonably representative of international moral norms. Geneva Conventions First Protocol (1977), Article 44.3, requires combatants to distinguish themselves from civilians by wearing uniforms or by some other recognizable identifying mark, when engaged in or preparing for attack, but excepts "situations in armed conflicts where, owing to the nature of the hostilities[,] an armed combatant cannot so distinguish himself," and extends combatant protections to the nonuniformed so long as they carry arms openly in combat.

The assumptions underlying these regulations are, ironically, made clearer by its exceptions. The law does not specify the relevant circumstances for exemption, but the most common scenario (and the historical impetus) is when one party is very resource-poor or lacks legitimate political authority, such as an insurgent political subgroup. In those cases, a combatant is not required to differentiate himself in any way from civilians in order to retain all the rights and privileges of lawful combatants, provided that he "carries his arms openly" while engaged in or deploying for an attack. He is then absolved of charges of perfidy under Article 37.1.c for "feigning . . . civilian, non-combatant status." It is implied that circumstances qualifying for exemption are to be narrowly construed, as this exception "is not intended to change the generally accepted practice of States with respect to the wearing of the uniform by combatants assigned to the regular, uniformed armed units of a Party to the conflict" (Art. 44.7).[31]

## "FAIR PLAY," INTERNAL, AND PROTECTIVE RATIONALES

The regulations and exemptions for uniformed combat reveal certain underlying assumptions of fair play in warfare.[32] Those who do not wear an identifying uniform of their own country into combat are considered to be lying, and therefore in the wrong—but why? After all, many occupations whose purveyors significantly impact people's lives do not require uniforms: IRS auditors, civil engineers, even doctors. In the United States, the highly recognizable white coat of medical doctors is a custom, not a legal obligation. It may be because, unlike others, soldiers are allowed to kill, not only other soldiers but also other civilians (under certain circumstances). In the domestic setting, officers of the government who have similar capacities to kill (notably, members of police forces) have similar uniform requirements, especially because they are integrated into the society in which they act. They live and work in the midst of the population, and they wear their uniforms for dual purposes, to project authority to both criminals and victims, as deterrent or enforcer to one and savior to the other.

Although modern soldiers are usually sequestered from the general populace and oriented toward foreign affairs, the rationales for their uniforms are analogous. The original objective of wearing uniforms was internal, to impose discipline and professionalism on previously disordered militia and to solidify the mercenaries' loyalty to the sovereign.[33] This purpose still holds, but the primary motivation has changed. It must have quickly become obvious that wearing uniforms disadvantaged the soldiers in them, particularly when moving through civilian populations. Yet, the expectation that this convention would be honored has persisted. It is not the case that warfare has only recently spread to civilian-populated areas and that, previously, soldiers could wear uniforms with impunity. Soldiers have always fought among or near civilians, yet the uniform's evident drawbacks have not overcome over three hundred years of this practice—certainly long enough to have figured out its hardships. Why would such a detrimental convention persist?[34]

Attitudes toward uniforms are influenced in part by their historical development during the early modern period in conjunction with the full-frontal assault of "linear battle," and this vision has captured both popular and military imaginations. Why would such a deadly practice continue for so long? It is not because people lacked the ability to predict the deadly combination of uniforming with new battlefield technology, especially long-range rifles. Individually, soldiers are clearly disadvantaged while in uniform—it takes resources and effort, and comes at great cost to themselves, so why not occasionally cheat to one's advantage? In fact, soldiers do try to cheat, and often. Other considerations have emerged to combat the natural tendency of every individual to abandon his uniform, including a practical need to "win hearts and minds."[35] But the uniform convention survives not out of expedience.

Although it makes him an easier target, the uniformed soldier allows himself to be recognized as such for several reasons. Added to the original internal intent of encouraging unit cohesion are now external motivations, including protecting civilians. Wearing uniforms makes it easier for soldiers and civilians to avoid each other and accidental civilian casualties. It also reduces intentional ones, as it prevents soldiers from hiding among civilians. A single readily identified soldier would not want to be caught alone in hostile territory, which encourages clumping for protection and helps keep soldiers away from civilians and war between soldiers. Every soldier wants to protect his own civilians, and the price of doing so not only makes himself more visible to the enemy but also protects the enemy's civilians, who can now identify and more easily avoid him. In order to safeguard their own populations, enemy soldiers cooperate by reciprocally wearing uniforms: they make themselves vulnerable on the understanding that their opponents do the same, because such cooperation has taken on an *ethical* salience in its own right, in the form of distinct moral justifications to limit harm to civilians (who have been designated as innocent through a separate cooperative enterprise).[36]

### ENFORCING THE UNIFORM CONVENTION

The ethic of cooperation in warfare to protect civilians by wearing uniforms has been formalized in domestic code, bilateral treaties, and international law. In the Geneva Conventions, moral expectations for safeguarding civilians—whether out of utilitarian or deontological (e.g., human rights) considerations[37]—are codified, and the Conventions seek to act as a third-party arbitrator in enforcing such cooperation.[38]

Protecting civilians requires *systematic* cooperation far beyond what can be accomplished by unilateral action or bilateral agreement. It relies on a multidimensional system of layered cooperation, a complex of agreements within each side and between opposing sides along many lines: soldier/soldier (fellow and opposing), soldier/civilian (own and opposing), civilian/government (own and opposing), soldier/government (own and opposing), government/government.

These agreements constitute a multifaceted contract between warfighters and their governments within a limited scope (the realm of war), premised on everyone's different statuses. Soldiers accept the disadvantages of wearing uniforms on the understanding that their opponents do so as well, with the intention of protecting civilians from both sides by clearly signaling their status. It is bolstered by an underlying and reinforcing agreement between governments (currently via the Geneva Conventions) to give uniformed fighters certain rights and protections as befitting their positions as government representatives (and not as independent, individual agents), and to discourage violation of the soldier/civilian distinction by categorizing and treating nonuniformed combatants differently.

This is not just a bilateral agreement between soldiers and their government, but rather a three-way understanding between soldiers, governments, and civilians.[39] Since civilians have not voluntarily relinquished their right to immunity, they have a right to not be unnecessarily attacked, as well as responsibilities to refrain from fighting or unduly obstructing it (e.g., disrupting the trajectory of a battle, purposefully or not). The parameters of noncombatant immunity form the basis of the uniformed combatants' rights. Combatants agree to exchange their right to immunity for a right to kill, with the understanding that the rules of engagement will be fair and reciprocal. The soldier/civilian distinction cannot work without agreement, cooperation, and reinforcement from all three parties—civilian, soldier, and government (see figure 3.1).[40]

Cooperation via international and domestic law is far less dramatic than a Christmas truce in the trenches or spontaneously stopping a firefight to rescue girls who have gotten in the way, but it is no less important or significant. What is unique about the ethic of cooperation when it becomes systematized in the international laws of war is that it no longer relies on one-on-one reciprocity. One's cooperation now takes place within a complex edifice and one's action is now directed toward an unspecified other, such that it can *appear* unilateral. Even if the opponent at hand defects and the cooperation is not immediately mutual, however, one continues cooperating within that larger institutional structure. Such formalized cooperation also breeds expectations of future cooperation, which affect how one engages the enemy, and may also create normative duties to cooperate.

For example, US troop members, including special forces, deployed to Afghanistan have frequently said that even if their opponents did not distinguish between civilians and combatants—for example, children were sometimes used as shields—they were themselves expected to maintain that distinction. One might nonetheless abide by the rules in order to promote future cooperation, as it is an important signal in all directions—not just to the immediate enemy, but also to the international audience and one's fellow soldiers.

## Weapons Bans

Civilians are the most prominent group protected by systematic, self-imposed cooperative restraint between enemies on the means they employ to kill one another, but this ethic also extends to protecting military personnel themselves.

Weapons bans safeguard both civilians and soldiers in different ways. Some reflect a desire to "fight fair" as there are improper ways for soldiers

```
┌─────────────────────────────────────────────────────────────────┐
│ • Soldiers exchange right to immunity for right to legally kill other soldiers. │
│ • Soldiers wear uniforms in order to identify themselves to other soldiers— │
│   they cannot pretend to be civilians.                          │
└─────────────────────────────────────────────────────────────────┘
                                │
                    ┌───────────▼───────────┐
            ┌──────▶│      Soldiers         │◀──────┐
            │       └───────────┬───────────┘       │
            │                   │                   │
            │       ┌───────────▼──────────────────────────────────┐
            │       │ • Soldiers are limited representatives of     │
            │       │   their own governments and immune            │
            │       │   from individual responsibility for their    │
            │       │   governments' political decisions.           │
┌───────────┴─────────────────┐ │ • Soldiers wear uniforms and take │
│ • Soldiers wear uniforms to │ │   precautions to protect all governments' │
│   remain identifiably separate. │   civilians.                    │
│ • Soldiers take on special  │ │ • Governments give their own soldiers the │
│   responsibilities to not harm │   legal right to kill other soldiers (so these │
│   civilians as appropriate. │ │   acts are not murder).           │
│ • Civilians cannot interfere with │ • Governments give other governments' │
│   soldiers' activities.     │ │   soldiers full POW rights, including fair │
│ • Civilians cannot pretend to be │   treatment and not holding them │
│   soldiers.                 │ │   individually responsible for their │
└─────────────┬───────────────┘ │   governments' political actions.* │
              │                 │ • Governments enforce the soldier/civilian │
              │                 │   distinction by punishing cheating parties. │
              │                 └──────────────┬───────────────────┘
              ▼                                ▼
     ┌────────────────┐                ┌────────────────┐
     │   Civilians    │◀──────────────▶│  Governments   │
     └────────────────┘                └────────────────┘
```

- Civilians do not interfere with governments' soldiers.
- Civilians do not pretend to be soldiers.
- Governments enforce protection of civilians and civilians' right to immunity by punishing soldiers and civilians who violate the agreement.

---

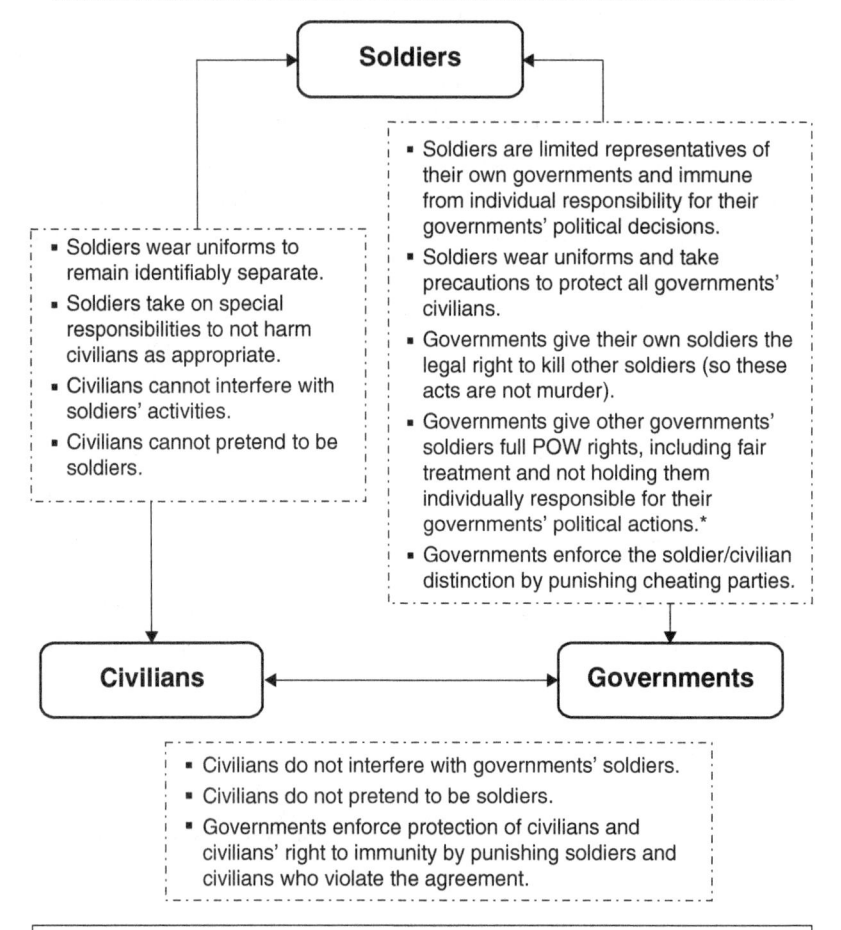

- This three-sided relationship is reciprocal, and their terms all go together. There cannot be one without the others.
- Civilians and soldiers who violate their terms of the agreement erode civilians' right to immunity and soldiers' rights as special government representatives.
- A second dimension can be laid on top of this, to represent the contract that governments have with each other to treat enemy citizens in particular ways.

*This covers soldiers in standard relationships to governments, though it also has implications for stateless individuals who act outside the authority of a state's recognized military. These fighters do not possess the right to kill soldiers or be treated in accordance with established international military conventions for POWs.

*Figure 3.1* The Soldier-Civilian-State Relationship

to die, as we saw in chapter 2. Others demonstrate an overlapping consideration for unnecessary suffering (e.g., chemical and poisonous gases), which speaks to the goal of minimizing harm done to soldiers in the course of taking their lives.

This latter rationale motivates the 1899 Hague Convention ban on expanding "dumdum" bullets (either hollow-point or soft-point), which swell upon impact, thus slowing down the bullet and creating a larger wound.[41] "Dumdum" bullets can stop the target very quickly, but also cause more damage if they do not kill, leaving soldiers in agony and more injured troops for their militaries to care for. It seems that maiming was considered worse than death, in this case, so they preferred weapons that were more likely to result in a clean kill.[42]

*Torture*

Torture is forbidden in international law, by all four Geneva Conventions and their two Additional Protocols, the Universal Declaration of Human Rights, the International Covenant on Civil and Political Rights, and the UN Convention Against Torture and Other Cruel, Inhuman, or Degrading Treatment or Punishment, among others,[43] as well as by various individual states in their domestic military regulations. The American case exemplifies the layers of motivation.

In the aftermath of revelations of torture at Abu Ghraib prison in Iraq (2003–04), the US passed the Detainee Treatment Act (2005), which prohibits "cruel, inhuman, or degrading treatment or punishment of persons under custody or control of the United States Government," regardless of location. This has been included in amended military manuals and highlighted in the new counterinsurgency (COIN) field manual (2006, rev. 2014; e.g., §7-38).

Setting aside the question of efficacy and whether torture actually works—top US military leaders are on the record saying that they believe it does not—banning torture aims to protect both civilians and soldiers through the mechanism of reciprocity. "A very practical reason is that it opens the door for our own troops to be tortured, and we have no basis to object," says then Rear Admiral Donald J. Guter.[44]

Use of torture also has long-term ramifications for winning a war. The original COIN manual from 2006 prominently declares in a large box,

"Lose Moral Legitimacy, Lose the War" (chap. 7, p. 7–9), and then recounts lessons learned from the official sanction of torture by French leadership and military in its Algerian colonial war (1952–64). These include rejecting extreme "ends justify means" consequentialism (§7-42) and understanding how to build legitimacy (§1-132):

> Torture and cruel, inhuman, and degrading treatment is never a morally permissible option, *even if lives depend on gaining information.* No exceptional circumstances permit the use of torture and other cruel, inhuman, or degrading treatment. (§7-42, emphasis added)

> Efforts to build a legitimate government though illegitimate actions are self-defeating, even against insurgents who conceal themselves amid noncombatants and flout the law. (§1-132)

The manual then buttresses this with an appeal to honor and virtue, as the practicality of winning should not be disentangled from the moral imperative of defending soldiers in all ways—including psychologically.

### MORAL INJURY

The ban on torture also protects soldiers from the moral injury it causes to themselves. The COIN manual's list of ten tactical and operational rules[45] distills the laws of war and defines the essence of a professional soldier to include rejecting torture. By presenting the prohibition in terms of what "Soldiers and Marines" do or do not, the manual ties the ethic of cooperation to protect certain classes of people to soldierly virtues, and cautions that anything less will cause them to lose the war on multiple fronts: torture will alienate and incite the opposition, as well as sow doubt and suspicion among those who fight for you and in yourself. Torture must be forbidden in order to maintain "moral high ground," says General James N. Mattis, who helped lead the effort to pass the Detainee Treatment Act, or else it "makes it easier for a soldier or a Marine to ask, 'What am I fighting for?' "[46]

I have argued that the "fair fight" ethic is motivated in part by a soldier's own conception of what it means to be a "soldier" instead of a "murderer," which requires a soldier holding himself to rigorous standards of behavior, for his own sake. In the same way, this torture ban protects soldiers not just from physical injury, but also from themselves: it defends their psychological well-being and, even more importantly, their character, which is inevitably twisted and misshapen through the employment of torture. As Rear Admiral Guter says, "If we torture, we've lost who we are."[47]

*Indiscriminate Weapons*

Toward the end of World War II, the British tried to repel the Japanese Burma Area Army's invasion of India in 1944 by holding the gateway town of Kohima, and were nearly thwarted by bureaucratic restrictions on the use of barbed wire, which had been implemented because it interfered with local farming.[48] It is not an exaggeration to say that civilian immunity is the centerpiece of contemporary international law on warfare and the ethic of cooperation to protect certain classes of individuals. That mandate is fulfilled in large part by banning weapons that disproportionately harm civilians, namely, ones that are by their nature indiscriminate.

The ICRC Commentary of 1987 considers Article 51 to be "one of the most important articles" in the Geneva Conventions Additional Protocol I. Among other protections, Article 51 prohibits "indiscriminate attacks," which include methods or means of combat that "cannot be directed at a specific military object" or otherwise limited as required and, consequently, "strike military objects and civilians or civilian objects without distinction" (§§4–5).

Most weapons bans are driven by overlapping considerations: for example, some of the suspect weapons discussed in chapter 2 and here were considered unfair precisely *because* they were indiscriminate, e.g., gas.

The discriminatory ability of weapons is a long-standing concern, perhaps first seen in international law in the Hague Convention of 1899 (IV, 1) Prohibiting Launching of Projectiles and Explosives from Balloons, a five-year ban.[49] It arises again during World War I with submarine battle, as the inherent nature, modes of attack, and incapacity of these vessels to save and accommodate crew and passengers of destroyed ships meant that they were "incompatible with the principles of humanity, the long-established and incontrovertible rights of neutrals and the sacred immunities of non-combatants."[50]

The Nyon Arrangement (1937) set provisions for defending and counterattacking against submarines, and declared that submarine attacks "constitute acts contrary to the most elementary dictates of humanity, which should be justly treated as piracy."[51]

Indiscrimination gets taken up again in later treaties, including the Geneva Conventions First Additional Protocol (1977) and the UN Convention on Prohibitions or Restrictions on the Use of Certain Conventional Weapons Which May Be Deemed to Be Excessively Injurious or to Have Indiscriminate Effects (1980), aka Convention on Certain Conventional Weapons (CCW). The latter's attached protocols address a number of other weapons (such as incendiary and blinding laser weapons). In particular, CCW's Protocol (II) on Prohibitions or Restrictions on the Use of Mines, Booby-Traps, and Other Devices (1980, amended 1996) bans "indiscriminate use weapons": those that are "not on, or directed against, a military objective," or that employ "a method or means of delivery that cannot be directed at a specific military objective" or that "may be expected to cause incidental" and disproportionate harm to civilians (Art. 3.8). This includes not laying mines in areas where civilians are concentrated without posting warnings or fencing off the affected territory (Art. 3.10) and not using booby traps under any circumstances (Art. 7). In addition, the locations of mines, minefields, and booby traps must be recorded and the information later made available (Art. 9) for their removal (Art. 10).

Mines are challenging weapons, as they are considered legitimate in standard land and sea military operations. Unlike later treaties that seek outright bans, the Geneva Conventions and the CCW accept their military function and try to regulate their use and handling during war and postwar. In general, factors such as the means of use and the power of the weapon (in relation to its objective) must be taken into consideration. The ICRC Commentary of 1987 takes pains to note that "in most cases the indiscriminate character of the attack does not depend on the nature of the weapons concerned, but on the way in which they are used" (§1965).

The Commentary distinguishes between that which can, depending on use, "have either a restricted effect or on the contrary be completely out of the control of those using them, causing significant losses among the civilian population and extensive damage to civilian objects," such as fire and water, and those whose "effects cannot be limited in any circumstances"

(§1963), such as biological weapons or poisoned drinking water (§1965) or nuclear weapons (§1966). In doing so, it acknowledges that some weapons are by their nature indiscriminate.

The very nature of a mine raises fundamental questions about when its use constitutes an attack: Is it when it is laid, or armed, or exploded, or when a person is endangered by it?[52] The verdict of these treaties is that the problem is less the nature of the weapon itself—mines can be laid in war zones away from civilians (and were traditionally used to ambush or to secure/fortify territory, like a moat) and later removed (albeit with difficulty)—but rather how it is deployed, and especially neglected or forgotten after placement.

Traditional mines are incredibly dangerous to civilians, long after they have been planted and abandoned. Embroiled in war from 1970 to 1998, during which countless mines of over thirty different types were laid, Cambodia, for example, is still demining *millions* of blast, bounding, and anti-tank mines, among other explosives:

> Pol Pot, whose regime was responsible for the deaths of some 1.7 million Cambodians between 1975 and 1979, purportedly called land mines his "perfect soldiers." They never sleep. They wait, with limitless patience. Although weapons of war, land mines are unlike bullets and bombs in two distinct ways. First, they are designed to maim rather than kill, because an injured soldier requires the help of two or three others, reducing the enemy's forces. Second, and most sinister, when a war ends, land mines remain in the ground, primed to explode. Only 25 percent of land mine victims around the world are soldiers. The rest are civilians—boys gathering firewood, mothers sowing rice, girls herding goats.[53]

Ongoing efforts have reduced casualties and deaths from thousands per year to 286 in the year 2010, but that so many mines are still active decades later speaks to their long-lasting threat.

The more recent "Ottawa Treaty" (The Convention on the Prohibition of the Use, Stockpiling, Production, and Transfer of Anti-Personnel Mines and on their Destruction, 1997) took an entirely different route in its development: the diplomatic campaign bypassed the usual governmental channels and was led by NGOs, in particular the International

Campaign to Ban Landmines (ICBL).[54] It also eschewed the traditional model of arms control treaties and their accompanying concern with arms races in favor of "establish[ing] . . . a new humanitarian norm against [widely used] weapons,"[55] according to then Canadian Foreign Minister Lloyd Axworthy, who participated in the push for the treaty.[56]

The treaty calls on signatories both to destroy existing stockpiles and to cooperate in removing existing mines, but proponents lament its focus on antipersonnel mines without addressing antivehicle mines that can be just as deadly, if not deadlier, to civilians. Opponents, on the other hand, criticize the lack of consideration given to legitimate and important military uses of mines, especially as no allowance is made for self-destructing or self-deactivating mines, which reduce the danger to unintended targets, e.g., those now used by the United States, which expire within four hours to fifteen days after being set.[57] Sometimes, political processes do not take into account technological innovations, and all arms control treaties struggle to balance military objectives with civilian protection. Arms control requires extensive cooperation on all sides, to abide by and enforce the terms of agreement and willingly give up whatever (sometimes considerable) advantages can be reaped from using mines.[58]

Unusually, the Ottawa Treaty explicitly and directly appeals to international humanitarian law, declaring its purpose to be "end[ing] . . . the suffering and casualties caused by anti-personnel mines that kill or maim hundreds of people every week, mostly innocent and defenceless civilians and especially children," and its content based

> on the principle of international humanitarian law that the right of the parties to an armed conflict to choose methods or means of warfare is not unlimited, on the principle that prohibits the employment in armed conflicts of weapons, projectiles and materials and methods of warfare of a nature to cause superfluous injury or unnecessary suffering and on the principle that a distinction must be made between civilians and combatants.
> (PREAMBLE)

The treaty's language demonstrates a significant development in cooperation to protect civilians. Several later weapons bans, including the Ottawa Treaty's Protocol on Explosive Remnants of War (Protocol V to the 1980 CCW Convention, 2003) and the Chemical Weapons Convention

(1993), also invoke this new moral landscape by including explicitly moral justifications, not just practical ones. The strength of these moral considerations at the inception of these agreements is a relatively recent adoption, in an environment in which ethical concerns for individual human rights are more fully developed and widely accepted. In these cases, collaboration was institutionalized on moral, not pragmatic, grounds.

Cooperation between enemies to ban weapons such as mines, booby traps, cluster munitions, and so on is primarily concerned with the disproportionate harm they cause to civilians, and often long after the war ends. By restricting the use of weapons that are difficult to aim, it attempts to make material what is in reality a vague concept of "civilian immunity." The military ban on hollow-point bullets (Hague Convention, 1899), which are still largely permitted in civilian use, primarily addresses the use of proportional means to achieve one's end (stopping the enemy soldier), as dum-dums seem unnecessarily barbaric. Meanwhile, biological weapons (multiple bans starting in 1925) and landmines (1997) cannot distinguish between military and civilian targets, so banning them attempts to protect especially civilians, who are likely to suffer collateral damage. Nuclear weapons, on the other hand, are restricted because they are too extreme and catastrophic. Most of these weapons, as well as poisonous gases and chemicals (multiple bans starting in 1899), are deemed unacceptable in part because they kill indiscriminately.

These weapons bans are driven by a variety of mixed motives and show that the ethic of cooperation in warfare is still evolving. Mutual gain through mutual disarmament is a motivating factor, but as time goes on, adherence to these agreements is driven more and more by the belief that there are "right," "honorable," or "civilized" methods of warfare that involve protecting both civilians and soldiers in certain ways.

## POW Treatment

Not only have practices and standards for the management of prisoners of war (POWs) changed over time but, as with wearing uniforms, its justifications have evolved, from more practical to more humanitarian. Although costly, enemies generally try to ensure decent treatment for their own soldiers in captivity by according their POWs the same. This cooperative behavior started informally, for self-interested reasons and with the hopes that the other side would reciprocate, and was eventually formalized in domestic code, bilateral treaties, and now international law.

Traditionally, it was commonplace to enslave prisoners of war (among others), and as late as 1625, Grotius declared that although ransom or exchange was preferable, it was the victor's right to enslave the losers. Two decades later, the Peace of Westphalia (1648) marks a major turning point by calling for prisoners to be released after the war without ransom,[59] although that still left many options.

Prior to the widespread contemporary practice of holding that first emerged in the nineteenth century, POWs were primarily dispensed through redistribution: (1) switching sides to serve their captors instead, as many were mercenaries; (2) equal exchanges of prisoners by numbers and rank, as it was expected that those released would reenlist; and (3) "paroling" prisoners on their word that they would not rejoin the war, whereupon they usually lived in the captor country until hostilities ended, but sometimes returned to their own country.[60]

The latter two methods of redistribution require extensive cooperation and trust between enemies, for obvious reasons, as does the system of mass detention that has since replaced it. Freeing prisoners on parole, for example, was risky, as it required honor on the part not only of parolees but also of their own governments to not reconscript them to the war effort upon release. Parole was a privilege, and violators were punished harshly by their captors if caught,[61] but this system could not have persisted as long as it did—captors' limited resources notwithstanding—if there were not *some* reasonable expectation that enough parolees and their governments would abide by their word. Otherwise, the captors would have been better off just killing prisoners (which they sometimes did), as that would have been equally untaxing on their resources while eliminating the risk of parole violation.

The nineteenth-century shift to large group holdings until the war's end came with a corresponding growth in international law to address it. Some of that was based on the Lieber Code (1863), which details important provisions for POW treatment, including that prisoners are considered captives of the government and not of individual captors or officers, the captive's private property belongs to him and cannot be seized by the captor, the prisoner must be fed "plain and wholesome food whenever practicable, and treated with humanity," unnecessary "intentional suffering or indignity" is prohibited, wounded captives should receive all possible medical treatment, and prisoners are not compelled to divulge information to the enemy and not to be punished for giving false information, as "honorable men, when captured, will abstain from giving to the enemy information concerning their own army" (Arts. 72–80).

The two Hague Conventions devoted great attention to the details of POW treatment, and current regulations are embodied in the Geneva Convention (III) Relative to the Treatment of Prisoners of War,[62] where, again, we see a shift in the rationale for this cooperation.

What was formerly considered mere convention or the product of ad hoc negotiation between belligerents is now considered a right, as POWs "may in no circumstances renounce in part or in entirety the rights secured to them by the present Convention" (Geneva Convention III, Art. 7), including humane treatment including adequate food, drinkable water, medical care, clothing, and basic necessities (Arts. 13, 20, 26, 28–32); protection against violence, reprisals, and torture (Arts. 13, 17); possession of identification documents (Arts. 17, 18); safe internment away from combat zones as soon as possible, and in hygienic places and conditions reasonably conducive to healthy living (Arts. 19, 22, 23, 25); questioning carried out in a language comprehensible to the captive (Art. 17); freedom of religious practice (Arts. 34–37); access to recreational activities (Art. 38); only reasonable and not unduly unsafe required labor, and payment for those services (Arts. 49–54, 62); retention of private property, including income accrued during captivity (Arts. 63–66); communication with the outside world, including parcels and relief shipments (Arts. 70–72), although subject to censorship (Art. 76); political organization and representation with the captor authorities (Arts. 79–81); trial by independent and impartial military courts, and due process for trials and punishments (Arts. 84, 96, 98–107), with punishments no harsher than those the detaining power would impose on its own military (Art. 88); no excessive punishments for attempted escapes (Arts. 93–95); and rapid and timely repatriation at war's end (Art. 118).

These comprehensive and demanding standards make cooperation between warring enemies all the more critical, especially as—unlike with exchanges or parole—there is little immediate interaction between enemy governments over their respective detainees or between governments and their captured soldiers (barring special exchanges or releases), as most prisoners are held for the duration of the conflict. Conditions of camps and prisoners may be inspected and are subject to oversight by neutral "Protecting Powers" (usually the ICRC or a neutral state) throughout the conflict,[63] but one cannot be certain how one's soldiers were treated until they are returned after the war and one can get their accounts, see their condition, and investigate alleged irregularities. Although external inspectors can help allay doubts, an enormous amount of trust is required for a state to pour its limited resources into treating its captives well, without immediate assurances that their own captured soldiers are simultaneously receiving like treatment.[64]

## *Arguments for Humane POW Treatment*

### 1. MILITARY NECESSITY

There have been three major arguments for humane treatment of POWs in the Western context, the first of which can be found in Emmerich de Vattel's *The Law of Nations* (1758), where he drew from the principle of military necessity to maintain that because a surrendered or captured soldier was no longer a threat it was therefore unnecessary and unjustified to kill or abuse him, as it serves no military purpose.

There are two sides to the coin of military necessity: in the pursuit of lawful ends, one has "a right to employ all means which are necessary for its attainment . . . for the purpose of bringing him to reason, and obtaining justice from him"—but only "barely the means necessary." "Right goes hand in hand with necessity and the exigency of the case, but never exceeds them," cautions Vattel. Thus, if anything short of killing is insufficient, then killing is permitted, but military necessity also contains its own limits, for when it is no longer necessary to exert force, such as "on an enemy's submitting and laying down his arms, we cannot with justice take away his life." Captor governments will be tempted to eliminate prisoners when they are unable to feed and otherwise care for their charges, which is difficult at the best of times and especially during a war: in those circumstances, Vattel advocates parole.[65]

Sustaining this particular interpretation of military necessity requires significant collaboration between enemies. It is not true that no military purpose is served by killing a surrendered or captured prisoner: one can destroy the other side's future military capacity and thus cripple it, as many future conflicts build upon previous ones, however long the interim or repackaged the catalyst. What reason is there to restrain oneself, unless some cooperative ethic over the *boundaries* of war restrains one from pressing immediate nonmilitary advantages that might otherwise have become future military gains?

## 2. NONPENAL KILLING AND DETENTION

The second major justification for humane treatment coincided with the nineteenth-century shift to mass detention for the war's duration, although there is no direct connection between them, as this rationale could have applied to exchanges and parole as well.

It is the argument that, barring war crimes or other violations, soldiers do no wrong by killing others in the context of war, no matter how many of the enemy one has killed. As they are considered to act only as agents of and at the behest of their state, soldiers are not held personally accountable for a state's decision to go to war and for the normal wartime consequences of doing so. As such, they are not to be individually punished with detention. This mutual recognition of the limits of warfighting liability emphasizes that soldiers are tools.

The Lieber Code makes one of the first explicit statements of this framework in codified military law:

> 56. A prisoner of war is subject to no punishment for being a public enemy, nor is any revenge wreaked upon him by the intentional infliction of any suffering, or disgrace, by cruel imprisonment, want of food, by mutilation, death, or any other barbarity.

> 57. So soon as a man is armed by a sovereign government, and takes the soldier's oath of fidelity, he is a belligerent; his killing, wounding, or other warlike acts, are no individual crimes or offences. No belligerent has a right to declare that enemies of a certain class, color, or condition, when properly organized as soldiers, will not be treated by him as public enemies.

As captured soldiers are not held as punishment, they should therefore be treated humanely.[66]

Nonpenal detention to shield soldiers from personal responsibility and punishment for war activities is a recent practice, one requiring enormous cooperation and trust between enemies. Funding large-scale military endeavors used to be much more difficult than it is now, so governments were always trying to deflect costs to the enemy, which included quartering troops on enemy territory and releasing captured soldiers instead of keeping prisoners—with the knowledge that soldiers would simply rejoin their own militaries, so there was in theory little net disadvantage from doing so.[67] One indicator of the strength of cooperation around nonpenal detention is that since the mid- to late nineteenth century, captor states have been expected to pay for prisoner upkeep.[68]

The great deal of prisoner abuse in practice[69] shows both how cruel humans can be and how expensive it is to maintain prisoners, but the cooperative ethic on POWs is strong enough that states often do hold prisoners for the duration of the war even though it is decidedly unremunerative. Captors are forbidden from ransoming prisoners, and there are limits to the amount and kind of work that can be demanded of POWs such that it would not normally offset the cost of holding them. Even permitted labor is highly restricted and must be compensated,[70] so nonpenal detention can command a significant portion of the captor's resources, which could be paid at the expense of locals' standard of living, as prisoners have many benefits and sometimes live better than the surrounding population.[71]

The soldier's dilemma when confronted with the prospect of having to take prisoners but being unable to keep them is aptly illustrated by T. E. Lawrence (aka Lawrence of Arabia) in his memoir:

> A young Circassian came in sight, driving three cows towards the rich green pasture of the ruins. This would not do, so . . . they brought him in, unharmed, but greatly frightened. . . . Now [the prisoner] was a nuisance, for if we left him he would give the alarm, and send the horsemen of his village out against us. If we tied him up in this remote place he would die of hunger or thirst; and, besides, we had not rope to spare. To kill him seemed unimaginative: not worthy of a hundred men. At last the Sherari boy said if we gave him scope he would settle his account and leave him living. He looped his wrist to the saddle and trotted him off with us for the first hour, till he was dragging breathlessly. We were still near the railway, but

four or five miles from Zerga. There he was stripped of presentable clothes, which fell, by point of honour, to his owner. The Sherari threw him on his face, picked up his feet, drew a dagger, and chopped him with it deeply across the soles. The Circassian howled with pain and terror, as if he thought he was being killed. Odd as was the performance, it seemed effective, and more merciful than death. The cuts would make him travel to the railway on hands and knees, a journey of an hour; and his nakedness would keep him in the shadow of the rocks, till the sun was low. His gratitude was not coherent; but we rode away, across undulations very rich in grazing.[72]

Ironically, the expectations that (a) prisoners will be held for the duration of the war in nonpenal detention under certain minimal standards of treatment and (b) the cost of prisoner maintenance will be borne by the captors combine to increase the burden on captor states (especially the resource-strapped)[73] to create a perverse *dis*incentive to capture soldiers, in favor of killing them or simply letting them die on the battlefield. Most would not have been as creative and merciful as Lawrence and his crew.

Given the net loss that can be expected from holding prisoners, the cooperative legal apparatus that is meant to protect and improve treatment of soldiers may actually worsen matters, as the existing rules make it much less costly to execute or abandon enemy wounded.[74] Actual battlefield deaths resulting from this consideration are impossible to measure, and are probably tamped down by expectations of reciprocity, but it certainly happens and is a serious and important unintended consequence of the attempt to better protect POWs.

### 3. HUMAN RIGHTS AND HUMANITARIANISM

One of the most important developments in the rationale for humane POW treatment is the conceptual shift from military strategic considerations to those of human rights, human dignity, and humanitarianism, regardless of any actual material benefits accrued. Says legal scholar Stephen Neff:

> The law on prisoners of war might be thought of as a sort of juridical miner's canary for the laws of war generally. Where the old law of

war, inherited from the Middle Ages and codified in increasing detail beginning in the nineteenth century, concerned itself chiefly with fairness and equity between the contending sides in the struggle, the later law—significantly relabelled "international humanitarian law"—has as its primary goal the overall minimization of suffering attendant upon the tragedy of armed conflict. International law, in short, has become, and continues to become, more people-centred. And prisoners of war, in the course of the nineteenth century, had the dubious honour of acting as advance scouts in that momentous, and ongoing, process.[75]

A human rights foundation for POW treatment only reinforces the Geneva Conventions' stipulation that POW rights cannot be renounced (III, Art. 7), even if the soldier does not want them.

While human rights doctrine can be seen to replace the convention-based foundations for POW treatment, it largely supplements and reinforces them to date, nicely complementing the limits contained within military necessity and the jurisprudence behind nonpenal detention. Some philosophers advocate radically overhauling modern military ethics with a human rights approach (see chapter 6 on the moral inequality of combatants), but human rights has thus far primarily buttressed the established rights of soldiers under existing political exigencies, which includes moral equality between combatants.

## The Modern Nation-State and Moral Equality Between Combatants

The approach to and standards for modern POW treatment are the objects of a broader and far-reaching consensus that is itself a major locus of cooperation in warfare: the modern nation-state and its accompanying reification. This, in turn, is the premise for the mutual recognition between states of a specific construction of the state/soldier relationship,[76] namely, the impersonal role that state representatives (including soldiers) are assumed to have with respect to their state, and the resulting "moral equality of combatants." (Cooperative conceptions of the modern nation-state and the state/soldier relationship will be revisited in chapters 5 and 6.)

Seventeenth- and eighteenth-century European prisoner-of-war exchanges were grounded in war's general ethos at the time, which was "largely lacking in ideological overtones, being more a matter of rational calculation than of patriotic fervor," argues Neff. As a result, the prospect of simply releasing captured soldiers to their governments—in part to reduce costs—even though they would rejoin the fighting "could be regarded with equanimity so long as it was understood that the conflict was not a war to the death," as the purpose was to position oneself for postwar negotiations, rather than deplete the enemy.[77]

War is not always regarded in this way, to be sure, but the idea that the purpose of war is to reach resolution rather than to kill everyone has generally combined with a geopolitical rather than an ideological approach that attempts to minimize harm to combatants who are considered not personally culpable within the standard boundaries of war. As the Lieber Code declares:

Modern wars are not internecine wars, in which the killing of the enemy is the object. The destruction of the enemy in modern war, and, indeed, modern war itself, are means to obtain that object of the belligerent which lies beyond the war. Unnecessary or revengeful destruction of life is not lawful. (Art. 68)

This is the moral equality of combatants, that soldiers on all sides are held to the same rules and have the same rights and privileges. Because decisions to go to war are made by civilian and military leaders, not by soldiers who are expected to obey, responsibility for the wrongs of war rests with the former. As mere representatives of the state—right or wrong—soldiers are thereby protected and not held responsible for their state's decision to go to war and their own subsequent actions within normal military limits. From this follows any number of military practices, including nonpenal detention and humane treatment of POWs, who are merely quarantined and then released to their respective governments at war's end without punishment.

In that sense, all combatants (whether just or unjust) are equally morally innocent, and should be treated the same way.[78] In addition, it is impossible to know with certainty which party to the conflict is wrong and which is right, if any; one common reason for war is intractable disagreement over this, and if the leaders cannot determine that, much less can their soldiers. I will address the severe implications of this epistemic problem as well as the geopolitical approach to war in chapters 6 and 7.

## The Relationship to Virtue Ethics

Like the "fair fight" ethos, cooperation to protect certain groups is often rooted in the virtue ethics idea that there is a "right" way for a soldier to behave. Especially when it comes to protecting civilian immunity, it is commonly believed that soldiers should bear extra risks in order to do so, because by the nature of their profession and privileges, they have special responsibilities to the more vulnerable.[79]

For example, Cicero, in his contemplation on practical ethics in *On Duties* (44 BCE), discusses the importance of honor and the benefit of virtue (e.g., 1.9), including martial virtue. Moderation is required with respect to one's enemies, for "certain duties must be observed even towards those at whose hands you may have received unjust treatment. There is a limit to revenge and to punishment" (1.33). Of the two types of injustices—inflicting injury and failing to deflect injury to others—the latter, "the man who does not defend someone, or obstruct the injustice when he can, is at fault just as if he had abandoned his parents or his friends or his country" (1.23). In fact, "justice must be maintained even towards the lowliest," i.e., slaves, for "the instruction we are given to treat them as if they were employees is good advice: that one should require work from them, and grant to them just treatment" (1.41).

In addition to being skilled fighters, then, justice and honor require soldiers and warriors to show restraint to one's foes and to protect the weaker. It is not an accident that many of the regulations to minimize damage to particular classes of individuals coincide with ideas found in preexisting traditions of military ethics. For example, the chivalric obligation to defend the helpless corresponds with the modern principle of civilian immunity. Says veteran samurai film actor Koji Yakusho:

> The samurai represents the refinement of the self, a way of living. How the samurai lives and the way he dies is a beautiful thing. Sacrificing oneself to help others over all else. Of course, the enemy has

the power and the numbers. But when someone stands up to that, whether it's Chanbara or Western, you have to root for that.[80]

This convergence in ideals is not a coincidence. Rather, traditional practices and virtue ethics have contributed to the development of these particular international laws and help to reinforce them, even as the conventions are now often justified by recourse to human rights claims.

## Assassination, Political Elites, and Responsibility for War

Perhaps the most striking—but overlooked—cooperation to protect certain classes of people is the disapproval of political assassinations, which amounts to nothing less than widespread collusion to shelter political elites.

There is ambiguity in the philosophical literature about what exactly constitutes assassination, and it is also not clearly delineated in the law. The various definitions tend to focus on three things, however: "treacherous" methods of killing, the targeting of specific individuals, and in particular the pursuit of political agents/leaders.

### *Treacherous Methods*

During peacetime, assassins kill private citizens for political purposes. During wartime, they target specific individuals with the use of "treacherous means," such as deceit or exploitation of protected statuses. One's status as a combatant or noncombatant in theory is irrelevant, but in practice is taken into consideration.[81]

Early thinkers generally focus on the form of the attack as a major determinant of its wrongness.[82] According to Vattel, killing by "surprise" involves sneaking and ambushing and killing generals or soldiers, i.e., military men on the campaign. Such clandestine killing "is nothing contrary to the natural laws of war—nothing even but what is perfectly commendable in a just and necessary war." Assassination, on the other hand, which also kills by surprise, is "treacherous murder," "criminal," "contrary to the laws of war, and equally condemned by the law of nature and the consent of all civilized nations."[83] This distinction carries over into military law. For example, the Lieber Code says:

### Section IX. Assassination

148. The law of war does not allow proclaiming either an individual belonging to the hostile army, or a citizen, or a subject of the hostile government, an outlaw, who may be slain without trial by any captor, any more than the modern law of peace allows such intentional outlawry; on the contrary, it abhors such outrage. The sternest retaliation should follow the murder committed in consequence of such proclamation, made by whatever authority. Civilized nations look with horror upon offers of rewards for the assassination of enemies as relapses into barbarism.

International customary law, as summarized by the ICRC, references the Lieber Code, the Brussels Declaration, the Oxford Manual (1880), and the Hague Conventions[84] in prohibiting "murder" through the use of "treachery."[85]

### *Targeting*

While domestic laws of many states prohibit assassination,[86] it is largely left undefined, perhaps deliberately so.[87] Customary international humanitarian law mentions targeting—singling out a "selected" individual to kill[88]—but codified international law such as the United Nations Charter allows states to target in the name of self-defense (Art. 51).[89] It is unclear how direct and imminent a threat must be in order to justify self-defense, and the United Nations has not condemned a variety of past assassinations. This opens the door to targeted killings, which have been a significant part of American strategy against terrorism, and would certainly be used by more states if they had the same capacity. The difference between assassination and targeted killing appears to hinge on whether or not one thinks one is at war,[90] which—in an atmosphere of fluid conflict—is easily exploited for one's purposes. In reality, it seems that most of the distinction is that one is forbidden while the other is not, which simply begs the question.

## Political Leaders and Agents

*Who* is a legitimate target of assassination? Historically, there has been no prohibition on assassinating political leaders, and thinkers such as Thomas Aquinas and Thomas More thought that assassination could be used if necessary to save innocents or to punish those who wrongly wage war, while Grotius condemned killing with treachery but also allowed that natural and civilized law permit killing an enemy at any time or place.[91]

In the modern period and in common parlance, however, assassinations generally refer to heads of state and their equivalents and to other politically "protected" persons such as diplomats or other political figures.[92] Even thinkers like Vattel who focused on the means of killing to condemn assassination were concerned with "the interest and safety of men in high command."

A precise definition that would meaningfully distinguish assassination, killing in war, and murder is unclear.[93] As Voltaire said, "Il est défendu de tuer; tout meurtrier est puni, à moins qu'il n'ait tué en grande compagnie, et au son des trompettes."[94] Despite the conceptual imprecision of assassination, however, there is widespread agreement on its rejection.[95]

Here, I focus on assassination insofar as it refers to targeting the political classes in particular. (There is ambiguity when the political leader is also the civilian commander-in-chief of the military, and even more opacity when the political leader is *in* the military, e.g., in many dictatorships.)[96] Lack of clarity notwithstanding, consistent criticisms of treachery and of singling out individual targets have a tendency in practice to protect political elites, who are considered civilians and treated differentially from soldiers.[97]

There are good reasons for defending the political leadership, including not wanting to open one's own leaders to being assassinated in turn. More important, however, is a concern with sowing resentment and geopolitical instability. Assassination destroys trust between nations, as Kant says, and generates political instability, as noted in chapter 2. Such deterrence is so important that Vattel considers it acceptable to impose cruel punishments even on those with justice on their side, for

> such [an] act is pernicious to human society;. . . the practice of it would be destructive to mankind;. . . whoever, by setting the example,

contributes to the introduction of so destructive a practice, declares himself the enemy of mankind, and deserves the execration of all ages.[98]

Stability between nations is especially critical because, unlike bonds between people within societies, there is little tying nations together—self-interest too easily diverges and even the constraints of trade are limited—so prudence suggests fostering whatever trust can be created, to reduce conflict, promote international stability, and thus better the lives of ordinary people.

This stability—along with its ensuing protection for political elites—comes at great expense to soldiers and civilians, however. While one kind of steadiness (geopolitical) is secured, a different kind can be made impossible for everyone else. The limited accountability of political leaders for their decisions to go to war—however unwise, unjust, or rash—means that countless soldiers (and civilians) are "slain without trial" (something that Francis Lieber decries about assassination) and without recourse. In the past, political leaders might have been executed or exiled upon losing a war, but this is now considered impermissible,[99] and there is little answering for having dragged a country and its people into an inappropriate war. Accountability comes only after the fact, and only if the just side won.[100]

## *Responsibility for War*

So while protecting the "interest and safety of men in high command" is undoubtedly beneficial for geopolitical stability, it is less justified in terms of moral and political accountability, as it is the political elites who drive and ultimately make the decision to go to war. Not only has "a word of command . . . made [them] our enemies [and] a word of command might transform them into our friends," as Remarque put it,[101] but soldiers largely die for the vainglories of others. What is war for? asks another soldier in *All Quiet on the Western Front*. Among other things, it is because "every full-grown emperor requires at least one war, otherwise he would not become famous. . . . Generals too, they become famous through war . . . even more famous than emperors."[102] Says the Chaplain in Bertolt Brecht's *Mutter Courage und ihre Kinder*, "It's not [the soldiers] I blame. They never went raping back home. The fault lies with those that start wars, it brings humanity's lowest instincts to the surface."[103]

Protecting political elites for stability's sake is sustained by cooperation between enemies—but is it warranted, given the harm to soldiers sent to war and to civilians put at risk? Like the distinction between soldiers and civilians, it might be a useful fiction to maintain that political elites should be off-limits from attack—but how useful, exactly?

This amnesty points to a troubling gap in the question of who is responsible for going to war. Soldiers are not held personally responsible, as we have seen, but neither effectively are their political leaders. Who, then, is to be accountable?

In fact, the Lieber Code, which greatly advanced the continued development of norms of "civilized warfare," also contained within itself some potential contradictions on this front. The Code takes a collective view of responsibility: "men live in political, continuous societies. . . . [They] bear, enjoy, and suffer, advance and retrograde, in peace and in war," so "the citizen or native of a hostile country is thus an enemy, as one of the constituents of the hostile state or nation, and as such is subjected to the hardships of war" (Arts. 20 and 21). Moreover, "war is not carried on by arms alone," so it is thus "lawful to starve the hostile belligerent, armed or unarmed, so that it leads to the speedier subjection of the enemy" (Art. 17). These sections actually erode the civilian/combatant distinction, and hold the civilian population partly responsible for the war. (See the disagreements over civilian responsibility discussed earlier.) Current international law vehemently rejects this view, however.

The collective corpus of contemporary international law sets forth three major principles that speak to who is blameworthy, and it is important to note that all three of these principles—civilian immunity, military nonresponsibility, and political nonaccountability—cannot be simultaneously held, as it leaves no one accountable for what is clearly a result of human agency. (I return to this problem of nonaccountability in chapters 5 and 6.)

## The Force of International Law, and Intended and Unintended Consequences

The particulars of modern-day schema to protect particular classes of individuals have developed through geopolitical struggle and negotiation, and there could easily have been a different set of protections in place now. As a result, even long-established and widely accepted institutions such as private property protections, civilian immunity for citizens of democracies, or medical immunity are still controversial, as we have seen, but the cooperative ethic that maintains these institutions to the extent that they are is strong. There is an element of rule-following involved in adhering to the law, but it takes much more than that to sustain the relevant international laws: it requires an independent and more compelling ethic of cooperation in warfare.

The cooperation between sovereign states required to adhere to these laws includes a certain amount of domestic enforcement on their own populations, as discussed earlier. That only enhances the legitimacy and standing of these various international protections, which then strengthens the independent moral imperative to obey the law.

Clausewitz declares international law's effectiveness to be "hardly worth mentioning,"[104] but in this respect he has been quite wrong. It is true that the law itself is a product of power politics and can be used as a formidable tool to gain advantage.[105]

No doubt many today think that the contemporary law of armed conflict (LOAC) privileges established and recognized nation-states and their formal militaries by imposing various costly and risky requirements—such as wearing uniforms into battle (with few exceptions), refraining from attacking vital civilian resources, or providing a humane and safe standard of living for prisoners—that are burdensome on poorer states or political organizations.

On the other hand, even strong states frequently try to break the law, and that is because there are considerable advantages to doing so. The law still constrains and is not *simply* a tool for the strong to further oppress the weak.

Shrouding the geopolitical origins of the law in the contemporary language of principles and rights can be sincere. Once established, laws can be used to hold others to account, and they can take on a moral life of their own and can command obedience even when detrimental to one's immediate interests.

### *Winning the War*

The irony is that sometimes the very laws that are designed to protect certain peoples and the ethic of cooperation that inspires or sustains them can lead to greater violence. As with the "fair fight," the ethic of cooperation to protect particular groups highlights an internal strain with the goal of warfare. For example, if one is fighting in crowded areas, then banning hollow-point bullets to protect soldiers sits in some tension with trying to shelter civilians, as dumdum bullets are less likely to pass through a human body and hit another target, who could be an innocent bystander.

Such well-intentioned restrictions can make it harder to win the war. Protecting classes of individuals during war is perhaps nowhere more visible than with cease-fires, humanitarian "pauses," and humanitarian corridors. These measures provide much-needed supplies to besieged civilians, but also turn out to be opportunities for opponents to rest and rearm for more fighting, which in turn prolongs the war and causes more damage overall. Unintended consequences will be addressed at greater length in chapter 5.

### Exclusion from the Laws of War

Laws necessarily create boundaries, and those frontiers can have pernicious consequences or be used to malicious effect. Although the soldier/civilian distinction gives the former privileges to kill in exchange for certain duties,[106] it says little about what punishments are warranted for violating those duties. At the birth of international laws of war in the eighteenth and nineteenth centuries, little was said about how to punish soldiers for wartime crimes, so warfighters were effectively legally immune under international law (although not necessarily under their own domestic laws).

They were certainly punished, and often violently so, but because there was no conception of punishing individual enemy soldiers for breaking the laws of war, such punishments were undertaken not as criminal punishment but rather as retaliation,[107] and the lack of consistency and rule of law sometimes made it harsher. Today, criminal punishments for most violations of the LOAC are left to domestic governments, also to uneven effect and great inconsistency.

In addition to giving soldiers largely unchecked privileges, drawing distinctions excludes some people from the law's protection, as it does with "fair fights." For example, in the lead-up to the American Civil War, Lincoln stated that secessionists were not enemies but rather criminals. "In one sense, his words were conciliatory" in considering secessionist acts to be "insurrectionary or revolutionary" crimes rather than acts of war, explains Witt, "but the words had a double meaning that was not lost on his listeners.... This was no mere lawyer's game. If the violence ... was a crime, then the humanitarian limits on war's destructive powers had no application." The public did indeed take note, as newspaper editorials all over the country declared that "secessionists were not 'entitled to the considerations belonging to a common humanity,' ... that if the limits of civilized war were inapplicable, then 'no quarter should be shown the rebels.' "[108] Given how the law was written, treason was a worse crime to commit than war (in terms of possible punishment), and the very designation of whether or not something was a war was used to bar people from protection under its laws.

The boundaries of the laws excluded in even more pernicious ways. The eighteenth-century laws of war had been "designed to set justice aside for the sake of humanity," and in incorporating concerns of justice into those laws, the Lieber Code did many things that were undoubtedly right from a moral standpoint, such as insisting on emancipation for slaves and equal treatment for black soldiers; but it also caused great tragedy, argues Witt:

> Asserting the priority of justice over humanitarianism had almost immediate practical consequences. International lawyers have long touted Lincoln's code for lessening the suffering of the Civil War. But this gets the president's order exactly backward.... [It] did not reduce the suffering in the conflict. To the contrary, Lincoln's code helped produce some of the war's most enduring humanitarian crises.[109]

The complexity of protecting classes of people is well illustrated by the legal struggles during the American Civil War.[110] In the attempt to codify the parameters of fighting between North and South, disagreement arose over whether blacks (both freemen and former slaves) qualified for handling as soldiers—and meanwhile everyone had already been treating Native Americans atrociously. The history of biological warfare begins at least as early as the eighteenth century, for example, when the British in America deliberately spread smallpox to Native Americans and blacks fleeing slavery, which they justified in part because these peoples were "savages."[111] Conduct in general toward Indians was so atrocious that respected war hero and West Point instructor Maj. Gen. Ethan Allen Hitchcock, who also served as president of the board that oversaw the writing of the Lieber Code, considered American military treatment of Native Americans to be "a picture of cruelty, injustice, and horror," and furthermore responsible for the Seminole Wars in the 1840s.[112] In reality, the Americans were no less barbaric than those they disdained.

With respect to blacks, although the Lieber Code accorded them the same protections (Art. 67), the Confederacy denied that they were legitimate combatants and placed them outside the jurisdiction of these laws. The South treated black soldiers and their white commanding officers as "fugitive slaves, insurrectionists, and criminals, not as soldiers" in some places, and refused to exchange them with the North. In many other places, blacks were reenslaved with former owners or sold to new ones, and there were frequent instances of summary executions and massacres on the battlefield or shortly thereafter.[113]

In response, Lincoln refused to exchange prisoners as long as the South persisted in treating black soldiers as criminals. Not only was this policy highly unpopular with white Northerners, but it also led to "the greatest humanitarian disaster of the last two years of the war," says Witt, as white Union soldiers languished and died in terrible prison conditions. There were strategic reasons for insisting on POW treatment for its black soldiers—the North was running short of available whites for military service and growing increasingly reliant on blacks to enlist, which they would only do if promised equal treatment—but, given widespread opposition to the policy, there was more to it than that. The North did not have to insist on POW treatment for its soldiers, says Witt, as the Lieber Code only warned that the South would risk Union reprisal if it discriminated between soldiers, so it was a separate Union decision to insist upon POW status for its soldiers, including the former slaves.[114] As a result, it created

> a startling paradox for the beginnings of the modern laws of war. For by insisting on nondiscrimination, Lincoln's code had a hand in the greatest humanitarian disaster of the last two years of the war. Some 55,000 men died in Civil War prison camps.... If the law of war's only goal were reducing human suffering, this would have been a searing indictment of its legacy. But the Union's code embodied a mix of purposes. Lessening humanitarian suffering was one. But so was justice for black soldiers and victory for the Union.[115]

The laws of war can serve different purposes—in this case, justice or humanity—and here, the two come into tragic conflict. This irony manifests many unintended consequences, especially when cooperation to protect certain groups of people inadvertently leads to the opposite, or when the formation of laws for the purpose of humanitarian protection also creates boundaries that are then used to exclude.

*Compensating Behavior*

The force of this ethic to protect certain peoples (especially civilians and political leaders) is both tenuous and surprisingly strong. It can overlap with other motivations such as self-interest[116] and with other types of cooperation in warfare, such as the "fair fight." One factor in determining who constitutes a legitimate target, for example—and therefore how enemies should cooperate in order to protect those with immunity—is whether the person is considered to be an "equal" or to have a fighting chance in some way.

This ethic of cooperation employs a variety of methods (e.g., uniforming, weapons bans), but it must act through mutual acceptance of a functional fiction—that people can be wholly innocent in war, despite their entanglements with the broader supporting society or even their direct responsibility for the conflict—and it yields certain tragic intentional and unintentional consequences.

There is no question that combining the *intention* to protect certain classes of individuals with more precise (if deadlier) and better-targeted technology has improved the lot of civilians. Still, deaths cannot be regulated out of existence, and these restrictions might make things worse in the immediate or longer run.

For example, the extensive damage from hurricanes, earthquakes, and floods is often attributed solely to nature, but part of the reason for the great destruction of natural disasters is precisely *because* engineers have made it safer to live in previously dangerous places (e.g., hurricane corridors, flood zones) and then people flock to those sites. Clustering the population allows for more efficient protection, which encourages even more people to live there, but concentrated population, infrastructure, and wealth also make for bigger disasters when the safety mechanisms fail.[117] This compensating behavior in response to the reduced risk offsets the gains in safety when nature does strike. When people think that something is less dangerous than it actually is—as they commonly do when disasters are rare or harm can be postponed—they also take more risks, which leads to greater destruction down the line.

The mass of regulations and institutions to protect civilians sometimes does the same: for example, people who live near a battle zone, and who must decide whether to flee now or wait in hopes that the fighting will move off and not come to their neighborhood, may take into consideration the fact that international law protects them and grants access to humanitarian organizations like ICRC or the possibility that humanitarian corridors might be negotiated. As a result, they may mistakenly calculate that in the event that they become trapped in a battle zone, they would be likely to receive assistance or to be able to leave later, so there would be no reason to evacuate now.

Relatedly, antiterrorism security measures in air travel may actually contribute to more deaths overall. Despite widespread fears, it is in fact far safer to travel by plane than by car, although not every mile in a plane is equal to a mile in a car. Because takeoffs and landings are the most dangerous times to be in an airplane, per-mile crash rates differ according to the length of the flight, so there is a point at which driving becomes more dangerous than flying, which in the United States in 1998 occurred at 150 miles: car trips shorter than that are statistically safer and less risky than flying, but longer ones are more dangerous.[118] How is this relevant to terrorism? As early as 1996, it was predicted that the delays and additional costs of increased security measures for air travel implemented in response to possible terrorist attacks, such as showing identification and being subjected to more questions and luggage searches, would drive marginal airline passengers to, well, drive, instead.[119] If driving over 150 miles is more dangerous than flying that distance in an airplane, however, then motivating people into their cars may have led to more deaths, and this was even before the additional post-9/11 security measures that have become quite prohibitive and off-putting to many travelers.

In conclusion, another analogy to safety measures is relevant. The dilemma over forest fire suppression strategy and the greater and far more disastrous conflagrations that later result has been described as "chaos today or chaos tomorrow."[120] While there are limits to analogizing war to fire suppression—war is not a natural disaster, although some may argue that as much as it can be circumscribed, it is ingrained in human nature and thus unavoidable—the question of whether to allow for some damage now or to sustain potentially more damage later cannot be avoided. There will ultimately be some kind of reckoning. If these protective measures ironically lead to more deaths or damage, is there some other way to fight war that would actually limit that?

CHAPTER IV

## Cooperation to End War Quickly

These Greeks are accustomed to wage their wars among each other in the most senseless way. . . . For as soon as they declare war on each other, they seek out the fairest and most level ground, and then go down there to do battle on it.

—MARDONIOS, 490 BC (HERODOTUS 7.9B)

Their Warres are farre lesse bloudy, and devouring than the cruell Warres of Europe; and seldome twenty slain in a pitcht field: partly because when they fight in a wood every Tree is a Bucklar. When they fight in a plaine, they fight with leaping and dancing, that seldome an Arrow hits, and when a man is wounded, unlesse he that shot followes upon the wounded, they soone retire and save the wounded.

—ROGER WILLIAMS, ON NATIVE AMERICAN WARS, SEVENTEENTH CENTURY

The well-intended complex of rules developed to minimize the inevitable destruction of war often yields tragic unintended consequences, as we have seen in the previous two chapters. Are there alternative approaches to war that might avoid this problem? Loopholes can be plugged by introducing additional regulations into the myriad that already exist, but perhaps it warrants considering an entirely different method: rather than trying to protect people with ever more regulation, enemies may be able to more effectively alleviate war's ravages if they cooperate on the *structure* of war such that it concludes quickly.

Such cooperation is actually unusual in practice, relative to examples of the other ethics of cooperation, and the historical record on this form of cooperation is sometimes contested. But this idea remains compelling across time, and there are enough historical specimens to build a viable (real-world) model.

This chapter examines some models of cooperation to end war quickly (classical Greek hoplite warfare, *monomachia* duel combat, and ritual warfare) and its misguided modern analogues, which omit the cooperative element entirely, to tragic effect.

The aesthetic appeal of decisive pitched battle remains highly influential, however, and these early models raise questions about what it means for a war to be decisive and what trade-offs might be made for brevity and conclusion. Ultimately, the question is whether there could be a genuine ethic of cooperation between enemies in any contemporary analogue of this scheme, given the present-day moral and political landscape and our accompanying expectations for what war should achieve.

## Pitched Battle, Shock Battle

An early example of cooperation to end war quickly is found with the classical Greek hoplites and their characteristic form of decisive shock battle (especially from 700 to 500 BCE), in which, according to historian Victor Davis Hanson,

> heavily armed and armored farmers [filed, in phalanx formation,] into a suitable small plain . . . where brief but brutal battle resulted either in concessions granted to the army of invasion, or a humiliating, forced retreat back home for the defeated. Ultimate victory . . . and enslavement of the conquered were not considered an option for either side. Greek hoplite battles were struggles between small landholders who by mutual consent sought to limit warfare (and hence killing) to a single, brief, nightmarish occasion.[1]

The harvesting demands of Greek agriculture (primarily olives, grapes, and grains) meant that there were only one or two months a year during which the small landholders had time to fight, and so hoplite battle grew out of this necessity for limited war. This "nightmarish" encounter was, at least, brief—sometimes wars lasted only an hour. Winners and losers alike wanted definitive resolution, as they needed to curb both casualties and time spent in conflict, so they opted for brutal yet bounded engagement.

Once invaders crossed the border and it became clear that an attack was coming, events unfolded very quickly in response to the threat of losing one's crops: "either the defenders usually marched out from their walled cities promptly to contest this occupation of their farmland," whereupon the two sides "attacked simultaneously," "or they simply submitted to the terms dictated in order to clear the intruder from their property as quickly as possible."[2]

The hoplites commonly wore body armor and took a spear and a shield into battle, and after the initial collision, "it soon degenerated into an enormous contest of pressure, as men used their shields, hands, and bodies in a desperate, frantic effort to force a path forward," all the while jabbing and thrusting with their spears.[3] The battle was brutal sea of "tortured," confused, animalistic anguish, but it had several important features.

### Simplicity and Low Casualty Rates

Despite the chaos and brutality, there was a "simplicity and clear order of hoplite combat," and casualty rates were "low by modern standards." The farmers could fight with frequency because they employed fairly straightforward phalanx tactics and strategy that did not require extensive drilling and training or significant public expenditure on arms and provisions.

Combat was not fatal to most participants, killing "only some 15 percent of their male citizens, many of whom were already past the prime of life," and leaving total casualties under 20 percent.[4] If such clashes had recurred in quick succession, as is often the case with modern battles, then repeatedly sustaining such casualty rates would have devastated the small hoplite armies of these small city-states, but as a one-off, it was an acceptable percentage in exchange for the second notable aspect of these classical hoplite battles.[5]

### Brevity

Crucially, while battles were "frequent," they were also short, and decisive, for related reasons. Modes of fighting often reflected the landscape, and this system of warfare developed out of both agricultural and geographic necessity. The flat plains of Thessaly and coastal Macedon lent themselves to equine husbandry and a cavalry-centric military, whereas the mountains (e.g., Crete, Acarnania, Aetolia) saw enclaves of herdsmen and their livestock favoring skirmishes and missile attacks. Those who preferred the pitched hoplite battle (e.g., Athens, Sparta, Thebes, Corinth, Argos,

Mantineia, i.e., most of the major states) lived on small, rolling plains in valleys, engaged in small farming, and were surrounded by mountains: the lack of natural protection or shelter meant that there was no advantage to the flanking horseman, and instead infantries marched to flat battlefields a short distance away.[6] Until the late fifth century BCE, there was no need for extended campaigns with long marches and repeated battles, because one's enemies were close, within a few hundred miles, usually just over the mountains.[7]

The hoplites were drawn from a "class of independent small farmers . . . [who] had little free time or desire for constant drilling."[8] Most hoplites owned enough land—usually ten to fifteen acres—for him and his family to subsist on.[9] Such agricultural production was very labor-intensive, timing was critical, and margins were slim:

> The enemy was usually nearby, on the other side of the range of mountains, no farther than a few hundred miles at most. Once the invader arrived in the spring, the entire "war," if that is the proper word, usually consisted of an hour's worth of hard fighting between consenting, courageous hoplite amateurs, rather than repeated clashes of hired or trained killers. The harvest demands of the triad of Greek agriculture—the olive, the vine, and grain—left only a brief month or two in which these small farmers could find time to fight.[10]

Partly, it was a question of resources, as Greek hoplites had neither the manpower nor the weaponry to fight for extended or repeated periods of time, or even to train frequently. Timing was essential in these wars, because the efficacy was not in destroying the opponents' underlying capacity for crop production (e.g., chopping down or setting fire to grain fields, orchards, and vineyards) but rather in seizing or destroying the crops themselves, and even this had to be timed carefully: too early in the season and the crops would be unusable for both consumption (seizure) and incineration, too late and the crop would have already been harvested and the people fortified with supplies to sustain them during battle. A perfectly timed invasion, however, also meant leaving one's own valuable crops unattended and vulnerable.[11] When they fought,

> The Greek battlefield was the scene of abject terror and utter carnage, but it was a *brief* nightmare that the hoplite might face only

once a summer, unlike the unending monotony of warfare in the trenches of the First World War or in the jungles of Vietnam. A man could focus all his courage upon one pure burst of frenzied activity; for an hour or two he overcame the limits of physical and psychological endurance.[12]

The intensity was such that one would not want to fight that way again anytime soon, but could do so for a short while. Such intensity and brevity were essential in making possible the decisive nature of these battles.

*Decisiveness*

The norms of classical Greek hoplite pitched battle were part of a larger set of unwritten "rules of engagement" that were considered "common customs." These included the following, says classicist Josiah Ober: "the state of war should be officially declared before commencing hostilities," and "a battle is properly prefaced by a ritual challenge and acceptance of the challenge"; "hostilities are sometimes inappropriate," especially during religious festivals; requesting the return of the bodies of one's dead is an indication of accepting defeat, and when requested, the opponent must return the dead; "battles should be fought during the usual (summer) campaigning season"; and "pursuit of defeated and retreating opponents should be limited in duration."[13]

Key to the brevity of classical Greek hoplite combat was that "long-drawn-out pursuit was rare," says Hanson, for "unlike Napoleon, the victors were not aiming for the complete destruction of an enemy army."[14] This interpretation is contested: for example, historians Peter Krentz and Hans van Wees argue that fleeing enemies were in fact sometimes chased from the battlefield and killed—so rather than some norm of restraint, it was the limitations of hoplite armor, whose design for use in close formation left one dangerously exposed outside of the phalanx, that generally stayed the hand of hoplite armies. Whatever the reason, one result and advantage of pitched battle that spurned extended pursuit was that battlefield victory produced limited claims over body and property:

In the battle's aftermath, permanent occupation of the defeated's prime lands, absolute destruction of his rural infrastructures, murder, rape, the enslavement of his people—the whole repetitious nightmare of the "campaign" of modern warfare—rarely followed in the Archaic and early Classical Periods. That belongs more to those terrible, final years of the Peloponnesian War (431–404 B.C.) when the agriculturalists' absolute monopoly and control over conflict vanished.[15]

The defeated side still kept its society, its culture, and much of its personal property. In fact, the structure of combat was "designed to *limit* war and martial gallantry, not to romanticize the warrior's inherent nobility."[16] Therein lies "the singular genius of hoplite warfare," argues Hanson: to limit the loss of civilian life and property from "constant and inevitable internecine struggles," battles had to be "demonstrably decisive to all involved—and therefore sometimes unusually brutal."[17] The trade-off was the ability to preserve Greek city-state culture and the very essence of these societies.

Extended maneuvers and use of "overwhelming force" were frowned upon because "battle was 'by convention,' a reciprocal agreement on both sides" to seek "decisive victory" through the risks of war:

> If it spelled certain death for hundreds involved, at least the intent was to limit, rather than glorify, war, and thereby save rather than destroy lives. The postmortem viewing of the dead, the exchange of bodies, the erection of the battlefield trophy, the lack of organized pursuit and further slaughter, and, above all, the mutual understanding to abide by the decision achieved on the battlefield—these were all rituals designed to reinforce the idea that further killing was not merely senseless but unnecessary as well. Surely, any continued fighting was a reproach to traditional values and to those who had gone down hours before and lay still on the battlefield.[18]

Unlike the other two ethics of cooperation discussed, this one does not limit what can be done while fighting—anything is permitted. Rather, it restricts the overall structure of war, primarily its location and duration. Although the fighters could and did suffer horrific injuries, the battle was short (from only a few hours to a day), the outcome was taken as definitive, and then everyone returned to their busy lives.

Historically, enlightened long-term self-interest alone has not been nearly enough to sustain this kind of cooperation, but the circumstances and ethics that made it possible have also been rare. It has required not only tight-knit communities clustered in close proximity but also ones who share a certain familiarity between them (e.g., common language) in order to uphold such structural constraints on warfare with any modicum of success.

### Duel Combat and Ritual Warfare

Some analogies to this ethic of ending war quickly can be found in duels and ritual warfare. Duels have been used not just for the resolution of personal rivalries or insults but also to render military verdicts. Although they are often portrayed in literature as preludes to or parts of mass battles, in fact "monomachia"—"duel combats . . . fought by chosen warriors instead of an all-out battle," after which both armies would battle only if neither warrior had won—was common in early warfare throughout the Mediterranean, says historian W. Kendrick Pritchett, pointing to examples from the eleventh to ninth century BCE in the Old Testament, earlier Egyptian literature, and Palestinian reliefs.[19] Although it has become a lesson about courage in the face of seeming impossibility and faith in God, the battle between David and Goliath may be the best-known instance of monomachia from that time period. As the Israelite and Philistine armies faced each other across the valley of Elah, the giant Philistine strode forward and challenged:

> Why are ye come out to set *your* battle in array? *am* I not a Philistine, and ye servants to Saul? choose you a man for you, and let him come down to me. If he be able to fight with me, and to kill me, then will we be your servants: but if I prevail against him, and kill him, then shall ye be our servants, and serve us.
> (1 SAMUEL 17:8–9)

Duels that settle battles are structurally similar to classical Greek hoplite warfare, in that they agree in advance to an artificial determinant of victory of some sort, in this case the outcome of a single fight, instead of time elapsed.

Ritual warfare among indigenous populations has long been an object of curiosity, fascination, and misunderstanding by Europeans, but it demonstrates a mode of battle that shares with Greek hoplites the desire to limit damage, although in a different way. In the North American Iroquoia Indian "mourning wars," the victors did not distinguish between killing in war and killing as a crime as Europeans did, so instead of taking prisoners, the victors would adopt and integrate them (usually women and children) into their tribe, in order to replenish their own numbers. Captured males were gruesomely killed with extended ritual torture, which horrified Europeans and Americans, but this not only served significant social functions,[20] but also constrained the violence wrought as everyone sought a delicate balance between killing enough to repopulate themselves (without losing too many in the process) and killing too many such that it would incite a new round of fighting. "Successful mourning wars required the maintenance of a fragile equilibrium, and when it worked properly the effect was to limit the destruction of native warfare," says Witt.

In seventeenth-century Rhode Island, Roger Williams observed that Indian war was "farre lesse bloudy, and devouring than the cruell Warres of Europe,"[21] and many Indians were shocked and revolted by the carnage of European fighting:

> In the Pequot War of 1637, observers reported that the Pequots "stamped and tore the Hair from their Heads" when they saw the extent of the colonists' devastation of their community. Even the colonists' Narragansett allies joined in the protest: "it is naught," they cried, "because it is too furious, and slays too many men."[22]

Tragically, when these two different cultures of warfare collided, their mutual lack of understanding meant that they quickly descended to the lowest common denominator: the Indians jettisoned their reservations about extinguishing whole villages, while colonists and settlers tortured and dismembered the Indians.[23]

In dealings with each other, however, the Iroquoians made a similar trade-off as the Greek hoplites: unconstrained violence in one context (postbattle ritual torture and execution, or on the battlefield, respectively) in exchange for otherwise limited harm to the people and their societies. The particular boundaries, practices, and structures of violence are artificially determined by each civilization, in accordance with their circumstances and priorities.

Here again, a sporting analogy might be useful. In sporting competition, when there is a tie at the end of regulation, there is usually a mechanism for producing a winner. This can be done in various ways, including flipping a coin, but if the rules call for further play, it usually comes in the form of an overtime period of a specified length (as many as is required to yield a winner), sudden death overtime (the first to score or to reach a designated score wins), or a separate decision-making process (e.g., penalty kicks). There is a certain artificiality to ending the encounter within a prescribed time limit (including overtime) and accepting whatever outcome results at the end of the designated process. While there was no hard-and-fast time limit to Greek hoplite warfare, it concluded within the day, once it became clear which side had prevailed on that day, and they did not revisit the result the next day in hopes of a different outcome or total annihilation of the other side.

### *Relation to Truces and Cease-fires*

Truces and cease-fires are important collaborative practices that can resemble cooperation to end war quickly, but they carry their own dynamics. They are often ad hoc and designed to serve a specific and limited purpose (e.g., a humanitarian pause), but can also recur regularly, such as those for the original Olympic games for over twelve centuries.

One approach to truces and cease-fires that overlaps with cooperating to end war quickly uses the lens of conflict management. For example, legal scholar Gabriella Blum argues that there is in fact no strict dichotomy between war and peace, as shown by various truces and cease-fires in the context of the ongoing India/Pakistan, Greece/Turkey, and Israel/Lebanon conflicts.[24] Rather, these states of being coexist within a larger, complex, ongoing relationship between parties. "Throughout history, rivals have frequently found a joint interest in limiting the scope of their conflicts, in excluding some spheres from them, and even in engaging in cooperative efforts for their mutual benefits," and these "islands of agreement" are used as part of relationship management, and do not interfere with the parties' ability to continue pursuing the conflict. Within the context of rivalrous relationships, accords can include confidence-building measures, phased peace agreements, stabilizing or status quo agreements (e.g., truces, cease-fires, armistices), or measures for limited warfare (e.g., weapons bans, limitations on acceptable targets).[25] This perspective on war is very much in line with my own, in that there can be self-imposed realms of constraint in the midst of horrific contention. Some of those confines clearly include certain ethics of cooperation, or can give rise to them over time.

Notable long-term cease-fires include the line in Kashmir established by the Karachi Agreement in July 1949,[26] the armistice that established the ongoing DMZ between North Korea and South Korea in 1953, and the ending of the Sino-Vietnamese War in 1979. In each of these protracted and deadly conflicts, both parties eventually recognized that the victory they had set out for was not possible, so they started looking for alternative endings that everyone could live with, and that would allow them to each claim victory to their respective constituencies.

A long-term truce merely prolongs war instead of ending it quickly, but at least the conflict takes a less directly violent form for the time being. This differs from an ethic of efficient resolution because, first, these are hardly rapid conclusions to the war, much less intentionally so (and therefore no agreement on the structure of the war), and second, there is no agreement on the winner, so it lacks the intentionally limited definitiveness of classical Greek hoplite warfare, for example. So while certain truces and cease-fires might reflect some form of the ethic of cooperation in warfare (e.g., humanitarian pauses manifest the ethic of cooperation to protect certain classes of people), others do not in any way.

## The Influence of Pitched Battle

Given how much it has influenced the way Westerners think of war, Greek hoplite battle may not seem unique, but it was an unusual way of fighting at the time. Although later supplanted with the addition of horsemen and light-armed troops, hoplite infantry (armored spearmen) battle was an essential method of settling disputes "instantaneously, economically, and ethically" for two centuries (around seven hundred to five hundred BCE and in much of the early fifth century BCE).[27]

Other Greeks fought in other ways, including with navies, cavalry, and missiles, employing skirmishes, artillery, and sieges. But the hoplites were "senseless," with their "heavily armored militiamen crashing together on flat plains during the long days of summer, each side after the initial collision seeking quite literally to push the other off the battlefield through a combination of spear thrusting and the shove of bodies."[28]

Contemporaneous observers critiqued the "wrongheadedness" of their approach. Notes Persian commander Mardonios, in 490 BCE:

> When they have declared war against each other, they come down to the fairest and most level ground that they can find, and there they fight. . . . Yet speaking as they do the same language, they should end their disputes by the means of heralds and messengers, and by any way rather than fighting; or if needs must that they wage war against each other, they should discover each where his strongest defence lies, and there make his essay.[29]

Not only was fighting itself irrational because their shared language and culture afforded opportunities for negotiation not present in other situations—although no more so than most wars between people comprehensible to each other—but the form of fighting was also militarily senseless: without reserves, flank attacks, or rear guards, and focused solely on the frontal assault.[30] Given its structure, it more resembled a "battle" than a "war,"[31] because "unlike modern battle, fighting in the ancient world ceased after a few hours, and the field of conflict fell silent. Ground was not fought over again and again."[32]

Modern warfare differs significantly in length and decisiveness, but classical hoplite battle's "folly" lives on. Its basic design of trying to "deliver fatal blows . . . without retreat" is an *aesthetic* that strongly influences modern conceptions of war, including "this Western desire for a single, magnificent collision of infantry, for brutal killing with edged weapons on a battlefield between free men,"[33] which I will discuss in chapter 6.

## Contemporary Echoes

Although the ethic of cooperation to end wars quickly has been abandoned, its appeal remains and modern analogues persist—but they have evolved and been distorted with time. The idea that quick wars cause less overall damage recurs persistently in the modern period. Circa 1517, Niccolò Machiavelli advised following the Romans' lead in making wars "short and massive," because "by fielding enormous armies, the Romans brought to a very swift conclusion all the wars that they waged against the Latins, the Samnites, and the Etruscans."[34] Over two hundred years later, Frederick the Great preferred "short and lively" conflicts,[35] as extended fighting only depleted one's own resources, population, and discipline,[36] so long wars should be conducted at low intensity. Therefore, even successful wars must be terminated "promptly and prudently,"[37] for "when it comes to battles we ought to be guided by the maxim of Sennerib of the Hebrews that it is better for one man to perish than an entire people."[38]

As Clausewitz theorizes in *On War* (1832), there is no way "of disarming or overthrowing [an] adversary" without violence, and kind-hearted efforts to minimize bloodshed misapprehend the logic of war (1.1.3).[39] So if there must be war, then perhaps the harsher, the better.

While some of the appeal of short, brutal conflicts was undoubtedly aesthetic and some practical, there were, surprisingly, significant humanitarian considerations as well. Although the losers' lot has improved over time due to rising moral and legal expectations, war is still fundamentally ruinous, and always in new ways. Wrote William Wheeler, a private in the Duke of Wellington's armies:

> On the 16th arrived at the City of Leyria. The enemy had commenced the destruction of this place, but . . . were obliged to leave the work of destruction half completed. The town had been on fire in several places, the houses were completely glutted, doors, windows, shutters, and in many places the floors were ripped to pieces for fuel, furniture broken to pieces and thrown into the streets, the churches did not escape, the graves were opened, and the dead dragged out. This was horrible. The dead lay scattered about, some had been burried [*sic*] many years, others only a few weeks. In one of the churches laid an inhabitant and a Priest, both stabbed in the side with a bayonet. They were both on the steps leading to where the Grand Altar once stood. They had no doubt retired here thinking the sanctity of the place would protect them, but no place would shelter the innocent and defenceless from such Hell hounds. There was not a living soul in the place but one solitary female. She was laying on a bed covered with blood, having received from the hands of the French soldiers eleven bayonet wounds.
> 
> (VILLA MAYOR, APRIL 20, 1811, LETTER NO. 22)

Despite the proliferation of international laws and their broadened and deepened protections, nothing seems to change in the conditions of war and technology only exponentially augments the carnage, observes international lawyer and legal scholar Mountague Bernard:

> Each age has its merciless soldiers and unfeeling statesmen; ambition spills more blood than cruelty; military science crowds together greater multitudes for slaughter; civilization itself multiplies a thousandfold the means of destruction, and forges more tremendous implements of carnage; from every country on which the curse successively falls the cry of anguish and rage goes up to Heaven, whilst faint and broken are the glimpses we obtain of anything like recognised custom or established law. Generally speaking, indeed, it is only when such usages are violated and trodden under foot that they proclaim their existence at all.

As a result, many nineteenth-century jurists threw up their hands in despair in the face of the inefficacy of the laws and the seeming impossibility of improvement, and reached for a "short, sharp, and decisive" approach instead—but without the cooperation. While Bernard disagrees, their instinct is understandable:

> Can we wonder if, with the latest complaints sounding in their ears, and fresh scenes of violence floating before their eyes, thoughtful men ask doubtfully whether anything has been really done to mitigate these evils within the last two hundred years? Nay, can we think it strange if, yielding to a kind of despair, they talk as if there were nothing to be done, nothing to be hoped for, but to make the calamity shorter at the cost of making it fiercer and more terrible?[40]

Francis Lieber himself, the author of General Orders No. 100, which helped lay the foundation for contemporary international laws of war, advised in 1861 that "the shorter war is, the better; and the more intensely it is carried on, the shorter it will be,"[41] and even wrote into the Code, "The more vigorously wars are pursued, the better it is for humanity. Sharp wars are brief" (Art. 29). He worried that trying to alleviate suffering in war by requiring fighters to use the least destructive means available would actually increase overall damage. In fact, it is "best and most humane," said Lieber, to fight "as intensely as possible so as to be through with it as soon as possible,"[42] because that would lessen suffering more than any direct attempts to do so. "The more earnestly and keenly wars are carried on, the better for humanity, for peace and civilization," he concluded.[43]

Lieber was not the only one who thought so at the time. Union General William T. Sherman actively rejected the humanitarian laws of war and their ethical constraints. When he burned Atlanta and devastated Georgia by "living off the land" on his infamous March to the Sea, he intended to destroy everything of possible military use to the Confederacy, and his scorched-earth operation helped fulfill his own later observation that war was not glorious and glamorous, but "hell."

The "only principle [is] which party can whip," he insisted, and said in 1865 that "the more awful you can make war the sooner it will be over."[44] When Sherman was offered a trade of all the Union soldiers held at the notorious Andersonville prison camp in exchange for his captured Confederate soldiers, he refused on the grounds that such trades would slow progress and prolong conflict. "I am almost satisfied it would be just as well to kill all prisoners," he mused, as "they would be spared these atrocities,"[45] and when he besieged Atlanta in 1864, he declared: "You cannot qualify war in harsher terms than I will," but "war is cruelty and you cannot refine it, and those who brought war into our country deserve all the curses and maledictions a people can pour out." Therefore, he suggested to Confederate Lt. General John Bell Hood, "If we must be enemies, let us be men, and fight it out as we propose to do, and not deal in such hypocritical appeals to God and humanity."[46]

Resistance to direct humanitarianism in war continued, and nearly two decades after the Civil War's end, Major General John M. Schofield stated in 1881:

> All the means, not condemned as mean or cowardly (such as assassination or poisoning), which tend directly and adequately toward the destruction of the military power and resources of the enemy, must be regarded as legitimate . . . good reasons for their adoption, as tending to make the contest "short, sharp, and decisive," and still more, as tending to prevent nations from going to war upon slight provocation.[47]

Although in 1892 Schofield ordered that the Geneva Convention of 1864 be incorporated into General Orders No. 100, he still publicly advocated brief and fierce fighting and decried what had been called "squeamish humanity." Around the same time (1896), editors of an influential military strategy journal wrote: "Terrible! Say you? Well, yes. War ought to be terrible. The trouble is that it has ceased to be terrible to altogether too many men."[48]

*Shortcomings of Modern Analogues: Omitting Cooperation*

Throughout the nineteenth century (when formal codification of the rules of war was still young and struggling) and beyond, officers and jurists resisted the shift in military ethics' focus to humanitarian constraints on the rules of engagement and POW treatment. Yet, the growing body of international law in this vein now assumes that there can be no other objects of cooperation, overlooking the fact that the structure of war itself can be.

Modern-era revivalists of this structural approach—the idea of short wars—advocated viciousness in order to end war more quickly and limit damage. It was an idea not devoid of humanitarian considerations, as we have seen, but rather, for some, a different idea of how to best care for humanity.

They erred in their response, however, by forgetting or being ignorant of the essential element of cooperation. When Machiavelli advocates "short and massive" wars, he praises the immediacy and decisiveness of Roman military response to declarations of war, which they used to secure ever-larger buffers for their empire, and thus "step by step . . . gain a reputation over that of their enemy and internal strength." Similarly, Frederick the Great's preference for short wars was born of concerns with his own resources and the effects of a prolonged conflict on his soldiers' morale and self-discipline, and he was far from unique in these considerations.

In these modern manifestations, the preference for "short and lively" wars completely neglects any collaboration that might accompany them. In hoplite battle, the rules of war were essential, even if one rule was that there were no rules on the battlefield. In losing that cooperative framework, the idea has been distorted so much that it bears only a superficial resemblance to the original—but more importantly, it then loses its ability to limit destruction and becomes enormously devastating both during the immediate conflict and later on, as unrestrained carnage breeds resentment and fuels future conflict. Once the cooperative element slips away, the humanitarian potential does, too—and the rationale for ending war quickly becomes simply to minimize damage to one's own side and without any kind of coordination on the format of war.

Most elements of the classical hoplite warfare, which was sustainable for only about two centuries,[49] were quickly abandoned. Only the idea of the pitched battle remains, which is still highly influential.[50] What classical Greek hoplites during this period wanted were "clear results,"[51] which were best achieved with short wars in the form of pitched battle. The outcomes would inevitably be a little arbitrary, but all sides could accept that in exchange for brevity. This crucial aspect of the structure has dropped out entirely, however.

Not only are modern wars not short, while being altogether too lively, but there is also no cooperation *with the enemy* to end the fighting quickly. What the moderns—including Lieber, Sherman, and Schofield—advocate instead is a one-sided effort to pummel the opponent into submission, which has been described in many different ways, including the ones mentioned earlier and more recently as "shock and awe."

This recurring and perennially attractive sentiment cannot be effective without cooperation, however, which is why such wars wreak even greater devastation while still ending in contested settlements. The reductio ad absurdum of this unilateral practice can be found in various places, including in some approaches to nuclear warfare.[52] For example, even though public justifications for the atomic bombings of Japan said that they shortened the war and ultimately saved lives, it was out of an unconstrained consideration for American lives only and not any utilitarian motivation to seek the least overall damage. Post hoc rationalizations sometimes adopt a utilitarian line by noting that it also spared military and civilian Japanese lives that would otherwise have been lost in a much bloodier invasion of the home islands. This is empirically debatable, but be that as it may, it was still a one-sided calculation at the time and not part of any broader cooperative understanding on the best structure of war to minimize damage, and as such is fundamentally disanalogous and vastly different from a moral standpoint.

## Trade-Offs and Conclusiveness

Short wars à la classical Greek hoplites offer immediate advantages, but are they preferable in the long run? Might there be a trade-off between short wars and long-term definitive outcomes? While hoplite wars—battles, really—were brief and conclusive, they were only temporarily so, as Greek city-states fought frequently; everyone expected that they would fight every summer, even if only once against a particular city-state that year. So were the outcomes of those battles definitive *enough*? Two major questions emerge when considering these circumstances: (1) What kinds of wars are more likely to yield definitive outcomes, and (2) when is an outcome "definitive"?

### *Types of Wars*

History tells the story of war through pitched battles, in part because it offers a more comprehensible narrative, as noted in chapter 1. Military leaders also prefer this focus because—in the same spirit as quantifying standards for military achievement—it is an easier metric by which to gauge themselves.

Succinct, intensive wars are not necessarily more conclusive, however. The first US-Iraq war (Gulf War), for example, was deliberately kept short: the United States spent four months building up troops and establishing ground operations, but actual combat lasted a mere six weeks (from January 17, 1991 to February 28, 1991). The US military and political leadership limited ground operations in order to keep combat brief, but that left business unfinished to this day.[53]

Military leaders continue to be seduced by the illusory promise of decisive (pitched) battle, when it is perhaps "grinding [through attrition] rather than genius" that ultimately wins instead.[54] When US Colonel Harry G. Summers, Jr., who fought in both the Korean War and the Vietnam War, said to his counterpart in Hanoi a week before Saigon fell to the North Vietnamese Army (NVA), "You know, you never beat us on the battlefield"—for the United States did indeed win most of the major battles in the Vietnam War—NVA Colonel Tu replied, "That may be so, but it is also irrelevant."[55]

But neither is it clear that longer, drawn-out, and more involved wars are better at yielding definitive outcomes. Some do, e.g., World War II against Germany and Japan, but many more do not. One can think of this problem along two dimensions,[56] resulting in four types of wars—all of which are just ideal types, as the real world is rather messy—with different dynamics and outcomes (see table 4.1).

Warfare fought within the framework of a cooperative ethic to conclude quickly can lead to outcomes with a certain kind of definitiveness, albeit limited. The lasting legacy of classical Greek hoplite battle is its spirit, according to Hanson, of concentrated and therefore efficient killing in order to yield a "clear victory."[57] The trade-off was, of course, limited opportunity and extreme brutality, but then at least everyone would have a decisive outcome. Or decisive enough such that they could return to the pressing matters of their daily lives (farming, harvesting, and the like), during their short windows of opportunity.

TABLE 4.1
Types of War Outcomes

|  | Cooperative | Noncooperative |
|---|---|---|
| Short | E.g., classical Greek hoplite battle, some forms of ritual or tribal war (ethic of cooperation to end war quickly). Definitive outcomes, but regular/repeated/recurring battles over the years. | E.g., Gulf War (1992), Six-Day War (1967). Definitive outcomes and short-term settlements, but renewed conflict usually ensues later. (Unless the winner is so brutal that it basically annihilates the losing population, including civilians.) |
| Open-ended | E.g., DMZs, conflicts with repeated truces and cease-fires. No definitive resolutions. Conflict is ongoing, generally at relatively low levels of violence. | E.g., World War II, Vietnam War. Massive casualties and destruction. Outcomes vary widely, but are usually not definitive. (World War II may be an exception that proves the rule.) |

Cooperative open-ended conflict, on the other hand, while lacking resolution, is usually conducted at lower levels of violence and more predictable, which counts for quite a bit when it comes to potentially losing one's life in war.

With warfare that is *non*cooperative on the structural front, however, the only hope for a definitive outcome depends on the aftermath of the war rather than the war itself: either annihilating the enemy population en masse after victory or overhauling the political, social, and cultural system such that the losing society is fundamentally transformed (e.g., Germany and Japan after World War II), which is not only a massive endeavor but also hardly guaranteed to yield the desired outcome. So open-ended and noncooperative warfare has the *potential* for more definitiveness, although that lies in paving the way for postwar transformation, and not in the outcome of the war itself. In doing so, it also destroys more, which may seed long-run resentments and eventual renewal of conflict. Overall, this model generates much higher variance in its results—and usually not positive and definitive ones.

## What Is a "Definitive" Outcome?

Which approach to warfare is better overall and in the long run? The answer to that question also requires asking what it means to have a "definitive" outcome. Does it have to be *completely* definitive?

Beyond injury and death, nothing is definitive about war: questions of right and justice, not to mention contestations of power, can be revisited again and again, at any time, over the years, decades, even centuries. Tactical decisiveness—on the battlefield—does not equal political conclusiveness, if the losing party does not choose to accept the outcome as determined by might. So what qualifies as definitive *enough*?

Are the outcomes of recurring wars, such as those of Greek hoplites, definitive enough? Ritual warfare as frequently used between aboriginal tribes does not seek final resolution. The Dani of New Guinea, for example, "do not enter into battle in order to put an end to fighting. They do not envisage the end of fighting any more than the end of gardening or of ghosts. Nor do they fight in order to annex land or to dominate people," observed anthropologists Robert Gardner and Karl G. Heider.[58]

Fighting begins with the ritual of—literally—calling a battle: once a tribe's leadership has decided to fight, a group of men will go to the border in the morning and shout a challenge to the enemy across no man's land. When the other side accepts, word is passed throughout the villages. "As with so many other points of procedure during a battle, it is understood that fighting will not start until both sides are ready,"[59] and that the "formal battle," which may be that same day, would begin with about a half hour of preliminary, ceremonial "sallies by forward groups."[60]

Once the fighting begins, it is brief: about ten to twenty engagements, lasting about ten to fifteen minutes at a time, usually with fewer than two hundred men on each side. They battle in spurts of "brief clashes and relatively long interruptions." During those lacunae, "taunts and epithets" are traded across the battlefield, and as most of the warriors across tribes are familiar with one another's names and have information about their private lives, "the insults are often personal and will elicit laughter from both camps." Then as night descends, everyone gradually withdraws.[61] The Dani also practiced other forms of warfare, including raids and ambushes, but these too included ritualistic elements, such as returning dead bodies to the opponents.[62]

One difference between the constrained combat of aboriginal ritual warfare and classical Greek hoplite warfare is the religious motivations involved in the former,[63] whereas the Greek structure was driven by scarcity in time and resources. Nevertheless, both examples can shed some light on the notion of definitive outcomes.

In all these cases—Greek hoplites, New Guinea Dani tribes, North American Iroquoia tribes, and anyone else who practiced similarly structured warfare—they were working on economic margins, and they had to contain the resources devoted to warfare or risk starving to death. At the same time, given their close proximity and competition with one another they could not avoid conflict altogether—hence a kind of bounded warfare that yielded outcomes whose decisiveness can also be considered limited. Although battles are taken to settle the conflict at the time, everyone expects that there will be future struggles, and indeed, combat recurs regularly.

This raises a question about what to make of the periods between clashes: Is it peace? Or is it merely a lacunae between hostilities? A comparison to the long-term truces and cease-fires that Blum studies is useful here. As noted earlier, these "islands of agreement" serve to prolong rather than end a war—the parties merely suspend their battle for the moment and postpone physical progress toward resolution—and this is altogether rather different from actually ending a war, even if full-blown fighting never resumes. Their immediate practical outcome resembles the limited definitiveness and later recurrence of classical Greek hoplite warfare, but they differ in that neither party to these truces or cease-fires thinks that the conflict is settled. In the case of the Korean DMZ, for example, they have simply paused the war, which they consider to be ongoing and unresolved, whereas classical Greek hoplites considered the war to be closed at the day's end. Although they would certainly fight again, perhaps as soon as the following summer, it would be viewed as a separate (even if related) conflict, and that was definitive enough.

## War's Capacity for Definitiveness

On the noncooperative "short and massive" model, in contrast, one must throw all one's resources into the fight in deliberate and organized fashion with the intention of generating a conclusive decision, according to Machiavelli, even if the enemy seems to be far weaker.[64] But while a short, intense, physical contest of pitched battle may be the only thing that can yield decisive victory, it is still unlikely to do so: miscalculations are surprisingly common. Wars comprising pitched battles can and do go on for years, even when one side possesses clearly superior firepower. Part of the problem is that whether or not the weaker side has ample resources, there can be many clashes before one party capitulates. The greatest challenge for this model, however, is that most wars are fought with mixed tactics: mostly attrition (e.g., guerrilla and other warfare), punctuated by the occasional pitched battle.

Pitched battle only yields a definitive outcome when both sides agree that it will determine the outcome, and usually only one party—the one with superior firepower—is interested in that. Suppose two opponents with vastly different resources—let us call them Imperium Romanum and People's Front of Judea—are in violent conflict over who will govern a people and territory. The weaker side (PFJ) will not entertain a structure in which it will lose as long as it can win by other means, and so it will refuse to let a particular battle determine the outcome of the war and will seek another pitched battle or turn to guerrilla warfare and slow attrition, all of which can extend the conflict for years without resolution. We do not need hypothetical quagmires: history is filled with such examples and recent ones include Afghanistan (American, Russian, and British attempts), Iraq,

Vietnam, Colombia and the FARC, and Sri Lanka and Tamil separatists, just to name a few.

What the "short and massive" model seeks is absolute conclusiveness—and the price for that is enormous destruction (preferably but not limited to the opponent). This approach can guarantee neither quick resolution nor final settlement, however, as results can always be contested with future wars[65]—and in fact, neither quick resolution nor final settlement is even particularly likely.

What we are left with instead is pitched battle without the cooperation, and therefore without the definitiveness of result. Modern warfare is far more intense, complex, and protracted than hoplite war; in combination with modern technology, this yields mutual slaughter, minus the benefit of quick resolution. Says Hanson:

> Whereas the polis Greeks discovered shock battle as a glorious method of saving lives and confining conflict to an hour's worth of heroics between armored infantry, their successors sought to unleash the entire power of their culture to destroy one another in a horrendous moment—and twentieth-century man has at last realized just that ability. *Like the Hellenistic Greeks, we have inherited the Hellenic idea of decisive battle, but not the confining circumstances of its birth. That can be a terrifying fact indeed.*[66]

The gross perversion of the spirit of decisive battle in contemporary times—by applying "wealth and ingenuity rather than the commitment of courage and muscular strength"—has made impossible the intended possibility of swift resolution through battle, says Keegan, and "it now demands more of man than any Greek was ever asked to give and threatens the devastation of all he loves and possesses."[67]

Perhaps limited definitiveness à la classical Greek hoplite warfare—which is what can be offered in exchange for limited damage—is the best that can be hoped for. But even this is difficult to achieve and, as we have seen, exceedingly rare in the history of war.

Understanding the limitations of military force to yield decisive, accepted political outcomes means that both political leaders and military strategists should take greater account of whether the way the war is fought and won will set the stage for future conflict, e.g., if it generates deep, simmering resentments that will eventually reignite. Considerations of postwar scenarios should not be limited to postwar peace (e.g., *jus post bellum*) but should also address future *jus ad bellum*.

## Could an Ethic of Cooperation to End War Quickly Be Revived?

Under what circumstances would it be possible to establish a structure of cooperation analogous to the classical Greek hoplite or ritual practices of bounded warfare, to check the ravages of war by limiting its breadth, scope, and time? Despite the historical rarity of clean models, there are enough examples that draw from the idea of cooperating for rapid resolution to develop an abstract type. Might such a model offer some guidance for contemporary times?

Obviously, the ethic of cooperation must be, well, cooperative. For this to work, neither side can defect from the agreement of the structure of war. This is difficult to achieve, for successful cases seem to require an extraordinary coincidence of shared language, religion, culture, and values, as well as close quarters, expectations of repeated interaction, and the ability to punish defection. Moreover, all sides must *perceive* one another as sharing these characteristics. It is not enough, for example, for different religious sects to hold significant theological beliefs and principles such that they would be categorized together in a typology of religions. If they do not recognize one another as fellow believers, e.g., different national Orthodox churches or different branches of Islam, then there is in practice no shared religion.[68] Clearly, these are necessary but insufficient conditions, as many peoples with shared characteristics have fought and continue to fight one another without a shared ethic to end war quickly, and have no desire to develop one.

In certain respects, this resembles the "live and let live" system that emerged in some of the World War I trenches, although there the trench soldiers were constrained in what they could establish because they had commanders compelling them to fight one another, around whom they then had to maneuver. (It would have been interesting to see what other systems of fighting—or rather not fighting—they might have developed otherwise.)

The contemporary oeuvre of humanitarian laws of war is well intentioned but has nonetheless contributed to some of the greatest tragedies in the history of human conflict. If it could be shown with some persuasiveness that warfare structured along the lines of classical hoplite or ritual warfare (in order to end conflicts quickly) actually does less damage overall, could this ethic be resurrected in some form?

Even if it could be empirically proven that wars conducted with a cooperative ethic to end fighting quickly are preferable on utilitarian grounds, significant challenges to its institutionalization would remain, including the way the moral landscape has changed. Such wars would still be troubling sights for participants and bystanders alike to stomach, especially with the development of a robust doctrine of human rights in international law.

First, not *any* short war would be preferable on utilitarian grounds. While the predominant rationale behind "short and lively" wars is to compel the enemy to surrender sooner and therefore avoid the losses from extended conflict, it is not obvious that such wars save lives—this is something that we cannot conduct controlled experiments on. Furthermore, the brutality of a "short and massive" war can instigate long-term resentments and lead to future reignition of the conflict. (See Kant's concerns with the difficulty of building trust between nations, for example.) For this kind of warfare to not engender an increase in future retaliatory or other related wars, all parties must be on board with this scheme: they must share this ethic of cooperation to end war quickly, the way classical Greek hoplites did, rather than just unilaterally attempt to impose this scheme on the other side as the moderns advocated.

Second, the potential gains and, more importantly, the potential losses from bounded wars in this vein must be restricted. Part of the cooperative ethic for the Greek hoplites and for ritual warfare was that the cost of defeat was also limited, which made it possible for losers to accept a quick but somewhat arbitrary procedure. (The wisdom of this condition can be seen in some historical demands for "unconditional surrender," including in World War II.)

Third, if some form of Kant's perpetual peace theory holds true, then there will be less conflict (military, economic, cyber, and so on) over time between enemies who share certain characteristics (e.g., due to trade, other economic ties, political commonalities, greater trust/communications), and then perhaps *serious* conflict will be reserved largely for enemies of different cultures, languages, or religions. Ironically, then, cooperation between enemies on this structural level would become relatively more difficult to establish and sustain.

Fourth, the international moral landscape has changed so much that it would now be hard to sell this approach to both soldiers and the public, given their existing expectations for *jus in bello* rules. The idea of warfighters meeting each other in an arena of sorts, battling without constraints for a few hours in order to settle the outcome of a conflict, would no doubt be appealing to some soldiers, especially when they face the alternative of a long and inhumane war of attrition. Not only would this more efficiently yield a result, but the image of gladiatorial-like combat also plays to a certain warrior ideal, as seen in the "fair fight" chapter.

But it would still be generally morally unacceptable to the broader community because at this point, not only the public but also many militaries are wedded to *jus in bello* restrictions on war and limited rules of engagement, as reflected in international law. The development of a robust doctrine of human rights and concomitant international law protections for soldiers will not be easily abandoned. Once safeguards are implemented and expectations established, it is difficult to roll them back. To address that concern, one might impose constraints *within* that battle, e.g., duel-like regulations on acceptable weapons or the like. But that would perhaps only exacerbate the next difficulty.

Fifth, the contemporary conception of the nation-state binds people together in such a way that both soldiers and civilians find the idea of compartmentalizing fighting in this manner to be distasteful—such gladiators would effectively be mercenaries fighting on the society's behalf. Although the brunt of the fighting does in fact fall on only a small portion of the population in modern societies and most other citizens are reluctant to shoulder the immediate physical costs of war, the picture of a soldier fighting for the love of his country and as the incarnation of his society is a strong and compelling one. Whether or not it bears any resemblance to reality in a particular case, this pervasive myth of the fervent citizen-soldier spurred onward by a greater cause (whether it be ideology, love of country/community, or the like) can be found repeatedly across time, from Pericles's Funeral Oration to Lincoln's Gettysburg Address to today.

In contemporary circumstances, any war/battle fought in cooperation to reach quick resolution would necessarily be a spectacle, an event to be viewed. That spectacle would only highlight that the spectators fall far short of this patriotic citizen-soldier ideal and that the societies are not embodied in their warfighters. Even if there were no literal arena, such a war would unwittingly call to mind an image of gladiators fighting to the death for the entertainment of others. So long as the citizen-soldier myth persists in modern societies that can function only with extensive division of labor, its shortcomings must be hidden in the fog and fireworks of a far-reaching war.

Sixth, both the public and most militaries are taken by the thought of a kind of definitiveness in war's outcome that hoplite or ritualized structure does not provide. Even though the conclusiveness they seek is impossible, they will still relentlessly pursue the possibility that war settles a conflict once and for all.[69] Even if one could overcome the objections raised by the abandonment of *jus in bello* restrictions and rules of engagement, people continue to be seduced by the vision of permanent (yet unattainable) definitiveness, and a contemporary ethic of cooperation to end war quickly that can yield only a more bounded decisiveness will be rejected. As a result, the narrow definitiveness of hoplite warfare, which existed within a larger modus vivendi that is in fact akin to our contemporary international system, will seem inadequate. We have greater expectations for war, now, and are clearly willing to do greater damage in order to pursue final resolution—even though we never have achieved it and can show that we never will.

CHAPTER V

## The Limits of Ethics of Cooperation in Warfare

> It is well that war is so terrible, or we should grow too fond of it.
> —GENERAL ROBERT E. LEE, REPORTEDLY (FREDERICKSBURG, 1862)

> I'd say there's peace in war too; it has its peaceful moments. War satisfies every human need, even for peace, it's got to or why else would we have wars? You can take a dump in wartime exactly like in the depths of peacetime, and between one battle and the next have a beer, then even when you're on the march you can prop your head up on your elbows and have a bit of shuteye in the ditch, it's entirely possible. While it's true that in the thick of battle you can't play cards, you can't do that in the thick of peacetime either, when you're ploughing furrows in the field—after a battle, at least, if you win, there are possibilities. You may get a leg blown off, and first thing you scream, then you calm down, then a glass of schnapps, and then in the end you're hopping around and the war's no worse off than before. And what's to stop you being fruitful and multiplying in the midst of slaughter, behind a barn or anyplace, in the long run you can't be held back from it, and then the war takes your progeny and can use them to carry on with. No, war always finds a way. Why should it ever end?
> —BERTOLT BRECHT, *MUTTER COURAGE UND IHRE KINDER*

As we have seen in the previous three chapters, each ethic of cooperation between enemies in warfare—for a "fair" fight, to protect classes of people, and to end war quickly—raises questions internal to that particular ethic, including (a) inconsistencies in applying the concept of "parity" across different weapons, (b) contradictions within the warrior ethic that heavily influence—and sometimes confuse—notions of the "fair fight," (c) the disconnect between what protections a category of persons receives and his responsibility for the war (e.g., political leaders), and (d) the decisiveness of outcomes generated by very short, recurring wars.

What should we make of the relationships *between* these ethics? While all of them seek to constrain war, they do so very differently. On the surface, "fair fights," protecting classes of people, and ending war quickly do not seem to have much to do with one another beyond the shared typology I have given them. A genealogy of the ethic of cooperation in warfare reveals them to be part of a multifaceted phenomenon, however, whose different manifestations have complex relationships with one another, conceptually, in practice, and across time.

Before situating the ethic of cooperation more broadly in the overall structure of modern warfare in chapters 6 and 7, I look here at where these ethics of cooperation converge and diverge. Taken as a set, commonalities emerge, such as an overlapping notion of "proper" fighting. Their simultaneous application also generates significant tensions, for example, with the use of discriminating weapons.

I then address the unintended consequences of these well-intended efforts to constrain war: adherence to "fair fight" and protective ethics can kill more people overall. This is especially concerning in the latter case, as that contravenes its very intention. Finally, both these collaborations can make it harder to win the war, so I question their proper relationship to the goal of warfare itself (to yield a political settlement or a justicial decision), and whether cooperation on the structure of war might provide better solutions for victory.

## Fighting "Properly"

Warrior virtues have shaped all three forms of cooperation discussed, especially for a "fair fight" and to protect classes of individuals. Both are either primarily or secondarily concerned with fighting "well," which can mean different things, as we have seen, but they strive to restrain soldiers in battle, whether it is with respect to fellow fighters or to bystanders.

Sometimes, they converge in their application. The "fair fight" and civilian immunity principles start from different motivations to agree on the practice of outlawing weapons such as poisonous gases, dumdum bullets, and torture. They also have overlapping misgivings about deceit—use of poisons and assassinations ("fair fight") and not wearing uniforms (civilian protection requires clarity about which category a person belongs to)—despite the obvious advantages, not to mention persistent use, of deception and the lack of an inherent connection between forthrightness and warfare.

At other times, there is convergence in their respective silences—and surprisingly so, for example, with aerial bombardments. Despite its many problems, use of this weaponry (within limits) is broadly accepted by both soldiers and international law and is not seen to inherently contradict widely accepted notions of "fair fights" or civilian immunity. The rules restrict targeting areas with heavy civilian concentration, but even increasingly accurate bombs are highly prone to causing collateral damage, and often more than traditional just war theory principles about proportionality permit. The struggle is the same as that over landmines, between a very useful combat tactic and the desire to protect civilians. Neither early limitations on ejecting projectiles from balloons (1899 Hague Convention [IV, 1])—which at the time anticipated the development of aircraft, their military use, and the subsequent impact on civilian populations—nor soldierly qualms about aerial bombardments have led to any serious efforts to outlaw this tactic.[1]

## Discriminating Weapons: Fairness Versus Protecting Civilians

Even as they converge in certain areas, the tension *between* the ethics of cooperation for a "fair fight" and to protect classes of individuals (especially civilians) inadvertently generates a number of problems. For example, one major target of the ethic to safeguard civilian immunity is indiscriminate weapons. Indiscriminate armaments can be addressed in multiple ways, however: not just by restricting or banning outright their use, but also through technological and scientific developments that make these weapons more discriminating, for example, time-limited landmines or precision-guided munitions of various kinds, including laser- and satellite-guided munitions fired from long-range or remotely piloted vehicles (i.e., drones).

This targeting ability actually arose much earlier, with the invention of optical and then adjustable telescopic sights and various technology (including hexagonal polygonal rifling and breech-loading) that made rifles far more accurate, and the use of snipers subsequently became an effective military tactic. "Because of their precision, snipers have proven their worth in combat where insurgents often hide among civilians. Using snipers shows the greatest amount of restraint," said Jim Lechner, a retired Army lieutenant colonel who served in Ramadi, Iraq, "Innocent people are not getting killed."[2]

## Technology's Double-Edged Sword

When targeted properly, "smart" (or at least "smarter") weapons can greatly reduce collateral damage to civilians,[3] and are much more precise than sending in ground troops for street sweeps, for example, with its concomitant collateral damage. Technological advancements are driven by a cluster of concerns, including increasing efficiency and protecting one's own soldiers from exposure—all of which have redounded to civilians' benefit.

Despite promoting civilian well-being, there are two major reasons why improved targeting capabilities are nonetheless troubling: (1) disconnect with expectations, and (2) "fair fight" considerations. While it is unclear that wartime atrocities are any worse in conventional warfare, it often seems so, perhaps because the large scale of conventional warfare and its concurrent technological developments are associated with the killing of both more and fewer civilians. Chemical and biological weapons as well as ever more powerful bombs can instantly kill on an almost-inconceivable scale, and scaling war up inevitably means killing more civilians in *absolute* terms. Yet, so long as reasonable attempts are made to properly target, increased accuracy means killing *proportionally* fewer civilians—and then expectations for fewer casualties rise alongside expanded technological capacity. This glaring gap between contemporary expectations and the practice of warfare enhances the perception that things have gotten worse. When there were no requirements for restraint, humanitarianism, or discrimination, there was, unfortunately, nothing to be disappointed about.[4]

Simultaneously, many people, including military members, view advanced targeted weaponry with ambivalence and suspicion, because it runs afoul of the notion of a "fair fight." In which direction the tension between fair fights and protecting civilians will ultimately be reconciled in practice is as yet unclear, but both present problems.

If it is resolved in favor of "fair fights," such that targeted long-range munitions (e.g., drone strikes) are restricted, then civilians will absorb more casualties, because closer-range combat (e.g., ground invasions) causes more collateral damage, especially in densely populated areas where drone strikes would be most effective. Given the existing rules of engagement for both scenarios, civilian casualties from ground invasions would greatly outnumber those by targeted drone strikes, so from the perspective of saving lives, it would be better to use remote technology. But *how* those civilians die makes a difference to how people perceive those deaths, and a larger number of civilian deaths from closer-range battle (where there might be at least the veneer of a possibility of fighting back) may seem more acceptable than fewer deaths of victims who may not even have known it was coming.

If the tension is resolved in the other direction, in favor of civilian protection, then targeted weaponry would be used as much as possible. Short- to medium-run utilitarian calculations of civilian deaths point to using targeted technology more frequently, but the long-run calculation is less clear. The perceived unfairness of those resulting deaths—even if they are fewer in number—would and do continue to further inflame resentments and aggravate the conflict in the long term. Said a Yemeni lawyer in 2012, "Dear Obama, when a US drone missile kills a child in Yemen, the father will go to war with you, guaranteed. Nothing to do with Al Qaeda."[5] Perhaps that antipathy would have been stoked for other reasons without the drone attack, but nonetheless, the fixation on the manner of attack and death is consequential.

In addition, there are questions asked of targeted killings using drones that generally are not asked about snipers: what a battlefield is and when one is in a zone of combat,[6] whether war should be confined to it, under what circumstances one can legitimately kill off of it, and who is a legitimate target. Snipers were generally aiming at fighters they could see (with optical assistance), but combat drones are piloted by soldiers far afield of the battleground and targets often include the enemy's political and religious leaders. This also returns us to chapter 3's discussion about protections for political leaders, and raises other questions as well: When are relations in a state of peace? Is targeted killing murder or acceptable military action?

## The Limits of Discrimination

Over time, these ethics of cooperation have exhibited increasing concern with discrimination, for example, disdain for the use of poison gas, which spreads of its own accord and cannot be targeted in the same way as some other weapons ("fair fight"), or maintaining the distinction between civilians and combatants (protecting certain groups).

Yet, there are limits to the amount of discrimination desired—in fact, it turns out that too *much* discrimination should not exercised either. For example, targeted killings or assassinations of key political figures, even of those who bear much of the responsibility for a war's injustices, still seem unfair from a fighting perspective, even as killing tens of thousands of soldiers who bear no responsibility for the decision to go to or continue war does not.

Similarly, both the moral equality of combatants and its corresponding moral equality of civilians divide the population into broad, crude categories that in most cases do not correspond to individual desert.[7] Yet it is done not just because of philosophical, epistemic, and practical limitations in determining distinct responsibility, but also because placement in one category as opposed to the other has enormous ramifications for one's chances of being killed, so the decision is made to err on the side of overinclusiveness in the civilian category. While the ethic of cooperation in warfare seeks to distinguish between people who are liable to be killed, and while there is a strong trend in international ethics over time to move toward a more individualistic lens of analysis (including in moral matters), there is some squeamishness about distinguishing *too* much in certain ways—perhaps to the detriment of the population at large.

## Unintended Consequences and Greater Harm

### *When "Fair Fights" Meet Technological Development*

In addition to making it harder to win, "fair fights" can cause more damage overall. For example, the kind of open, linear engagement that is stereotypical of eighteenth- and nineteenth-century European battles—soldiers dressed in national uniforms, lined up in formation, shooting in unison—did not adapt well to technological advancements, especially of long-range, more accurate artillery. Too many instances demonstrate the tragedy of preexisting (cooperatively based) tactics meeting new machinery: e.g., the Napoleonic Wars and the Battle of Solferino, the American Civil War, and the World War I trenches, to name but a few.[8]

The negotiated cooperation of a "fair fight" yields behaviors that draw from certain antecedent ideas about what it means to be a soldier, about right and honorable ways to do battle. As a result, this conduct becomes entrenched in individual soldiers as not just expedient, but moreover virtuous and ethical. Military tacticians might otherwise have been quicker to adapt to the horrific carnage, but such connections between negotiated behaviors and the seemingly "eternal" soldierly virtues hindered the evolution of the ethic of cooperation in warfare in response to modern technological developments. In part because these modes of engagement had become associated with and grounded in virtue ethics,[9] however, soldiers mistakenly thought they were locked into a narrow—calamitous—choice set.[10]

Sadly, the catastrophic lessons from the full-frontal fighting of the Napoleonic Wars had not yet been pushed beyond the limits of tragedy, and the vicious interaction between tactical conservatism and technological progress continued in the American Civil War (1861–65), as with Pickett's Charge at Gettysburg (1863). Officers and soldiers alike knew they were doomed, but they marched anyway—deliberately, in unison, and aligned—across three-quarters of a mile of open fields, climbing over fences along the way, all the while taking heavy artillery fire. Only when within a few hundred feet of the enemy did they charge, and by then, their mile-long front had shrunken to half the length, as men fell steadily and their neighbors filled in the gaps.

The linear battle tactics that had been used for over sixty years and accompanying field works met with modern artillery and firepower that had longer range, improved accuracy, and more rapid fire, such as Minié bullets and—by the end of the war—repeating rifles. Once again, there was little adjustment away from frontal assault tactics, except in ways that only made things worse, including digging into field works and trenches that presaged World War I. Technology was rapidly outpacing tactical evolution, and these and other resulting deaths throughout the war were all the madder because little was learned from them—European observers at the American Civil War only honed these techniques for the stalemated trenches of the First World War.

It should be apparent by now that some "unfair" actions or situations might actually be more beneficial than "fair" ones. After all, says Hastings, "Sniping merely represented the highest refinement of the infantry soldier's art. Its exercise required courage and skill."[11] Targeted killing, especially as enhanced by technology, is potentially more accurate and can kill fewer people more efficiently, in comparison with the chaos and destruction of throwing troops against one another in large-scale, pitched battle, or house-to-house searches, during which many bystanders can be killed. Yet, somehow, those are often seen as more fair because everyone is subject to the randomness, even as more people must die in order to reach a conclusion. As courageous as it is to adhere to "fair fight" ethics in pitched battle, it unfortunately does not make much sense given that the object of war is not its physical action, but rather its political outcome. There is something to be said for being more efficient about warfare, especially since the major resource in question is not equipment or other material goods, but rather human life.

## *When Protections Backfire*

### CEASE-FIRES AND HUMANITARIAN PAUSES

Like the cooperative "fair fight" ethos, the collaborative ethic to protect certain classes of people could make it harder to win the war and, ironically, ultimately do more harm. Ethically motivated cooperation to distinguish between fighters and civilians manifests in striking ways, such as cease-fires (usually in the context of peacekeeping) and their related humanitarian pauses and humanitarian corridors, which operate in stark contrast to the sieges they are meant to relieve. They seek to supply the basic needs of residents caught in conflict zones and provide safe passages out and corridors for food, medical supplies, medical treatment, fuel, and other essentials into the community. These cease-fires are usually brief, lasting anywhere from a few hours to several days per agreement, during which aid workers must work furiously to reach as many people as possible, after which fighting immediately resumes if no longer-term agreements have been reached. They have been used in a variety of places, including Yemen, the Gaza Strip, and Syria, and it can be inspiring to see people set aside their visceral hatred and intractable differences in order to allow attendance to otherwise besieged civilians swept up in the carnage.

Problems arise, however, when participants are insincere. People often continue fighting because of the obvious advantage in attacking while the other side has laid down arms. Cease-fires and humanitarian pauses have also frequently been opportunities for combatants to rearm.[12]

This raises the question of what a cease-fire is for. Although it is often thought of as a step in progress toward peace, it does not have to be intended as such.[13] Temporary stays of combat without any such implications have historical precedents. Toward the end of *The Iliad*, Achilles is moved by the plight of Priam, who has braved great danger to personally and humbly beg for the return of his son's body. Achilles asks:

> ". . . Tell me, be precise about it—
> How many days do you need to bury Prince Hector?
> I will hold back myself
> and keep the Argive armies back that long."
> And the old and noble Priam answered slowly,
> "If you truly want me to give Prince Hector burial,
> full, royal honors, you'd show me a great kindness,
> Achilles, if you would do exactly as I say.
> You know how crammed we are inside our city,
> how far it is to the hills to haul in timber,
> and our Trojans are afraid to make the journey.
> Well, nine days we should mourn him in our halls,
> on the tenth we'd bury Hector, hold the public feast,
> on the eleventh build the barrow high above his body—
> on the twelfth we'd fight again . . . if fight we must."
> The swift runner Achilles reassured him quickly:
> "All will be done, old Priam, as you command.
> I will hold our attack as long as you require."
> With that he clasped the old king by the wrist,
> by the right hand, to free his heart from fear.
> (24.771–90)

In this case, the cease-fire was a gesture of respect, to allow fulfillment of certain paternal and religious obligations.

A cease-fire can also be seen as good in and of itself. For example, there are separate Arabic and Hebrew terms for temporary truce or cease-fire (*hudna* هدنة or *hafsakat esh*) and for calm/calming down or lull (*tahadiya* or *hafuga*, respectively). While both suspend military action for a period of time, the former is generally seen as a binding arrangement and could be years long,[14] while the latter is usually short and more informal.[15] There is disagreement, however, about their parameters[16] and respective purposes: while some view *hudna* as a potential means to and part of the peace process, rather than as an end in itself,[17] others intend it as merely a tactic in warfare. "It means the cessation of hostilities, which does not necessarily imply the end of conflict. It's the standard term for an armistice," says Rashid Khalidi, Columbia University Middle East Institute director.[18] For example, a West Bank Hamas leader, Sheikh Hassan Yousef, emphasizes that *hudna* "articulates the status of conflict with the enemy, . . . it expresses the continuity of conflict," and, according to sources, Hamas "conditioned [*hudna*] upon the Palestinians' continued ability to prepare for a future stage of conflict."[19] Exiled Hamas leader Khaled Meshaal has said that cease-fire can be "a tactic in conducting the struggle. . . . It is normal for any resistance that operates in its people's interest . . . to sometimes escalate, other times retreat a bit. . . . The battle is to be run this way and Hamas is known for that."[20] Viewing it in this light starts to blur the distinction between *hudna* and *tahadiya*.

Whether or not a cease-fire includes humanitarian provision, if one party contextualizes it within a process toward peace (e.g., by giving people time to assess their respective situations, creating space for less-heated negotiations, or serving as a confidence-building measure), then the other side using the cease-fire as simply a pause without intent to work toward resolving the conflict (e.g., by taking the opportunity to rearm) will appear to constitute cheating on the agreement, whether in letter or in spirit. The ensuing bad faith between parties may ultimately do more to derail the possibility of peace than if the fighting had simply been allowed to continue until its natural end.[21]

Despite the best of intentions and enormous resources and effort, both humanitarian pauses/cease-fires and humanitarian aid can prolong conflict and have often unwittingly done so. At any given point in a war, one side or another expects to win, so any cessation in hostilities will favor one side or another, leaving the unfavored party wanting to continue fighting. Says political scientist Edward Luttwak:

> An unpleasant truth often overlooked is that although war is a great evil, it does have a great virtue: it can resolve political conflicts and

lead to peace. This can happen when all belligerents become exhausted or when one wins decisively. Either way the key is that the fighting must continue until a resolution is reached. War brings peace only after passing a culminating phase of violence. Hopes of military success must fade for accommodation to become more attractive than further combat.[22]

As a result, pauses that enable the flailing side to recuperate and resupply (including arms) only "snatch[es] from the party that is prevailing the consummation of the victory it believes it has earned through its expenditure of blood and treasure," explains legal scholar W. Michael Reisman. Victory by one side or another is what ends conflict, so pauses may merely exacerbate matters.[23] As one of my university history professors once said of the endless cycles of violence, cease-fires, and renewed fighting in the Middle East, "Sometimes, you have to let them fight it out, or there will be no resolution." (Others may object, of course, that "no resolution" may be the least worst resolution.)

Money is fungible, and it and other resources given for humanitarian purposes are easily diverted, if not outright stolen, in ways that indirectly prop up bad regimes, allow them to shirk their essential responsibilities, or contribute to rearmament. Drawn by the benefits, combatants pretend to be noncombatants, or harass and coerce both aid beneficiaries and aid workers—and the more resources to contest, the fiercer the fighting can be.[24] Peacekeepers and other enforcers, as well as warring parties, sometimes lose leverage as it becomes clear that there are certain things that they will not do in prosecuting the peace.

Cooperating to limit damage to both civilians and opposing soldiers (through particular regulations for POW treatment, humanitarian pauses, and so on) is born of the best of intentions, but it *can* make it harder to win the war and therefore prolong the fighting and cause more net destruction (death, injury, starvation, hardship) over the duration of the conflict than, perhaps, if the suffering had been more intense but the war had ended sooner. Again, this is not to say that all shorter, sharper engagements will be less harmful overall than longer ones with greater attention to humanitarian concerns—but it is certainly a possibility that must be taken seriously.

Whether or not wars should be approached in such a utilitarian manner cannot be settled here, but it is important to note that sincere cooperation between enemies in order to ameliorate harm can lead to inadvertent, and sometimes contradictory, consequences. Cease-fires and humanitarian pauses are hardly the first time in the history of warfare that this has happened.

It is an irony embedded in the laws of war that their good intentions can nonetheless cause greater violence. Contrary to common belief that the lesson to be learned from the devastation of the American Civil War was "that the laws of war cannot constrain the machinery of industrialized warfare" and that General Orders No. 100 were merely a shield to deflect the hypocrisy, in fact, argues Witt, Sherman's assault on Atlanta and ensuing path of destruction from there to Savannah "was not a betrayal of the law of war. It was the practical embodiment of the code's unsettling critique of the orthodox laws of war."[25]

The Enlightenment project's "moral logic of war" tried to limit war's damages by rejecting the idea that the pursuit of justice legitimizes almost any action. It saw the destruction wrought in the name of justice, and argued that because only God could know which side was just, humans must therefore fight with some restraint and artificial impositions, for humanity's sake. In recognizing that there would always be some uncertainty about which side—if any—possessed *jus ad bellum*, it imposed complementary constraints on what soldiers were responsible for and what they could do to one another.[26] The problem was, as Witt describes,

> [Sherman's] humanitarian critics evaluated each case . . . in isolation, as if unconnected to the broader war effort, its aims, or its future ramifications. They condemned no-quarter warfare or violence against civilians without regard to the ends in view. What Sherman had keenly grasped was that the laws of war in the modern age had set aside the just war tradition's concerns with right and wrong and replaced them with a new ethic of humanitarian constraint, an ethic that dismissed questions of justice as ultimately unresolvable.[27]

Sherman, as well as Lieber, believed that pursuing those Enlightenment-inspired humanitarian goals in such narrow, piecemeal ways missed the forest for the trees, for no matter which way you cut it, war was "barbarism" and "cruelty," so better to end it quickly—and "the more awful you can make war the sooner it will be over."[28] Sherman was stepping back, says Witt, and taking the importance of humanitarianism more broadly, and looking at the war as a whole.

### THE PARADOX OF PRIVATE PROPERTY PROTECTIONS

This distressing paradox in the history of humanitarianism can be aptly illustrated with the American attempt to promote civilian livelihood by protecting their private property. At the time of the Revolution, safeguarding private property during war was a radical move, and was seen as related to civilian immunity. European jurists considered all enemy private property to be fair game for seizure. Alberico Gentili was hardly alone in considering it eminently "clear" that the law "grants the rights of war (*belli iura*) to both contestants, makes what is taken on each side the property of the captors, and regards the prisoners of both parties as slaves," and even if "injustice is clearly evident on one of the two sides," the "general principle" still holds.[29] For example, Vattel argues,

> We have a right to deprive our enemy of his possessions, of every thing which may augment his strength and enable him to make war. This every one endeavours to accomplish in the manner most suitable to him. Whenever we have an opportunity, we seize on the enemy's property, and convert it to our own use: and thus, besides diminishing the enemy's power, we augment our own, and obtain at least a partial indemnification or equivalent, either for what constitutes the subject of the war, or for the expenses and losses incurred in its prosecution:—in a word, we do ourselves justice.[30]

The new American nation birthed in the late eighteenth century took a different legal approach, however, in questioning the unmitigated right to spoils, and this inevitably became embroiled with the slavery question.

Early on, Benjamin Franklin tried to expand the treaties of war to encompass property rights. In 1780 and 1781, he argued that wars should be fought only between armies of professional soldiers so that everyone else may peacefully work for the "common benefit of mankind," that "farmers, fisherman & merchants" should be protected, and that property owners should be compensated for goods seized or pillaged. This idea was picked up in the Supreme Court's *Brown v. United States* 12 U.S. 110 (1814) ruling (which reaffirmed the "right to confiscate enemies' property" but did not automatically grant that right with an official declaration of war), James Kent's *Commentaries on American Law* (1826–30), and Henry Wheaton's *Elements of International Law* (1836) (which pointed to the "progress of civilization" and declared "private property on land . . . exempt from confiscation").[31] While this trajectory seems positive from a humanitarian perspective, there is more to the story. Says Witt:

> American statesmen embraced tight limits on the destructive powers of warring armies; they embraced greater limits on war's destruction than European jurists had ever thought possible. But for many Americans, the preservation of private property in slaves counted as one of the law's chief humanitarian accomplishments.[32]

The push to protect private property was motivated in part by the desire to protect slaveholders' property in their slaves (e.g., Jefferson, Quincy Adams), and the laws of war protected slave property and forbade inciting slaves into "servile insurrection," which Lincoln would upend part way through the American Civil War.[33]

During that war, the Lieber Code adhered to the dominant view that private property could be seized out of military necessity: "all captures and booty belong, according to the modern law of war, primarily to the government of the captor," subject to the standard restrictions on private gain and "wanton" or unauthorized violence (Arts. 37–38, 44–46).

When it came to slaves, however, the Lieber Code acknowledged that they "complicat[ed] and confound[ed] the idea of property . . . and humanity," and then declared that slavery was contrary to natural law and "exist[ed] according to municipal or local law only." As a result, escaped slaves to free territories were "immediately entitled to the rights and privileges of a freeman," and these rights belonged to him in perpetuity, so freemen could not be enslaved again after the war (Arts. 42, 43).

The opposition, however, appealed to the "basic standards of civilized conduct in wartime. 'Every civilized nation on earth,' they insisted, compensated property owners for property destroyed in wartime, including slave property."[34] In this respect, the international norms of "civilized" warfare were indeed on their side.

Two contrasting approaches throw the complexity of wartime humanitarianism into stark relief. Alexander Hamilton was one of the few prominent dissenters from early American advocacy of the sanctity of private property: he believed that the laws of war entitled one to plunder the private property of one's enemies—which included slaves—and he thought that the British army had been permitted to seize and free American slaves during the Revolutionary War.[35] On the other hand, Lincoln himself invoked the idea of slaves as property to argue for freeing them, writing to a Unionist opponent to the Emancipation Proclamation (1863):

> You dislike the emancipation proclamation; and, perhaps, would have it retracted. You say it is unconstitutional—I think differently. I think the constitution invests its commander-in-chief, with the law of war, in time of war. The most that can be said, if so much, is, that slaves are property. Is there—has there ever been—any question that by the law of war, property, both of enemies and friends, may be taken when needed? And is it not needed whenever taking it, helps us, or hurts the enemy? Armies, the world over, destroy enemies' property when they can not use it; and even destroy their own to keep it from the enemy. Civilized belligerents do all in their power to help themselves, or hurt the enemy, except a few things regarded as barbarous or cruel. Among the exceptions are the massacre of vanquished foes, and non-combatants, male and female.[36]

In making the case for emancipation, Lincoln reaches for the very norms of expansive conquering rights to property and person that are contrary to the more recent "advanced" understanding of warfare that seeks to distinguish between combatants and civilians and to leave civilians some modicum of livelihood. Although Lincoln championed emancipation for its own sake and makes that clear in this same letter, he was no stranger to political expediency, and his and Hamilton's uses of this wartime-claim-to-property argument show that humanitarian ideals can cut both ways. In Lincoln's case, the property argument was used to free slaves, but that same argument also has far nastier implications that would be difficult to block in other contexts. Protecting private property in order to defend civilian livelihood on humanitarian grounds had complicated, unintended implications, including for the concept of property and the ultimate fate of slaves/human property.

## ASSASSINATION AND THE ACCOUNTABILITY GAP

Similarly, collusion between elites to shelter political leaders may lead to many more deaths. The Lieber Code, for example, prohibits assassinations (Art. 148), as does contemporary international law. As discussed earlier and in chapter 3, assassination may be a case of too much discrimination. In the context of war as an instrument of politics, considering top political leaders to be civilians is at least as artificial as the civilian/combatant distinction, if not more. Not only is it questionable why one can legitimately kill a private or a seaman but not a civilian commander-in-chief, but political assassinations could certainly prevent or end wars as much as they can start them.

There may be good reasons to override considerations of individual desert and short-term military calculations in the service of building rapport between nations or limiting the spirals of recrimination and revenge in international affairs that would otherwise lead to an endless cycle of war. It is, after all, not so far-fetched to imagine that sanctioning political assassinations would also open the door to using that permission as cover to instead eliminate personal, economic, and political rivals, rather than attend to the rectification of geopolitical justice.[37] In a sentiment later echoed by Vattel and Kant, Cicero says,

> The foundation of justice . . . is good faith—that is, truth and fidelity to promises and agreements. . . . While wrong may be done . . . in either of two ways . . . by force or by fraud, both are bestial: fraud seems to belong to the cunning fox, force to the lion; both are wholly unworthy of man, but fraud is the more contemptible. But of all forms of injustice, none is more flagrant than that of the hypocrite who, at the very moment when he is most false, makes it his business to appear virtuous.[38]

Preserving whatever geopolitical stability there can be is essential, of course, but given that a mere "word of command" turns peacetime soldiers into mortal enemies and just as easily transforms them back again, more attention should be paid to how to hold political leaders responsible in a more systematic way for killing thousands, hundreds of thousands, or millions for their own petty feuds and vainglories. Unfortunately, ad hoc trials like Nuremberg or even the International Criminal Court are not nearly enough. I return to this persistent and troubling accountability gap in chapters 6 and 7.

### COMPENSATING BEHAVIOR

Unintended consequences are actually a common byproduct of trying to make safer various aspects of life.[39] For example, the implementation of safety equipment in American football and boxing prevents some injuries, but also causes others. Football helmets have reduced the incidences of broken teeth, noses, and jaws, as well as skull fractures and subdural hematomas,[40] and the number of deaths from football has declined by 10 percent. At the same time, they have increased spinal injuries, quadrupling the number of broken necks and permanent paraplegia.[41] This is because helmets became a tool for use in the game: players, ever enterprising, use it to "spear" and "gore," which can injure both the offensive actor (especially in the spine) and the recipient (especially in the head). Although helmets can reduce the chances of a concussion, they in fact increase that possibility if the player is hit harder and more often, as became the case with the mandate to wear helmets, because it seemed safer. Players changed how they played in response to the adoption of helmets, in ways that offset many of the benefits of helmet use—they compensated for these new regulations, and have made similar adjustments with every rule change in football.

A similar phenomenon occurred in boxing. Gloves were introduced for two purposes: to protect the hands of bare-knuckle fighters and to make fights more exciting by speeding them up (bare-knuckle matches could drag on for hours) and encouraging more shots to the head (bare-handed punches to hard facial and head bones injure the attacker). Freed of such concerns with their own hands, boxers now pummel their opponents' heads with heavy, padded gloves, resulting in more concussions, long-term mental deterioration, subdural hematomas, and death.[42]

As with injuries in sports, civilian casualties and deaths cannot be regulated out of war. Actors adjust their behavior in response to new conditions, which may in some cases reduce overall damage, but may also simply shift it to other areas.[43] Mandating equal medical care or a high standard of POW treatment for the enemy, for example, may lead some to kill injured adversaries or leave them to die in the field in order to avoid that burden, as opposed to collecting them but providing lesser treatment, a problem noted in chapter 3.

As with the "fair fight" ethic, we see tension between the cooperative ethic to protect classes of individuals and the purpose of warfare. In the course of trying to fight "well" and to reduce harm to groups of people, the parties' ability to reach a settlement through fighting is hindered. Insofar as combat is the chosen (willingly or not) method of conflict resolution, such attempts to bring some order and meaning to the senselessness of war and to minimize injury may in fact ironically cause more damage and render it more meaningless.

The adverse effects of cooperation to protect particular classes of people are actually even more serious than that of "fair fights." Both can wreak more havoc, but in the case of "fair fights," that harm is merely an unintended consequence, whereas in protecting classes of people (such as through cease-fires or humanitarian pauses), the damage runs directly counter to the intention of that ethic.

## Sabotaging Victory

The ultimate aim of most wars is to end the fighting and enact a sustainable political solution as quickly as possible. "Fair fight" considerations (including parity) and humanitarian protections, however, have no direct relationship with producing a result for war. These purposes run along nonintersecting and contradictory tracks, and this dilemma can be succinctly illustrated by POW treatment, which, like other areas of cooperation, is motivated by multiple considerations.

### *Limited Resources*

POW status and treatment are negotiated conventions, ones that can siphon valuable resources from war efforts. For example, German POWs in the United States during World War II served notably high-quality detention, such as in various Texas camps. In between reveille at 5:45 AM and lights off at 10:00 PM, they were paid for their work through local labor programs and received many perks, including a variety of educational programs and the ability to learn, make, and sell handicrafts. There were POW-taught courses on a range of topics such as English or engineering, performances by the POW orchestra and theater troupe, team sports in soccer, handball, and volleyball, and news dispensed through the camp newspaper. Prisoners who took correspondence courses from local colleges and universities received academic credit from German institutions when they returned.[44]

As disturbing as any POW experience would be, this was, all things considered, a rather good state of existence. It was undoubtedly provided so that word of such conditions might encourage Germans to surrender and Germany to treat its American POWs well, but it also cost significant resources and yielded a standard of living sometimes higher than that of the surrounding civilians. Might these resources have been better used to try to win the war more quickly, which would have checked overall harm to soldiers and civilians alike? Even for a country with resources as vast as the United States' and certainly for losing parties in a war, that would be a consideration.

### Parity of Randomness: Snipers and Drone Warfare

In modern warfare, the purpose of physical engagement in war is not to kill the enemy per se, but rather to kill enough of the enemy's soldiers such that he surrenders. As American General George S. Patton reportedly said, "I want you to remember that no bastard ever won a war by dying for his country. He won it by making the other poor, dumb bastard die for his country."[45] Any opportunity that the soldier has to get closer to that goal should be taken.

Yet, those aforementioned Austrian soldiers, World War I snipers, and Indian and Pakistani air forces from chapter 2 all refrained, despite having legitimate—even good—reasons to shoot or bomb, because at the moment, they were stricken at least in part with concern for a certain kind of "fairness" in war. Yet, any "fair fight" restraint simply makes it harder to win.

Snipers have been used by Western militaries for centuries, but have only recently acquired a noble and heroic reputation. Historically, they were disdained for unfairly and dishonorably killing from afar someone unaware of his presence. For example, filmmaker Michael Moore declared publicly upon the release of biopic *American Sniper,* "My uncle killed by sniper in WW2. We were taught snipers were cowards. Will shoot u in the back. Snipers aren't heroes. And invaders r worse [sic]."[46]

The fair fight ethic leads to shooters sometimes holding back as well as a general hatred of snipers, both of which are attempts to constrain some of the randomness of war and impose what modicum of order can be imposed. Nonmilitary are not alone in harboring this sentiment. Snipers themselves have felt ambivalent about their tasks, as evidenced in chapter 2, as well as here: During the American Civil War, a Whitworth rifleman with a Georgia cavalry regiment missed a Union horseman surveying the Confederate line when the horseman unexpectedly urged the horse to move, and he hit the horse instead: "By golly! I missed him, and I was sure I'd get him. Well, his time had not come to die to-day, and I am not sorry that he got away. It looked too much like murder. . . . He was a brave fellow, and I hope he'll get through all right."[47]

Moreover, snipers have been feared, loathed, and sometimes jeered by their own colleagues, as being both bloodthirsty and unjust.[48] Recalls US Marine sniper Jack Coughlin, "Back in Vietnam, our own people called us 'Murder, Inc.' They thought we were psychopathic killers,"[49] and in the 1980s, a British infantry battalion referred to its own sniper section as "The Leper Colony."[50] Snipers were held in such contempt that they were sometimes summarily executed by the other side upon capture, in contravention of established laws of war[51] and with the approval of senior officers. There were certainly more than a few instances of extrajudicial revenge. During World War II, US First Army Assistant Division Commander Lt. Col. Chester B. Hansen wrote in his diary:

> [General Omar] Brad[ley] says he will not take any action against anyone that decides to treat snipers a little more roughly than they are being treated at present. A sniper cannot sit around and shoot and expect capture when you close in on him. That's not the way to play the game.[52]

Although snipers play an important role in military operations, they are frequently considered by enemy and associate alike to be more murderers and killers—assassins at best—than soldiers.

Why is this the case? One reason, as journalist Max Hastings explains, is that "sniping made the random business of killing, in which they were all engaged, become somehow personal and thus unacceptable to ordinary footsoldiers."[53] Adds military history writer Martin Pegler:

> Generally, most soldiers can abandon their peacetime beliefs, when faced with killing to survive or to protect comrades, and such a choice is regarded as morally acceptable. Yet the concept of a soldier deliberately stalking a human quarry as one would an animal was to most infantrymen a repugnant one. One reason for the discomfort of combat soldiers was undoubtedly that among them the sniper was unique in literally having the ability to hold life or death in his hands and, suddenly, death was personal. . . . Few other soldiers ever had the questionable luxury of deciding whom to kill or when. To the average soldier, war was a matter of obeying orders, so the majority were able to treat fighting as a relatively impersonal job to be done as quickly and at as little risk as possible.[54]

War—especially the large-scale conflicts between conscripted nation-state militaries, utilizing broad- and long-range weapons such as artillery and machine guns—is a haphazard, confusing, anonymous, and accidental affair. Surviving is largely a matter of luck, so it is easy to see how soldiers would resent being personally targeted by snipers in that way.

Animosity toward snipers reflects the sense of foul play that is repeatedly invoked. For example:

> Sniping, as far as I know, is recognized as a legitimate means of warfare. And yet there is something sneaking about it that outrages the American sense of fairness [said journalist Ernie Pyle on the World War II European theatre].[55]

> There was a general feeling among other troops that the sharpshooter did not "play fair," and in some way violated the unwritten rules of war. One Northerner complained that sharpshooters would "sneak around trees or lurk behind stumps" and from this vantage point "murder a few men."[56]

This attitude is understandable and had much to do with the traditional ideals of waging "sporting" warfare.[57]

Even though the skill and bravery of sharpshooters earned the respect of many, there was a general feeling that they did not play fair, taking advantage of the burdens endured by the troops on both sides of the line. A Union infantryman recalled the unwritten code of honour that forbade soldiers firing on an enemy when "attending to the call of nature, but these sharpshooting brutes were constantly violating that rule." Another Union soldier succinctly expressed a revulsion felt by many: "I hated sharpshooters, both Confederate and Union, and I was always glad to see them killed." As the Civil War drew to a close, so the ambivalent picture of the sniper was completed: a figure halfway between an elite infantryman and a common murderer.[58]

Over and over again, the word *sporting* or *fair* shows up in discussions about warfare ethics and *jus in bello*. War is not an athletic game, and the influence has largely run in the other direction—from war to sports—yet the vocabulary of athletic competitions is repeatedly used to succinctly describe a sentiment that has much in common with its sports counterpart. As we saw in chapter 2, in both sports and war, fairness or sporting-ness often refers to some kind of parity between opponents: of ability, equipment, exposure to risk, and opportunity to win.[59]

Yet, for however much these sentiments and concepts resonate, sniping is an effective way of killing, and insofar as wars are won by killing, considerations of fairness should have no part in a narrow, purely functional vision of war.

### Battle Function Versus War Function, Revisited

On some understandings of warfare and certainly most modern ones, physical comparability between soldiers or nations has no place because, ironically, war is not really about the physical fight. The military objective of defeating the enemy on the battlefield is only relevant in the service of an overarching political goal—"to impose our will upon the enemy"[60]—because the fight is ultimately about geopolitics. In Clausewitzean terms,[61] warfare is a political tool, not an end in itself, so striving for parity within these means seems crazy. Although war will never be "purely rational," it will always be political:

> 23.— . . . war has its origin in a political object, we see that this first motive, which called it into existence, naturally remains the first and highest consideration to be regarded in its conduct. But the political object is not on that account a despotic lawgiver; it must adapt itself to the nature of the means at its disposal and is often thereby completely changed, but it must always be the first thing to be considered . . .
>
> 24.—*War is a mere continuation of policy by other means.*
> . . . war is not merely a political act but a real political instrument, a continuation of political intercourse, a carrying out of the same by other means. What now still remains peculiar to war relates merely to the peculiar nature of the means which it uses. . . . The political design is the object, while war is the means, and the means can never be thought of apart from the object.[62]

To that end, war is actually not a contest of physical prowess, military expertise, or strategic acumen. It is all those things, of course, but it is also a method of dispute settlement, whether a geopolitical contest or a disagreement about justice.

This becomes especially salient as combat technology advances: the more "high-tech" war becomes, the less it is related to application of martial skill, to the degree that it may in some forms of fighting have nothing to do with martial prowess at all (e.g., RPA operators, despite the US Air Force's continued insistence that they be trained pilots). This lack of martial exercise is one of the reasons drone warfare seems unfair, and it raises the question of whether someone launching an attack in Yemen from a base in Nevada, for example, is engaged in soldiering, per se. While RPA piloting requires an enormous amount of skill, is it *martial* skill?

Even if so, martial skill bears no direct relation to Clausewitzian rational war aims and may even counter them—its exercise and display are relevant to the activity of soldiering and warfighting, but not, strictly speaking, to the political objective of the victory. In some sense, the physical activity of war is incidental—its primary object is to induce a political or judicial rendering.

## The Search for Significance

Those who are moved to practice "fair fight" ethics in combat are usually not thinking about the war's overarching political or justicial objective: they often hold independent reasons for a "fair fight." Obviously, maintaining parity between states is not possible in geopolitical conflicts. In fact, the opposite might be true: one might tend toward picking fights against opponents one can win against. Still, among individual soldiers, there is ample evidence of repeated concern for equality of risk and opportunity, within certain parameters, when none is required or advised.

The cooperative "fair fight" ethic reflects a circumscribed conception of war as an activity in itself, as a self-enclosed contest between soldiers in some way. This reaction is challenging, but understandable. For many warfighters, especially modern-day ones in large national militaries, there is little connection between their actions or interests and the larger geopolitical conflict, and as a result, the activities of their daily lives—killing the enemy and surviving—become ends in themselves. It is unsurprising that soldiers would want to both become better at these tasks and establish some norms for them, for it is the only thing that allows them to continue on in so barbaric and horrific an activity. Said Korean War MASH surgeon Otto Apel of the desperation he confronted every day: "Like all aspects of war, with time we relegate the misery to the far side of our memories, and we glorify the mythical, the heroic, the things that justify the loss and the pain of conflict. That is the only way we can fight the next war. We forget the human consequences."[63]

Even as we forget, however, there is an equally strong human desire to make sense of the often inexplicable and incomprehensible calamity of war, all the more so for those who suffer it. Says Lt. Gen. Harold G. Moore, of his time in Vietnam, "It wasn't our place to question. We were soldiers and we followed their orders. In times and places like this, where the reasons for war are lacking, soldiers fight and die for each other."[64]

For most warfighters, the physical engagement is the only world they know, so they focus on bringing order to that which they can control. Confronted with war's inescapable inanity, soldiers look for meaning. Establishing codes of conduct internal to the activity—such as fulfilling martial virtues or maintaining norms for a certain kind of fairness in the contest—is one way of coping with tragedy beyond one's control or understanding.

## What Is the Best Way to Win?

As the rules and norms of war are also subject to compensating behavior, unintended consequences, and adverse effects, so we must revisit the question of how best to achieve whatever purpose that war serves. Here, perhaps, there may be a certain complementarity between different types of the ethic of cooperation in warfare, and problems within one might be addressed by another. One major shortcoming of the "fair fight" ethic is that this courtesy is not extended to every warrior one meets—only to some (chapter 2). Throughout history, people have exercised their discretion to fight in one way against one set of peoples and simultaneously quite differently against another. The respect accorded by a "fair fight" has been used to draw boundaries between civilized and uncivilized, between acceptable and unacceptable, between worthy and intolerable—to pernicious and sometimes genocidal effect.

One way to combat the delineation of exclusionary boundaries is to impose a different ethical categorization that trumps this one. In effect, that is what happened with the prioritization of civilian immunity through both international ethical evolution and legal instantiation. Now, the dominant ethical and legal distinction between people in war is whether one is considered a fighter or immune. As such, all the courtesies that are due to another fighter are owed to *all* fighters, as dictated by international law, regardless of one's personal or tribal beliefs about the opponent's worthiness. Concurrently, all considerations due to bystanders are now due to *all* civilians. Thus, the LOAC declares that the ethic of cooperation to protect certain classes of individuals takes precedence—ethically, socially, and legally—over "fair fight" considerations.

But these restrictions, too, can prolong the conflict, cause more damage, and make it harder for one side to win and thus for a conclusion to be reached. And as with any typology, what falls within and without the boundaries of categorization can be problematic.

## Structural Cooperation to End War Quickly

Perhaps this is where the ethic of cooperation to end war quickly might be of service, as that is its primary function, after all. Although the contemporary world would be hard-pressed to accept such an ethic, because of both an unachievable desire for permanent definitiveness to war and an unreasonable ideal of a soldier fighting not as a gladiator and only for love of his country (chapter 4), this possibility should be explored.

### POLITICAL DUELS

The proposal from 2002 for a duel between then Iraqi and American presidents Saddam Hussein and George W. Bush, instead of going to war, nicely illustrates this difficulty. Challenged Iraqi vice president Taha Yassin Ramadan:

> Bush wants to attack the whole Iraq, the army and the infrastructure. If such a call is genuine, then let the American president and a selected group with him face a selected group of us and we choose a neutral land and let [UN secretary-general] Kofi Annan be a supervisor and both groups should use the same weapon. A president against a president and vice president against a vice president, and a duel takes place, if they are serious. And in this way we are saving the American and Iraqi people.[65]

The American White House and population scoffed at the idea, of course, but why should the proposal not have been seriously considered? Ramadan could not have argued it better: Rather than invading an entire country, killing tens or hundreds of thousands of soldiers and civilians, and crippling a country for decades by destroying infrastructure, why not "[save] the American and Iraqi people" with a *monomachia* duel between those responsible for the political decisions leading these countries to war?

The idea was dismissed out of hand for two main reasons. The first is the ethic of cooperation to protect political leaders (chapter 3), even as they remain both the most responsible and the least accountable for the damages of war. The second is that a cooperative ethic to end war quickly is so difficult to develop and sustain that few would take any form of this seriously as a way to reach a political settlement.

But why not? Why is throwing hundreds of thousands of soldiers into war to kill one another a better way of resolving the conflict? The practice of dueling to settle political disputes has not always been frowned upon. While many duels are fought over matters of personal honor, a significant number have tried to settle political disagreements. In addition to the early Mediterranean practice of *monomachia* (chapter 4), the famous Burr/Hamilton duel (1804) between the sitting US vice president and the former secretary of the treasury was a product of not just personal animosity but also long-standing political rivalry, which included charges of corruption, abuse of office, and the like. Indeed, throughout most of history, there has been little separation between the two, and political accusations are intended and taken as personal charges. Even Abraham Lincoln was challenged and agreed to a duel (albeit reluctantly) in 1842 when he wrote a satirical letter insulting Illinois state auditor James Shields over the refusal to accept now-invalid notes from the recently defunct State Bank of Illinois for tax payments.[66] Of course, one cannot forget Greek antiquity, when Paris and Menelaus swore that they would

> . . . fight it out for Helen and all her wealth.
> And the one who proves the better man and wins,
> he'll take those treasures fairly, lead the woman home.
> The rest will seal in blood their binding pacts of friendship.
> [The men of Ilium] will live in peace on the rich soil of Troy,
> [the Achaeans] sail home to the stallion-land of Argos.
> (3.85–91)

"The Achaean and Trojan forces both exulted, / hoping *this* would end the agonies of war" (3.135–36), but the gods intervened to spark the breaking of this truce,[67] and by the end of "that day ranks of Trojans, ranks of Achaean fighters / sprawled there side-by-side, facedown in the dust" (4.629–30). Paris and Menelaus's duel is one of the early and poignant examples of this long-standing desire, revisited again and again, to resolve conflicts neatly and minimally. For all its potential virtues, that this monomachia failed to settle the outcome of the war speaks to the instability and inconclusiveness of bounded fair fights—if the gods want war, they will get war, and humans are no different.

One of the few advantages to a broadly engaging war as opposed to limited duels between leaders or champions is that the more the population is involved, the more they will buy in to the endeavor and the outcome, which may be necessary to win.[68] But it is not obvious that the population at large would be heavily and personally entangled in a war effort, especially given the division of labor and technological advancements in modern societies;[69] even if it were, would that be worth the trade-off and cost in human lives?

In between the extremes of impunity for guilty political leaders and rampant, chaos-inducing political assassinations, and aside from duel combat between political leaders, might there be other ways to address responsibility for starting an unjust war? Historically, exile has actually not been uncommon, although it is usually not the first thing that comes to mind when thinking of possible punishments for political injustices. Both coerced and self-imposed exile have been used for a variety of purposes, including for retribution or other punishment, to serve political justice, and to smooth tenuous political transitions. (Exile can also be more literal and comprehensive, i.e., physical banishment from a territory, or can take a more limited form, e.g., excommunication from a religious community.)[70]

Despite soldiers bearing the brunt of the war, political leaders have been loath to extend humanitarianism into actual combat beyond neutral medical care, some of which is provided by third parties such as International Committee of the Red Cross (est. 1863). For example, Field Marshall and Prussian/German Chief of General Staff Helmuth Karl Bernhard Graf von Moltke acknowledged the importance of international ethical norms and believed they should be reflected in the law,[71] but nonetheless doubted that better conditions for soldiers could be codified into existence:[72]

> Success can come only from the religious, moral education of individuals, and from the feeling of honour and sense of justice of commanders who enforce the law and conform to it, so far as the exceptional circumstances of war permit. . . . Increased humanity in the mode of making war has in reality followed upon the gradual softening of manners.

In the meantime, soldiers are not saints, and in their suffering, they will behave badly. "It is impossible for the soldier who endures sufferings, hardships, fatigues, who meets danger to take only 'in proportion to the resources of the country.' He must take whatever is needful for his existence. We cannot ask him for what is superhuman," concedes Moltke, therefore, "the greatest kindness in war is to bring it to a speedy conclusion. It should be allowable with that view to employ all methods save those which are absolutely objectionable."[73]

So while many political leaders would prefer nonviolent means of settling disputes and, if it did come to violence, they would of course be quite concerned for the well-being of their valiant soldiers, it is still never in doubt that it is *soldiers*—as opposed to other parties—who must die in order to violently settle disputes.

Despite its certain advantages, structural cooperation to settle conflict quickly such as duels between political leaders is politically unacceptable and a nonstarter in the contemporary world.

Yet, nothing about war requires that it have a monopoly on yielding political solutions, and in fact, political agreements are frequently reached through other means, such as diplomatic negotiations or coercive measures short of violence (e.g., sanctions). When it comes to overt violent resolution, however, political determination is generally not permitted in other violent arenas and is confined to traditional battlefields, and responsible political leaders remain troublingly unaccountable.

## OTHER VIABLE STRUCTURAL ALTERNATIVES

Although collaboration for succinct warfare is usually limited to its structure, it does not have to be; it can govern the way people fight. The first formal weapons ban agreement, the Saint Petersburg Declaration (1868), actually bans explosive bullets *under* a certain weight (four hundred grams), in order to prevent unnecessary anguish. Explosive bullets that are too light are unlikely to kill and would only cause suffering, so the treaty intended for warring parties to use heavier explosive bullets or regular bullets, to help ensure lethality. The pact serves two stated purposes: reducing harm to soldiers and military necessity, as presented in its rationale:

> That the progress of civilization should have the effect of alleviating as much as possible the calamities of war;
> That the only legitimate object which States should endeavour to accomplish during war is to weaken the military forces of the enemy;

That for this purpose it is sufficient to disable the greatest possible number of men;

That this object would be exceeded by the employment of arms which uselessly aggravate the sufferings of disabled men, or render their death inevitable;

That the employment of such arms would, therefore, be contrary to the laws of humanity.

The logic seems to be that doing full damage to a soldier (killing him) better realizes war's purpose (the opponent's surrender), and the treaty does not mince words: the way to achieve the object of war is to kill as many men as is necessary.[74] So while this treaty can and should be seen as a groundbreaking moment in the history of cooperation to protect certain classes of individuals (soldiers) and in the history of weapons bans, it can also be viewed as cooperation to end war more quickly: more efficiently destroying the opponents' resources (here, people) means quicker resolution.

There are other ways to cooperate to end war quickly, however. Any number of structures for warfare and methods of victory could be agreed upon, so why should soldiers' lives be sacrificed on behalf of political leaders who are generally held unaccountable, as opposed to merely wounding soldiers, dueling between political leaders, fighting gladiatorial matches between selected soldiers, or some other format?

Unfortunately, while solutions to problems stemming from one form of cooperation can be found in another, there may ultimately be no definitive resolution because one always has recourse to violence. Resorting to (greater) violence is a trump card: even if parties agree to a limited violent structure to settle a dispute, that may not be the final word, as there is always the possibility—perhaps likelihood—that the losing side refuses to accept the outcome and turns to larger-scale violence in the hopes of a more favorable settlement.[75]

The fact of this trump card does not mean, however, that once there is open violence, participants should immediately move to the large-scale format, as is often done now. Aside from division of labor, nation-states use soldiers in part because they are attached to the myth of the patriotic citizen-soldier as the nation-state writ small (chapter 4); but if that is the case, then large-scale warfare (see chapter 6 on trial by combat) is not needed for modus vivendi. Small-scale trials would do just as well.[76] We have neglected smaller-scale possibilities for settling violent disputes: form should follow function here, and there are viable limited-structure alternatives for cooperation that can minimize harm while reaching a conclusion quickly. Whether or not this is a case of making the best the enemy of the good, it is blindness to that possibility that ultimately does the most damage of all.

---

The ethic of cooperation in warfare arises in part from the desire to make people better off in the face of inevitable destruction: the question is whether its methods succeed or whether it might, ironically, make things worse by causing more damage. We saw in chapter 3 how existing standards for POW treatment and prisoner exchange might slow down the war effort, as it saps resources that could have been used to fight and win the war. We have also seen in this chapter that humanitarian provisions like ceasefires can backfire, and how stereotypical eighteenth- and nineteenth-century European *bataille rangée*, which was influenced by the "fair fight" ethic, met the latest technology to yield horrific results that only compounded the tragedy of the war. The "fair fight" and protective/humanitarian ethics operate simultaneously in warfighting, but in tension with each other and with the aim of war. In chapter 7, I will discuss how the debate over who is a legitimate combatant and therefore subject to certain immunities and privileges also necessarily creates boundaries that exclude whole groups of people from the law's protection, thus exposing many of them to arbitrary treatment, and sometimes worse than they otherwise would have received.

Given the chaotic nature of war, it is unsurprising that the combination of its myriad moral principles generates similarly messy results. An ethic built around structuring short wars (as they should be, that is, genuinely cooperative) can address some of those problems generated by the friction between the other ethics of cooperation; however, as mentioned, it is as difficult to sustain as it is historically rare.

With this sober look at the adverse effects and devastating costs of "fighting well" and trying to make war more humane, we have asked fundamental questions about what war is for and whether the norms of war should more directly address the *function* of war (to settle political disputes).

Now, we should also interrogate the relationship between the ethic of cooperation between enemies and other moral principles of war, such as just war theory. The political view of war is not the only approach in play.

War has another major goal as well, which is to render deontological justice more broadly, to achieve *jus ad bellum*. (This is a wider mandate than the three ethics of cooperation discussed here, which are focused on *jus in bello* or on utilitarian justice.) The pursuit of *jus ad bellum* is a question that has been largely vacated in modern warfare—but perhaps we should inquire into what *content* should occupy the conclusive political settlement that war is trying to achieve. Now, war is utilized primarily to resolve geopolitical disagreements, but in a way that effectively constitutes trial by combat, as we shall see, and remains largely silent in response the *jus ad bellum* question.

# CHAPTER VI

## Cooperative Ethics, Just War Theory, and the Structure of Modern Warfare

> This is the nature of war, whose stake is at once the game and the authority and the justification. Seen so, war is the truest form of divination. It is the testing of one's will and the will of another within that larger will which because it binds them is therefore forced to select. War is the ultimate game because war is at last a forcing of the unity of existence. War is god.
>
> —CORMAC MCCARTHY, *BLOOD MERIDIAN*

This chapter puts the ethic of cooperation in a broader context, first by addressing its relationship to other principles of warfare, and then by showing how the superstructure of modern war itself is informed by the ethic of cooperation, and in particular three aspects of that structure: (1) the political nature of war, (2) how abdication from *jus ad bellum* judgments has led to concentration on justice within war (*jus in bello*), and (3) the ways in which modern nation-states collude to define "legitimacy" in war—and who has standing to fight.

These structural features add up to modern warfare being a form of trial by combat that confers only effective right, with all of its accompanying attributes and ensuing doctrines (e.g., moral equality of combatants) as well as its practical and moral problems. In addition to leaving questions of justicial right and responsibility for war disturbingly unresolved, this arrangement faces new challenges in this geopolitical context in which cooperative and noncooperative (e.g., contemporary terrorism) forms of warfare prominently clash.

## Contemporary Norms of War

As significant as is the ethic of cooperation between enemies, it is not the only principle in play, and it alone is insufficient for getting through all of war's stages and scenarios. Not only is its sustainability questionable—cooperation tends to erode over the length of a conflict, the longer it drags on—but it is often overridden in practice and does not always take priority in the hierarchy of practical and ethical principles of war. Furthermore, it does not address certain key questions, including how to determine whether the cause for war itself is just.

Nonetheless, it is one of a few major influences on the contemporary norms of war and, along with what is generally referred to as traditional just war theory,[1] it has extensively shaped the international laws of war. All three (the ethic of cooperation, traditional just war theory, and international law) play substantial roles in the present-day body of warfare norms, which has several major pillars, including civilian immunity, proportionality in attacks, medical neutrality and protection, and returning remains of the dead, among others. There are two essential ensuing institutions not mentioned in most discussions of fighting practices, however, that I will focus on here: (a) war as trial by combat, and (b) the emphasis on internal justice (within the fighting of the war) and internal virtue (e.g., warrior virtues) (see figure 6.1).

The existence of an ethic of cooperation has worked its way into both the practice of warfare and the theory of just war, with little notice. In

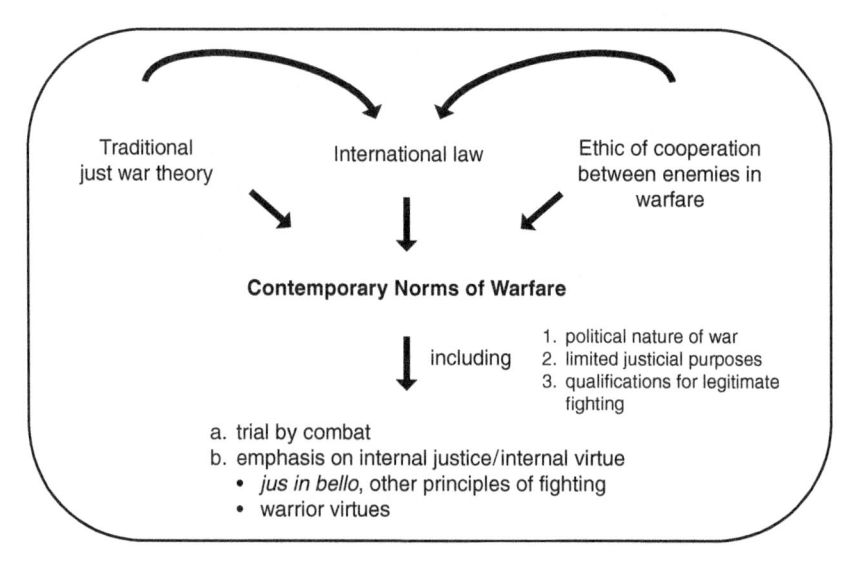

*Figure 6.1* Contemporary Norms of Warfare

doing so, this anomaly has unconsciously created expectations for reciprocity and future cooperation and has generated certain practices that are now taken for granted. It is commonly thought that some of those institutions (especially collaboration to protect certain classes of individuals and elements of "fair fight" cooperation) are the only ways that war should be fought, but this raises at least two sets of broader questions.

## The Ethic of Cooperation and Just War Theory Principles

First, morally motivated cooperation creates challenges for other operating ethical principles of warfare. Tensions persist between it and important pillars of traditional Western just war theory, such as principles of neutrality, just cause, and right intention, some of which are enshrined in international law.

For example, the ethic of cooperation to protect civilians can conflict with the principles of double effect, military necessity, and proportionality, which feature prominently in Western *jus in bello* doctrine. Whether one uses the traditional or Walzer's more demanding variant of the doctrine of double effect,[2] the embedded requirement of right intention and its accompanying side constraints of military necessity and proportionality speak to essential criteria for immanent justice that are not inherent in cooperation to respect civilian immunity. While many are motivated by deontological beliefs, the protection of civilians in and of itself and the particular forms it takes are matters of convention, and it can and is often pursued in ways that are contrary to those immanent justifications.

The soldier/civilian distinction has not always been strictly observed, for example, even in the law, especially when it comes to making allowances for military necessity. General Orders No. 100 (Lieber Code), for example, says that

> Commanders, whenever admissible, inform the enemy of their intention to bombard a place, so that the non-combatants, and especially the women and children, may be removed before the bombardment commences. But it is no infraction of the common law of war to omit thus to inform the enemy. Surprise may be a necessity.
> (ART. 19)

According to traditional just war theory, the principle of military necessity[3] must be restricted by the principle of proportionality and the doctrine of double effect, but both constraints allow for civilians to be *knowingly* (if not technically intentionally) killed. Rather, what protects civilians is a conscious decision to cooperatively and reciprocally abide by an artificial designation of "innocent"—or at least functionally innocent (i.e., "civilian")—for certain groups.

Both the principles of military necessity and civilian immunity are core to widespread understandings of just war theory, but usually work at cross purposes, and it is unclear which takes precedence when they conflict, as neither law nor philosophy offers much guidance on this issue. Civilian immunity *seems* to have priority in philosophy—although not the law—but even there, allowances are made for "supreme emergency," for example, which is an extreme case of military necessity.[4] The relationship between the ethic of cooperation and these traditional principles is a complex and difficult one, and it is not clear how they should accommodate each other, if that is even possible.

### The Ethic of Cooperation in the Practice of War

Second, morally motivated cooperation generates challenges in the *practice* of war, especially internally, in tension with other operating ethics of cooperation (chapter 5) and the inability to deal with noncooperative warfare (chapter 7). The latter difficulty is highlighted by the question of terrorism, which has been of great international concern recently. It is not much of an exaggeration to say that war between modern nation-states is premised on cooperation, not merely in their use of warfare as a political tool, but also in their mutual recognition of one another as entities who can legitimately wage war and of their soldiers as representatives who can legitimately kill on their governments' behalf. This becomes problematic when they encounter groups such as stateless terrorists whom they do not recognize as legitimate killers, which can lead to branding them as "illegal enemy combatants" and thus trapping them in legal limbo, or when terrorists target civilians, which violates one of the central pillars of contemporary international law.

## Structure as a Locus of Cooperation

Beyond "fair fight" norms, protections for certain peoples, and the echoes of the idea of ending war, there are other cooperative ethics; ending war quickly is one specific manifestation of a broader collaboration over the *structure* of war, including its conduct, boundaries, and purposes.

I argue that modern warfare is also collaborative at the structural (macro) level, insofar as it is intended as a tool for conflict resolution rather than a primarily destructive act. After all, it was not so long ago that unconditional surrender was the norm, but expectations for how victors are to cooperatively engage with losers after their defeat have changed dramatically since the Second World War. These intervening seventy-odd years are only a fraction of the modern era, however, so how can the whole of modern warfare be characterized as cooperative? Exactly how strong is the claim I am making?

Certainly not that every war or every action in war since the sixteenth century (roughly when the modern era began) has been or is cooperative, nor that not a single person has waged war nihilistically. Rather, I am making a broader, more abstract statement, viz., that cooperation informs and hangs over our thinking about war. This has developed slowly over centuries and is not necessarily universal, but even as other types of warfare are practiced, a cooperative framework has evolved to dominate and generally characterize the way modern nation-state militaries approach war. When someone argues that it is unfair that the enemy does not wear uniforms, imposes crippling postwar reparations, executes POWs who have surrendered, or uses chemical warfare, he is often approaching the conflict with a cooperative mindset, even if unknowingly.

We found an early example of structural cooperation with classical Greek hoplites and their characteristic form of decisive shock battle to end war quickly. Although hoplite pitched battle can be seen as an antecedent to modern pitched battles,[5] this is not to say that the Greeks practiced modern warfare, but rather that the ethic of cooperation in warfare is not so far-fetched and has manifested in various ways.

Classical hoplite warfare is also but one way to cooperate on the structure of war.[6] Modern structural cooperation takes multiple forms: strategically, modern war is used to settle political disputes, such as who will rule a territory, the legitimacy of how one comes to rule, or the acceptability of particular ideologies. As such, one goes to war with the goal of getting the enemy to surrender. There are historical exceptions, of course, but generally, the intent is not to annihilate the other side. We bind ourselves in fighting not only with legal conventions, but also with moral considerations such as proportionality, right intention, and the doctrine of double effect. Many of these guidelines originate from the medieval period, but they have since taken on a secular life of their own.

Most tellingly, this cooperation also extends to the postwar period. Long gone are the days when the victor killed all the men and raped and enslaved the women and children. Since World War II, agreement on a surrender treaty is no longer enough. We now frown upon terms dictating unconditional surrender or harsh reparations, and increasingly even expect the victor to help the vanquished rebuild their infrastructure or install an independent political system, sometimes pouring vast sums of money into the defeated country (e.g., the Marshall Plan). The restrictions we moderns place on ourselves and our goals in war would be unrecognizable to the ancients. Describes jurist Mountague Bernard:

> The cruelties, as we now consider them, of very early times, are natural incidents of a society in which life is cheap; because it is insecure,—a society violent in its enmities, brutal in its legislation, and fierce even in its pleasures. No established principle, no recognized moral obligation, is then violated by refusing quarter to a vanquished enemy, or by murdering in cold blood captives whom it is dangerous or unprofitable to keep; and the slaughter of peasants on whose blood, even in peace, the law set a trifling value, could be no great crime in war. Mercy pleaded only for women, children, and *genz de l'Eglise*,—or, more falteringly, for the *poures genz*,—when there was no separation between the citizen and the soldier, and every able-bodied layman was therefore deemed an enemy.[7]

Even as massacres, tortures, and barbarities are perpetuated today, they occur less frequently, and it is hard to overstate how significant it is that we now consider them to be outrageous. The international moral landscape has changed. These new expectations contradict our archetypal images of war and reflect the mind-set that war is about something more than simply winning—it is meant to advance the political process and must do so in cooperative fashion.

## Three Features of Structural Cooperation

Cooperation is an interactive process, not just an end result. Even under conditions of international anarchy, there is not always a constant state of war—cooperation is sometimes attained and organization in some areas achieved.[8] Even under duress, there are ways to communicate, for example, through deterrence.[9] One can use one's behavior to motivate the other side's calculus to make cooperation possible (e.g., cooperation hinging on reciprocity, such as World War I trenches' "live and let live"). In this way, cooperation and conflict exist along a spectrum of communication methods. Structural cooperation in modern war has myriad aspects, three of which I discuss here: (1) the political nature of warfare, (2) its limited justicial purposes, and (3) qualifications for legitimate participation.

### 1. The War/Politics Continuum and the Political Purpose of War

Systemic approaches to war have generated opposite claims about the relationship between war and politics. Clausewitz formulates war as an extension of politics, and Foucault contends that it is actually the other way around, that politics is a continuation of war.[10] Historically, Foucault is more correct. Once upon a time when violence was more prevalent in interpersonal relations,[11] politics helped tame the primal instincts to survive, seize resources, and otherwise dominate those around you, by sublimating those desires into cooperative political structures and competitions. Although Foucault did not refer to classical Greek hoplite warfare or the outgrowth of certain traits of modern warfare from those practices, they encapsulate the phenomenon that he describes: parties agree to a particular process and condone what outcomes result, regardless of personal preference.[12]

It is the nature of competitions that there must be a winner, however, and as the ultimate arbiter of a conflict is death, every loser of a nonviolent confrontation has a trump card: he can always choose to kill his adversary. As we have seen, this is why it is sometimes difficult to sustain cooperative ethics in warfare.

When nonviolent politics become the primary form of societal interaction, it inverts the relationship between politics and war. Then, war becomes its tool in the way Clausewitz describes: useful to have in the arsenal as a negotiation instrument, a not-so-veiled threat, or an exit strategy.

Despite their differences and without saying as much, both Clausewitz's and Foucault's analogies think of war as a collective decision-making process about the most fundamental question of politics: Who gets to rule a given territory? This contrasts with Aristotle and J. S. Mill, who think that there are rather *two* fundamental questions of politics: who gets to rule, and *how* they should rule. The belief that the right answer to the first question obviates the second is dangerously incorrect, says Mill. In modern times, we tend to agree. So, as the relationship between war and politics circles back around in Clausewitzean fashion, we demand more specificity in the first query, e.g., how to decide rightful rule and what qualifies as legitimate, including which means of killing and violent conflict resolution are acceptable. This requires limitations on the use of force and cooperation on adhering to and enforcing the rules of war.

### A TOOL FOR CONFLICT RESOLUTION

War is not merely a counterintuitive way of resolving disputes—it is downright insane—and it would not seem possible to cooperate on precisely the most fundamentally destructive act of mutual harm. Yet, modern warfare indicates a form of structural cooperation insofar as enemies utilize it to resolve disagreements, especially political contests, e.g., who will rule, how one comes to do so legitimately, and which ideologies will prevail. Rather than being purely destructive, unconditional, or nihilistic, warfare is a way of reaching sustainable agreement.

### PITCHED BATTLE AS LEGAL PROCEEDING

Embedded in questions of right authority for war is the idea that war functions as a mechanism for conflict resolution, because there is no higher adjudicating power from whom recourse could be had. Said Alberico Gentili in the sixteenth century:

> War on both sides must be public and official and there must be sovereigns on both sides to direct war. This is the view both of Augustine[13] and of the other theologians, and reason shows that war has its origin in necessity; and this necessity arises because there cannot be

judicial processes between supreme sovereigns or free peoples unless they themselves consent, since they acknowledge no judge or superior. Consequently, they are only supreme and they alone merit the title of public, while all others are inferior and are rated as private individuals. The sovereign has no earthly judge, for one over whom another holds a superior position is not a sovereign.[14]

Later, he says more explicitly that "there may be reasonable doubt as to the justice of the cause," and sometimes even "a justifiable ignorance (*ignorantiam iustam*)." As a result of "the weakness of our human nature, because of which we see everything dimly," we cannot perceive true and pure justice, he says, yet "if it is doubtful on which side justice is, and if each side aims at justice, neither can be called unjust."[15]

If it is impossible to say which side is in the right, then the implication is that war will adjudicate this question. In fact, argues legal scholar James Whitman, the pitched battle was for centuries considered a form of "trial or legal proceeding": in contrast to raids or sieges, they were intended to *limit* damages by producing a decisive outcome. Even if pitched battles dragged on, they were still better than "more savage" possibilities. Whitman compares this to the advantages of a public system of justice—as opposed to private meting, e.g., vigilantism—for this structure of warfare constitutes "a kind of rule of law."[16] It may seem horrific to use war as a legal mechanism, but Whitman repeatedly reminds us that the alternative, like private justice, is worse.

Despite the contemporary image of eighteenth-century pitched battle as the outgrowth of chivalry, the aristocratic conception of warfare was in fact invented later, in the 1830s during the Romantic era.[17] Instead, European warfare in the 1700s was fought according to *jus victoriae*, the law of victory, which sought to answer the questions of how one knows who won and what is gained by winning.[18]

In setting ground rules, *jus victoriae* actually constrained war more than its modern humanitarian counterpart did, argues Whitman, and more effectively, because "monarchical monopolization of legitimate military violence," à la Weber, crushed the priority of the aristocrats and imposed public warfare over private warfare. It was *jus victoriae*, rather than aristocratic or humanitarian morality, that "civilized" war.[19]

This "wager theory of battle," as Whitman calls it,[20] is the idea that war is a way of making decisions—in this case with an "enforceable wager," a "contract of chance."[21] Eighteenth-century political commentators, such as Éléazar de Mauvillon who said that "sovereigns recognize no arbiter of their quarrels except the chance of arms," used this language of chance and contract/agreement.[22] Although these rules of law were different in conception from rules of games and were not binding, they did nonetheless guide behavior,[23] and treating war as a wager bounded and civilized it.[24]

After a battle, there is often still debate over who won as well as what rights the victor gains,[25] so why should battles "decide the fortunes of states" at all? It was because, Whitman argues, people accepted the role of "fortune" and chance, and, in choosing this method, bound themselves to their outcomes.[26] Rather than shy away from the arbitrariness of the fight and its accompanying questions about the legitimacy of luck, premoderns viewed battle as a "chance of arms," and early modern lawyers took a "workmanlike attitude toward the legal significance of even the most arbitrary slaughters."[27] One can liken the process to pure procedural justice or a single-day sporting event, for unlike extended and grinding wars, fortune plays a large role in pitched battles and "on any given day, either side [has] a chance to win."[28] In fact, "Mars," the Roman god of war, was a premodern Latin synonym for "the unpredictability of battle," and in legal language, a pitched battle was described as *sors*, which is a "decision-making procedure that uses chance," such as drawing straws.[29]

Two of the essential questions of war are (1) *jus ad bellum*: was the invasion right?, and (2) *jus victoriae*: should international law respect the victory and should the victory count for a legitimate and durable claim of right?[30] These are answers to which a theorist like Clausewitz, who believed that only wars of annihilation (with or without the use of pitched battles) could bring ultimate strategic victory,[31] has no answers, because many influential battles do not annihilate and in fact let the other side get away afterward.[32] Technical victory can be enough to make peace,[33] and this is reflected in the legal and moral philosophy of war. Pitched battles were deemed to carry more legal weight than other methods, e.g., raids, and thinkers such as Pufendorf and Vattel thought that the victor of pitched battles was entitled to "dictate terms."[34]

There are certain advantages to using wagers such as pitched battles to answer legal questions, says Whitman: (1) outcomes can be attributed to God, which gives them more legitimacy; (2) wagers relieve people of the responsibility of making decisions,[35] as well as make results unchallengeable; (3) given the absence of monopolistic state power, wagers are a way of making results binding; (4) wagers are consistent with other institutions that confer rights through risk-taking; and (5) with a wager, limited battles are sufficient to settle disputes, which helps to contain war.[36]

Understanding pitched battle as a gamble helps us to see how, despite its greater risks, what looks like irrational behavior actually makes sense, because the potential payoff was such that some people were willing to take the chance. It also explains why eighteenth-century warfare could be bounded, because if the method of decision-making relied on chance and irrationality, then participants preferred a quick and decisive outcome that was also difficult to challenge.[37]

### ABANDONING THE WAGER MODEL: RETURNING TO QUESTIONS OF RIGHT

All of these advantages were true for classical Greek hoplite warfare, so why did that cooperation collapse after two centuries? Why did the "verdict of battle" lose force and decisiveness after the eighteenth century? Why could something merely resembling these systems not be sustained now? According to Whitman, the American Civil War demonstrates a modern break point, because the Confederacy thought that their pitched battle victories should and would win them rights of secession and support from European governments—but they did not, because the meaning and significance of pitched battle victory had already changed such that "verdict of battle" was no longer readily accepted.[38]

First, military theory at the time was transforming, and strategists were being seduced by the illusion that scientific methods and techniques could guarantee results.[39] If this were so, properly planned and executed battles would be less risky to individual fighters, and their outcomes more certain. Therefore, there was no reason to take the gamble or "wager" of war.

More important, however—and more controversial—was political change. When wars were waged by monarchs, they tended to adhere to the eighteenth-century pitched-battle framework even well into the nineteenth century, says Whitman, because they were focused on acquisition of property. It was when wars were waged by republics, whose popular movements were ideologically motivated to impose particular forms of governance on others, that fighting became unbounded, much more "chaotic," and out of control. People then imparted "millenarian" significance to battles and saw them as "turning points in history," which meant that "war ceased to belong to the realm of Fortune and entered the perilous realm of Destiny"—and no limits were placed on what could be done to fulfill that.[40] Throughout human history, warfare has been almost singularly vicious, and the unusual "interlude of relative calm in the eighteenth century came during an exceptional moment of princely success in monopolizing violence," says Whitman, and he cautions, "Wars enter their most dangerous territory not when they lose touch with chivalry but when they aim to remake the world."[41]

While Whitman persuasively rejects alternative explanations for the particularly deadly combination of eighteenth-century structure (war as wager and pitched battle as decisive) with nineteenth-century ideology (and its imperative to conquer), such as technological advances,[42] it cannot be denied that new technology added a fair amount of lethality to the mix. The degeneration of pitched battles' decisiveness also coincided with the rise of international law on war, which pursued multiple purposes including the clarification of property rights, and reflected a shift of emphasis in thinking about morality of and within war.[43]

Although the particular political purposes of war may have changed in their relative distribution and the weights of their various components—from more acquisitive to more ideological—war is, however, ultimately still a method to resolve disagreements that are wholly independent of the process. How can a war determine who rightfully owns a piece of property? How can a war determine which political system is better or more (morally) correct? While it is the case that democracies win more wars than nondemocracies,[44] for example, this fact in and of itself does not prove the greater *justice* of a particular political system—only its greater ability to provide for the security of its people. I will return to these questions later.

## 2. Limited Justicial Warfare—Vacating Questions of Jus ad Bellum

Despite *jus ad bellum* claims becoming increasingly moral and ideological in the nineteenth century, the international laws of war have become less so and, with limited exceptions, have in fact largely ceded questions of *jus ad bellum*. Rather than try to eliminate war, which would be impossible, international law tries to bound, regulate, and codify its violence, but with reference to the existing geopolitical structure, for "whatever their views on war itself, nearly all legal thinkers agreed that if international law posited an abstract ideal too far in advance of actual practice, it would be a dead letter," says historian Peter Holquist. During its conception in the nineteenth century, "international law . . . meant essentially law between the states—and the defining attribute of state sovereignty was precisely the right to go to war."[45] That could not be taken away, but it could be limited, and ethical discourse and the law slowly evolve until we get the UN Charter, which forbids "the threat or use of force against the territorial integrity or political independence of any state" (Art. 2.4), permits wars only in "self-defence," either by individual or collective states (Art. 51), and outlines procedures for responding to "threats of the peace, breaches of the peace, and acts of aggression" (Chap. VII).[46]

This is, of course, a consideration of sorts of *jus ad bellum*: it amounts to saying that all aggressive wars are unjust[47] and that only defensive wars are just.[48] In tying justice to preexisting territorial boundaries, however—regardless of how they came to be drawn in those positions—this formulation de facto privileges the status quo, as "peace" is here considered merely the absence of violent conflict, and makes no judgment on the justice of present circumstances or how those circumstances came to be. This then becomes a time-slice principle, arbitrarily implemented from when the UN Charter was established or whenever a condition of peace is deemed to exist, and reflects a limited conception of what qualifies for *jus ad bellum*.

As such, considerations of *jus ad bellum* have *effectively* dropped out of the international laws of war.[49] The narrow bounds of legitimate war mean that many standing injustices—such as oppressive domestic rule or previous invasion and conquest—will not and cannot be addressed with warfare, even though that is still the main currency of international political negotiation. In doing so, it excuses in practice past unjust wars and rejects all claims to rectify those injustices with force, even if that is the only means possible. By removing evermore frequently asked questions of international justice from consideration, international law has left only narrow geopolitical goals, namely, "peace," referenced against an arbitrarily chosen point in time.

As a result, the voluminous international laws of war focus almost exclusively on questions of *jus in bello*—how one is permitted to fight *during* a war—independent of the justice of one cause or another. Previous chapters have discussed several different categories of *jus in bello* regulations, including civilian immunity, cultural protections, and so on, but here, I would like to return to ethics of cooperation related to POW treatment and in particular medical immunity and medical neutrality, which grow out of this secession of *jus ad bellum* territory.

## MEDICAL IMMUNITY AND MEDICAL NEUTRALITY

When Benjamin Franklin tried to establish wartime protections for commercial interests (including merchants, farmers, and fishermen) in bilateral treaties during the American founding period, he also noted, "It is hardly necessary to add that the hospitals of enemies should be unmolested."[50] Nearly a century later, the Lieber Code called it "customary" to identify hospitals in or near battle zones with designated "usually yellow" flags "so that the besieging enemy may avoid firing on them" (Art. 115). Furthermore, it was "honorable" for fighters to take preventive measures and request that their enemies so mark hospitals in their own territory (Art. 116), and both religious and medical staff (chaplains, medical officers, apothecaries, and hospital nurses and servants) if captured were not to be considered POWs except under extenuating circumstances (Art. 53).

At the same time, Europe's own horrors prompted the establishment of the International Committee of the Red Cross (ICRC) in 1863, which sprung out of Henry Dunant's struggles to provide humanitarian care to the wounded in the fields outside Solferino (1859).[51] In the aftermath, he institutionalized the provision of such services with the creation of an international organization. The resolutions from the ICRC's founding conference recommended that "in time of war the belligerent nations should proclaim the neutrality of" official and volunteer medical personnel, hospitals and ambulances, locals providing relief, and the wounded.[52] Since then, a variety of international laws and domestic military regulations have delineated the respect, immunity, and protection that should be afforded to medical personnel of all kinds.[53]

Some providers, marked by distinctive arm badges and symbols, are explicitly and broadly neutral, e.g., MSF or ICRC, in that their purpose is to service everyone equally. Immunity is also legally granted to members of state militaries or providers associated with particular states (e.g., local ambulances, domestic and military hospitals, and medical personnel and local residents).

In return, even medics of national militaries are supposed to act neutrally by caring equally for wounded enemy soldiers.[54] Surprisingly, this is not an uncommon occurrence.[55] The Israeli military, for example, makes no secret of the fact that it frequently treats not just wounded Syrian civilians injured along their shared border/battlefront, but also injured Islamic fighters battling Assad who are likewise hostile to Israel.[56] Former US Marine Phil Klay recounts during his deployment in Iraq when a wounded Marine arrived at the base and then died on the table:

> Normally, there'd be a moment of silence, of prayer, but the team got word that the man who killed this young Marine, the insurgent sniper, would be arriving a few minutes later. That dead Marine's squadmates had engaged the sniper in a firefight, shot him a couple of times, patched him up, bandaged him and called for a casualty evacuation to save the life of the man who'd killed their friend.
>
> So he arrived at our base. And the medical staff members, still absorbing the blow of losing a Marine, got to work. They stabilized their enemy and pumped him full of American blood, donated from the "walking blood bank" of nearby Marines. The sniper lived. And then they put him on a helicopter to go to a hospital for follow-up care, and one of the Navy nurses was assigned to be his flight nurse. He told me later of the strangeness of sitting in the back of a helicopter, watching over his enemy lying peacefully unconscious, doped up on painkillers, while he kept checking the sniper's vitals, his blood pressure, his heartbeat, a heartbeat that was steady and strong thanks to the gift of blood from the Americans this insurgent would have liked to kill.[57]

While there are obvious strategic interests in saving potential POWs, the medics themselves often just see it as their job and view the wounded merely as patients in need of care. In a short *Al Jazeera* documentary shot during nearly two weeks in Afghanistan with the medical crew of the US Army's 214th Aviation Regiment, Major Patrick Zenk estimates that about half of their missions serviced local nationals, "We'll go in for anybody, we go in for locals, we go in for soldiers, we go in for coalition forces, we even go for enemy POW." The filmmaker himself, Vaughan Smith, recounts:

> Everybody was treated equally. There was no distinction, in these crews and the medics like [Sgt.] Tyrone [Jordan], in the effort they made to save any life . . . and that could be a Taliban life. We would only know if a Taliban had come into the helicopter, or an enemy

insurgent, because a Marine would accompany them . . . and they'd normally be handcuffed if there wasn't a good medical reason why that was inappropriate. And we had people who had been making bombs—there was one person who got blown up by the bomb they were making—and we'd have quite a few Taliban come into the helicopters. But Tyrone would apply the medical assistance to everybody universally, and that was quite an impressive thing to see.[58]

This is not without historical precedent. Jewish-American medic Pfc. Louis Cooperberg writes home during World War II about treating Nazi soldiers:

> They have robbed and murdered and raped, and they lie on my slab, innocent like and in pain, and I give them the same care, the same treatment I give our own boys. Yet all the while, I know these same men have killed my cousins and aunts and uncles in Poland, have tortured and killed without compunction, and despise me because I am a Jew. But I treat them.
>
> Occasionally, when I am through and Jerry blubbers out his thanks, I tell him I am a Jew. He seldom believes me. He may say, hurriedly, it matters not to him, he has never killed any Jews, but fear is on his face and I see the lie, but still I treat them. . . .
>
> An old fellow, his face and his bearing attesting his fear of what his propagandists told him he might expect at our hands, kept me busy reassuring him we were not savages. I hated every minute of it. An SS trooper arrogantly refused a blood transfusion because it was American blood, we forced it into him, we should have let him die. I fixed a German when gas gangrene had set in, and my friends marveled that I, a Jew, should touch him, much less clean his infection. But I can't explain that. How can you hate one defenseless man? (August 28, 1944)[59]

During the Korean War, MASH surgeon Otto F. Apel describes multiple incidences of ministering to North Koreans and Chinese, against whom the United States was fighting.[60] In 1951, non-American soldiers treated in his MASH unit tallied 3,750: about half South Korean, a quarter from the UN fighting force (from all over, e.g., Colombia, Ethiopia, France,

Netherlands, Turkey, Philippines, Thailand, New Zealand), and about a quarter (874) POWs, which means they were wounded enemies (largely North Korean and Chinese).⁶¹ The POWs did not always appreciate their medical treatment, however:

> In the 8076th, a Chinese soldier who had been taken prisoner came in for surgical care. After the operation, he was taken to post-op for recovery. A MASH nurse tended to him as he came to. When he recognized where he was, he looked at the American nurse and immediately spit in her face. Ed Ziegler, our aviation officer, was present in the post-op tent. When the Chinese soldier spit on our nurse, Ed immediately and instinctively belted him across the face. . . . No one in the operating tent blamed him one bit.⁶²

Medical neutrality reflects the idea that war is merely an instrument of policy-making and dispute-settlement: the killing is not the goal and is, therefore, nothing personal. War is a circumscribed and artificial activity, and as such, soldiers are mere tools.

There is certainly a potential public relations benefit from word of lifesaving Israeli medical treatment spreading among the neighboring Syrian and Islamic militant population. Ulterior motives cannot be ruled out, not least because Israeli medics on the border seem to treat only Sunni militants, who share some common enemies with Israel, and not Shia fighters, who are more likely to support Israel's more threatening enemies, e.g., Assad and the Syrian government, Hezbollah, and Iran.⁶³

Many people also believe that national personnel should privilege fellow co-nationals. A "charity begins at home" guideline established by the Israeli Medical Association's Ethics Bureau in 2008 was replaced in 2015 by a new rule requiring medics at the sites of terror attacks to treat the wounded according to their medical need—which means that some attackers might be treated before some victims. The head of the ethics panel explained that there had been cases of mistaken identity, because it is difficult to properly ascertain attackers: "Doctors are not judges. The implication of the previous directive was that the doctor needs to investigate who was responsible and punish him by not giving him treatment." This new standard is so controversial, however, that it was not widely publicized at the time of decision or implementation.⁶⁴

Limited resources and national loyalty are realities that cannot be ignored. Said an Israeli Golan Brigade commander, Lt. Col. Itzik Malka:

> My dream is that one day, the Red Cross will say, thanks guys, we'll take it from here, you go back to your unit and take care of injured Israelis. I am proud of what we are doing here, but it is a great burden. For every Syrian in hospital, there is one less bed for an Israeli. One day we will have to make a choice between an Israeli life and a Syrian one. When that happens it will be hard, but I have to say my first duty will be to Israelis.[65]

Although medical neutrality is the flip side of medical immunity, the policy is not without its controversies, and the service providers themselves are ambivalent. A report about extended POW camp riots in the Korean War observed: "American doctors were in a strange situation, confronted by patients who were also enemies, uncertain whether to halt food and treatment in hopes of restoring order or to follow their ingrained professional instincts to minimize suffering and loss of life despite all provocations."[66]

In comparing the American field hospitals that also treated North Koreans with a South Korean hospital in Pusan, one doctor noted bitterly in 1950 that "our enemies were receiving much better care at our hands than were our allies [South Koreans] at the hands of their own people."[67]

Soldiers have long been outraged at the equal treatment of their enemies, and understandably so. It is especially jarring to wake up in a medical ward next to those who have just been trying to kill them and who might still wish to do so. Said anonymous British soldiers fighting in Afghanistan:

> My friends who were injured were waking up in the hospital to find Taliban in the bed next to them. A lot of people are getting injured out there and the last thing they want to see when they come round is the Taliban on the same ward. It's just not right.
>
> I'm appalled that Taliban are being treated in the same room at the hospital. I know we have to treat them under the Geneva Convention, but no one should have to wake up in the same place as someone who may have injured them or their mates.[68]

It is difficult to adhere to the policy of equal treatment when it conflicts with the interests of one's co-nationals. If both co-national and enemy are equally injured and equally likely to die, but the enemy soldier arrives at the treatment location first, can the military doctor wait for the co-national? Who receives treatment first when resources are limited? What if the co-national is slightly less injured than the enemy soldier, but there are only enough means (including time) to save one person, or there are enough resources to either restore the co-national to full bodily function or save the life of the enemy soldier but leave the co-national permanently maimed? With all respect to medical professionals in national militaries, there remain reasonable doubts about how strictly they *could* correctly decide and adhere to the requirements of equal treatment—much less want to—especially as resources grow scarce.[69]

Still, many military medics take seriously this duty of equal care and regularly perform these heroic, counterintuitive—and overall rare—feats. Only a handful of (wealthy) militaries have the capacity to provide this dramatic, life-saving treatment with any frequency. One could argue that only such rich countries could wage war as much as they do, so they should hardly be praised for treating injuries that would not otherwise have been inflicted. We know from history, however, that war can be and more often is conducted on the cheap, and that wounded enemy soldiers could easily be and often are left to die—so exceptions to this convey something meaningful about how soldiers view one another and the shared cooperative ethic they engage in to save others.

## MULTIPLIER EFFECTS—CAN MEDICAL CARE BE GENUINELY NEUTRAL?

Significant normative questions remain, however, two of which are different sides of the same coin: *Should* national medics provide equal treatment to soldiers/prisoners and *should* there be immunity for medical personnel from attack? If the answer to the former question is "yes,"[70] then the answer to the latter would seem to be the same—as it is that professionalism and neutrality that earn medics immunity—but it is actually not so straightforward.

Medical personnel in modern militaries are not simply doctors. Many are also militarily trained and often carry weapons, even if only intended to be used in self-defense. Their military capabilities and sometime participation in fighting raise questions about their claims to immunity, but more problematic are the outcomes of their main missions.

The military doctor's primary job is to heal—but it is not simply that. Rather, the job is to "salvage," i.e., to heal soldiers such that they return to active duty as soon as possible.[71] The nature of the injuries and curative limits of medicine mean that many wounded soldiers will be unable to fight again after recuperation. Some will, however, and especially with medical and transportation technology advancements, medics have been able to keep more soldiers alive and deliver more of them back to the battlefield.

One reason that soldiers are legally entitled to equal medical treatment is the assumption that the wounded would be *hors de combat*, especially since they would physically no longer be able to fight. As such, injured enemies would be removed from the field of combat (literally and figuratively), given medical treatment as is their humanitarian right, and detained for the remainder of the conflict. Immunity for medics is tied to this assumption,[72] and therefore based on a background agreement or convention—one that historically has not always existed. In fact, argues military ethicist Michael Gross:

> There is nothing about the practice of medicine that morally compels anyone to protect surgeons and nurses on the battlefield. As a military asset, they are vulnerable to death and injury. There is no compelling moral reason to distinguish between a doctor and a tank driver except for the fact that the sides *agree* to protect medical personnel. They do so out of mutual self-interest in the same way they agree not to harm one another's political leaders.[73]

If the basis of this convention is debatable, then so should it be interrogated. High-quality medical care heals more soldiers and increasingly puts some of them back in the field to fight rather than being permanently *hors de combat*. From 1980 to 1988, only 2.3 percent of the 469 American soldiers who received an amputation and later underwent a physical evaluation remained on active duty, but 16.5 percent of 448 did so from 2001 to 2006, for example.[74] In fact, from 2001 to 2012, an impressive 171 of the 881 US Army soldiers who had major amputations (above the wrist or ankle) as a result of battle wounds in Iraq and Afghanistan were restored to military service in some capacity.[75]

While the absolute and even relative number of soldiers returned to the field contribute little when all is said and done, the enormous efforts and tremendous success of military physicians boost military performance in less direct but more significant ways. The *Al Jazeera* documentary *Blood and Dust* observes their great impact on the morale of American and British troops in Afghanistan, because they know that their militaries' medical capabilities drastically lower the probability of being killed (15:39–15:56), which has knock-on effects for their military decisions and actions:

> I think it's tremendously important—they have confidence knowing that if they get injured or if they get hurt, we'll come and get them. And we do so in all environments, day and night . . . under very low-illumination periods. That gives a soldier confidence that they can continue to fight and we'll be there for them.
> (US ARMY'S 214TH AVIATION REGIMENT,
> MAJOR PATRICK ZENK; 15:19–15:38)

> I believe that they wouldn't go out there and do what they do, they wouldn't go probing for insurgents and doing ops and fight as hard as they do without us, without knowing that we're going to come get them no matter what the odds, no matter where they're at, no matter what they're doing.
> (US ARMY'S 214TH AVIATION REGIMENT,
> CREW CHIEF SPECIALIST DENNIS CATER; 15:57–16:20)

Medical treatment can thus directly and indirectly contribute to the prosecution of a war, not to mention that reducing the number of deaths overall makes the war more politically palatable at home and protracted conflicts therefore more sustainable.[76]

Given the artificiality of the convention of medical immunity, perhaps military physicians should be valid military targets. Asks the documentary's filmmaker Vaughn Smith:

> It begs the question . . . are the rules of war, the Geneva Conventions . . . a little out of date? Because they were designed for a period of time where a battle would be decided and then the problem would be looking after the wounded. Whereas now, you can have a helicopter

with a red cross, which would suggest that you shouldn't shoot at it. But if that helicopter, with the medicine inside it, is a force multiplier, then does that not make it a valid target?
(16:54–17:25).

Military medics demur. US Army's 214th Aviation Regiment Crew Chief Specialist Dennis Cater argues that they should not be valid targets because they rescue everyone, including opposing soldiers and local civilians and, as such, are not directly in the fight (17:25–17:56).

Insofar as military medics do rescue and treat ally and enemy alike, they are not necessarily privileging one side or the other. In this respect, it is more like the reciprocity of earlier POW arrangements, when both sides might release prisoners knowing they would rejoin the fight, so parity was roughly maintained.

What is different from historical and contemporary POW arrangements, however, is that the burden of medical neutrality is actually greater on those with superior military and medical capability, e.g., the United States and the United Kingdom in Afghanistan and Iraq, because they have a larger capacity to treat their own wounded and therefore must service *all* wounded in the same way. So while it may seem that medical immunity merely provides yet another benefit to the already-mighty militaries, it actually advantages those with lesser resources, for without medical immunity, there would also be no medical neutrality: each military would be left to care for its own wounded, and emergency medical evacuation and treatment capacities of poorer military forces are extremely limited.[77]

### STRUCTURAL IMPLICATIONS

Expectations for and treatment of military personnel aptly reflect and demonstrate key parts of modern warfare's complex structure. Because medics are force multipliers and substantively contribute to the prosecution of the war, but are still off-limits, the institution of medical immunity indicates the power of the ethic of cooperation to protect classes of people.

Its accompanying medical neutrality is more complicated. As wars are instruments of dispute settlement for geopolitical disagreements (here, structural feature 1), rather than any imposition of deontological right, soldiers are merely tools of their governments (or gladiators in trials by combat, as argued later) and they do not prosecute their own agendas or beliefs in waging war. As such, they focus on acting rightly in the context of war (e.g., protecting civilians, not committing war crimes, and other *in bello* requirements) and neither are responsible for nor make judgments about broader questions of *jus ad bellum* (structural feature 2), which is why medics treat all soldiers equally. This neutrality reinforces the medics' immune status; it is also an acknowledgment of the moral equality of combatants, which will be discussed later.

## 3. Qualifications for Legitimate Warfighting

Before any contest begins, it must be determined who is eligible to participate. International law has sought to delineate how one would qualify as a legitimate warfighter and therefore be eligible to receive prescribed treatment. Here, I focus on qualifications for individuals, but the same questions should be asked of what constitutes a legitimate political organization—whether it claims to be a state or otherwise—that utilizes soldiers on its behalf.[78] As the Geneva Conventions on this issue are more stringent than and supersede the Hague Conventions' efforts,[79] I will reference the former here. To be eligible for "prisoner of war treatment," one must be a member of an armed forces or militia that has an established hierarchy and chain-of-command, uses a fixed and distinctive emblem, carries arms openly, and acts in accordance with international laws and norms of *jus in bello*. POW protections are also extended to accompanying civilian and crew members of military forces, as well as to inhabitants of unoccupied territories who spontaneously "levée en masse" when invaded—under those circumstances, they need only carry arms openly and adhere to international laws and norms of *jus in bello* (Geneva Conventions [III] [1949], Article 4[A]).

Additional Protocol I (1977) significantly expands combatant status and accompanying treatment to a fighter in revolutionary, secession, or independence movements who "owing to the nature of the hostilities . . . cannot so distinguish himself" (as an armed combatant, through the use of distinctive emblems) so long as he carries arms openly (Art. 44.3). Most importantly, POW protections are extended to practically every fighter regardless of his actions: although "forfeit[ing] his right to be a prisoner of war" by eschewing combat requirements, "he shall, nevertheless, be given protections equivalent in all respects to those accorded to prisoners of war by the Third Convention and by this Protocol" (Art. 44.4).

While the treaty goes on to clarify that it "is not intended to change the generally accepted practice of States with respect to the wearing of the uniform by combatants assigned to the regular, uniformed armed units of a Party to the conflict" (Art. 44.7), it does blunt the legal justification for distinguishing between types of participants in wars, and is one of the reasons that the United States, for example, has never ratified this treaty and that these provisions remain controversial among a wide range of states.

### RESTRICTING THE DEFINITION OF LEGITIMACY

This broad umbrella for POW protections per international law actually represents an agreement between sovereign states to recognize only certain types of fighters as legitimate. Here, I use the United States' approach to "unlawful enemy combatants" to illustrate the general problem this creates. After the attacks of September 11, 2001, US officials transferred many detainees to a prison at its Guantánamo Bay Naval Base, where they were held in legal limbo, via a legal loophole through which the detainees were deemed "unlawful enemy combatants."[80]

At first glance, this is a puzzling category, because what would make a combatant "unlawful"? Both the Department of Justice and White House counsel advised the president and the Department of Defense that existing international laws of war did not pertain to treatment of al Qaeda and the Taliban because (1) al Qaeda ("merely a violent political movement or organization and not a nation-state"), the Taliban ("not a government"), and Afghanistan ("failed state") are "non-State" actors, and "a non-State actor cannot be a party to the international agreements governing war"; and (2) although the Geneva Conventions' "Common Article 3," which places restrictions on actors in non–inter-State conflicts, was written with insurgencies (e.g., civil wars, internal conflicts) in mind, it should be interpreted to apply "only to 'armed conflict not of an international character occurring in the territory of one of the High Contacting Parties,'" as the drafters cannot be said to have been thinking of "armed conflict between a Nation State and a transnational terrorist organization, or between a Nation State and a failed State harboring and supporting a transnational terrorist organization."[81]

While there was some resistance from other parts of the government, this rationale prevailed for several years, long enough for nearly eight hundred detainees to be sent to the Guantánamo prison under its auspices.

(The United States eventually repatriated or released most of them without charges, instituted military commissions to review or try the detainees, and established certain detainee rights, such as habeas corpus.)[82] The legal limbo symbolized by the Guantánamo Bay prison is perhaps the most notorious example of privileging certain conceptions of the soldier and the state, but it is by no means unique to the United States.

Why were fighters such as those in al Qaeda considered "unlawful"? Then US Deputy Assistant Attorney General John Yoo explained in a later essay:

> Unlike previous wars, the *current enemy is a stateless network of religious extremists* who do not obey the laws of war, who hide among peaceful populations, and who seek to launch surprise attacks on civilian targets with the aim of causing massive casualties. *They have no armed forces to target, no territory to defend, no people to protect*, and no fear of killing themselves in their attacks. *The front line is not solely a traditional battlefield*, and the primary means of conducting the war includes the efforts of military, law enforcement, and intelligence officers to stop attacks *before* they occur. Information is the primary weapon in the conflict against this new kind of enemy, and intelligence gathered from captured operatives is perhaps the most effective means of preventing future terrorist attacks upon U.S. territory.[83]

Ironically, Yoo invokes the untraditional nature of the enemy to strip it of its rights, while in the same breath advocating a nontraditional approach to warfare against them. The author and context make it easy to dismiss this explanation as the fevered ramblings of a fascist apologist, but these simultaneously contradictory views are firmly embedded in the international geopolitical system and in the international laws of war.

The very idea of limitations on lawful soldiering is in fact quite old. Cicero recounts Cato's demand that his son should swear his military oath anew if he wanted to remain in the army, "since he could not in justice fight the enemy when his former oath became void," and the Elder Marcus Cato's letter to young Marcus to refrain from battle after he had been discharged, for "it is not lawful for one who is not a soldier to fight with the enemy."[84]

What makes for a lawful soldier has changed, and is currently delineated in international law in the Third Geneva Convention (Art. 4), which specifies mostly regular members of armed forces, militias, or resistance groups meeting certain conditions, and various support or related personnel.[85] While it is a separate question *how* to treat unlawful combatants, it follows neither that they can be held indefinitely in legal limbo and subjected to "enhanced interrogation techniques" nor that they should be given protections fully equivalent to those afforded lawful combatants turned POWs.

That the category of lawful combatant (Additional Protocol I's Article 44 amendments notwithstanding) is so narrow is noteworthy and telling. Not only does the requirement to carry one's arms openly (and for regular armed forces or militia to wear distinctive emblems) preclude certain types of raids, but it also passes judgment on who can claim to legitimately fight in a war. But why should external forces determine whether a person counts as a legitimate warfighter?

### STATE PRIVILEGE

Setting aside for the moment any expediency considerations: there is no real political reason to restrict legitimate warfighting in this way *except* in order to privilege a certain conception of the state. If the political government or organization that one pledges allegiance to considers one to be its soldier, and if in the course of war one declares oneself to be a soldier (and does not falsely claim civilian immunity) and otherwise obeys international law,[86] then the relevant relationship is that between the soldier and his claimed government. Why are martial allegiance and military designation permitted only to and for certain forms of government as determined by outsiders?

For example, the US Department of Justice in 2002 denied that the Taliban was the legitimate governor of Afghanistan, calling it a militia, and argued that their fighters—they never called them "soldiers"—did not merit full POW treatment under the Geneva Conventions: "To the extent that the Taliban militia was more akin to a non-governmental organization that used military force to pursue its religious and political ideology than a functioning government, its members would be on the same legal footing as al Qaeda."[87]

While the Taliban was at the time—and still is—being challenged for governing control of the territory of Afghanistan, using military coercion to impose religious and political ideologies is hardly disqualifying when it comes to international recognition and thus political legitimation: viz., Saudi Arabia,[88] Iran's religious police and its Ministry of Promotion of

Virtue and Prevention of Vice, and numerous others who enjoy international legitimacy. Similarly, Syria's extended civil war left its embattled government with questionable control over significant parts of its claimed territory, yet it was still broadly recognized across the international community.

In terms of instability of monopoly on the use of force—to use the widely accepted Weberian definition of sovereignty—the Taliban is hardly unique. In terms of other standard measures of legitimacy (e.g., respect for human rights, democratic political participation), there are many illegitimate governments whose international recognition is never questioned (e.g., Saudi Arabia, China), as well as legitimate governments that are not recognized (e.g., Taiwan). Judgment can go either way, but the convention, for it is merely that, should be consistently applied: recognize the legitimacy of existing Saudi Arabian, Syrian, *and* Taliban governments, or none of them at all.

Instead, the international structure arbitrarily privileges the status quo by prioritizing existing governments with a time-slice principle, regardless of how they got there. This legal loophole that drops "unlawful combatants" outside of the law is a product of collusion between states to restrict access to "legitimacy" by using an assumption that ignores (and thus legitimates) all the past injustices along the way to achieving or maintaining a monopoly on the use of force over a territory.[89]

Rationalizing that the war against al Qaeda is new because "the front line is not solely a traditional battlefield" rings hollow, because no war, even those fought primarily in pitched battles, has ever not utilized other forms of conflict and conflict management. What seems to be most relevant in this situation is that the enemy is "stateless." Yet contrary to Yoo's claim, it does have armed forces to target—ones that are not organized and recognizable in the ways that a standard nation-state's troops are expected to be. At the time, it is true, they did not have "territory to defend," but they sought to establish one, and indeed, a different Islamist group, ISIS, controlled a significant swath of territory from 2013 through early 2019. To say that organizations such as al Qaeda have "no people to protect" is simply absurd, as is the idea that they are the only fighters who disobey the laws of war.

The major features that make a fighter "unlawful" are not all that different from those possessed by many "lawful" fighters—what is at work here is less the characteristics of the fighters themselves and more the privilege given to existing and recognized states, which is conferred not for any reason relating to their moral and political legitimacy. This is the ethic of cooperation at work, this time with respect to war's structure, via collusion among existing nation-states to limit the playing field. It is a product of widespread agreement within the dominant form of political organization about the preferred structure of war and its acceptable participants, whose facets have little to do with whether or not a combatant is really "lawful."

## LEGITIMATE STATE/SOLDIER RELATIONSHIPS

The fundamental nature of a soldier is that he represents his political organization or government in carrying out acts of political coercion. He is a representative, and that is a matter of the relationship between him and his government, and should only be determined by them. Whether the soldier obeys the laws of war in fighting and whether the government with monopoly on the use of force in that territory has legitimate claim to such are separate questions.

There are several reasons why it is advantageous from an international perspective to dictate who qualifies as a legitimate fighter: it helps preserve the modus vivendi between nation-states largely respecting one another's claims to sovereignty (for the opposite would be much worse, as we have seen), it tamps down more generally on political anarchy, and it incentivizes individual soldiers to moderate their behavior in war in order to receive certain treatment should they be captured. This particular structure of warfare yields many benefits, but it is still important to recognize the nature of the principles being used—that they are the result of cooperation, negotiated agreement, and convention, rather than that they reflect some deontological rightness—and to understand the trade-offs made in employing them.

## MARGINALIZING NONSTATE ACTORS

The danger lies in marginalization, which becomes the default in practice. When there is exclusion from certain *jus in bello* treatment grounded in an ethic of cooperation, as with Native Americans or any others deemed "barbarians" (chapter 2), horrific injustice ensues because there are no compelling grounds offered for a group's inclusion in that otherwise-proffered treatment. When they then fall into a legal loophole, as many fighters do, they can end up in a place like Guantánamo Bay, where, on the grounds of this international agreement, they have no legitimate claim to any rights or particular treatment.

To where one repatriates stateless fighters is an additional problem. It is all well and good to criticize existing international boundaries and the monopoly of states on forms of political organization as both arbitrary and conventional, but the fact remains that this is the international structure in place, and that leaves no room for people who do not wish or are not permitted to be categorized according to existing states. The contemporary conception of sovereignty in relation to territory is a convention that has very real and practical implications.

Ultimately, this structural application of the ethic of cooperation sits in tension with the pursuit of both: (a) domestic justice, as the criteria for designating legitimate soldiers should hinge on their relationship with their governments rather than on the judgments of international arbiters, and (b) international justice, as the criteria for legitimacy are applied inconsistently to soldiers and their political organizations to privilege existing states.

The external agreement between existing sovereign nation-states to recognize only certain fighters as legitimate on the basis of external features, rather than the internal relationship between a fighter and his government, generates this contemporary problem of "unlawful enemy combatants" falling into a legal void and leaving their treatment to the whims and mercies of the states that captured them. Although Geneva Convention Additional Protocol II urges that "at the end of hostilities, the authorities in power *shall endeavor* to grant the broadest possible amnesty to persons who have participated in the armed conflict" (Art 6.5, emphasis added),[90] it is not required—and in the case of "illegitimate" fighters, what constitutes the "end of hostilities" is often highly subjective. Common Article 3, which appears in all four of the 1949 Geneva Conventions, is broader in application than Protocol II,[91] and it protects participants in "armed conflict[s] not of an international character occurring in the territory of one of the High Contracting Parties" from murder, mutilation, cruelty, torture, "outrages upon personal dignity," and unfair trials, but it does not cover *non*international conflicts *not* on a contracting party's territory. The scope of Common Article 3 could and perhaps should be interpreted generously, as the US Supreme Court did in *Hamdan v. Rumsfeld*, 548 U.S. 557 (2006).[92] Narrower legal interpretations are also reasonable and possible, however, especially in cases of noninternational conflicts (not state-against-state) that occur on a noncontracting party's territory or on territory of unrecognized governance (e.g., failed states).⁹³ Furthermore, the law as it is written still privileges traditional conceptions of nation-states and territoriality, and still begs the fundamental question of legitimacy. The international consensus (as expressed through international law) might decide to grant "illegitimate" fighters criminal trials, military tribunals, or nonpenal detention (on the order of what "legitimate" POWs are supposed to receive), but that is subject to cooperative agreement and can always change.⁹⁴

Ironically, the ones who ended up in the American prison camp at Guantánamo Bay are lucky, in the international scheme of things: forces within American government and society themselves (including the US Congress and the ACLU) worked to mitigate and constrain the treatment of these detainees and bring them under the umbrella of Geneva Conventions protections, and ultimately have been reasonably successful in doing so. Military detainees of other, especially illiberal, societies would not have and have not been so fortunate, however, and leaving this issue up to the vagaries of fortune demonstrates one tension between the ethic of cooperation and other influential principles from traditional just war theory that focus more on deontological determinations of justice.

The monopolization of the definition of "legitimate" warfighting and warfighters by the existing cabal of nation-states solves one problem, but generates another when it runs into contemporary terrorism and other noncooperative forms of warfare, which reject these definitions of legitimacy. This challenge will be addressed in chapter 7.

## Trial by Combat

These various forms of cooperation on the contemporary structure of war—(1) war as political/verdict of battle, (2) limiting questions of justice to *jus in bello*, and (3) restricting who qualifies as a legitimate fighter, among others—combine to point to something larger about the nature of war. Although pitched battles are no longer as decisive as they were in the eighteenth century, the structure of war itself still constitutes trial by combat. By effectively abdicating questions of *jus ad bellum* beyond self-defense, international law has decreed that a war's outcome determines effective right (and who is *considered* to have had *jus ad bellum*); this assumes that wars are merely political, because those are the only types of questions that combat can answer in a secular world. This effectively turns modern war into a trial by combat.

As a legal proceeding, trial by combat (here, war) must still attend to its legitimacy as a process, which it maintains in part by permitting only certain types of player/participants to determine the outcome. Not just anyone can play—only those who have standing to effect a judgment via trial by combat. Those deemed legal participants then receive equal moral standing (moral equality of combatants).

Also known as judicial duel or "wager of battle," trial by combat is a way of judicially resolving conflict—the favor of God was invoked equally by both sides, but it was the winner who was declared to be in the right. Regulations guiding it appear in Germanic legal codes, but it was not exclusive to Germanic people. The historical record shows its usage as early as the eighth century, throughout the medieval period, and into the early seventeenth century. Manifest use of wagers has declined in other areas of life since the thirteenth century—trials by combat are now seen as bizarre and have been nearly eliminated[95]—but it lingers on unseen in the contemporary structure of warfare.

### *Pure and Perfect Procedural Justice*

Trial by combat can be categorized as either pure procedural justice or perfect procedural justice. If trial by combat is pure procedural justice, then whatever outcome is yielded is the legitimate one. If it is perfect procedural justice, then we know what the desired outcome looks like: whatever the material result, it is the revelation of God's truth.[96] Although most military victories are no longer followed by a formal rendition of "Te Deum,"[97] military conflicts cannot help but be imbued with an undertone—or perhaps overtone—of the fulfillment of destiny. Even in the heyday of the eighteenth-century wager through pitched battle (which was grounded in fairly nonideological and nonreligious claims to property), it is no accident that victors sung a religious thanksgiving afterward. In the nineteenth century, Lincoln mused privately about why this devastating American civil war continued:

> The will of God prevails. In great contests each party claims to act in accordance with the will of God. Both *may* be, and one *must* be

> wrong. God can not be *for*, and *against* the same thing at the same time. In the present civil war it is quite possible that God's purpose is something different from the purpose of either party—and yet the human instrumentalities, working just as they do, are of the best adaptation to effect His purpose.[98]

Maybe every victory was not so significant as to warrant interpreting it as God's active will, but every victory is at least something that God did not actively oppose.

Although pure procedural justice and perfect procedural justice are quite different, when it comes to the question of war and divine will, they are functionally the same—because the question of who is in the right (deontologically) can never be answered by martial contestation.

The correlation between democratic governance and wealth, which is frequently noticed, offers a useful comparison. Despite disagreement about causation and whether the trend is changing, the majority of the richest 40 percent of countries in the world are considered "free" according to the Freedom House rubric, and nearly all of the remainder are petro-states.[99] Whatever the cause, this association between democracy and wealth may be epistemically revealing: insofar as governments are supposed to improve their citizens' lives, greater wealth and the ability to provide higher standards of living might show that democracies "know" better ways of structuring political society.

Another, less-noticed correlation is that democracies have also produced greater military achievement. Contrary to the image of authoritarian societies being more successful in war because they are more disciplined, democracies have in fact won about 80 percent of the time, in the past two centuries.[100] While some attribute this to the greater likelihood of democracies assisting one another,[101] or their superior ability in marshaling resources from their society to fight,[102] others argue that their system of governance means that democracies usually only engage in wars they are likely to win (selection effect) because their leaders are accountable to the population,[103] that their military leaders are more skilled because they are less likely to have been chosen for political reasons, and that their soldiers are more willing to fight than those of nondemocracies as evidenced by surrender rates.[104]

Whatever the reason, democracies' greater military effectiveness means they are more capable of protecting their populations' security and pursuing their populations' interests. More security is, however, a necessary but insufficient condition of providing better lives to one's citizens, so at best democratic systems have shown through military prowess that they are more capable of securing the *underlying conditions* for justice and right—stability and security. This builds on the wealth correlations: insofar as democracies have demonstrated greater ability to generate wealth, which is highly correlated with better standards of living, democracies are superior forms of governance; and one of the conditions for greater wealth is more security and stability, which democracies are also better at realizing; as such, when democracies win wars, they demonstrate superior ability to secure the conditions for better livelihoods and thus create the necessary if insufficient conditions for justice.

Although the democratic form of governance can be said to be demonstrably superior in this particular way, democracies are not then necessarily right in violently and coercively imposing like governments[105]—much less when they war for other reasons—and neither does this give us a way to adjudicate between two democracies fighting each other.

### Effective Right in the Pursuit of Justice

In the international arena, where there is no consensus or acceptance of how to determine who is in the right, military force is used to *impose* right. This is where trial by combat conflicts with other principles of just warfare. Military victory cannot *prove* right, because nothing about military success directly demonstrates the justice of one's international cause, and is even unlike the tighter connection between the form of governance and the creation of public policies that improve citizens' lives or the correlation between democracy and wealth.

In the practice of international politics, however, might ultimately makes right, and insofar as war is a way of determining *effective* right in the international arena (as in the Westphalian system we currently live in), democracies are "right" more often than nondemocracies. But no matter who wins, the triumph takes on an ideological bent regardless of any actual correlation between victory and justice. This is one way in which the two approaches to war as trial by combat—pure procedural justice and perfect procedural justice—come together. Even if one thinks of war as a purely procedural matter whose result is legitimate whatever it is, there is a post-hoc tendency to ascribe justicial or teleological significance to the outcome.[106] Here it is worth quoting at greater length Judge Holden from Cormac McCarthy's *Blood Meridian*, who speaks to war's neutral and arbitrary nature but simultaneous power to divine:

> Games of chance require a wager to have meaning at all. Games of sport involve the skill and strength of the opponents and the humiliation of defeat and the pride of victory are in themselves sufficient stake because they inhere in the worth of the principals and define them. But trial of chance or trial of worth all games aspire to the condition of war for here that which is wagered swallows up game, player, all. . . .
>
> This is the nature of war, whose stake is at once the game and the authority and the justification. Seen so, war is the truest form of divination. It is the testing of one's will and the will of another within that larger will which because it binds them is therefore forced to select. War is the ultimate game because war is at last a forcing of the unity of existence. War is god. . . .
>
> A moral view can never be proven right or wrong by any ultimate test. A man falling dead in a duel is not thought thereby to be proven in error as to his views. His very involvement in such a trial gives evidence of a new and broader view. The willingness of the principals to forgo further argument as the triviality which it in fact is and to petition directly the chambers of the historical absolute clearly indicates of how little moment are the opinions and of what great moment the divergences thereof. . . . Man's vanity may well approach the infinite in capacity but his knowledge remains imperfect and howevermuch he comes to value his judgements ultimately he must submit them before a higher court. Here there can be no special pleading. Here are considerations of equity and rectitude and moral right rendered void and without warrant and here are the views of the litigants despised. Decisions of life and death, of what shall be and what shall not, beggar all question of right.[107]

Modern warfare bears a disturbing resemblance to trial by combat and its cousin, trial by ordeal. Both are premised on the belief that an inscrutable God would favor the innocent. Insofar as we prefer that wars be won by the party in the right, then, like trial by ordeal, trial by combat—which rewards the stronger or more skilled fighter—is by contemporary standards barbarously arbitrary in its adjudication of justice.

## SOLDIERS AS "CHAMPIONS"

This use of champions, who could be engaged to fight in one's stead, is another analogous aspect to trial by combat. Champions generally have nothing to do with the underlying conflict, yet they bear the physical costs (which can include maiming or death), while the parties to the conflict avoid any physical harm. This is precisely the role that soldiers play on behalf of their governments, and it should raise the same questions about unethical use of proxies to fight on one's behalf in modern warfare as it does in trial by combat.

Yet, the institutional organization of modern warfare and the moral equality of combatants doctrine allow states to engage in trial by combat. (Historically, it was probably the other way around, that combatant equality developed in response to the trial-by-combat structure of warfare.) Winners may or may not be in the right—the outcome of a physical contest tells us little if not nothing about the justice of that party's claim, and yet, that is effectively what war as an institutional practice purports to determine. This essentially theological way of thinking about immanent justice—whether or not there is any *stated* recourse to God's favor of the innocent—is somewhat tempered by other principles in play, such as human rights and the traditional Western *jus ad bellum* criteria of just cause, right intention, and legitimate authority, which seek to ensure that the correct (i.e., just) outcome will come to pass. But the fundamental problem of trial by combat remains, and sits in tension with other equally influential approaches to war ethics.

## ABDICATING *JUS AD BELLUM* JUDGMENT, PRIORITIZING *JUS IN BELLO*

Whatever justicial or teleological meaning is imputed to a war's outcome, military victory confers effective right—and the body of international law reflects and accepts this judgment. In deeming self-defense to be the only legitimate cause for war, international law is either taking a selectively pacifist stance or declaring that any other *jus ad bellum* cannot be determined by man or political process definitively enough to act on it. This abandons a "natural law" understanding of war as constrained by or consistent with justice, and embraces instead a conventional, positivist conception of war.[108] In doing so, it privileges the status quo of existing state boundaries and contemporary claims of legitimate governance. There are, of course, many good reasons to do so, especially if the status quo promotes a relatively peaceful or stable modus vivendi. Yet, it implicitly condones the extensive use of violence and military conquest that had previously established *effective* right to these borders, and is ultimately a *practical* approval of the status quo. In this way, modern and contemporary warfare—supported by its component institutions, e.g., international law, the cooperative structure of war, and the moral equality of combatants—is effectively trial by combat.

This should raise concerns insofar as we are interested in justice. Whether or not it takes religious overtones, trial by combat is essentially an appeal to "heaven," for it attempts to establish some claim of natural law right that cannot be determined via this process. The only right it establishes is conventional right, to which the existing body of contemporary norms of war then accords the status and privileges that would be conferred to natural law right. Yet, short of annihilating all competing claimants, war (trial by combat) cannot in and of itself definitively settle anything about justice, because people have to accept the legitimacy of the outcome, and in the international arena, they do so largely on practical grounds.

Because war cannot say much about *jus ad bellum* rendered, the past centuries have seen increasing efforts to imbue *jus in bello* with meaning and to pursue justice there—some of which have been discussed in this book—which generates tension between certain ethics of cooperation and the justicial concerns of traditional just war theory. Classical just war theory is more concerned with rightness than fairness, as demonstrated, for example, by Aquinas's allowance for ambushes and the lack of restrictions on how soldiers are killed (the crossbow ban against fellow Christians notwithstanding). Rather, the focus is on proportionality constraints—is it "worth it" for the goal? As such, restrictions on how one is permitted to fight can conflict with the ability of the side in the right to win, which would hinder the pursuit of justice.

The ethic of cooperation's influence on the structure of warfare leads to a system that recuses itself from addressing natural law claims of *jus ad bellum*. This generates a fundamental contradiction between the ethic of cooperation and aspects of classical and traditional just war theories, the latter of which are largely concerned with the determination of justice across the areas of warfare.

Once people recognized the limitations of warfare in a more secular world driven by maintaining modus vivendi, and moved to a primarily conventional/positivist model, they sought justice elsewhere, and focused on making actions *within* war just, such as with "fair fights," honor, not "taking advantage" of opponents, protections for people during fights, efficiently finding a winner of the war, and so on. These have little to do with justice rendered by war itself, and only in some cases have anything to do with justice *during* war, with *jus in bello* in a natural law sense. *Jus in bello* is extremely important, of course, but the contemporary emphasis on it for its own sake tends to lose sight of the original problem, which is that *jus ad bellum* cannot be adequately determined through methods of adjudication currently available to man.

### *Moral Equality of Combatants: A Useful Fiction?*

Within modern warfare's "trial by combat" structure, the use of soldiers as proxies of the state has led to the doctrine of moral equality between combatants, which is buttressed by many of the cooperative institutions explored here (e.g., contemporary POW treatment, medical immunity, medical neutrality). As discussed in chapter 3, one major justification for extending the same protections to every POW regardless of the justice of his cause is the belief that he is merely an agent of his state and only kills as such: a soldier is a vessel, and thus there is nothing personal, criminal, or punishable in killing other soldiers in the context of war. This is grounded in assumptions of the modern nation-state, its reification, and its soldiers, who are considered its impersonal representatives. The modus vivendi sought after the devastation of the religious wars and its accompanying abdication of *jus ad bellum* judgment lead to the doctrine that combatants in war are morally equal—that they cannot and should not be held responsible for considerations of *jus ad bellum*, which are the responsibility of political leaders. Instead, they should only be judged on *jus in bello*, and therefore all have equal rights of self-defense and privilege to kill. This is known in contemporary just war theory as the moral equality of combatants. From this has followed numerous practices such as humane treatment of POWs and nonpenal detention (i.e., quarantine rather than punishment) and medical neutrality.

The doctrine of moral equality of combatants is a crucial part of the broader attempt to codify war and limit its destructiveness: wars are not intended to secure total annihilation or result in the death or enslavement of every man, woman, and child. Instead, they serve a bounded political purpose to resolve disagreements, not to establish cosmic rightness or wrongness. The realities of epistemic limitations are such that soldiers cannot determine with certainty whether or not they fight on the right side. Once the door to uncertainty about the correctness of one's cause was opened, international law and contemporary just war theory then predominantly treated soldiers as moral equals, rather than criminals. Says Michael Walzer:

> They can try to kill me, and I can try to kill them. . . . Though there is no license for war-makers, there is a license for soldiers, and they hold it without regard to which side they are on; it is the first and most important of their war rights. They are entitled to kill, *not anyone*, but men whom we know to be victims. *We could hardly understand such a title if we did not recognize that they are victims too.* Hence the moral reality of war can be summed up in this way: when soldiers fight freely, choosing one another as enemies and designing their own battles, their war is not a crime; when they fight without freedom, their war is not their crime. In both cases, military conduct is governed by rules; but in the first the rules rest on mutuality and consent, in the second on a shared servitude. The first case raises no difficulties; the second is more problematic.[109]

Even if the war's cause is unjust, soldiers do no wrong by fighting for it, as they are considered apolitical and not held directly responsible for *jus ad bellum*—that is the responsibility of the leaders who make the decision to go to war.[110] This presumption of moral equality means that soldiers are not to be punished for killing in the name of that injustice, as normal fighting is no wrongdoing, and from that follows certain nonpenal detention and medical treatment due to soldiers.[111] The historical rise of states and their large national armies has also "nationalized" soldiers' lives, thus further removing soldiers from personal responsibility for ordinary acts of war, including killing.

Interestingly, the only major contemporary theory of just war that directly addresses the recusal from *jus ad bellum* judgment is revisionism, which argues instead for the moral *in*equality of combatants.[112]

It may be that moral equality is well suited for a system in which there is so much fundamental uncertainty and dispute over the justice of everyone's respective causes that there could be no agreement on an adjudication procedure other than the resort to force. This is largely the global system we have now, in which the limit of epistemic possibility combines with self-interest for an unfortunately stalemated outcome.

While it is undoubtedly difficult if not impossible to know whether the cause one fights for is just, however, there is an epistemic asymmetry such that it is easier to know if one's cause is *unjust*[113]—and given the experience of human history, it is perhaps wise to assume that one's cause is most likely unjust, which would make combatants' moral equality less defensible on epistemic grounds, argues Jeff McMahan.[114]

Revisionist just war theorists like McMahan contend that soldiers who fight for an unjust cause have no right to attack opponents fighting for a just cause, because the opponent is innocent in the relevant sense and therefore not liable to attack. Similarly, soldiers for an unjust cause have no rights of self-defense (and are not morally entitled to fight back) if attacked by a soldier fighting for a just cause.[115]

Even if one assumes the philosophical truth of this moral inequality and the empirical truth of the relevant epistemological capacity, one reason to nonetheless retain the moral equality of combatants is that soldiers are bound by their professional oaths to trust and obey. Treating combatants as morally equal alleviates some of the ensuing burden on soldiers for decisions that their governments made. As Walzer says, soldiers are victims, too.

The more democratic, participatory, and accountable—and the less strictly top-down—the political system is, however, the more plausible a principle of moral *in*equality becomes, and the less that argument holds true. Nonetheless, the structure of civil/military relations and the normative expectations for military subordination and active-military abstention from politics in liberal democratic systems might obviate the force of that epistemic argument somewhat.

## THE COST OF MORAL INEQUALITY

Should moral symmetry between combatants be eliminated if its justifications are inconsistent with determinations of responsibility, epistemology, and justice?[116] Replacing it with moral *in*equality comes at a cost. Nonpenal detention for POWs and battlefield immunity for national medics rest in large part on this doctrine of moral equality, which is premised on the particular political and limited-justicial structure of modern nation-state warfare.

Even though soldiers would still have basic moral rights as human beings, it would follow from the *in*equality doctrine that soldiers from an unjust side are not owed any inherent *moral* considerations to be treated *as POWs under existing international law*. If transporting, feeding, and otherwise caring for them in particular ways—per costly international agreements[117]—would drain resources that would prevent the just side from winning the war, then those unjust soldiers could be handled in other ways instead. The contemporary concept of and required treatment for a prisoner of war (apolitical and not responsible for *jus ad bellum*) rests on the moral equality of combatants—this is a complex apparatus whose parts hang together.

With a moral *in*equality doctrine, however, responsibility and liability for *jus ad bellum* are applied individually, and analogously to criminal behavior. Even accounting for human rights constraints, judging individual warfighters on the basis of criminal responsibility and liability would have implications for the validity of the entire structure of warfare including the very concept of "prisoner of war," as well as many of its accompanying privileges. For example, the Geneva Conventions respect national military hierarchies by stipulating that both commissioned and noncommissioned officers held as POWs are not required to work; in contrast, there is not only no moral or legal obligation to respect criminal organization hierarchies (which soldiers would be more akin to, if they are viewed through the individualistic lens of the moral *in*equality doctrine) but in fact compelling reasons to break up those chains of command. The knock-on effects of treating soldiers through this individualistic, criminal lens (as opposed to being nonresponsible agents of the state) would be varied and far-reaching. Put in practice, it would also contradict the structural cooperative ethics that frame current international law protecting POWs.

Abandoning the moral equality of combatants may also open the door to punishments for soldiers, as they would then be held responsible for the unjust fighting—at great cost to them. Although certain protections and services could still be provided on humanitarian grounds, those reasons would justify far less than is currently expected and given—and one cannot rely on individual soldiers to follow the logic of epistemic asymmetry and avoid this problem altogether.

Unfortunately, one cannot have it both ways: we cannot get rid of moral equality while keeping moral immunity for combatants and equal protection for POWs. Equal protection for all soldiers is instituted in part by the ethic of cooperation's influence, and it could not realistically be sustained in conjunction with a doctrine of combatant moral *in*equality. One can make the distinction between law and morality, as McMahan does, and argue that despite the moral asymmetry of combatants, it is still important to retain equal treatment of all sides as a matter of law. Given the ways in which the law strives to reflect morality and how the institutional structure of war as a whole seeks to integrate morality and law where possible, however, moving to a moral system of combatant *in*equality would necessarily open the door to the possibility of punishing *soldiers* for the wrongdoing of fighting an unjust war, which may include incarceration and death penalties (common punishment in criminal law) for ordinary wartime activities. This is a serious implication of the doctrine of moral *in*equality of combatants, and one that it is not clear revisionists would be willing to accept.

## REVISITING STRUCTURAL ALTERNATIVES

The use of soldiers as champions for what is essentially trial by combat is deeply morally problematic, so perhaps that should point us to moral *in*equality of combatants. But given the accompanying difficulties with moving to such a system—including the harm to soldiers that will follow—perhaps that should point us instead to considering, once again, as in chapter 5, different structures for war, such that there are fewer champions called upon, and thus fewer deaths. The large scale of contemporary war and its accompanying destruction are part of the problem, and at some point, the quantitative difference becomes a qualitative one.

CHAPTER VII

## Abdication of Judgment, Noncooperative Fights, and the Meaning of War

> Later, in the darkness, a mortar round landed on a truckful of wounded men and flung [him] to the ground, stunned. He woke under the same brilliant moon. Chinese soldiers walked among the wounded and the dead, probing bodies with their rifle butts. Both kindness and cruelty walked with them. "If there was a response they would offer the casualty a drink from a steaming canteen, if not they searched for watches." Later on another soldier thrust his bayonet into a body. His companions laughed.
> —ALBERT E. COWDREY, *THE MEDICS' WAR: UNITED STATES ARMY IN THE KOREAN WAR*[1]

Despite enormous advances in the ethics of warfighting, especially in protecting civilians and soldiers and otherwise limiting damage, there has been little progress made on the fundamental function and role of war, which is to yield a "correct" or just outcome beyond a modus vivendi. So if war cannot render human justice, perhaps there is something to be said for the classical Greek hoplite approach, which is at least short and efficient.[2] Unfortunately, "part of the modern condition [is] that we have lost the capacity to limit the conflict of war to pitched battle," says James Q. Whitman,[3] or to any other such bounded structure, so even the eighteenth-century model of pitched battle as wager is unlikely to be revived, much less a contemporary version of Greek hoplite war or something less deadly such as ritual combat.

Perhaps that is because war will always be with us. After all, what reasons would one have to accept the outcome of gladiatorial duel-combat (*monomachia*) or small-scale wars if one loses? Further violence is always available as a last resort, a trump card that someone will always be willing to use in the service of both right and wrong—usually without knowing which—and political leaders are unlikely to implement processes to hold themselves more accountable for those decisions.

We have seen that some buy-in to war as a decision-making procedure has been possible in the past, however, and the cost of doing otherwise makes it worth exploring whether similar structural agreement can be had again in a different way. The choice is not between ideal and nonideal worlds, but rather between different (often still horrific) nonideals.

Path dependence means that in all likelihood we will be unable to deviate from existing structure,[4] but it compounds the tragedy of contemporary warfare that these models are available to us but cannot be implemented for other—often well-meaning—reasons. The paradox of eighteenth-century warfare, as Whitman argues, is that while its laws systematically deferred to sovereigns and permitted many things that would be illegal now, it still managed to maintain certain standards of restraint that we admire.[5] Although the current prevailing method of limiting warfare relies on humanitarianism, it is not the only thing that can constrain war—as we have seen, alternatives have and are still used, perhaps to better effect, and could be revitalized.

Cleaving too narrowly to the contemporary model, which abjures making judgments on *jus ad bellum* (with the exception of self-defense) and focuses *within* war by heavily regulating *jus in bello*, can run the risk of falling into a view that believes something to be lost if we did not fight. It is, of course, human nature to make the best of an unavoidable bad situation. Each expression of the ethic of cooperation between enemies is in some way an attempt to comprehend the incomprehensible, whether by finding or creating meaning within the senselessness of war's violence (e.g., through honor, virtue, or self-sacrifice on behalf of one's country, fellow soldier, or the innocent) or limiting it so that it minimally intrudes on the rest of one's life where one does find purpose.[6]

The various manifestations of the ethic of cooperation are driven by a variety of motives—ranging across aesthetic, humanitarian, justicial, professional, utilitarian, and so forth—but they also reflect deeper moral reasons. They are fundamentally concerned with both living well (insofar as one must fight, one should do so with dignity and give one's opponent his due) and dying well (cleanly, without grotesque suffering, and with good conscience).

Still, some consider war to be necessary violence under certain circumstances, for example, in decolonization, as Frantz Fanon argues: in the Manichean world of colonial society, in which one breathed an "atmosphere of violence, that violence which is just under the skin," there must be a role reversal between "native" and "settler" in order to complete decolonization. "The last shall be first and the first last" only when "the colonized man finds his freedom in and through violence." Violence is a language common to both colonizer and colonized; its brutality becomes embedded in the colonized, and so thoroughly deforms their souls in subjugation that only through that same language can they throw off the colonial yoke. Violent overthrow "invests their characters with positive and creative qualities," "mobilizes" and "binds them together as a whole," and "introduces into each man's consciousness the ideas of a common cause, of a national destiny, and of a collective history." As such, "violence is a cleansing force" that develops the colonized's personality in ways necessary for self-rule: "free[ing] the native from his inferiority complex and from his despair and inaction[,] it makes him fearless and restores his self-respect," and re-creates him as the author of his own actions, for "when the people have taken violent part in the national liberation they will allow no one to set themselves up as 'liberators,'" and in producing the possibility for unity, they thus finally become free.[7]

Like Fanon, a very different figure believes that martial suffering can bring a person to fruition as a human being. Two years into World War II, boarding school students sing "not less we praise in darker days," but Prime Minister Winston S. Churchill replies: "Do not let us speak of darker days: let us speak rather of sterner days. These are not dark days; these are great days—the greatest days our country has ever lived; and we must all thank God that we have been allowed, each of us according to our stations, to play a part in making these days memorable in the history of our race."[8]

This must be filtered through Churchill's hawkishness, of course, but it was his job to maintain the population's morale and put the war's hardships in the best possible light, and he may have been sincere in attempting to find some purpose for his people in a vicious and recurring activity that often seems bereft of any.

However, both Churchill and Fanon verge on forgetting that violence is merely a means, made necessary only by circumstance, for the cultivation of certain traits. Sometimes people overlook the *unavoidable* part: that the destruction of war should be eschewed as much as possible and that only when there is genuinely no other choice should we seek meaning in it. Even as Moltke (the Elder) supported the evolution of international law toward greater protections for soldiers and civilians, for example, he still warned:

> Perpetual peace is a dream, and it is not even a beautiful dream. War is an element in the order of the world ordained by God. In it the noblest virtues of mankind are developed; courage and the abnegation of self, faithfulness to duty, and the spirit of sacrifice; the soldier gives his life. Without war the world would stagnate, and lose itself in materialism.[9]

Unsurprisingly, Nietzsche takes things further, in seeing violence as a form of liberation from abnegating self-loathing, while the ancient Greeks of Homer glorified the martial arts and virtues.[10]

Warfighters themselves are not immune. Even as they are forced by circumstance to find meaning where they can in war, they, too, are seduced by its horrors. "Many men both hate and love combat. They know why they hate it; it is harder to know and to be articulate about why they love it," explains J. Glenn Gray. "For some of them the war years are what Dixon Wecter has well called 'the one great lyric passage in their lives.'" There is, moreover, a certain aesthetic quality to warfare, Gray astutely grasps:

> The ugly can please us too, as every artist knows. And furthermore, beauty in various guises is hardly foreign to scenes of battle. While it is undeniable that the disorder and distortion and the violation of nature that conflict brings are ugly beyond compare, there are also color and movement, variety, panoramic sweep, and sometimes even momentary proportion and harmony. If we think of beauty and ugliness without their usual moral overtones there is often a weird but genuine beauty in the sight of massed men and weapons in combat.

Gray cautions, however, that reveling in the sublimity of war's spectacle is incorrect, or at least misleading, for it should not be "triumph" that one feels but rather humility—"a recognition of the power and grandeur to which we are subject," à la Kant's contemplation of the starry skies above.[11]

The tendency to venerate war and violence is understandable insofar as it is a common human instinct to try to survive whatever one's circumstances, or to try to make sense of and impose order on one's insensible conditions. There are many different ways to do that, however, and it might behoove us to consider more bounded alternatives that run less risk of prolonging a war for its own sake or in the pursuit of greatness and glory through violence. Extended conflicts often last so long that their geopolitical goals change and the original objective is lost. The Korean War, for example, dragged on for years longer than necessary, at great cost to human life, in part because the opposing sides could not come to an agreement about repatriating POWs who did not want to return to their home country, an issue that had little to do with the catalyzing conflict.

The loss of sense of purpose could be seen in the widespread adoption of body armor by American troops in the Korean War. Body armor was available in World War II, but at the time, soldiers ridiculed it and officers considered it inefficient and burdensome. While the wholehearted embrace less than a decade later had also to do with the military becoming accustomed to this innovation and seeing its enormous utility in protecting life and limb, there was another reason as well. An Army investigation in 1952 surmised that changed attitudes toward and use of body armor was a result of the "unique" aimlessness of the Korean War: "the lack of specific battle goals and the prolonged truce talks [have] resulted in a feeling of caution in all combat echelons. Commanders, under these conditions, are not quite so ready to sacrifice personnel on the battlefield."[12] This is but one of the many pitfalls of the structure of contemporary warfare.

Alternatives to the current model of war will seem ludicrous to the contemporary warrior who understands war to be about efficiency in the narrowest sense—i.e., killing, as it is the quickest way to establish dominance—but examples can be taken from more ritualistic warfare, which settled disputes as well. For example, when Joseph Medicine Crow, last chief of his tribe, was called up in 1943 to fight in World War II, he felt ambivalent:

> He wanted to prove himself in Europe, but in a Crow way. For them, warfare was seldom about killing. Rather it was an endless series of raids and horse-stealing in which young men showed how cunning, noble and resourceful they were, decorating their coup sticks with beads and feathers to prove it. It was, he thought, the finest sport in the world. He went on raids along the Siegfried Line with red warpaint under his uniform and a yellow-daubed eagle feather, symbol of his spirit-helper, tucked inside his helmet. In one village he collided with a German soldier. Rather than simply shooting him, he threw away his rifle and wrestled him into submission, as he had the Sioux boy long ago.

In the course of repeated courageousness, then and at other times, in the conventional Western war, he "unconsciously performed—by grabbing the explosives, manhandling the enemy soldier, seizing his rifle, and stealing the horses—the four deeds that established him as a war-chief of his people."[13]

Given the state of international moral discourse and human limitations, however, we are nowhere close to even considering a major change in the structure of war—wars are only becoming more protracted (in part with the help of new technology and new arenas and mediums of conflict) and increasingly ideological, and it is difficult to conceive of circumstances under which a more limiting structure could be widely implemented.

If that is the case, it behooves us to ask: In the human spirit of survival and resourcefulness in the face of an impossible situation, is there anything that can be said for war? While Kant speaks at great length in other places about the wrongness of war, in his *Critique of Judgment*, he invokes its beauty and sublimity, including the aesthetic appeal of the soldier and the greatness that can come with war:

> For what is that which is, even to the savage, an object of the greatest admiration? It is a man who shrinks from nothing, who fears nothing, and therefore does not yield to danger, but rather goes to face it vigorously with the fullest deliberation. Even in the most highly civilised state this peculiar veneration for the soldier remains, though only under the condition that he exhibit all the virtues of peace, gentleness, compassion, and even a becoming care for his own person; because even by these it is recognised that his mind is unsubdued by danger. Hence whatever disputes there may be about the superiority of the respect which is to be accorded them, in the comparison of a statesman and a general, the aesthetical judgement decides for the latter. *War itself, if it is carried on with order and with a sacred respect for the rights of citizens, has something sublime in it, and makes the disposition of the people who carry it on thus, only the more sublime, the more numerous are the dangers to which they are exposed, and in respect of which they behave with courage. On the other hand, a long peace generally brings about a predominant commercial spirit, and along with it, low selfishness, cowardice, and effeminacy, and debases the disposition of the people.*[14]

This passage has vexed many a reader of Kant, for it seems inconsistent with his many stern and unequivocal criticisms of war elsewhere, but it may offer some answers to what function war can serve in teleological history. For Kant, some types of conflict offer the possibility of developing essential human capacities for reason, rational thought, control of the passions, and self-regulation.[15] This passage, especially Kant's lamentation of degradation into corrupted commercialism, may seem no different from Churchill's and Moltke's exhortations for rising to the occasion of war and its cultivation of the most noble of virtues. While there is significant overlap between the virtues they all invoke, including self-discipline, sacrifice, and courage, Churchill and Moltke are focused on the development of martial virtues—which are important—qua martial virtues, whereas Kant was after something greater, namely, the virtues necessary for peaceful and lawful autonomy.[16]

While always tragic, war can be pursued in more barbaric fashion (especially but not exclusively in colonial conquests) or, alternatively, "with order and with a sacred respect for the rights of citizens." The latter approach helps cultivate traits of honor, courage, restraint, discipline, generosity, and cooperation, argues Kant, all of which are required in order to develop and sustain a lawful constitution for self-governance, which is only one of many steps necessary for eventual perpetual peace.

Kant's philosophy of history may or may not prove true—thus far, the record is mixed at best—but there is reason to find some alleviation of despair in the enormous progress that has been made over time in constraining the worst excesses of war, including with the continued development of different types of ethics of cooperation (e.g., international law).

## Noncooperative Warfare

Much analysis of military strategy and tactics uses game theory, while most contemporary work on military ethics and just war theory argues from first principles in order to explicate the rights that are owed to and duties incurred by individuals or various groups of people. But unilateral moral duties (God-given or otherwise) alone cannot explain explicit conceptions of and the language of reciprocity and the use of negotiated agreements in developing and enforcing warfare regulations and military ethics. While war brings out the worst in humanity, it also inspires the best—not just impromptu acts of moral rectitude, but also concerted efforts to do right by one's opponents.

This book has explored a significant yet overlooked principle at work in the thinking and practice of war. Different aspects of the ethic of cooperation between enemies have been discussed by others, and at times extensively, but the cohesive overarching phenomenon has gone largely unrecognized as such—understandably so, as it takes different forms that often appear to have little to do with one another. As noted in chapter 1, the explicit laws and treaties of modern international law are unique in their universalizability, nonreliance on comprehensive doctrines, and legal specificity; and adherence to the international legal apparatus constitutes a form of cooperation motived by self-interested, moral, and deontological motivations.

The ethic of cooperation in warfare is so pervasive and influential that the dominant contemporary symbols of humanitarianism are grounded in it and recognize the practical limitations of convention. Argues former Canadian politician and historian Michael Ignatieff:

> *The [Geneva] Conventions make no ringing claims about human brotherhood. Instead, they accept war as a normal anthropological ritual—the only way that certain human disputes can be resolved.* They seek only to ensure that warriors conform to certain basic principles of humanity, the chief principle being to spare civilians and medical personnel. *These two traditions—human rights and the laws of war—inspire humanitarian activists in all the world's danger zones, but they are in fact two different practical moralities.* Even within the Red Cross itself, the conflict between these moralities remains unresolved. There are those who insist that the Red Cross's ultimate responsibility is to attack the causes of war, while others believe it is only there to tame the beast.[17]

Convention is a major driving force of morality. Especially to make claims about something as grounded in human practice and human nature as warfare, theoretical arguments should take into account broad-ranging historical and existing practices. It is, in fact, by exploring existing warfighting norms and their moral implications from the bottom up, building cases from principles, that we can shed light on essential aspects of warfare that are otherwise overlooked by a strictly top-down methodology. It also permits us to develop normative prescriptions and philosophical arguments that would not otherwise be available to us.

In exploring the overlooked but equally, if not more, influential normative force of *convention* on warfare, we gain a better understanding of the moral dimension of key military practices. This helps us to better see certain contemporary military challenges for what they really are; in the case of the extensive use of cooperative ethics, it enables us to understand that it is the source of some critical tensions in one of the most significant developments in warfare in recent years.

*Contemporary Terrorism*

Terrorism itself is nothing new. It has always been used, but is perhaps more significant now, as expectations for what constitutes acceptable warfare and who qualifies as legitimate participants have only narrowed over time, especially after the Second World War (chapter 6). In addition, the nature of terrorism today takes a different tone: unlike the prominent terrorist groups of the 1960s and 1970s, their contemporary counterparts are more likely to be organized in ways and to make demands that do not fit within the existing Westphalian state-centric international structure, which is predicated on various underlying ethics of cooperation.

This has generated a fair amount of confusion about what terrorism is, where it fits into the international system, and how one should respond to it. For example, it is common to consider terrorism synonymous with non-state groups, so can states commit terrorism? The answer to that question is, emphatically, "Yes."[18] The horror that contemporary terrorism provokes is warranted, but much of the ensuing confusion was not, and resulted from the unknowing application of certain aspects of the ethic of cooperation in warfare that are nonetheless taken for granted.

Not only is terrorism an ancient form of warfare that has been consistently employed even alongside "conventional" warfare, but it is also utterly unsurprising that those who cannot win conventionally might turn to terrorist tactics. Victor Davis Hanson notes this in 1998, when he describes the dilemma of modern Western warfare: "excellence at frontal assault and decisive battle" holds within it the very seeds of its destruction, as its practitioners have become so skilled that few are willing to fight them that way anymore, so they will turn to stealthier forms of combat, and their opponents will have to follow suit.[19]

While noncooperative forms of warfare are not new challenges per se, the moral landscape has changed in the past few centuries. Terrorism as a strategy or tactic is now controversial because it rejects the dominant ethical framework in war, as embodied by the international laws of war, which are based in significant part on certain cooperative ethics, as we have seen.[20] If these cooperative expectations were not in play in this way, terrorism would actually become less of a moral problem. Its noncooperative approach rejects the widely accepted model of contemporary international law and runs up against now-established expectations for cooperative behavior in war, which is why both their tactics and their status as fighters are deemed illegitimate, and they have been liable to fall into legal loopholes of various kinds. The chapter 6 discussion about "unlawful enemy combatants" is relevant here: such restrictions on legitimate participation in warfare are conventional and arbitrary, but abandoning these cooperative principles also leaves us with few tools for condemning actions that seem, to many, to be beyond the pale, and would return us to a premodern period in which nearly anything in the service of a just cause would be acceptable.

The first chapter of this book discussed the concerns American citizens had about its government negotiating prisoner exchanges with the Taliban, in part because of the political legitimacy it might confer to the latter: that apprehension is firmly grounded in the complex web of international law that draws heavily from the ethic of cooperation in warfare and in turn generates normative expectations to adhere to that cooperative framework.

That terrorists do not abide by the "rules of warfare" makes them suspect in all matters—deservedly or not—in the eyes of their opponents. When questioned about the possibility of a cease-fire between Hezbollah and Israel in 2006, US Ambassador to the United Nations John Bolton encapsulated the blanketing doubt that is cast: "I think it's a very fundamental question how a terrorist group agrees to a cease-fire. How do you hold a terrorist group accountable? Who runs the terrorist group? Who makes the commitments that the terrorist group will abide by a cease-fire? What does a terrorist group think a cease-fire is?"[21]

Bolton may have been exaggerating for effect, because terrorist organizations are not internally anarchic, and in the case of Hezbollah, there is a clear leadership structure and people to hold accountable, but his questions reflect a widely held uncertainty about whether organizations that reject most accepted understandings and conventions of the international laws of war could nonetheless share common conceptions of some military ideas (here, the cease-fire) and furthermore be trusted or motivated to abide by its commitments.

The broader struggle for any military group in this contemporary context is how to engage when confronted with acts of terrorism in violation of international law. After all, Cicero says, one need not keep one's own promises to an enemy who does not share the same understanding. Then, Cicero was referring to the pirate, who is counted not among "lawful enemies," but rather as "the common foe of all the world" (*communis hostis omnium*). Such inherent insincerity and duplicity that rely on the opponent doing the opposite can also be said to apply to terrorists, and would also place them outside of the law, as *hostis humani generis* (the alternative term that is more commonly used).[22]

Should one respect international rules of engagement (e.g., civilian immunity, POW protection, and so on) and still obey the laws of war oneself if the other side does not, for how is cooperation sustained without some (even if not immediate) reciprocity? As we have seen, strict reciprocity is not necessary to sustain an ethic of cooperation overall, although it does require *some* others to participate, even if indirectly or at various degrees removed.

In chapter 3, I argued that a military will have interests in nonetheless following the rules in order to promote future cooperation as well as to signal the enemy, the international community, and one's own personnel. But for soldiers on the ground, it is understandably difficult to adhere to the rules when opponents flaunt their noncompliance, and in a way that is likely to kill you; as the saying goes, "Better to be tried by twelve than carried by six."

This dilemma surfaces in many situations, including whether to adhere to POW regulations or provide equal medical treatment to opponents who violate international laws and norms (chapters 3 and 6).[23] It also harkens back to chapter 6's exploration into the price of a doctrine of moral *in*equality of combatants and the implications of making *jus in bello* dependent on *jus ad bellum*,[24] namely, what to do about hinging *jus in bello* treatment on possession of *jus ad bellum*.

Once we investigate the bases of the laws of war, they turn out to be built—more frequently than is commonly believed—not on rights, but rather on an ethic of cooperation between enemies. For that reason, there may not be as much owed to one's opponents as is frequently proclaimed. On the other hand, there may be other purposes for continuing to maintain one's own practices even in the face of the opponent's violations—but we should be clear about that. I will mention two here.

### Normative Obligations for Future Cooperation

All conventions and rituals, even if they originate purely out of expedience, eventually take on meaning of their own, as practitioners inevitably imbue them with significance. Just as the wager of battle is conducted with full understanding that it is a gamble whose outcome does not speak to the inherent justice of one's cause, but still acquires justicial or theological import after the fact, so too does formalized cooperation (e.g., wearing uniforms, respecting civilian immunity, treating POWs in a particular way) eventually breed expectations of future cooperation that become infused with a moral valence even stronger than that of entering into a wager of battle. Those engendered moral expectations in turn affect how one engages the enemy and may create normative duties to cooperate, independent of the original positivist approach. One already sees this phenomenon in the major warfare conventions discussed here, where the reasoning behind these practices is starting to blur with more recent human rights justifications in the contemporary period.

### Universal Consistency

The second reason is especially important for liberal democracies. The realism-based Westphalian international system considers domestic and international politics to be separate, and both states and individuals overwhelmingly operate according to that principle. Because of the specific content of their domestic governing principles and values, however, it ought to be of particular concern to liberal democracies—and to any society that espouses a universal ideology—to make their foreign policy (including the practice of war) more consistent with their domestic politics. Liberal democratic countries *should* have an interest in fighting wars in ways that are informed by their underlying domestic principles—or at least consciously, rather than inadvertently, making exceptions. (Hence the importance of signaling to one's own population and soldiers, and to the international community.) This is a challenge not only for political and military practice, but also for academic and philosophical study, which usually treats military affairs and just war theory separately from other issues of global justice. The increasingly urgent questions about whether and how to extend domestic systems of governance and justice to the global realm frequently overlook problems of war. There are no easy answers to this and many other inquiries in this book, but it is essential to at least recognize the source of some of the serious challenges that have arisen in contemporary warfare, such as (il)legitimacy of certain types of fighters and political organizations or the use of terrorist tactics.

## Evolving Norms and Sustainable Practice

In the conduct of warfare, the ethic of cooperation between enemies does not have absolute priority. It can be and is frequently overridden, as deception and subterfuge are also highly prized across all martial cultures, and the practice of cooperative ethics is often rife with hypocrisy, reserving gentler treatment for some while simultaneously butchering others deemed unworthy. At the same time as the United States was laying down the revolutionary and enormously influential Lieber Code to govern and constrain its domestic disturbance, it acted quite differently in other spheres. In the Indian Wars, for example, US troops frequently embraced the belief that if they killed the "nits," there would be no more "lice," and in the Philippines in 1901, General Jacob Smith retaliated for the massacre of fifty-nine of his soldiers by ordering the slaughter of the inhabitants of the entire island of Samar: "kill and burn all persons who are capable of bearing arms in actual hostilities" apparently meant anyone over the age of ten.[25]

The ethic of cooperation alone, even when it does work, is often not enough. Cooperation between enemies can be used to attempt a great deal of good and can be sustained for long periods of time, but it can also be used for ill, including colluding to shield responsible peoples from justice. The ethic of cooperation in warfare is often born of other virtues, but by itself is mostly neutral. Safe havens in Srebenica and elsewhere during the Bosnian War, for example, needed more than just a cooperative morality to sustain them.

There are serious concerns about how these shared strategies of cooperation fare over the course of a protracted conflict, and at least anecdotally, the strength of rules and norms appear to erode over time. The longer a war lasts and the more desperate the situation becomes, the more likely participants are to abandon the rules of war and any cooperation, such as with the eventual breakdown of "live and let live" as World War I wore on.

Despite repeated violations and erosion, however, the ethic of cooperation between enemies exists, is still practiced, and remains quite forceful. Cooperation in warfare defines the idea of modern warfare, through its use in international law, mutual recognition of sovereignty, limited mutual recognition of opponents' soldiers, and so on. Not only do modern states monopolize the use of force within their territory, they also monopolize the definition of legitimacy, whether it is for fighters, states, or actions. This has both benefits and costs, and conflicts with other important influences on warfare, as we have seen. In order to begin to address these tensions, one must properly identify the problem, and the problem is not always a result of (unresolvable) moral differences—some conundrums arise out of conflicting approaches to these underlying cooperative principles.

Most modern nation-state soldiers are trained in ways complementary to the pervasive cooperation in the structure of and regulations governing war, but this means they are generally unprepared to cope with the way war will be fought when rules, norms, and cooperative ethics break down. For example, because the American military—and most militaries, for that matter—is accustomed to thinking about war while in a peacetime situation, its soldiers have not been adequately prepared for those late-war scenarios. Says US Office of Net Assessment Associate Director Andrew May, "We must be prepared to do things [then] that we don't want to think about doing, and we must spend more time thinking about the fact that we're extending peacetime norms into conflicts."[26]

Given the relative brevity of the era of classical Greek hoplite warfare, which was still embedded within a broader Greek context of very uncooperative warfare, we cannot shy away from difficult questions about how to engage in brutality when faced with possibly existential scenarios, even if they do not rise to the level of "supreme emergency." It is also worth thinking about how the life of a cooperative framework might be extended in prolonged conflicts, as well as what types of laws have greater chances at longevity.

It is possible that humanitarian laws, given the nature of the content, would hold up better under existential pressure. The difficulty there, however, is that it is harder to get genuine buy-in for humanitarian law, precisely because of the demanding nature of its content, than it is for the ethic of cooperation in warfare, so the threshold required for its effectiveness is much higher. Perhaps the ethic of cooperation in warfare is more easily sustained because it appears to demand less. Or perhaps an ideal solution is a mixed strategy of some sort.[27]

The major shift in just war theory that occurs in the early modern Western period is normatively and epistemically correct: we cannot know *jus ad bellum*, so all we can hope to accomplish, even if far too imperfectly, is *jus in bello*. But the manner in which we have approached and concentrated on *jus in bello* may do more harm to the very people that these *jus in bello* principles and regulations are trying to protect. And it still does not mean that we have abstained from *jus ad bellum* judgments in the right way. As such, it is worth considering what the ethic of cooperation—a parallel yet intertwined approach to war—can offer, and perhaps revisit the very structure of war, in particular what cooperation could end war quickly.

Consider jurist Mountague Bernard's reflections on the modern laws of war:

*The growth of professionalism tends naturally . . . to banish high-minded and chivalrous sentiment, and establish a medium standard of principle and practice.* Less in soldiership, because here the professional standard itself is in some respects a most exalted one, demanding nothing less than the nicest honour and the most absolute self-devotion. Yet Henry V., if he had lived in the nineteenth century, would not have granted four days' grace—no, nor one—to a besieged city expecting to be relieved; on the other hand, he would not, when that city surrendered, have beheaded as rebels men who never were his subjects, or expelled a multitude of helpless women from house and home. *The mechanical and commercial spirit, again, sees too clearly the work to be done, and the shortest way to do it, to be in its own nature merciful or generous; it is apt to be impatient of scruples as well as disdainful of forms. The ceremonial of the law of war has been curtailed.* . . . There was a time when sovereigns stipulated with each other against the use of chain-shot, and a keen controversy raged among military men towards the end of the seventeenth century about the lawfulness of a sort of huge bomb-ship which was employed at the siege of Antwerp. Now invention racks itself to produce the biggest gun, the deadliest projectile, the most frightful engine of wholesale slaughter, and the shallows of Kertch and Cronstadt are planted thickly with infernal machines.[28]

This can be taken as a requiem for the decline of chivalry or as a warning against the seductiveness of technological prowess, but what is striking about his Henry V counterfactual is the observation that the growth of professionalism will tend toward the perpetuation of a "medium standard of principle and practice."

Given the depths of human depravity and cruelty, a "medium standard" is actually fairly good, and probably much better than average. Unfortunately, more recent principles of human rights—as desirable and just as their content may be—might be trying to do too much now.

In aiming to do more, humanitarianism sometimes sabotages its own mission, and lets the best be the enemy of the good. Perhaps the best that can actually be done is something much more modest, but at least possibly achievable: move to a less suboptimal equilibrium and limit damage by cooperating to end war quickly somehow.

War is a multifaceted phenomenon, simultaneously many different things. It is a normal part of the political process (à la Clausewitz) and at the same time a "radical break" from civil society (à la Walzer); it is simultaneously a tragedy and an adventure; it is both a "disease" (à la Antoine de Saint-Exupéry) and a nutrient;[29] it is at once a parasitoid and a fertilizer.

Human history is in some ways the story of trying to concurrently wage and tame war. In making sense of the complexities of warfare, the ethic of cooperation requires more recognition and study, for it is far more central to the practice and thinking of warfare than has been realized. Its various manifestations present certain values, priorities, and solutions, but they and the particular structure of cooperation in modern warfare also generate their own problems. A potential resolution to those challenges can be found *within* the ethic of cooperation (through structural collaboration to end war quickly), although in reality such a structure is unlikely to ever be implemented on a large scale. In that respect, the ethic of cooperation in warfare carries within it the seeds of its own Greek tragedy: many of the damages of war are avoidable, yet also foreseen and foreordained, in part because the way out of this dilemma that it offers would in all likelihood be refused.

# Notes

## Preface

1. *The Vietnam War* 2017: episode 2, "Riding the Tiger" (1961–1963), 36:15–37:24.

## 1. The Horrors of War and the Nature of Cooperation

1. Hedges 2002:3, 103–4.
2. Remarque 1975 (1928):100, 102.
3. The easy, monotonous freedoms of civilian life seem "empty," "undirected and insignificant," describes J. Glenn Gray (1998:45). Recent depictions of this phenomenon include Boal 2005 and *The Hurt Locker* (2009). Said Chris Hedges:

    > I learned early on that war forms its own culture. The rush of battle is a potent and often lethal addiction, for war is a drug, one I ingested for many years. . . . Even with its destruction and carnage it can give us what we long for in life. It can give us purpose, meaning, a reason for living. Only when we are in the midst of conflict does the shallowness and vapidness of much of our lives become apparent. Trivia dominates our conversations and increasingly our airwaves. And war is an enticing elixir. It gives us resolve, a cause. It allows us to be noble. (2002:3)

4. There are exceptions, of course, such as Winston S. Churchill, who combined fascination with and horror at war. During his military academy days and as a war correspondent in Cuba, on the field of battle in Sudan, as a naval officer in World War I, and through his tenure as prime minister during World War II: even in the line of fire, where he often put himself, he "regularly manifested great personal courage" and "found the fury and romance of the battlefield deeply alluring" (Rosenberg

1999:172–73). He longed to join the D-Day invasion troops in 1944, and had to be dissuaded by the king ("Churchill's Request to Accompany Invasion Force" 2004). At one point during World War I (February 1915), he raved, "I think a curse should rest on me, because I am so happy. I know this war is smashing and shattering the lives of thousands every moment—and yet—I cannot help it—I love every second I live" (Carter 1965:361). In 1909, however, he had confessed, "Much as war attracts me and fascinates my mind with its tremendous situations—I feel more deeply every year . . . what vile and wicked folly and barbarism it all is" (Gilbert 1971:481).

5. Eisenhower 1946.
6. For good sweeping histories of warfare, see, among others, Keegan 1993; Parker 2005; Paret et al. 1986; Chaliand 1994; and Gat 2006.
7. Boot 2013:9–10. Max Boot's account of five thousand years of guerrilla warfare notes that

> throughout most of our species' long and bloody slog, both before the development of urban civilization and since, warfare has been carried out primarily by bands of loosely organized, ill-disciplined, lightly armed volunteers who disdain open battle. They prefer to employ stealth, surprise, and rapid movement to harass, ambush, massacre, and terrorize their enemies while trying to minimize their own casualties through rapid retreat when confronted by equal or stronger forces. (2013:10)

8. Boot 2013:9.
9. Whitman 2012:35–36.
10. Boot 2013:4.
11. Hanson 2005:94.
12. Pritchett 1974:chap. 9, "Ambuscades," 177–89.
13. McCullough 2005a:chap. 7, esp. 280–84, 293.
14. McCullough 2005b:minutes 27:44–28:15. After an ignominious beginning to his relationship with the laws of war, George Washington rebounded by trying to diligently enforce the "moral structure of the Enlightenment laws of war," which included forbidding plunder and otherwise protecting civilians (Witt 2012:20). For example, he had the Continental Congress's Articles of War (September 20, 1776)—which included punishments for those "beating or otherwise ill-treating," "disturbing," "committing any kind of riots," "us[ing] violence or committ[ing] any kind of offense against the persons or property" or "fair or markets" "of the good people of any of the United States of America" (sections 9.1, 10.1–2)—distributed throughout the army, and required every officer and soldier to sign a copy.

There are practical limits to this adherence, of course. Upon realizing that many soldiers and officers objected to signing the new Articles because that might extend their length of service, Washington acknowledged that "it is in vain to attempt to reason away the Prejudices of a whole Army," and allowed those already enlisted to remain under their prior conditions (letter to John Hancock, September 21, 1775; footnote no. 5 to General Orders, August 9, 1775).

15. McCullough 2005b:minutes 34:54–36:07.
16. Boot 2013:8.
17. Hobbes 1996 (1651):chap. 13.
18. Arkush and Allen 2008; Johnson and Thayer 2013; Holmes 2008. There are disputes about whether the propensity for war is biologically determined and whether violence has decreased over the course of human history: Pinker 2012; Barash 2013; Hart and Sussman 2005 argue that humans evolved as prey; and Fry 2009.

19. Holmes 2008; Fisher 2006; Callaway 2009.
20. See, e.g., the Price Equation: Frank 1995; Smith and Price 1973; "Selflessness of Strangers" 2010.
21. "The cost of early selfishness is greater than the cost of trust," evolutionary psychologists have found. "The Evolution of Generosity" 2011.
22. "Human Behavior" 2002; Fehr et al. 2002. There can be some sense of morality even in nature's endemic scarcity. A variety of animals seem to possess some understanding of the concept of "fairness"—including elephants, chimpanzees and other monkeys, dogs, and even rats—to varying degrees.
23. Samuel Bowles found that "in the absence of war, a gene imposing a self-sacrificial cost of as little as 3% in forgone reproduction would drop from 90% to 10% of the population in 150 generations," but predicts that "much higher levels of self-sacrifice—up to 13% in one case—could be sustained if warfare were brought into the equation." Self-sacrifice of a certain kind in warfare thus enables "the evolution of collaborative, altruistic traits that would not otherwise be possible." "Warfare, Culture and Human Evolution" 2004. See also Bowles 2009.
24. Makos and Alexander 2012.
25. Decades later, they randomly met at a Vancouver Association for Survivors of Torture (VAST) meeting, realized their connection, and became friends and "brothers." *My Enemy, My Brother* 2015. Another notable example is Gandhi telling a Hindu man, who had killed a Muslim boy out of vengeance for Muslims killing his son, to adopt a Muslim child and raise him as such. *Gandhi* 1982.
26. Bairnsfather 1917; Brown 2004; Brown and Seaton 1999; Ekstein 2000; "Fraternization Between the Lines" 1914; Edward Hamilton in Housman 1930; Jürgs 2005; "Bertie Felstead" 2001; Vinciguerra 2005; Weintraub 2001.
27. Ashworth 2000 (1980).
28. Gray 1998 (1959):189.
29. Ashworth 2000 (1980):131.
30. Van Emden 2013:154–56.
31. E.g., when the British took over French sectors, they "generally found a kind of unofficial suspension of arms or truce prevailing." Edmonds 1928:156.
32. Van Emden 2013:157.
33. Charles Sorley, British 7th Suffolks 12th Division, letter to Mrs. Sorley, July 10, 1915. Sorley 1919:283.
34. Herbert Read, British 21st Division. Ashworth 2000 (1980):104.
35. Ashworth 2000 (1980):30.
36. This is part of a broader phenomenon, that the "the farther we are from dangerous contact with this image [of the enemy], the more we are consumed by it. A civilian far removed from the battle area is nearly certain to be more bloodthirsty than the front-line soldier whose hatred has to be responsible, meaning that he has to respond to it, to answer it with action," says Gray. "Progression in abstract hatred was detectable at every level, from company to regiment to division to army and farther back" (1998:135).

    See also Feaver and Gelpi 2005, on the greater enthusiasm for use of military force by civilians with no military experience, compared with military officers or veteran civilians. (Although once it is determined that force will be used, nonveteran civilians are more supportive of restraints on the manner of force applied.)
37. Ashworth 2000 (1980):174–75.
38. Ashworth 2000 (1980):109–10, 121.
39. Arnold 1867.

40. Remarque 1975 (1928):chap. 8, p. 166.
41. Remarque 1975 (1928):chap. 9, p. 191.
42. Along the southern front, for example, Italian officer Emilio Lussu (2014 [1939]:187) wrote that with a few exceptions, the Austrians "normally . . . respected the religious holidays. On the important feast days there was no shooting from their trenches and their artillery remained quiet, too."
43. At the siege of Petersburg, Swiss national Rudolph Aschmann, who fought for the Union, explained some of the workings of the North-South "live and let live" system across trenches just three hundred steps apart:

   > For a while the guards at our front were on the best of terms with each other. . . . One day when we were on picket duty a shot fell from the Confederate side without, however, striking anyone on our side. Indignant at this breach of the peace we made ready to shoot back but the enemy immediately gave a sign that this disturbance was due to a mistake. Soon after, the delinquent appeared in front of the enemy line where as a penalty he had to parade back and forth for two hours in plain view of both picket teams, carrying a heavy beam on his shoulder. Loud shouts of applause indicated to the Southerners that this was satisfaction enough and that peace had now been completely restored. Occasionally the higher command of one or the other side would give orders to open fire on the opposite patrols. In such case they usually gave each other a warning signal, and once we even heard a Southerner call: "Yankees, lie down! We have orders to shoot!" Immediately fire was opened and kept up all day with intensity. (1972:170–71)

44. The *M.A.S.H* television show dramatizes a similar incident, although there the pilot is portrayed as inept rather than intentionally abstaining. "5 o'Clock Charlie" 1973.
45. Apel and Apel 1998:114–16.
46. Mallett 1974:193.
47. Mallett 1974:2.
48. Letter no. 2, Riding Street Bks., February 13, 1809; letter no. 45, Moimento, April 28, 1813; letter no. 3, Maidstone, April 12, 1809. Wheeler 1993 (1951):15, 108–9, 17.
49. Lussu 2014:218, 221, 226.
50. While the soldiers largely suffered the cavalier use of their lives, they occasionally managed to exact revenge. Ottolenghi recounted an incident in which a platoon was ordered to execute twenty soldiers randomly selected from a company that refused to stay in its cave during a bombardment in which they thought the cave would collapse on them: the platoon first fired high and missed all twenty soldiers, then when the commanding major started shooting the soldiers himself, the platoon turned their fire on the major and shot him to death. Lussu 2014 (1939):240–44. See also the arbitrary scapegoating and execution of select soldiers for a failed, but impossible, assault in Humphrey Cobb's *Paths of Glory* (1935), which Stanley Kubrick later dramatized in film (1957).
51. Clausewitz 2000:1.1.2, pp. 264–65.
52. Clausewitz 2000:1.1.24: "Der Krieg ist eine bloße Fortsetzung der Politik mit anderen Mitteln."
53. In evolutionary biology, cooperation refers to any direct or indirect adaptations in fitness that have evolved usually, but not always, in order to increase reproductive success (Gardner et al. 2016). In noncooperative game theory, "cooperation" describes joint non-defection in something like a Prisoner's Dilemma—this invokes a common usage of the word. In cooperative game theory, what makes it "cooperative" is

that communication within it is not merely "cheap talk" (Ordeshook 1986:302–4). This is a highly specialized use of the term *cooperation*, and can sometimes be misleading. (Perhaps it should more descriptively be called "coordinative" game theory.)

54. Military strategy had trended in this direction for a while, but its *reductio* may have been reached by the United States in the Vietnam War, in its excessive emphasis on measuring, quantifying, and calculating on paper its way to victory, in utter defiance of the reality on the ground and the fact that no matter how many more Vietcong were killed than Americans, the North was willing to keep fighting. Says then Army advisor James Willbanks, "The problem with the war [is] the metrics. If you can't count what's important, you make what you can count important." *The Vietnam War* 2017: episode 4, "Resolve" (January 1966–June 1967), 25:41–26:00. This led to tragic tactics that tried to win the war through numbers, such as attempting to maximize the "body count" and optimize "kill ratios," all in service of determining a futile "victory index." See also Summers 1995 (1982):18; Madrigal 2017.

55. Clausewitz 2000:1.1.3, "The Use of Force Theoretically Without Limits," 265–66, emphasis added.

56. Hume 1896 (1738–40):bk. 3, pt. 2, sec. 2, 490.

57. Parametric action is not "joint," but rather effectively isolated, for example, if my interactions with others are so mediated by institutions that I do not take into account their particular strategies. Suppose the joint behavior of a continuum of producers and consumers has created an equilibrium market price: that price is taken as given by everyone, so my behavior is in no way responsive to others' actions. When one asks, "What's the weather today," there is no response from nature—one simply decides how to dress according to the given conditions. Similarly, in an equilibrium market, the only question is, "Given that this is the price, what do I do?," with no interaction between producers. (This differs from monopolistic or oligopolistic behaviors, even.) Later, I discuss interaction between actors mediated through international law: while it may appear similar to parametric action, it differs in that the law is a dynamic institution, constantly being interpreted, reinterpreted, and changed as a result of such interactions.

58. Group agency requires that

   1. Members intend to participate in the group and see themselves as acting for the sake of some shared goal, share overlapping (but not necessarily the same) conceptions of the goal, and jointly will the goal, although they need not believe the goal can be achieved.
   2. Members mutually expect one another's participation in achieving the shared end.
   3. Members intend to achieve the goal, even if it is not any particular action but rather simply the constitution of a group.
   4. There is some essential connection between members' ends, such that they share the same (if general) goals. It is not enough that a private says, "My end is to follow orders, so therefore my officer's ends are my ends." Their content must overlap to some extent, beyond just the procedural connection.
   5. Participants share and condone at least a general conception of the means. (Tacit acceptance is enough.) To preserve a notion of individual agency within groups, acceptance of the ends cannot automatically include concurrence on the means (Chiu 2011:445–47).

   For more on collective agency, both explicit and implicit/tacit, see Chiu 2011.

59. For more on focal (or Schelling) points, see Schelling 1960, esp. pp. 55–64.

60. Hume 1896 (1738–40):490. Along these Humean lines, see also Lewis 1969.

61. What does it mean to *intend* to act cooperatively? In an iterated prisoner's dilemma, players' responses to opponents' actions are strategic. Opponents could be hard-wired to behave in certain ways, however, e.g., to always cooperate, always defect, or always reciprocate. Such preset behavior might generate cooperative outcomes, but the lack of conscious choice makes it less interesting. For example, responding to the equilibrium price in a market and responding to live-and-let-live trench warfare are both joint behaviors, but the former is parametric action, while the latter is strategic, and therefore more puzzling and noteworthy, especially in the context of warfare.

62. When the United States and the United Kingdom fought the War of 1812 (which lasted three years), both sides agreed to recognize truce flags for allowing continued mail services between them (Witt 2012:67).

63. Ashworth 2000 (1980):30.

64. Rosenberg and Gall 2014. American discomfort was partly due to reports that Bergdahl had deserted his post shortly before his capture by the Taliban. Bergdahl had shipped home his personal belongings in advance, which raised questions about how much he had contributed to his own capture and to the casualties incurred by units who searched for him in the aftermath of his disappearance. Schmitt, Cooper, and Savage 2014; Savage and Schmitt 2014; Bethea 2014. The latest developments are summarized in Oppel 2017.

65. Restrictions included a one-year travel ban, but there were questions about whether the Taliban would be appropriately monitored. Schmitt and Savage 2014; Rosenberg and Gall 2014; "Qatar Allowing Freed Taliban Men to Move Freely in Country" 2014.

66. Some questioned the legality of the exchange, as US president Barack Obama did not give a thirty-day notice to Congress before releasing the Taliban prisoners from Guantánamo, as required by law. Baker 2014.

67. The US administration initially sought a broad peace agreement for Afghanistan that would involve the Afghan government and the Taliban, but soon realized that it would be impossible at the time. Sanger and Parker 2014.

68. Rosenberg and Gall 2014; "Freedom for Sgt. Bergdahl, at a Price" 2014.

69. Clinton 2014:153, 158, 163.

70. Schmitt and Savage 2014.

71. "The Iran-Contra Affair" n.d.

72. Lubold and Hudson 2014.

73. For example, both Japan and South Korea have much to gain from jointly fending off threats from China, yet these two liberal democracies, with many shared values, harbor a deep, mutual, historical hostility, and their bitter relationship prevents effective resistance against what is at this geopolitical point in time a greater shared enemy.

74. There is some confusion about the relationship between terrorism and political legitimacy in this context. Some supporters of the prisoner exchange point out that there is no reason not to negotiate with the Taliban, because it is not a terrorist group; rather, it is "a political faction and a military force in Afghanistan; they are combatants in a war that the United States is fighting," and therefore Bergdahl was not a hostage but rather a prisoner of war. E.g., Kaplan 2014. This makes the mistake of thinking that being a terrorist and being a political force (e.g., a state government) are mutually exclusive—in fact, many have been both. See, e.g., Scheffler 2006. This misconception says something about the way war is perceived: despite ample historical evidence to the contrary, it is often assumed that a negotiation partner must be "official" in some way that fits the framework of contemporary state sovereignty.

75. "Obama Was Right to Strike a Deal with the Taliban" 2014.

76. Kaplan 2014.

77. "Obama Was Right to Strike a Deal with the Taliban" 2014.
78. Oikonomides 1991; Toynbee 1973.
79. Lubold and Hudson 2014; Boot 2014.
80. Israel Ministry of Foreign Affairs 2004; Reuters 2011; Bronner and Farrell 2011; Londoño 2011.
81. Onuah and Kingimi 2017.
82. See, e.g., Blum 2007.
83. For example, it can result from mistaken beliefs about the outcomes of one's actions or from nature-selecting situations or parametric choice, when benefit is entirely incidental.
84. Cooperation occurs at different levels and between varied actors, and there is no single or consistent way that this ethic is always manifested. There are also conflicting or cross-cutting interests—within each side, across sides—as in the World War I trenches, where noncommissioned officers (NCOs) seemed like bullies to their own men, and officers and high command tried to break up the truces. "Live and let live" required certain background conditions, such as the parallel internal societal struggles that promoted cooperation between enemies against those of a different status from one's own side.

    Cooperation at one level can also affect that at a different level: for example, agreements between states about how to treat POWs can motivate the behavior of the individuals who must implement them, or NGOs and private organizations can secure international law ultimately signed by sovereign states, such as the international land mine ban treaty.
85. Anonymous, United States Marines 2014.
86. Modern warfare's distinctive characteristics reflect broader developments in the modern era (roughly the seventeenth century to the twentieth): rapid population increases (from the Industrial Revolution and other scientific advances), increased bureaucratic centralization, the rise of nationalism as a driving political force, and the growth of secularism.
87. A comprehensive doctrine of belief addresses all major aspects of human life, especially foundational philosophical principles, a moral code, and religious beliefs, in a way that ties these areas together, whether or not it does so consistently. Rawls describes comprehensive doctrines as general and comprehensive moral conceptions:

    > A moral conception is *general* if it applies to a wide range of subjects, and in the limit to all subjects universally. It is *comprehensive* when it includes conceptions of what is of value in human life, and ideals of personal character, as well as ideals of friendship and of familial and associational relationships, and much else that is to inform our conduct, and in the limit to our life as a whole. A conception is *fully* comprehensive if it covers all recognized values and virtues within one rather precisely articulated system; whereas a conception is only *partially* comprehensive when it comprises a number of, but by no means all, nonpolitical values and virtues and is rather loosely articulated. Many religious and philosophical doctrines aspire to be both general and comprehensive. (Rawls 1993:13)

    Examples include J. S. Mill's and Kant's doctrines of liberalism, as well as the three Abrahamic faiths (Judaism, Christianity, Islam), all of which offer "systematic judgments on a wide array of ethical and political issues in a variety of contexts," including what is valuable about human life, which virtues humans should develop, and what principles should govern our lives. Taylor 2011:241.

88. Plato 2013:bk. 1, 338c, LCL 237:48–51.
89. Machiavelli 1998 (1513):chap. 18, "In What Mode Faith Should Be Kept By Princes."
90. Pinker 2012:32–33.

## 2. Cooperation for a Fair Fight

1. Walzer 2015:138–43.
2. Orwell 1970:291–92.
3. Walzer 2015:143.
4. Marshall 2000 (1947):50–51.
5. Marshall 2000 (1947):78.
6. Marshall's work and that of those he influenced—e.g., former US army ranger and military psychologist Dave Grossman (Grossman 1995 and Grossman and Christensen 2008)—have become required reading at some military institutions.
7. Spiller 1988; Smoler 1989; Chambers 2003; Engen 2011.
8. In later conflicts, such as the Korean and Vietnam wars, Marshall (1951) found that the portion of soldiers who fired their weapons at all had doubled from World War II numbers, to more than half.
9. Gertz 2014:32–33.
10. G. E. M. Anscombe (1958:7) differentiates those who fight or supply the means of fighting from those who "are not fighting and are not engaged in supplying those who are with the means of fighting," such as farmers growing food that would be consumed regardless of one's current occupation. See also Anscombe 1961; Ford 1944; and Nagel 1972. This issue relates to the broader question of collective responsibility. Specifically in the context of war, see, e.g., Arendt 1987; Chiu 2011; Crawford 2007; Estlund 2007; Jaspers 1961; Levinson 1974; and Wasserstrom 1971.
11. Lussu 2014 (1939):161.
12. Lussu 2014 (1939):162, 163.
13. Walzer 2015:142.
14. *Politics*, I.1256b.
15. Lussu 2014 (1939):161–63.
16. Lussu 2014 (1939):162–63.
17. For example, Chinese scholar Frank A. Kierman, Jr., calls a declaration of hostility at Ch'eng-p'u (*Tso Chuen*, Hsi Kung, Year 28) "outstanding," for

    > It bears a remarkable resemblance to the sort of things that two reasonably literate quarterbacks might say to one another before some crucial game, while talking before newspapermen. This sporting atmosphere is perhaps not entirely inappropriate, since warfare had in those days so close an affiliation with hunting, which constituted training for war and shared with it the aura of augury, with bags of game being scrutinized to see what they meant. (1974:41–42)

18. Young predator animals do the same—their play is a version of the hunting and fighting they will do later in life.
19. "Alumnus Football" (1908), by American sportswriter Grantland Rice, ends:

    > Keep coming back—and though the world may romp across your spine—
    > Let every game's end find you still upon the battling line;

> For when the One Great Scorer comes to write against your name,
> He marks—not that you won or lost—but how you played the Game.
> ★★★
> Such is Alumnus Football on the white-chalked field of Life—
> You find the bread-line hard to buck, while sorrow crowns the strife.
> But in the fight for name and fame among the world-wide clan,
> "There goes the victor," sinks to naught before "There goes a man."
>> (Fountain 1993:95)

20. In the *Oxford English Dictionary*, "sporting" (adj.) is defined as

    1c. Practising or exemplifying the ideals of a particular sport; characterized by sportsmanlike conduct; (also more generally) fair, generous; resilient, "game."
    2b. Providing good sport, esp. good hunting . . .
    Special uses include: sporting chance n. *colloq.* (originally) an uncertain or doubtful likelihood (of success); (now chiefly) a reasonable but not certain chance; a fair opportunity.

    In fact, the connection between sports and fairness is so tight in some cases that the British phrase "it's just not cricket," means something that is dishonourable and "contrary to traditional standards of fairness or rectitude." See "It's Just Not Cricket" n.d.; and the definition of "Cricket" in the *Oxford English Dictionary*.
21. "Do the Right Thing" 2012.
22. Smyth 2010; "World Cup 1987" 2012; "The Gracious Mr. Walsh" n.d.
23. Girardot 2015.
24. Sometimes, prescribed sanctions for rule-violating conduct will require one to play man-down and therefore at a disadvantage, e.g., FIFA-level soccer players are sent off the field after incurring one red or two yellow cards and NHL hockey players can be put into the penalty box.
25. Tour officials have neutralized the race if there is a large-enough crash and especially if the race leader is caught in it, to attend to the injured and also so that those behind do not fall too far away.
26. Although the race commentator says at the time that Armstrong is waiting because he still needs Ullrich's help given how far they are from the race finish, the strong norm of not taking advantage of the leader's misfortunes was still in play. Hanstock 2012.
27. "Schleck Loses Chain" 2010; Landau 2013; Gallagher 2010.
28. Pucin 2003.
29. Pucin 2003.
30. As with most sports, cycling outcomes are never purely the result of the athlete's physical and mental skill, because the sport utilizes equipment, namely, the bicycle. Because everyone has different instruments (within set parameters), it is not just how one handles the equipment but also one's choice of tool that is being tested.
31. Cases in which riders crash because they were following too closely to a rider crashing in front of him are ambiguous—sometimes it is bad luck, sometimes it is poor skill or judgment on the part of the follower.
32. Even inclement weather, the ultimate "act of God," does not warrant similar allowances. In time trials, the cyclists ride the route with staggered starts, which span several hours, and it is common for the weather to change over the course of the day, but there are no handicaps given for those suffering poorer weather.

33. This approach continued with Reconciliation Plaza and Wall at West Point, which commemorates the reunion of northern and southern soldiers after the Civil War by referring only to the gallant fighting from both sides, while studiously ignoring the object of the war. (See also chapter 6, on abdicating *jus ad bellum* judgments.)
34. Witt 2012:209.
35. Singh 2006; Srivastava 2006:199; Fricker 1979:37.
36. Fricker 1979:37.
37. Fricker 1979:37; Chaudhry 2012.
38. Srivastava 2006:199; Ganguly 2014.
39. Fricker 1979:37.
40. Unlike in sport where one can stall or play a nonscoring offense until time runs out in order to try to keep the contest close enough, there is no time limit in war, so this form of self-imposed parity is not available there. In fact, one usually tries to win a war precisely by running up so much of a lead that the other cannot win and then surrenders. (The one exception might be the ethic of cooperation to end war quickly, to be discussed in chapter 4.)
41. Although customary, using identical weapons was not necessary, so long as both sides agreed.
42. There is a long-standing connection between dueling and the military, in part because the military made that connection and because of the historical overlap between aristocracy and military service. Duels were often about honor (LaVaque-Manty 2006:729), and this lasting influence on broader military culture resulted, unfortunately, in a high number of officer/military deaths by dueling in the modern era.
43. In the West, this included in Ireland (*Code Duello*, 1777), France (originating in part from Irish and English sources), the United Kingdom (Joseph Hamilton, *The Dueling Handbook* or *The Only Approved Guide Through All the Stages of a Quarrel*, 1829; A Traveler, *The Art of Duelling*, 1836), and the United States (John Lyde Wilson, *The Code of Honor; or Rules for the Government of Principals and Seconds in Dueling*, 1838).
44. The ritual elements of pilots' encounters were present from the beginning. In perhaps the first aerial dogfight, between two American mercenaries in the Mexican Revolution, Colonel Dean Ivan Lamb recounted spotting an enemy plane on a reconnaissance flight:

> As I neared the machine close enough to note details, the pilot pushed up his goggles. Sure enough, it was Phil Rader. He seemed to recognize me and while trying to edge a bit closer we nearly locked wings. He quickly sheered off shaking his fist at me, then straightened out flying parallel. He drew a pistol and fired downward below my machine. For a second my heart stopped beating as I drew my own ornate gun, but before starting action it occurred that he had not actually aimed at me, but beneath. Following his example, I fired twice and as he suddenly tilted his plane my heart jumped into my throat, thinking that by accident he had been hit. He straightened out again and copied my example by firing two shots. We then fired spaced shots until our guns were empty at about the same time. . . . He succeeded in reloading in some manner as we both edged in to continue the "battle," but Rader's pistol was in his holster as we neared and he was waving his hand; then I caught the signal to turn and nodded. He turned first and motioned for me to come on. In a moment I was alongside as we headed back over Naco. In five minutes we were directly over the town and I saw him shoot directly downward. I picked out a certain

disliked cantina and took a shot at it. At short intervals Phil's shots could be heard but I gave them no heed knowing they were not meant for me. . . . Phil waved his hand and continued straight to the east while I turned back over Naco and landed as gasoline was running low. (1934:93–95)

45. Richthofen 1918:chap 8, "My First English Victim, 17th September, 1915."
46. The sport of fencing, which systematizes the duel, actually codifies certain principles of "fair" fighting. While *épée* most resembles the duel's deadly conditions, both foil and sabre restrict the valid target area and employ "right of way" rules, in which a fencer scores a hit only if he has first established priority by initiating the attack. Subsequently, the defender can score not with just any counterattack but only if he takes away the priority and establishes it for himself, with one of a number of specified actions.
47. Says Lancelot, "I shall proffer you large proffers,. . . that is for to say, I shall unarm my head and my left quarter of my body, all that may be unarmed, and let bind my left hand behind me, so that it shall not help me, and right so I shall do battle with you." Malory 2003 (1485):bk. 19, chap. 9.
48. The chivalric and romantic reputation of Round Table knights was greatly at odds with their everyday lives. What honorable behavior occurred was heavily circumscribed. For example, Lancelot earned his chivalric reputation because he "had the custom of never killing a knight who begged for mercy, unless he had sworn beforehand to do so, or unless he could not avoid it," according to the thirteenth-century *Lancelot-Grail*. Otherwise, he was pleased to kill horses and knights, sever limbs, and "[leave] a sorrowful wake behind him, so that the whole earth was bathed in blood wherever he passed." Kaeuper 2000:24, 31. Knights preferred and regularly used ambushes and raids. They also plundered, raped (especially among the lower classes), seized women as property, and killed in myriad horrific ways, including decapitation and torture.
49. Sinha 2005:288.
50. *Mahābhārata* (c. 400 BCE).
51. The *Mahābhārata* describes an epic battle between two sons of kings, Bhima and Duyodhana, in which the former wounds (and kills) the latter by breaking his thighs. Although Krishna permitted Bhima's actions, Rama was furious, and raged, "Oh, fie on Bhima! Oh, fie, that in such a fair fight a blow hath been struck below the navel! Never before hath such an act as Vrikodara hath done been witnessed in an encounter with the mace! No limb below the navel should be struck. This is the precept laid down in treatises! This Bhima, however, is an ignorant wretch, unacquainted with the truths of treatises!" (chap. 9, §§58–60).

Krishna reasoned that the end justified the means (consistent with *kutayuddha/realpolitik*), but this contravenes *dharmayuddha* (righteous war) and within it *gadayuddha* (combat between fighters armed with maces). Says historian Kaushik Roy,

> it was considered unethical to engage an unarmed enemy. . . . Generally, it was considered unethical to attack an opponent's thigh. The rules of *gadayuddha* (combat between two fighters equipped with maces) noted that an opponent could not be struck below the navel. . . . Mehendale says that the *Mahābhārata* [when Bhima followed Krishna's unethical advice] shows that, due to the operation of *dharma* on a cosmic scale, nemesis or retributive justice overtook even Krishna in the end. Krishna was killed accidentally by a hunter. (Roy 2012:36; Mehendale 1995:45, 57)

52. *Manusmrti/Mānava-Dharmásātra* (c. 200 CE), chap. 7, "The Law for the King," §§90–93: War and the Warrior Ethic" (*Manu's Code of Law* 2004:113).
53. Mehendale 1995:5, 59.
54. Thapliyal 2002:90.
55. Kierman 1974:27, 29–30.
56. *Zuo Zhuan Zhu*: Lord Xi year 26, year 33; Lord Wen year 10; Lord Xuan year 12; Lord Zhao year 5. *Zuo zhuan zhu*, Lord Zhuang year 11; Lord Xi, year 15, year 28, year 33; Lord Wen year 12; Lord Cheng year 2; Lord Xiang year 23, year 28; *Gongyang zhuan zhushu*, Lord Xuan year 12. Lewis 1990:23, 34, 38. Ritualization did not mean that battle was not deadly: no fewer were slain in these battles, dead bodies of defeated enemy were often used to erect monuments to victory, there are reports of trophies of heads or ears being taken for postbattle rituals, and there were at least some instances of human sacrifice. Lewis 1990:25–28.
57. "This principle was so routinely observed that in one case a state successfully secured the departure of an invader by staging a mock funeral." *Zuo zhuan zhu*, Lord Xi year 26, Lord Wen year 7, Lord Xuan year 12, Lord Xiang year 4 (Lewis 1990:38).
58. *Zuo Zhuan Zhu*: Lord Zhuang year 28, Lord Xi year 26, Lord Wen year 14, Lord Ai year 7. Kierman 1974:44; Lewis 1990:38.
59. *Zuo Zhuan* 1960 (c. fourth century BCE):6.12.7, 261.
60. *Zuo Zhuan* 1960 (c. fourth century BCE):10.21.5, 689.
61. *Zuo Zhuan* 1960 (c. fourth century BCE):5.22.4, 183.
62. Kierman 1974:66n57, 321.
63. His defeat is described in the *Zuo-zhuan* as "shameful," and his own minister of war argues, "Your Grace does not know the rules of fighting:—Given a strong enemy, in a defile or with his troops not drawn up, it is Heaven assisting us. Is it not proper for us to advance upon him so impeded with our drums beating, even then afraid *we may not get the victory?*" (*Zuo Zhuan* 1960:5.22.4, 183).
64. "K'wang Këaou (狂狡) engaged a man of Ch'ing (鄭人), who jumped into a well, from which the other brought him out with the end of his spear,—[only] to be captured by him. The superior man will say that K'wang Këaou transgressed the rule of war, and was disobedient to orders, deserving to be taken. What is called the rule of war is to be having ever in the ears that in war there should be the display of boldness and intrepidity. To slay one's enemy is intrepidity; and he who does otherwise deserves death" (*Zuo Zhuan* 1960:7.2.1, 289).
65. Mao 1938.
66. French 2017:229.
67. Geneva Convention 1977, Protocol I, Article 44.3. It should be noted that this regulation is not solely about "fair fights," but also about shielding civilians and fellow soldiers. The latter motivation will be addressed in chapter 3.
68. Chiu 2010:46–47.
69. See arguments regarding the role of uniforms in protecting civilian immunity in Chiu 2010.
70. *The Art of War*, 1.18.
71. Aquinas cites Deuteronomy 16:20 ("Thou shalt follow justly after that which is just"), Augustine, who says it is wrong to lie (Contra Mend. 15), and Matthew 7:12 ("Whatsoever you would that men should do to you, do you also to them"). Aquinas 2017 (c. 1265–1273):2.2.Q40 (War).A3.
72. QQ. in Hept. qu. x super Jos. Joshua 8:2.
73. Aquinas 2017 (c. 1265–1273):2.2.Q40 (War).A3.

74. This form is fighting is sometimes called "linear battle" or *bataille rangée* (lined-up battle) (Whitman 2012:58).
75. There are some historical precedents for pitched battles, and classical Greek hoplite warfare will be discussed at length in chapter 4.
76. Connor 1988:11–12. Surprise attacks were expected in sieges or naval battles or by light-armed troops, but it was not the norm between hoplite armies then. "Before the large-scale use of peltasts [light infantry], Greek warfare was limited to pitched battles, and these more or less prearranged. In Greek hoplite warfare in the plains, the Greeks resorted little to tactical maneuvering, and like two bulls, horns against horns, the armies preferred to clash in open combat. " Pritchett 1974:chap. 8, "Surprise Attacks," 156–76, esp. 173–74.
77. Quintus Curtius 1946 (c. 41 CE):vol. 1, bk. 4.13.3–10, LCL 368:278–81.
78. Polybius 2010 (c. second century BCE):6, bks. 28–39, LCL 161:410–13; Pritchett 1974:chap. 9 "Ambuscades," 187.
79. Written for the American Civil War, the Lieber Code (General Orders No. 100) (1863) sets forth comprehensive guidelines for how war should be fought, including the ethical treatment of prisoners of war, spies, slaves, and so on, many of which served as foundational standards for later domestic and international laws of war.
80. Walzer 2015:143.
81. Deuteronomy 20:10.
82. Connor 1988:9.
83. Pritchett 1974:chap. 7, "The Challenge to Battle," 147–55, 149–50.
84. Romans were not the only lovers of legal form. In early Chinese combat, "the classic set piece declaration of hostility in the *Tso-chuan* is a lengthy 'speech' in which Lü Hsiang apprises Ch'in that Chin is breaking off friendly relations (8.14.3). This elaborate and literary rationale is a forerunner of many comparable items attached to incidents in Warring States times." Kierman 1974:41.
85. Neff 2008:27–28; Dionysius of Halicarnassus 2006:bk. 2, chap. 72; Livy 1919:bk. 1, chap. 32, §§5–14.
86. Neff 2008:28.
87. If the *fetiales'* demands for justice were rejected, then "he called both the celestial and infernal gods to witness and went away, saying no more than this, that the Roman State would deliberate at its leisure concerning these people. Afterwards he, together with the other *fetiales*, appeared before the senate and *declared that they had done everything that was ordained by the holy laws*, and that, if the senators wished to vote for war, there would be no obstacle on the part of the gods." Dionysius of Halicarnassus 2006:bk. 2, chap. 72, emphasis added.
88. Declarations of war should also serve important political purposes, argues Brien Hallett (1998), in articulating justifications for the war itself and its ensuing violence, and guiding the military in pursuit of legitimate operations. Ritualization of this aspect of a fair fight—giving the opponent notice—is seen on a small scale in martial arts bouts. Not just in sport competitions, but also in real fights, martial arts tradition usually calls for opponents to square off and bow to each other before beginning to fight, which then starts with the two combatants immediately adopting a "ready" stance. In film depictions, the classic move of the dishonorable villain is to strike his opponent as he is midbow, looking down, unaware of the impending blow before the bout has started.
89. Clay 1819:637, 640.
90. Cobb 1819:588.

91. Witt 2012:107.
92. The Lieber Code previews this distinction, when it "admits of deception, but disclaims acts of perfidy" (§16). Most states also consider spying and assassination to be unprotected forms of deception, and usually punishable by death. International law is mostly silent on the issue of spying, except to define it (Hague Convention IV, Chap. 2, Art. 29–31, October 18, 1907), which de facto condones the nation-states' assertion of the severity of this crime. The Lieber Code deemed it acceptable to execute spies by hanging (§88), which indicates the contempt in which spies were held.
93. This passage also speaks to the importance of maximizing buy-in to the Law of Armed Conflict (LOAC): people will not accept regulations that guarantee they will lose the conflict, so they must be giving a fighting chance, so to speak, of winning. In this case, it means that the LOAC, "if it is to be respected," must provide for fairer terms of engagement.
94. An early—largely unsuccessful—attempt at a weapons ban can be found under Pope Innocent II's Second Lateran Council (1139), which declared, "We prohibit under anathema that murderous art of crossbowmen and archers, which is hateful to God, to be employed against Christians and Catholics from now on" (canon 29). In this case, however, the ban privileged only coreligionists, as crossbows were allowed against non-Christians and heretics, and may have been partially motivated by sociopolitical concerns that these weapons made it too easy for low-class soldiers to kill aristocratic knights. Hefele 1912:721–22; Bernhardi 1883:153–59; Breiding 2014.
95. Baker 2013.
96. Moore et al. 1918.
97. Graves 1958 (1929):146.
98. Moore et al. 1918.
99. Pruszewicz 2015.
100. Cushing 1936:chap 2, 69.
101. Military historian Simon Jones (2014): "It was honorable to fight with conventional weapons, rifles, artillery, perhaps. But it seemed somehow dishonorable just to exterminate your enemy with gas as if you were exterminating vermin or pests."
102. Kershaw 2008; Hitler 2016 (1925).
103. Erlanger 2013.
104. M. Fisher 2017.
105. Churchhill 1942.
106. Witt 2012:118–20.
107. Charges included "murder, premeditated murder, injuries or mutilation, rape, assaults and malicious beatings; robbery, larceny, desecration of Churches, cemeteries or houses, and religious buildings; and the destruction of public or private property that was not ordered by a superior officer." General Orders No. 20, US Army, Tampico, Mexico, February 19, 1847.
108. Witt 2012:122–24.
109. "The Balance of Terror" 1966.
110. Contrast this with Achilles's analogy to men and lions and to wolves and lambs when he confronts what he considers the lesser Hector (*Iliad*, 20.302–315), as well as Priam's and Achilles's mutual admiration while squaring off over Hector's body. When Priam first emerges, "Achilles marveled, beholding majestic Priam," admired his "daring" and "heart of iron," recognized his suffered, offered him a chair, slaughtered a sheep, and served him fine food and drink, which they shared in mutual respect (24.563–67, 605–11, 728–55). Likewise:

> Priam the son of Dardanus gazed at Achilles, marveling
> now at the man's beauty, his magnificent build—
> face-to-face he seemed a deathless god . . .
> and Achilles gazed and marveled at Dardan Priam,
> beholding his noble looks, listening to his words. (24.740–44)

Achilles agrees to return Hector's body, which had been cruelly defiled, and orders it first bathed and anointed, for:

> He feared that, overwhelmed by the sight of Hector,
> wild with grief, Priam might let his anger flare
> and Achilles might fly into fresh rage himself,
> cut the old man down and break the laws of Zeus. (24.684–87)

Priam then asks for eleven days to mourn and bury Hector, to which Achilles quickly acquiesces, and Priam sleeps the rest of the night outside Achilles' lodge (24.786–90).

111. "I thought it eminently fitting to show some token of our feeling, and I therefore instructed my subordinate officers to come to the position of 'salute' in the manual of arms as each body of the Confederates passed before us. It was not a 'present arms,' however. . . . It was the 'carry arms,' . . . with musket held by the right hand and perpendicular to the shoulder. I may best describe it as a marching salute in review. When General Gordon came opposite me I had the bugle blown and the entire line came to 'attention,' preparatory to executing this movement of the manual successively and by regiments as Gordon's columns should pass before our front, each in turn. . . . By word of mouth General Gordon sent back orders to the rear that his own troops take the same position of the manual in the march past as did our line. That was done, and a truly imposing sight was the mutual salutation and farewell." Chamberlain 1901.
112. "Baron von Richthofen" 1918; "Funeral of the Red Baron" 1918.
113. Beaugé 2007; Boot 2010.
114. Aussaresses 2001.
115. Ahmad 2006:92–93.
116. August 28, 1780, emphasis added.
117. Marshall 2000 (1947):79, emphasis added.
118. Lussu 2014 (1939):123–25.
119. In the afterword, historian Mark Thompson notes that similar episodes were chronicled elsewhere on the Italian front. Lussu 2014:272.
120. Art. 148, emphasis added. Article 148 of the Lieber Code was written in the context of Confederate outlawry orders raised against Union commanders David Hunter and John W. Phelps, who created black regiments populated by contraband slaves in the South, and Benjamin Butler, who led Union troops in New Orleans (Witt 2012:244). In declaring these generals to be "outlaws," the Confederacy made them subject to summary execution, without trial, by any capturing officer. The law is subject to independent readings, however.
121. "*Sine ira et studio, quorum causas procul habeo,*" "without anger and without partiality, from the motives of which I stand sufficiently removed." Tacitus, *Annals* 1.1, 244–45.

   This ethos is captured by Max Weber, who describes the "special virtue" of a "fully developed" bureaucracy as its "dehumaniz[ation]" (*entmenschlicht*), in that it "succeeds in eliminating from official business love, hatred, and all purely personal, irrational, and emotional elements which escape calculation" (1946 [1922]:216). "Ihre spezifische . . . Eigenart entwickelt sie um so vollkommener, je mehr sie sich, 'entmenschlickt,' je vollkommener, heißt das hier, ihr die spezifische Eigenschaft, welche ihr als Tugend nachgerühmt wird, die Ausschaltung von Liebe, Haß und allen rein persönlichen, überhaupt aller irrationalen, dem Kalkul sich entziehenden, Empfindungselementen aus der Erledigung der Amtsgeschafte gelingt" (1922:662).

122. For example, the American Medical Association's Council on Ethical and Judicial Affairs references its code of professional ethics when it exhorts physicians to go beyond the law in looking out for signs of abuse and says that they have responsibilities to both "share in providing care to the indigent"—including making it "a normal part of" their practice—and engage in improving their communities and public health more generally. It reminds physicians that "the practice of medicine is a privilege" and that the "essence of the physician" includes not just treatment of illness but also the "moral virtues of beneficence and charity." Clarke et al. 1993.
123. United States Army 2013, emphasis added.
124. United States Army n.d. and United States Air Force 2007.
125. While the recovery of personnel has only recently become more possible, the sentiment has always been in the US military (Daileda 2014), although the US Army's FM 3–50 *Army Personnel Recovery* (2014) says that "4–7. The mission is always paramount. The Soldier's Creed and the Warrior Ethos (ADP 1 and TC 3–21.75) make it clear that the Army values its members, but the mission is foremost."
126. *Budōshoshinshū* (武道初心集) 1984 (seventeenth century CE).
127. *De Officiis*, 1.39–41.
128. Shortly afterward, the British declined to grant a reciprocal request. Van Emden 2013:1–3.
129. "American Cryptology" 2015.
130. Note Adam Smith's conception of sympathy, which is actually quite demanding: it is an imagined empathy of how one might feel in another person's situation and *in that body*, as that person and not as oneself, rather than a direct reflection of the sufferer's sentiment. Smith 1982:I.i.1.2, I.i.1.11, VII.iii.1.4.
131. FM 6–22, August 2012, emphasis added.
132. The connection between virtue and the law in warfare is long-standing. Even the Geneva Conventions, which seek to supersede cultural specificity and traditional mores with rational legality, acknowledge the significance of traditional virtues in buttressing the international laws of war:

> There are "three powerful spirits, which from time to time have moved over the face of the waters, and given a predominant impulse to the moral sentiments and energies of mankind. These are the spirits of liberty, of religion and of honour." . . . This sense of honour, which was nourished during the Middle Ages of Europe by chivalry, particularly in tournaments and in jousting, has contributed to the establishment of the rules which finally became assimilated into the customs and practices of war, in accordance with the principle that the law of the powerful tends to become common law. There were rules for attack and rules for defence, and the knight always trusted the word of another knight, even if he were an enemy. Perfidy was considered a dishonour which could not be redeemed by any act, no matter how heroic. (International Committee of the Red Cross 1987a:on Art. 37, §1498)

133. Ficarrotta 2001:61–71. The breadth of virtues required may be quite wide: For example, the Round Table knights swore: "never to do outrageously nor murder, and

always to flee treason; also by no means to be cruel, but to give mercy unto him that asketh mercy, upon pain of forfeiture of their worship and lordship of King Arthur for evermore; and always to do ladies, damosels, and gentlewomen succor, upon pain of death. Also that no man take no battles in a wrongful quarrel for no law, nor for no world's goods." Malory 2003 (1485):bk. 3, chap. 15.

134. French 2017:8–12.
135. Shay 2003 (1994):115.
136. *Contra Faustum*, 22.74.
137. Hedges 2002:26.
138. Depending on the end to which the virtues are oriented, they can bring good (as virtues are commonly believed to do) or evil. Cf. Kant:

> It is impossible to think of anything at all in the world, or indeed even beyond it, that could be considered good without limitation except a *good will*. Understanding, wit, judgment and the like, whatever such *talents* of mind may be called, or courage, resolution, and perseverance in one's plans, as qualities of *temperament*, are undoubtedly good and desirable for many purposes, but they can also be extremely evil and harmful if the will which is to make use of these gifts of nature, and whose distinctive constitution is therefore called *character*, is not good. (*Groundwork*, section 1, 4:393; Kant 1996:49)

139. Kulish et al. 2015; Cole 2017; Ismay et al. 2017.
140. Cole 2017.
141. See Smith 1982:VI.iii.27.
142. Although uttered in a different context, the words of Colonel Chabert are apropos here: "Les souffrances morales, auprès desquelles pâlissent des douleurs physiques, excitant cependant moin de pitié, parce qu'on ne les voit point." Honoré de Balzac, *Le colonel Chabert* 1997 (1832):31. "Physical pain pales beside moral suffering, but arouses more pity since it can be seen."
143. It is unclear whether poison would be an acceptable "ruse" under the Geneva Conventions.
144. Kant thought that the *right* kind of warfare could help develop people's dispositions for moral behavior. Valdez 2017.
145. International Committee of the Red Cross 1987a:on Art. 37, §1500, emphasis added.
146. *Perpetual Peace* (1795), §1.6, 8:346–47 (Kant 1996:320); *The Metaphysics of Morals* (1797), §57, 6:347 (Kant 1996:485). The connection between morality in warfare and morality in other aspects of life is not uncommon. For example, in Chinese literature, notes Kierman:

> Early Chinese historians could not conceive of—or could not admit that they could conceive of—a great victory won by a morally disreputable sovereign ruling a state which lacked any virtues except military strength. Sovereigns and generals may in fact have had no trouble conceiving of it. But at least in the written account, every victor had to display correct attitudes before, during, and after his battle. (1974:46)

The highly influential *Seven Military Classics*, including Sun Tzu's *The Art of War*, also links good governance with victory. Chiu n.d. That this connection would be made in both Eastern and Western philosophy is unsurprising: people want to see virtue rewarded. There may even be some truth to these stories in the literature—but they are also surely meant as heuristic, as pedagogy, and as instructive of the idea that morality and victory are tied.

147. Vattel 2008 (1758):bk. 3, §155.
148. For example, Union Army Major General John M. Schofield, who was otherwise happy to dispense with the laws of war, still considered assassinations and poisoning to be "mean" and "cowardly." Witt 2012:325.
149. Art. 16, 70.
150. The Law of War Manual (updated 2016) explicates further:

> Honor may be understood to provide a foundation for obligations that help enforce and implement the law of war or special agreements between belligerents during armed conflict. For example, honor may be understood to provide the foundation for the requirement for persons to comply with the law of war in good faith. (§2.6.2.1, p. 67)

151. Payne-Gallwey 2007.
152. The exact ratio of forces is disputed. The low-end estimate says it was 4:3 in favor of the French (twelve thousand French troops to nine thousand English), while most other estimates say it was upward of 4:1.
153. This is not to say that asymmetry has never raised questions before. On the contrary, it has prompted cries of unfairness and uneasiness from both losers and winners on many occasions of slaughter, e.g., when Polish cavalry met German machine-gun fire (not tanks, as is commonly believed) in World War II; when British and Egyptian breech-loading and repeating rifles, machine guns, and field cannon met Sudanese muskets, swords, and spears at the Battle of Omdurman in 1898 (Headrick 2010:275; Churchill 1902 [1899]); or when "Daisy Cutter" bombs meet AK-47s.
154. Thucydides 1998 (431–400 BCE):4.126. LCL 109:428–31.
155. Plutarch 1931 (c. 100 CE):§234:E5, E46. LCL 245:394–421. Cf. Herodotus 2015 (c. 440 BCE):9.72.2.
156. What was seen as problematic can become acceptable, even trivial, and vice versa. For example, the contemporary norm in professional tennis of "apologizing" for a "net ball" or mishit winner was not expected some forty years ago. Even if apologies are merely pro forma rather than sincere, it reflects an idea that such balls are in some way "unfair." This contrasts not only with a previous era of tennis but also with other sports, both team (e.g., baseball, soccer, football) and one-on-one (e.g., fencing).
157. See the development of nuclear weapons, for example, as well as the spread of drone technology. Although American use of unmanned aircraft receives by far the most attention, as of 2016, over eighty countries have drones among their military equipment, over thirty-five of which are major systems, and thirteen have weaponized drones (of which at least six have employed them in combat). As of 2017, even Hezbollah, Hamas, and ISIS have developed—however rudimentary—unmanned aircraft capable of dropping bombs and inflicting casualties. Abbott et al., 2016; Bamford 2016; Warrick 2017; Kesling 2017.
158. Bowden 2013; *Eye in the Sky* 2015. Another unexpected cause of distress has been the cognitive dissonance between the RPA pilots' jobs and their environments. What was thought to be a benefit (the ability to live and work comfortably and to go home to one's family at the end of the shift, while deployed) has instead been a significant source of psychological strain. One solution could be to separate pilots from their families, such that they serve more traditional deployments. Or their jobs could actually be made more video game–like, à la *Ender's Game* (1985). If they thought their activities were merely simulations, that might ease the mental burden and possibly even improve performance—but may also incur significant costs in terms of moral injury. There may be value for the warrior in experiencing the trauma of his job.

159. Evans 2013, emphasis added; Thompson 2013; Tilghman 2013.
160. Ferdinando 2016; Seck 2016; Londoño 2013; Terkel 2013; Tilghman 2016.
161. There are separate questions about whether drone warfare is both effective and superior at reducing collateral damage. Targets, their populations, and other critics have legitimate complaints about civilians being killed. In comparison with civilian casualties from more boots-on-the-ground, however, the evidence is fairly compelling, although there are certainly dissenting views. See Fisher 2016; Hayden 2016; Zenko and Wolf 2016; Friedersdorf 2016; Shane 2015. The discomfort with drone warfare may be largely driven by a sense of "unfairness."
162. Galliott 2016:chap. 7. See also Williams 2015; Kahn 2002; Simpson and Sparrow 2014.
163. The idea that RPA pilots are not in the field makes intuitive sense, but it also reveals another common assumption in the ethic of cooperation for a fair fight: that there are more or less accepted "battlefields" or even vaguely defined "areas of conflict," outside of which war should not be waged. While I certainly do not advocate total war, the presumption is incorrect. If opponents could get to Nevada, USA, and attack RPA pilots in their bases, they would—ceteris paribus—be permitted to do so under any standard understanding of the rules of engagement.
164. Chairman of the Joint Chiefs of Staff, Marine Corps general Joe Dunford, has repeatedly said that American soldiers should never enter into a fair fight: "Rather, we have to maintain a joint force that has the capability and credibility to assure our allies and partners, deter aggression and overmatch any potential adversary" (Garamone 2016).

    Similarly, while RPA pilots seem to be *emotionally* affected by their intimate knowledge of the targets and civilians they kill, they are generally not particularly concerned with fairness as parity, and sometimes note that "unfairness" is precisely the point. For example, said an U.S. Air Force RPA pilot on not putting oneself at risk by being in the battlefield, "Isn't that the goal? That's what archers did. . . . [We] increasingly look for stand-off weapons capability. . . . [We're] always looking for asymmetrical advantage, just like suicide bombings. . . . No one wants a fair fight, but you want an ethical fight. That's why we don't use gas" or fire on someone surrendering or target civilians. "It's unfair that we outnumber the enemy ten to one, but it's not a *mano a mano* fight. You want it to be unfair. You want to meet the enemy with overwhelming force" (Weaver 2015).

    At the risk of overgeneralization, there seem to be broad differences between the different military branches in how strongly they are influenced by the "fair fight" ethic, which probably stems in part from the historical development and trajectory of their respective kinds of warfighting.
165. Pruszewicz 2015.
166. *Report of the Permanent Advisory Commission for Military, Naval and Air Questions to the Council of the League of Nations* 1920.
167. Still, Germany, Britain, and France frequently used and strove to develop new and more effective gases.
168. Pruszewicz 2015.
169. Thousands have been "gruesome[ly]" slaughtered by machetes in Rwanda, for example, but "the production and sale of machetes is not considered a threat to international security." Erlanger 2013.
170. Jones 2014.
171. Anonymous, United States Army, 2015.
172. Although ancient Greeks did not think that "barbarians" could be converted to civilization, the classical Chinese thought of them as akin to criminals, who could be culturally rehabilitated.

173. The *Hoplitenpolitie* had "standards of warfare for conduct in inter-polis wars which were not observed in war against barbarians." Pritchett 1974:chap 8, "Surprise Attacks," 173. See also H. Berve, *Neue Jahrbuecher fuer Antike und deutsche Bildung* 1 (1938):6–7. Cf. R. Lonis, "Les usages de la guerre entre Grecs et Barbares," *Annales littéraires de l'Université de Besançon* 104 (1969).
174. This also happens when the notion of parity goes awry, such as when it focuses on the wrong features. For example, military historian Martin Pegler attributes some of the social stigma against snipers not only to revulsion against surprise attacks but also to class divides in killing. When American Col. Daniel Morgan advised his sharpshooters to "shoot for the epaulettes" during the American Revolutionary War, "this deeply unsporting concept was not embraced by the British who believed that the specific targeting of officers should not be normal practice for the common soldier in battle" (Pegler 2004:39). "It was an officer-class attitude," Pegler explains, "The British thought shooting an enemy from great distance in cold blood was unacceptable, in a way that blasting them to pieces with artillery was not" (Wood 2015).
175. Witt 2012:98–99.
176. Witt 2012:101–2.
177. Witt 2012:107–8.
178. "The tomahawk and scalping knife; about Indian enormities, and foreign miscreants and incendiaries. I, too, hate them; from my very soul I abominate them. But I love my country and its Constitution; I love liberty and safety, and fear military despotism more even than I hate these monsters. . . . You have no right to practice, under color of retaliation, enormities on the Indians. . . . [Common law is the] principal foundation of all public or international law. . . . We have constantly abstained from retaliating upon the Indians the excesses practiced by them towards us, we were morally bound by this invariable usage, and could not lawfully change it without the most cogent reasons. . . . [Given that this has been the predominant practice (except for destroying their towns)], the other principles of the laws of civilized nations are extended to them, and are thus made law in regard to them. When did this humane custom, by which, in consideration of their ignorance and our enlightened condition, the rigors of war were mitigated, begin?" (Clay 1819:638, 639).

# 3. Cooperation to Minimize Damage

1. Clausewitz 1873 (1832):bk. 1.1.6.
2. David 2009:17.
3. Witt 2012:251.
4. Nuremberg Trial Proceedings 1946:58–59.
5. Gouré 1962:98–99.
6. Gouré 1962:158–59.
7. Gouré 1962:161, 163, 218, 180, 216.
8. Gouré 1962:164.
9. Gouré 1962:192.
10. Appian 1912 (second century CE):§132.
11. For summary, explanation, and relevant case law on Rule 1, see the ICRC's Customary IHL Database.
12. ICRC 1958.

13. One of the primary motivations behind this provision was indiscriminate attacks of various kinds during World War II. ICRC 1987a:§1946. Civilian protection, however, was not intended to hinder the ability to fight in self-defense against an invader, as many fear, as "nothing in the present Charter shall impair the inherent right of individual or collective self-defense if an armed attack occurs against a Member of the United Nations, until the Security Council has taken measures necessary to maintain international peace and security" (United Nations Charter, Art. 51). See also Geneva Convention—Additional Protocol I, Art. 51, Section 7; ICRC 1987a:§§1925–27.
14. Complicating that calculation is the possibility that the bombing campaigns were in fact crucial to and decisive for the Allied victory, for their effect not only on morale but also on Axis operational capacity and military effectiveness, as Richard Overy argues, e.g., by reducing production as well as prompting the redirection of Axis military resources toward defense against the bombers, in ways that ultimately made them less militarily effective. Overy 1996:chap. 4, esp. 127–33, chaps. 9–10.
15. Walzer 2015:146.
16. Walzer 2015:146.
17. bin Laden 2002b. See also Blanchard 2004; bin Laden 2002a.
18. Mir 2001.
19. Some have argued that the distinction between combatant and civilian is not as stark as it might seem, that there may be moral or political liability for civilians (especially democratic citizens), although they differ on the ultimate implications of that responsibility for civilians' liability and permission to be killed. See McMahan 2009:chap. 5; Frowe 2014:chap. 6; May 2005; Primoratz 2002; Stilz 2011; and Kutz 2000. Even some forms of political participation in nondemocratic, authoritarian regimes can render one responsible in some way for the government's actions: see, for example, Chiu 2011.
20. Other ways of arguing for the elimination of the civilian/combatant distinction include German Imperial Navy Zeppelins commander Peter Strasser's, during World War I:

> We who strike the enemy where his heart beats have been slandered as "baby killers" and "murderers of women." What we do is . . . but necessary. Very necessary. Nowadays, there is no such animal as a noncombatant. Modern warfare is total warfare. ("Zeppelin Terror Attack" 2014; Lawson and Lawson 1996:79.)

This argument from "necessity," however, is less philosophically and normatively successful.
21. This question is relevant in a variety of settings. For example, on the date of the *RMS Lusitania*'s departure from New York back to Liverpool, German diplomats published the following warning in fifty American newspapers, including in New York, in some cases next to advertisements for the Lusitania's sailing:

> NOTICE! TRAVELLERS intending to embark on the Atlantic voyage are reminded that a state of war exists between Germany and her allies and Great Britain and her allies; that the zone of war includes the waters adjacent to the British Isles; that, in accordance with formal notice given by the Imperial German Government, vessels flying the flag of Great Britain, or any of her allies, are liable to destruction in those waters and that travellers sailing in the war zone on the ships of Great Britain or her allies do so at their own risk.— IMPERIAL GERMAN EMBASSY, Washington, D.C., April 22, 1915.

The Lusitania was torpedoed on May 7 off the Irish coast, and 1,198 of the 1,962 crew and passengers died.

Was the warning sufficient? Should the passengers have been made aware that military arms were being transported on the ship? Although the *Lusitania* was officially listed as an auxiliary war ship, had carried ammunition in the past, and at the time was carrying about 4.2 million rifle cartridge rounds among other items that were publicly listed in the cargo manifest, the general public did not know of the *Lusitania*'s status and its additional mission at the time. Was the presence of those arms enough to make the Lusitania fair game for military attack, whether or not the public and passengers were aware? Should the British government have done more to protect its citizens, knowing beforehand that the *Lusitania* was at risk?

After the sinking and in response to American protests—there were 128 Americans among the deaths—the German military agreed to some restrictions on submarine warfare, which lasted for two years.

22. There is further disagreement about whether soldiers must shoulder undue risk to protect *other* countries' civilians as well, as opposed to just their own. See, e.g., Margalit and Walzer 2009; Kasher and Yadlin 2009.

    The limits of the strength of the principle of noncombatant immunity and the imperative to protect the weak are especially evident when it comes to other countries' civilians. For example, a poll of US adult citizens found that a sizeable majority of the American public value the lives of their own soldiers at least five times more than those of the opponents' civilians. Well over 60 percent would prefer (67.3 percent) or approve of (63.1 percent) a conventional air strike that deliberately killed one hundred thousand of the opponents' civilians rather than fight a ground war that killed twenty thousand US soldiers. It made some difference if it was a nuclear strike: preference dropped to 55.6 percent while approval fell to 59.3 percent. The ratio of lives valued was also affected: even if the opponents' noncombatant casualties were two orders of magnitude greater than those of US soldiers, a staggering 47.7 percent would still prefer and 59.1 percent would approve of a nuclear strike that killed two million opponent civilians rather than take twenty thousand American military deaths. Sagan and Valentino 2017.

    It should be noted, however, that this poll does not speak to the force of the principle of noncombatant immunity within the warrior classes themselves, and the ethic for civilian protection may well be more strongly held within some militaries or subunits.

23. Goldstein 2006. See also Roberts 2016; Angers 1999; and "My Lai" 2010.
24. When Japanese general Tomoyuki Yamashita was convicted in 1945 of command responsibility for war crimes against civilians and prisoners of war in the Philippines and Singapore, he appealed to the US Supreme Court, challenging the American military commission's authority and jurisdiction. His appeal was rejected, although the decision was not unanimous (US Supreme Court 1946). Yamashita then petitioned directly to US president Harry Truman for clemency, and Truman asked MacArthur to review the case. MacArthur 1946.
25. See Chiu 2010:esp. 52–56.
26. Anonymous, United States Armed Forces 2014.
27. There were also artillery and cavalry, and advance light infantry was often sent to ambush or screen. For an overview of fighting in the 1770s and 1780s, see the similar Napoleonic period, described in Bruce et al. 2008.
28. Letters by officers during that time often praised the manliness of standing and taking fire bravely.

29. Keegan 1988.
30. Parker 1988:71–72; Holmes 2001:931–35; Pfanner 2004:95–99.
31. Chiu 2010:45–46.
32. See chapter 2 on why the ethic of cooperation for a fair fight persists, despite the effectiveness of guerrilla warfare.
33. Cf. Michel Foucault, on corporal inscription and the use of uniforms, such as in military schools to indicate variations in status, privilege, and punishment, as well as their relationship to biopolitics. See, e.g., Foucault 1995 (1975), 2003, 2010.
34. Chiu 2010:48–49.
35. The *Seven Military Classics* 武經七書, for example, admonishes would-be conquerors to wage war righteously and humanely, in order to better establish their claim to rule over that of the despots they are trying to overthrow.
36. The ethic of cooperation to protect certain classes of people is not always consistently applied or developed across categories of people. For example, in the "war on terror," the United States has taken the principle of discrimination (protection of civilians) more seriously than it has the protection of POWs (e.g., regulations on legal representation, torture, conditions of imprisonment), complying far more strictly with Protocol IV (and even going beyond its official obligations to comply with Additional Protocol I, to which it is not a signatory) than with Protocol III of the Geneva Conventions. Kinsella 2005.
37. See Chiu 2010 for justifications for the uniform convention and its exceptions.
38. Even the legal exceptions reflect this ethic of cooperation, as the regulations specify that those who are deemed unequal are exempt from reciprocating and not required to cooperate. (Whether those affected parties are in fact unequal in a relevant sense and whether those are grounds for not cooperating are separate matters.)
39. At first glance, figure 3.1 appears to resemble the famous Clausewitzean trinity: people, army, and government. This is a misconception of trinity, however. Clausewitz says that the dominant tendencies in war are a "wonderful trinity" of "the original violence of its elements, hatred and animosity, which may be looked upon as blind instinct; of the play of probabilities and chance, which make it a free activity of the soul; and of the subordinate nature of a political instrument, by which it belongs purely to reason" (Clausewitz 1873 [1832]), which often get simplified to "emotion, chance, and reason."

    Several contemporary interpreters—including Summers 1995 (1982) and Keegan 1993—have mistakenly identified the trinity as the people, army, and government. Clausewitz, however, refers to the people, army, and government as the primary—though not exclusive—exemplars and manifestations of the trinity's elements, and not the trinity itself. Bassford and Villacres 1995.
40. Chiu 2010.
41. Hague Convention (IV, 3) Declaration concerning the Use of Bullets Which Expand or Flatten Easily in the Human Body, July 29, 1899.
42. The ICRC, an observer at the negotiations for the later Protocol on Blinding Laser Weapons (Protocol IV to the 1980 Convention on the Use of Certain Conventional Weapons) (October 13, 1995), makes the same judgment here that maiming is worse than death. It deemed the "prohibition, in advance, of the use of an abhorrent new weapon . . . before a stream of victims gave visible proof of its tragic effects" of permanent blinding to be a "significant breakthrough in humanitarian law" (ICRC 1995).
43. For a summary of international criminal, humanitarian, and human rights law, see ICRC 2011.
44. Fink and Cooper 2017.

45. Appendix §D-11 (p. D-3):
    - Soldiers and Marines fight only enemy combatants.
    - Soldiers and Marines do not harm enemies who surrender. They disarm them and turn them over to their superiors.
    - Soldiers and Marines do not kill or torture enemy prisoners of war.
    - Soldiers and Marines collect and care for the wounded, whether friend or foe.
    - Soldiers and Marines do not attack medical personnel, facilities, or equipment.
    - Soldiers and Marines destroy no more than the mission requires.
    - Soldiers and Marines treat all civilians humanely.
    - Soldiers and Marines do not steal. They respect private property and possessions.
    - Soldiers and Marines do their best to prevent violations of the law of war.
    - Soldiers and Marines report all violations of the law of war to their superior.
46. Fink and Cooper 2017.
47. Fink and Cooper 2017.
48. "Kohima, a village 5,000 feet above sea level surrounded by peaks 10,000 feet high to the west and 8,000 feet to the north and east, has been described as 'an ocean of peaks and ridges crossed by bridle paths.' [1st Assam Regiment Colonel Hugh] Richards had been trying to fortify the place for a month, stymied by a quartermaster in Dimapur who would not release barbed wire to him as there was an administrative regulation forbidding its use in the Naga Hills" (Roberts 2011:270).
49. This prohibition was renewed in the 1907 Hague Convention Declaration (XIV) Prohibiting the Discharge of Projectiles and Explosives from Balloons. Due to the foreseen use of aircraft in warfare, many desired to permanently ban the use of projectiles from the air, not just those ejected from balloons, so delegates inserted a separate prohibition on the "attack or bombardment, by whatever means, of towns, villages, dwellings, or buildings which are undefended" (Hague Convention [IV] Laws and Customs of War, Annex to the Convention—Art. 25). Schindler and Toman 1988:201.
50. US president Woodrow Wilson, April 19, 1916, in response to a number of submarine incidents, including the sinking of the *Lusitania* the previous year. Garner 1920:374.
51. Preamble, Nyon Arrangement, September 14, 1937. This agreement was prompted by neutral merchant ships being targeted by submarines during the Spanish Civil War. See Heller-Roazen 2009 for a genealogy of the pirate in legal and political thought.
52. The International Society of Military Law and the Law of War meeting (Lausanne, 1982) "conceded that from the legal point of view the use of mines constituted an attack in the sense of the Protocol when a person was directly endangered by . . . a mine." ICRC 1987a:on Art. 51, §1960.
53. Jenkins 2012.
54. Davenport 2002–3.
55. Beyond a vague mention of "other severe consequences for years after emplacement," which could refer to the physical effects of the active mines themselves, the Ottawa Treaty makes no mention of other humanitarian concerns, including economic prospects; yet economies are also crippled by mines.

    Farmers cannot work or feed their families when untold numbers of mines litter the fields. For a country like Cambodia, for example, where over 60 percent of the population is engaged in farming, this is devastating. "There's a clear link between land mine contamination and poverty," says the Mines Advisory Group (MAG), a major demining operation (Jenkins 2012).

56. Sigal 2006:99. See also ICRC 2007.
57. US Department of State 2004, 2014.
58. Restrictions on mines also show how recourse to an ethic of cooperation between enemies is not the only mechanism at play, and civilian protection can be undertaken unilaterally. For example, although the United States has not signed the treaty and holds a stockpile of around ten million landmines, it has not used, exported, or produced antipersonnel mines since 1991, 1992, and 1997, respectively. It has also "done more to counteract mines than any other country, spending $1.9 billion during the past 18 years through the Humanitarian Mine Action Program—roughly a quarter of the total spent on demining and other remediation activities around the world" (Jenkins 2012).
59. "CX. Moreover, all Prisoners on the one side and the other, without any distinction of the Gown or the Sword, shall be releas'd after the manner it has been covenanted, or shall be agreed between the Generals of the Armys, with his Imperial Majesty's Approbation."
60. Neff 2010:57–58.
61. Neff 2010:61.
62. The Convention Relative to the Treatment of Prisoners of War (1929) has been superseded by the Convention (III) Relative to the Treatment of Prisoners of War (1949).
63. Geneva Convention (III), Arts. 4, 8, 10–12, 56, and so on.
64. Although reprisal is now banned by the Geneva Conventions, it was common and quite understandable to many, as the cost of prisoner upkeep can be prohibitive. For example, in June 1862 of the American Civil War, when Lincoln learned that dozens of pro-Union prisoners were being maltreated in a Confederate jail in Tennessee, Lincoln approved the same treatment for the same number of Confederate prisoners. Later, Secretary of War Edwin Stanton cut rations by 20 percent for Confederate prisoners in Union detention, in response to reports that Union prisoners were being inadequately fed. Neff 2010:67. See also Neely 1991:151–52; Tap 1998:207.
65. Vattel 2008:bk. 3, chap. 8, §§136–37, 139–40, 150–51. The Lieber Code echoes this when it bars the intentional infliction of additional harm to enemies "already wholly disabled," upon punishment of death (§71).
66. Neff 2010:64.
67. Neff 2010:59.
68. Brussels Declaration 1874:Art. 27. Hague Convention (IV) Laws and Customs of War, 1907—Annex Art. 7; Geneva Convention (III) Relative to the Treatment of Prisoners of War, 1949:Arts. 12 and 15. Prior to that, sometimes the home rulers of captured soldiers would pay for their maintenance, e.g., during the Seven Years War of 1756–63, when the French king paid the British government for a certain level of care of French prisoners held there. Abell 1914:4–8. This seldom happened, however, as reimbursement/collection was difficult and because prisoner exchanges were frequent.
69. This includes not only skimping on conditions provided but also the illegal use of POWs as slave labor, such as was prevalent in World War II.
70. POWs may be compelled to work during their internment, but no more than their enemy counterparts, not on military operations, and not on excessively dangerous missions, and they must be compensated with fair wages for their work and provided with certain working conditions. Geneva Convention III, Art. 51–55; IV, Art. 40, 51.
71. This dilemma is discussed in chapter 5.

72. Lawrence 1973 (1926), chap. 51.
73. When the Confederacy faced this dilemma in 1863, they started releasing Union prisoners on parole, thus "free[ing] Confederate resources that would otherwise have been taken up feeding, transporting, housing, and guarding" them. The Union declared those parole oaths null and void because they were promised without authorization from the parolees' own government. So when Lieber wrote into General Orders 100, "Art. 131[,] If the government does not approve of the parole, the paroled officer must return into captivity,"

> This played right into the hands of the Confederate practice. All through the Gettysburg campaign, Confederate officers gleefully issued unlawful paroles, relying on the Union's own statement that such paroles obligated the prisoner himself to report to his captor's lines. Even as the battle raged on the third day at Gettysburg, embarrassed Union high officials were forced to issue an awkward amendment, insisting that illegally paroled soldiers were actually free to resume fighting. (Witt 2013)

See also Witt 2012:254–56.
74. Killing the wounded on the battlefield is obviously illegal, but leaving them to die is ambiguous. Geneva Conventions Common Article 3 stipulates that "the wounded and sick shall be collected and cared for" (§2), and that impartial NGOs may assist warring parties in doing so, but there would be reasonable disagreement on the time frame required for collection, and ample opportunity for plausible deniability. See chapter 6 on medical neutrality.
75. Neff 2010:70.
76. Chiu 2010:esp. 53–54. See also Figure 3.1.
77. Neff 2010:59.
78. See, e.g., Walzer 2015:esp. chap. 3 "The Rules of War." In contrast, see McMahan 2012.
79. See Luban 2014, and again Margalit and Walzer 2009, Kasher and Yadlin 2009, and Sagan and Valentino 2017.
80. *Mifune: The Last Samurai* 2015:~10:00–11:00. Of the continued—and doomed—fight against impossible odds, adds director Sadao Nakajima, "The ronin acts out his frustration and rage, knowing in the end, it's hopeless. He knows that death is inevitable. He fights for his own sense of justice" (~12:00–13:00).
81. Wiebe 2003; Schmitt 1992:609, 613.
82. See also Schmitt 1992:609, 613, *supra* note 5 at 616.
83. Vattel 2008 (1758):bk. 3, §155, "Whether an enemy may lawfully be assassinated or poisoned."
84. Hague Convention (IV) Laws and Customs of War, 1907:Art. 23(b) "it is especially forbidden . . . to kill or wound treacherously, individuals belonging to the hostile nation or army."
85. ICRC n.d.:Rule 65. Perfidy.
86. E.g., US Executive Orders 11905 (1976), 12306 (1979), 12333 (1981): "No person employed by or acting on behalf of the United States Government shall engage in, or conspire to engage in, assassination" (§2.11).
87. E.g., Zengal 1991.
88. ICRC n.d.:Rule 65. Perfidy.
89. Maxwell 2012. US Department of Defense 2015.
90. Pickard 2001:esp. 9. Maxwell 2012; US Department of Defense 2015.
91. Wingfield 1998:287, 295; More 1965 (1516):111; Zengel 1991:123, 149.

92. Pickard 2001:9; Schmitt 1992:611–13. Increased protection over time for political elites is analogous and perhaps related to the repositioning of Western military leaders to the back of the field. Says Victor Davis Hanson:

> For the most part, this novel Greek idea—that the battlefield commander, along with his small staff of subordinates, should at least be near the hard fighting, if not an active participant in the killing—survived in the West until the onset of the twentieth century. Yet, by the First World War, at least, it had eroded entirely, as the general receded to the rear, to a point completely detached from the fighting, and a position undreamed of by the men of antiquity. (2009:108)

By the time of the Vietnam War, US Marine Corp officers were only supposed to draw their weapons if something had gone badly wrong, for an officer who had to draw his weapon was distracted from directing his men, said a first lieutenant who had served in the war.

There is an ostensible strategic explanation: modern battle requires more specialized attention to planning, communication, coordination, and management. (Advanced communications technology also no longer requires military leaders to be on the battlefield as frequently, and increasingly "scientific" approaches to tactics and strategy in war would seem to rely less on immediate leadership there.) This tactical evolution comes at a cost in terms of troop morale and efficacy, and raises questions about why certain classes are privileged to an extent beyond their actual utility.

93. Many contemporary definitions simply beg the question, e.g., Newman and Van Geel 1989:434: "assassination refers to the intentional killing of a high-level political figure, whether in power or not." Brandenberg 1987:55n1: "intentional killing of an internationally protected person," as defined in the Convention on the Prevention and Punishment of Crimes Against Internationally Protected Persons, Including Diplomatic Agents 1973:Art. 1, para. 1, 28 U.S.T. 1975, 1035 U.N.T.S. 167 (New York Convention).
94. *Dictionnaire philosophique*, "Droit" (1764).
95. David 2003; Addicott 2004; Melzer 2008; Iran Human Rights Documentation Center 2008; Teplitz 1995; Vlasic 2012; Human Rights Watch 2011. Discomfort with the subterfuge of assassination is not necessarily universal, however. For example, ancient Chinese philosophy leaves treatment of assassination primarily to historical texts where, with few exceptions, moral judgment depended on whether or not the assassin was successful: "勝者為王 敗者為寇," the winner is the king, the loser is the villain. (Or, in contemporary parlance, "might makes right," for history is written by the victor.)
96. For example, killing Martin Luther King, Jr., was strictly political, but people like Abraham Lincoln or Archduke Franz Ferdinand are ambiguous as they merge political and military concerns, while those like Julius Caesar, Ahmad Shah Massoud (head of Northern Alliance, Afghanistan, 2011), and Manchurian warlord Zhang Zuolin 張作霖 (1928) were also military commanders, so it is not obvious that these were assassinations as opposed to acts of war.
97. Soldiers are subject to military courts, for example, although these distinctions can be manipulated, such as when Union commanders used military court-martials to avoid charging those soldiers with war crimes and Union judge advocates charged noncombatants with violations of laws of war so that they would be considered military, rather than political, prisoners and therefore subject to greater detention and trial. Witt 2012:269.

98. Vattel 2008 (1758):bk. 3, §155.
99. They might still be punished for war crimes or domestic oppression, but that is a separate matter.
100. This is a tension with contemporary geopolitical reality. Once upon a time, political heads went to war because kings, emperors, and lords were also military leaders, which meant they incurred risk (albeit far less than their soldiers) in going to war and were fair game on the battlefield. The spread of a civil/military leadership divide in most contemporary societies means that decision-makers are no longer accountable via their participation in battle.
101. Remarque 1975 (1928):chap. 8, p. 166.
102. Remarque 1975 (1928):chap. 9.
103. Scene 6.
104. Clausewitz 2000:1.1.2: "Force, to meet force, arms itself with the inventions of art and science. It is accompanied by insignificant restrictions, hardly worth mentioning, which it imposes on itself under the name of international law and usage, but which do not really weaken its power" (264–65).
105. For example, in codifying certain European maritime laws of war, the Paris Declaration Respecting Maritime Law (1856) demonstrated international law to be "a creature of power, not of humanitarian ideals. The laws of war suddenly seemed a body of rules for strong European states to manipulate at the expense of the weaker military forces of the United States." Witt 2012:136.
106. Chiu 2010.
107. Witt 2012:128.
108. Witt 2012:142.
109. Witt 2012:249.
110. This struggle actually began earlier, in the debate over Andrew Jackson's behavior in the Indian wars, when Henry Clay accused Jackson of abandoning the humanitarian aspect of the law, while Jackson's supporters argued that there was severity in the law as well and that the humanitarianism did not apply to Indians. Witt 2012:106–7. See also chapter 2.
111. The effectiveness of these attacks (which can never be known for certain, given how disease spreads) is beside the point—the evidence shows that it was deliberately attempted. Fenn 2000; Dixon 2005:152–55; Peckham 1947:170, 226–27.
112. Witt 2012:253.
113. Witt 2012:256–58.
114. Witt 2012:262. Lincoln did not want the Emancipation Proclamation to encourage uprisings among the slaves, which is why the Lieber Code declares that those fighting "without commission" and otherwise "divesting themselves of the character or appearance of soldiers . . . are not entitled to the privileges of prisoners of war, but shall be treated summarily as highway robbers or pirates" (Art. 82). Witt 2012:249.
115. Witt 2012:262–63, 249, 256–63.
116. For example, Judaic prohibitions on felling fruit trees during sieges can be taken as a reflection of environmental concern, but are actually intended prudentially, to preserve the invaders' own possible resources. Said Jewish studies scholar and rabbi Norman Solomon:

> We must be careful not to read later concepts into the text. For instance, someone might read the commandment to spare the lives of women and children as a primitive form of non-combatant immunity, all adult males being regarded

by default as combatants. But the Deuteronomic context is not about the human rights of citizens of an opposing state, but about whether Israelites might retain heathen women and children as booty (in war against the Canaanites women come under the *herem* ban and must be killed). Likewise, the commandment not to cut down fruit trees has been utilized as a "proof-text" for environmental responsibility in time of war; in its context, however, it is a counsel of prudence, that the conquering army should not destroy its own potential food sources. (2009:40)

117. Ip 2015:136, 149. In contrast, imagine getting caught in an earthquake in an area in which there were no buildings. Except for land/mudslides or tsunamis or perhaps the fault line opening up beneath your feet, you would simply fall down, and be otherwise unharmed.
118. Barnett 1998.
119. Hahn 1996.
120. Ip 2015:chap. 8.

# 4. Cooperation to End War Quickly

1. Hanson 2009 (1989):4.
2. Hanson 2009 (1989):33, 137.
3. Hanson 2009 (1989):28–29, 35.
4. Hanson 2009 (1989):35–36, 221, 224, 35–36.
5. Mortality rates alone in the most devastating modern wars (e.g., Napoleonic Wars, American Civil War, World War I, World War II, Korean War) hover around 20 percent, for much larger militaries. Gabriel and Metz 1992:esp. chap. 6 and tables 1 and 3.
6. Hanson 2009 (1989):xxvi.
7. Hanson 2009 (1989):35.
8. Hanson 2009 (1989):32.
9. Ober 1994:14.
10. Hanson 2009 (1989):35.
11. Hanson 2009 (1989):33–35. See also Hanson 1983:30–63.
12. Hanson 2009 (1989):25.
13. Ober 1996:56. There is some disagreement about the nature and significance of these "rules of engagement" as presented by Hanson and Ober. For example, Krentz, van Wees, and Lanni have argued that these "rules" were not norms but rather a result of the military tactics used at the time: for example, confining war to the summer season was out of necessity and convenience, rather than due to obligation. Furthermore, Lanni posits that any reduction in the damages of war during this time were due to the military tactics used, rather than any norms or laws to limit them, and that when siege tactics were introduced, the correlating destructiveness ensued. Krentz 2002:27; van Wees 2004:115–50; Lanni 2008:486–87.
14. Hanson 2009 (1989):36.
15. Hanson 1991:5.
16. Hanson 2009 (1989):25.
17. Hanson 2009 (1989):222.
18. Hanson 2009 (1989):223.

19. Pritchett 1985:15–16. Pritchett cites Y. Yadin, *The Art of Warfare in Biblical Lands* (1963):72–73, 267, 354; and J. J. Glück, "Reviling and Monomachy as Battle Preludes in Ancient Warfare," *Acta Classica* 7 (1964):25–31.
20. Witt explains, "For the captor, torturing captives served as a kind of spiritual replenishment and as a celebration of the supernatural. The captive, in turn, derived honor from the experience of being tortured. As one historian has put it, Indian warriors 'earned posthumous esteem by bearing themselves stoically under the ordeal'" (2012:90–91).
21. Williams 1988 (seventeenth century):1191.
22. Witt 2012:91.
23. Witt 2012:91–92.
24. Blum 2007.
25. Blum 2007:19, 20, 24–27, 28.
26. Blum 2007:58–59.
27. Hanson 2009 (1989):xxv–xxvi. Along with essential social institutions such as religion and agriculture (Hanson 2009 [1989]:24), the form of warfare both reflected and contributed to the particular political structure in place. Hoplite battle, Hanson says, emerged from the Greek city-states' unique political system, in which soldiers were also "free landowning citizens"—simultaneously fighters, farmers, and voters—who had vested political and economic interests in short, decisive wars. The courage to bear the brutality and suffer the carnage of hoplite phalanx battle was also honored in Greek literature, art, culture and politics (Hanson 2009:xxiv–xxv).
28. Hanson 2009 (1989):xxiv.
29. Herodotus 1922 (c. 440 BCE):7.9B.
30. Hanson 2009 (1989):10.
31. Hanson 2009 (1989):17.
32. Hanson 2009 (1989):197.
33. Hanson 2009 (1989):9.
34. "Fare le guerre . . . corte e grosse." Machiavelli 1997 (1531):bk. 2, chap. 6, "How the Romans Proceeded in Waging War."
35. "A toutes ces maxims, je joindrai encore que *nos guerres doivent être courtes & vives*, puisqu'il n'est pas de notre intérêt de traîner l'affaire; qu'une longue guerre ralentit insensiblement notre admirable discipline, & ne laisse pas de dépeupler notre pays, & d'épuiser nos ressources." Frederick II 1747:Art. 23, "Par quelle raison & comment il faut donner Bataille," 167–73, esp. 171, emphasis added.
36. These concerns about discipline and commitment echo Machiavelli's. "Short and sharp" wars require passion, ferocity, and brutality, which carry with them enormous possibility for victory, but also inherent danger, especially if the war lasts too long and soldiers become disillusioned and start looting or otherwise pursuing their own interests over that of army and city-state. Natural courage would never be enough to win wars, which is why leaders must attend to questions of training and discipline, Machiavelli believed. Paret et al. 1986:24–25.
37. This tactic complements Frederick's broader strategic approach in his early days, in which he thought that war should aim at destroying the enemy's forces, rather than at occupying or defending a particular territory, and that therefore the most efficient wars maintain a mobile offensive: engaging the enemy on his own soil, keeping him on the move, and forcing him to respond subordinately to one's own movements. Robson 1957:172.
38. Luvass 1966:141.

39. Clausewitz cautions against faith in the ability of "philanthropy" or "civilization" to resolve conflicts without war or in an "artistic" way to limit the bloodshed:

    *In affairs so dangerous as war, false ideas proceeding from kindness of heart are precisely the worst. As the most extensive use of physical force by no means excludes the co-operation of intelligence, he who uses this force ruthlessly, shrinking from no amount of bloodshed, must gain an advantage if his adversary does not do the same. Thereby he forces his adversary's hand, and thus each pushes the other to extremities to which the only limitation is the strength of resistance on the other side. . . . If the wars of civilized nations are far less cruel and destructive than those of the uncivilized, the reason lies in the social condition of the states, both in themselves and in their relations to one another. . . . The demand for the destruction of the enemy, inherent in the theoretical conception of war, has been in no way actually weakened or diverted by the advance of civilization.* (2000:1.1.3, emphasis added)

40. Bernard 1856:133–34.
41. Witt 2012:170.
42. Witt 2012:235.
43. Witt 2012:184.
44. Witt 2012:279.
45. Witt 2012:278.
46. Witt 2012:252.
47. Witt 2012:325.
48. Witt 2012:357–58.
49. Subsequent civilizations "had forgotten or indeed not understood that the old style of hoplite conflict was by deliberate design somewhat artificial, intended to focus a concentrated brutality upon the few in order to spare the many." Hanson 2009 (1989):224.
50. Most major nation-state militaries, including that of the United States, have developed and emphasize military institutions and culture designed for pitched, frontal battlefield clashes, e.g., with Soviet tanks. Extended guerrilla wars like Vietnam or the ongoing conflicts in Afghanistan and Iraq make these militaries uncomfortable, as their traditions and institutions are designed to end wars as quickly as possible, rather than to survive a quagmire. (Although the U.S. Training Doctrine Command is concerned that upcoming officers only know how to deal with counterinsurgency and not with conventional warfare, given their recent wartime experiences, the military remains structured for conventional warfare.) Blaker 2017.
51. Hanson 2009 (1989):14.
52. As the possibility of annihilating all of civilization became clear, the theory and doctrine of MAD (mutually assured destruction) and various disarmament treaties attempted to pull back from the brink of nuclear war and systematize some restraints on the use of this "short and massive" force, including establishing direct phone contact between the United States and the Soviet Union (1963) after the Cuban Missile Crisis (1962).

    Some proponents of MAD argue that the widespread possession of nuclear weapons actually forces enemies to cooperate with one another to deescalate conflicts, because no one wants a nuclear war. Skeptics question the validity of this theory—including whether all enemies would always be deterred by the prospect of nuclear annihilation, if they thought they could survive a nuclear attack or because survival was not the goal at all—as well as its morality.

Once nuclear technology had proliferated to the degree that it was no longer such a scarce resource, theorists also started thinking about how to *conduct* nuclear war, including how to signal intent to the opponent about what kinds of targets one would hit or avoid (e.g., if one plans to spare civilian centers such as large cities and begin by striking military targets, and is willing to stick to those target classes)—in other words, how to bring deterrence into the conflict itself if necessary, not just to prevent conflict. This interaction remained theoretical (e.g., Schelling 1960), and was never actualized in explicit discussion between Americans and Soviets (May 2017).

53. The unfinished business does not necessarily mean that the brevity of the initial war was incorrect: perhaps it was the *form* of the brief fighting (a relative underemphasis on ground troops) or its limited goals (containment and reversion to status quo ante), or perhaps it was the length, involvement, and greater ambitions (regime change) of the second war starting in 2003 that was the mistake.

    The United States also stayed its hand in 1991 out of humanitarian concerns (not wanting to annihilate the remaining, disorganized Iraqi forces) and political miscalculation (believing that Hussein was so weakened that he could be deposed).

54. The historical record may point to long-term and gradual attrition—the ability to exhaust the enemy with one's reserves of manpower and military hardware and capacity—winning the day and deciding the outcome of a war, rather than major battles and landmark collisions of troops. See Nolan 2017; Beckett 2017.
55. Summers 1995 (1982):chap. 1.
56. Other dimensions may be added, such as low-to-high intensity, which would gauge how involved the war is, in terms of amount of resources used (fire power, manpower, and so forth).
57. Hanson 2009 (1989):225.
58. Gardner and Heider 1968:135.
59. Gardner and Heider 1968:137.
60. The preliminary "*weem iya* [is] a sort of ceremonial thrust in the direction of the enemy. As a rule, a similar party of the enemy . . . respond[s] to this gesture by advancing in cautious stages: running, then stopping, then running forward several more paces. When the two groups are fifty yards apart, bowmen are likely to loose one or two arrows at their opposite numbers, more as a gesture of readiness to engage than in a serious attempt to do harm. After a few minutes, both groups will turn and fall back in the direction of their main forces. At a shorter distance from the enemy than before, they will stop and wait until the time has come to make another sally toward the front. This preliminary fencing is almost entirely ritual, like that of Japanese wrestlers, who confront each other with characteristic squats and bows before the sudden furious struggle begins." Gardner and Heider 1968:138.
61. Gardner and Heider 1968:141.
62. Gardner and Heider 1968:144.
63. Demands for revenge from both ghosts and surviving family members generated a sense of obligation to go to war. Gardner and Heider 1968:136.
64. Paret et al. 1986:24–25.
65. See Whitman (2012:76) on challenges to the results of the wager of battle. Whitman's theory will be discussed in chapter 6.
66. Hanson 2009 (1989):xxviii, emphasis added.
67. John Keegan, introduction to Hanson 2009 (1989):xiii.
68. This differs in other religions, e.g., ancient Greece or Buddhism, where different cities prioritize different gods among the pantheon, but most would recognize one another as practicing the same religion.

69. This is related to contemporary demands that war serve some ideological, rather than mere geopolitical, purpose, as we shall see in chapter 6.

## 5. The Limits of Ethics of Cooperation in Warfare

1. The Rann of Kutch (chapter 2) was an exception, and in general, air forces are less concerned with "fair fights" than armies.
2. Michaels 2015.
3. Increasingly accurate weaponry has reduced the number of sorties required by the American military to hit a 60' x 100' building, for example. Over the past century, the number has been as follows: World War I–N/A, World War II–3,024, Korean War–550, Vietnam War–44, Persian Gulf War–8, US-Iraq War (2003)–1 ("A Nation at War: A Historical View," April 20, 2003).
4. For a sobering reminder of how pervasive yet casual violence permeated human life before anyone expected otherwise—and how much our circumstances and expectations have changed—see Pinker 2012: chap. 1, "A Foreign Country."
5. Haykal Bafana هيكل بافنع (@BaFana3). 5:50 AM, May 11, 2012. Tweet. See also Mothana 2012; Abbas 2013b, 2013a.
6. See chapter 2, inc. note 163.
7. See, e.g., Walzer 2015: Postscript, "A Defense of Just War Theory," 342–43.
8. In Stendhal's *The Charterhouse of Parma* (1839), young Italian nobleman Fabrizio del Dongo finds chaos and misery on the battlefield, contrary to the noble romance he expected in joining Napoleon's war, and suffers thievery and a severe wounding by his own adopted side.

    Truth was perhaps more brutal than fiction. British Pvt. William Wheeler (1993 [1951]) describes a number of tragic battles, including at Waterloo (Letters Nos. 73–75, 19–23 June 1815, pp. 164–75), and recounts of other occasions:

    > We entered the trench and fixed our ladders, when sudden as a flash of lightening the whole place was in a blaze. . . . The top of this wall crowded with men hurling down shells and hand granades on the heads of them below, and when all these are expended they have each six or seven loaded firelocks which they discharge into the trench as quick as possible. Add to this some half dozen cannon scouring the trench with grape. . . . Heaps of brave fellows killed and wounded, ladders shot to pieces, and falling together with the men down upon the living and the dead. Then ever and anon would fall upon us the body of some brave Frenchman whose zeal had led him to the edge of the wall in its defence, and had been killed by their own missiles or by the fire of our covering party. (Letter No. 25, Campa Mayor, June 20, 1811, 61)

    > The battle was now raging with double fury. . . . I never before witnessed such large masses of cavalry opposed together, such a length of time. I am at a loss which to admire most, the cool intriped courage of our squares, exposed as they often were to a destructive fire from the French Artillery and at the same time or in less than a minute surrounded on all sides by the enemy's Heavey Cavalry, who would ride up to the very muzzles of our men's firelocks and cut at them in the squares. But this was of no use, not a single square could they brake, but was always put to the rout, by the steady fire of our troops. . . . I went to see what effect our fire had, and never before beheld such a sight in as

short a space, as about an hundred men and horses could be huddled together, there they lay. Those who were shot dead were fortunate for the wounded horses in their struggles by plunging and kicking soon finished what we had begun. In examining the men we could not find one that would be like to recover, and as we had other business to attend to we were obliged to leave them to their fate. (Letter No. 75, Camp Cato plains, June 23, 1813, 173–74)

9. This situation demonstrates the sometimes-catastrophic interaction between habits, norms, and technology. What is the relationship between habits and norms, and which tracks which? Might there have been a brief period in which certain habits (e.g., linear battle) and particular norms (e.g., virtue ethics motivations for a "fair fight") interacted to produce an equilibrium of sorts, but with the development of new technologies, that pairing then becomes a misalignment and generates a very suboptimal equilibrium? If so, then the habits must be decoupled from the norms in order for the former to adapt to the technological developments.
10. This is not the first time that attachment to an existing strategy produced a tactical choice set that contained only extremes. For example:

> When envoys from Epeiros urged Fulvius in 189 B.C. to make an expedition against the Aitolians, their recommendation took the form of two alternatives (Polybios 21.26). The Romans should march to the city of Ambrakia. Here the Aitolians might choose to meet the Roman legion in the field; the country round that city was described as suitable for a pitched battle. Or, if the Aitolians declined battle, they would be besieged within a city easy to attack. The alternatives epitomize the choices for the Greek in phalanx warfare, a pitched battle or a siege. (Pritchett 1974:chap. 8, "Surprise Attacks," 174, FN52)

In this situation, the strategic decision to use the phalanx limits the other available battle tactics, and so if they cannot engage in pitched battle, the Greeks are then left with the stark choice of siege warfare, which is much worse in terms of overall damage to the population.

11. Hastings 2004:88.
12. Shannon and McGirk 2006; Cody 2006; Teslik 2006; Chu and Daragahi 2006; Prothero 2007; United Nations 2003b; Burg and Shoup 1999:chap. 3, 91; Jett 1999:116; Brown 2012; Eisikovits 2015; Cordesman et al. 2007; Karami 2016; "Al Houthis Deliberately Misused the Ceasefire to Rearm" 2017; Stedman 1997; Cordesman 2009:23; Stedman and Tanner 2003; Berman 1996; Eisenstadt and Satloff 2014; Collins 2008; Ben-David 2008.
13. See Blum 2007.
14. Islamic tradition holds the defining *hudna* as the Treaty of Hudaybiyyah (صلح الحديبية), a ten-year agreement in 628 CE, between Muhammad and the Quraysh tribe in Mecca, although the peace lasted less than two years.
15. Eisikovits 2015:chap. 1, pp. 6, 15–16. See also Metz 2017.
16. Questions include minimum and maximum lengths of a *hudna*, whether it could be renewed, and so on, based in part on interpretations of the history and the Qur'an. See Fahim 2006; Abu Sway 2006; "Hudna" 2005; MacEoin 2008; Crane 2008.
17. "The *hudna* is a means to a goal, rather than a goal in itself. Nevertheless, the *hudna* represents something more than simply a tactic. In Arab and Islamic tradition, a *hudna* constitutes a phase within a larger process: first the ceasefire, *hudna*, then the *sulh*, reconciliation. The most common outcome of the *hudna* phase is a final peace agreement. Ideally, the purpose of a *hudna* is to resolve a conflict by forcing the parties to use the ascribed period to seek a nonviolent resolution to their differences" (Taustad 2010).

18. Fahim 2006.
19. Scham and Abu-Irshaid 2009:11.
20. "Hamas Awaits Truce Offer Reply" 2008.
21. See, e.g., Charny 2007:223n18; Cohen 2014.
22. Luttwak 1999:36.
23. Reisman 1998:16–17.
24. It is difficult to give aid effectively and in a way that does no further harm, even when just dealing with bad governance. When there is also war to contend with, it may be impossible. Nunn and Qian 2014; Polman 2011, 2010; Narang 2015; Tanguy 2000; Keating 2012; LeRiche 2004; Chang 2016; Cambanis 2014; Bauer 1969; Deaton 2013:esp. chap. 7, "How to Help Those Left Behind," 267–324.

    There are questions about whether the harms caused are worth the benefits, as well as whether humanitarian aid is the real culprit or whether the causes of conflict lie elsewhere, e.g., bad governance, historical legacies, inequality, corruption, rent-seeking, preying on natural resources. See, e.g., The Humanitarian Policy Group at ODI 2010; Kahn and Lucci 2009; Perrin 1998; Slim 2015:esp. 23; Stewart 2013; Singer 2009.
25. Witt 2012:252.
26. Classical and traditional Western philosophy's attempts to "civilize" war provide further grounds for the ethic of cooperation for a "fair fight" and the doctrine of "moral equality of combatants."
27. Witt 2012:17–18, 279.
28. Witt 2012:279.
29. Gentili 1933 (1598):bk. 1, chap. 6: That War May Be Waged Justly on Both Sides.
30. Vattel 2008 (1758):bk. 3, §161: "The right of seizing on them."
31. Witt 2012:45, 70–72.
32. Witt 2012:77.
33. Witt 2012:70–77, 199, 245.
34. Witt 2012:206–7.
35. Witt 2012:72.
36. Lincoln 1863.
37. See, e.g., the recent spate of political assassinations among South African ANC officials, even without moral permission to assassinate. Onishi and Gebrekidan 2018.
38. Cicero 1991 (44 BCE):1.23, 1.41.
39. Compensating behavior occurs in all walks of life, not just safety improvements. For example, in a controlled study, those wearing activity monitors lost less weight than those without them, perhaps because wearing the monitor subconsciously counted in the person's mind as having exerted effort toward the goal, and then the person compensated for that by expending less effort elsewhere, thus inadvertently stymieing achievement of the goal. Reynolds 2016; Carroll 2017.
40. Bleeding between the brain and skull that can cause death.
41. Ip 2015:90.
42. See, e.g., "Hanging Up the Boxing Gloves" 2015.
43. For example, the required use of seatbelts in automobiles has saved lives, whereas the installation of anti-lock braking systems (ABS) has led to at least no reduction in the number of crashes: according to some studies there are either fewer frontal collisions but more rear-end ones, or no increase in rear-end collisions but increases in roll-overs and running off the road. Greg Ip (2015:100–2) argues that whether or not offsetting behavior emerges depends on how the technology is being used. In the case of seatbelts, they are meant to increase the possibility of surviving an accident,

whereas ABS are meant to reduce or prevent accidents altogether, so drivers then take greater risks because they think they will not get into an accident at all.
44. Krammer 1996.
45. *Patton* 1970.
46. Moore 2015.
47. Minnich 1922:295–96.
48. Pegler 2004:21.
49. Wood 2015.
50. Pegler 2004:23.
51. Says Max Hastings of World War II, "Almost every soldier on both sides shared a hatred of snipers, which frequently caused them to be shot out of hand if captured" (2004:88). This occurred in the American Revolutionary War and Civil War as well (Pegler 2004:17).
52. Hastings 1984:209–10.
53. Hastings 2004:88.
54. Pegler 2004:20–21.
55. Pyle 2001 (1944):397.
56. Gilbert 1998:46.
57. Pegler 2004:21.
58. Gilbert 1996:27–28.
59. The idea of equal exposure to risk is important not just between warring humans, but also between humans and animals in the activity of hunting. Several soldiers analogized shooting an unarmed and unaware enemy to game hunting, but even game hunters have a sense of "fairness" that involves some idea of parity of exposure to risk. For example, NRA spokesman Kelly Hobbs's statement on Internet "hunting" argued: "The NRA has always maintained that fair chase, being in the field with your firearm or bow, is an important element of hunting tradition. Sitting at your desk in front of your computer, clicking at a mouse, has nothing to do with hunting." Safari Club International, a group dedicated to hunting large and exotic trophy animals, agreed that Internet hunting "doesn't meet any fair chase criteria." Humane Society of the United States n.d.

One difference is the purpose of hunting as an activity: "Hunting is totally experiential. You immerse yourself in it: You're outdoors, the animal has a fair chance," said Kirby Brown of the Texas Wildlife Association, "This falls off of the ethical charts" (Moreno 2005). As with war, however, here too the notion of fairness can be arbitrarily manifested: for example, it is nonetheless generally considered acceptable for human hunters to use blinds to cloak themselves from detection by the wildlife they hunt.
60. Clausewitz 2000:1.1.2. See also chapter 1.
61. While Clausewitz's conception of war is much narrower than that of earlier Western and non-Western writers, his vision is the prevailing one in modernity. Earlier conceptions of war focused on morality, religion, or justice/rectification, but for Clausewitz, war was simply the use of force, in the service of a larger political goal. Any ethical considerations and restraints, such as who could fight or be attacked or the subsequent political impact, were merely instrumental. Clausewitz's works assume a state-centric political system, in which soldiers have both special privileges and responsibilities (see Chiu 2010:esp. 52–56), in part because there is uncertainty about which side has just cause.
62. Clausewitz 2000:1.23–24.
63. Apel and Apel 1998:122. Forgetting helps soldiers survive, but it also makes the next war more likely, as its forgotten horrors fade away to glorious propaganda, all too quickly. In a letter to his wife, Apel recounts:

It makes strong men break down and cry to see these boys come in caked with mud and blood, bled white under it all, all of them in shock of one type or other, saying nothing, asking nothing, and not one out of a hundred complaining about anything. They just lie there and say, "Yes, Sir," or "No, Sir," or "Thank you, Sir" until you want to tell them to yell or cry or do anything but just lie there. God never has before nor ever will again make anything to equal the G.I. They are so wonderful it makes a lump in your throat every time you look at them. I wish every last person in Washington could be compelled to walk through our hospital during a push to see just what these poor guys are going through. But instead they sit back and listen to the stories of the heroes on the front lines taking a whole hill single handedly and telling others what a wonderful thing they have done stopping the Reds in Korea. No one knows what war is until they have seen these hospital tents filled to overflowing with G.I.'s. (Apel and Apel 1998:122–23)

64. Moore and Galloway 2008:108; Roberts 2017.
65. Wallace 2002.
66. Donald 1995:90–92.
67. In the course of the duel, Paris is whisked away from death's blow by Aphrodite, and Hera badgers Zeus to allow her and Athena to break the truce and spark the resumption of war, in the service of ultimately razing Troy to the ground (Homer 1998:bk. 4).
68. Cf. J. S. Mill ("A Few Words on Non-Intervention," 1859) on not interfering with native/domestic despotism.
69. Many other factors are relevant here. When the crew of the USS Enterprise finds two advanced, seemingly peaceful societies (Eminiar VII and Vendikar) locked in a war that supposedly inflicts millions of civilian casualties per year yet causes no infrastructure or other damage, it turns out that the war is being simulated on computer, and designated casualties then report to machines where they are neatly disintegrated. This method of warring allows the civilizations to persist in a way that would be impossible with conventional warfare ("A Taste of Armageddon," 1967). In this case, war engages the breadth of the populations, but the extreme sanitation of death and destruction removes all motivation to end or prevent war.

"Death, destruction, disease, horror—that's what war is all about. . . . That's what makes it a thing to be avoided. You've made it . . . so neat and painless, you've had no reason to stop it," says Capt. Kirk as he destroys the simulation computers. "I've given you back the horrors of war. . . . You can either wage it with real weapons, or you might consider an alternative. Put an end to it. Make peace. . . . The instinct [to kill] can be fought. We're human beings with the blood of a million savage years on our hands—but we can stop it. We can admit that we're killers, but . . . that we're not going to kill today."

Afterward, Kirk justifies the gamble he took, with reasoning reminiscent of a "short and massive" approach (chapter 4): "They have been killing three million people a year. It had been going on for five hundred years. An actual attack wouldn't have killed any more people than one of their computer attacks, but it would have ended their ability to make war. The fighting would have been over—permanently."

70. Some unjust wars might be a case of "dirty hands" and the impossibility of governing innocently, and if so, some form of exile might be a fitting option for punishment when one does the right thing from a utilitarian perspective but is nonetheless guilty of moral wrong—especially if employing the socially expressed while socially limited "Catholic" model of punishment, per Walzer (1973).
71. Moltke the Elder.

72. Addressing European geopolitical tensions at the time, Moltke similarly believed in the necessity—and improbability—of religious and moral education to shape views on the enterprise of warfare itself:

> Happier circumstances cannot be expected until all nations come to the conviction that every war, even a victorious one, is a national misfortune. To persuade people to take this view, even the power of our Emperor would not avail; it can only arise from the better religious and moral training of nations, which again must be a fruit of centuries of historical development, which neither of us will live to see. (Letter to Karl Friedrich August Hauschild, March 1879; Moltke 1893:270)

73. Letter to Johann Caspar Bluntschli, December 11, 1880; Moltke 1880:15–18.
74. This treaty appears to thread the needle: it acknowledges that decision-makers would balk at the use of weapons that "render . . . death inevitable," alleging that soldiers merely need to be "disabled" to win, but the content of this treaty belies that. In reality, with heavier bullets, "disabl[ing]" is a mere euphemism.
75. This is why it is so hard for monomachia to successfully settle the outcome of a war, as seen earlier in *The Iliad*. Some militaries already have a variety of nonlethal weapons, e.g., lasers, Tasers, stun guns, or "pain rays," but in addition to the training and budgetary constraints on their effective use, there is always the question of what to do when the opponent escalates the level of violence to a point where lethality is necessary to neutralize the threat.
76. I do not refer to clandestine special operations here, as they are not considered official wartime activities.

# 6. Cooperative Ethics, Just War Theory

1. For the long and complex history of Western just war theory's development and the many different schools of thought and their approaches, see, among others, Orend 2006:chap. 1; Reichberg 2015; and Reichberg et al. 2006.
2. The traditional formulation requires, among other things, that "3. The intention of the actor is good, that is, he aims only to the acceptable effect; the evil is not one of his ends, nor is it a means to his ends." Walzer argues, however, that a greater obligation is actually carried by soldiers who have rights of war, and they must take into consideration the rights of civilians whose lives they put at risk, so he proposes to make the doctrine of double effect more stringent: "3. The intention of the actor is good, that is, he aims narrowly at the acceptable effect; the evil effect is not one of his ends, nor is it a means to his ends, and, aware of the evil involved, he seeks to minimize it, accepting costs to himself" (2015:153, 156).
3. Pursuing only those military actions that will actually contribute to defeating the enemy and winning the war, in proportion to the military advantage gained.
4. I set aside human rights arguments for civilian immunity, because they are underdeveloped and have not been the largest influence on this principle. In fact, the humanitarian impulses that led to the distinction between combatants and civilians only arose with the realization that there was no way to definitively know or determine *jus ad bellum*.
5. Hanson further claims that cooperation to limit both the damages of war and time spent in conflict also contributed to the development of another significant form of cooperation—Greek democracy—around the same time period, as decisive political

outcomes rendered by vote were preferable to protracted disagreement. In one poignant example, "regardless of the personal preferences of the combatants involved, the Greeks who died at Charoneia [in 338 BCE] had voted to fight there; the phalangites in the army of Philip who killed them had not" (2009 [1989]:xxvii–xxviii).

That democracy, however, eventually brings an end to the hoplite system, which had relied on a more limited conception of citizenship. Democracy in Athens led to experimentation that challenged traditional military practices and strategies, says Josiah Ober, which unwittingly

> precipitated an unprecedented series of innovations in military strategy, personnel, and technology. And these innovations in turn did overthrow the rules of war, and in the process undermined the social and political order on which independent polis culture depended. Athenian democracy was, in this sense, the condition of its own impossibility.

This proved ultimately proved "fatal to the regime of 'war by the rules.'" Ober 1996. See also Hanson 2009 (1989), 1995, 1996.

6. See chapter 5 for other alternatives.
7. Bernard 1856:109–10.
8. Axelrod and Keohane 1985.
9. See theories of bargaining and conflict strategy.
10. Clausewitz 2000:1.1.24; Foucault 2003:"7 January, 1976," 15–16.
11. Pinker 2012.
12. This structural similarity to democratic politics is one reason why some thinkers tie Greek hoplite warfare to democracy.
13. Augustine 2017 (c. 400 CE):22.71.
14. Gentili 1933 (1598):bk. 1, chap. 3, "War is Waged by Sovereigns," 15.
15. Gentili 1933 (1598):bk. 1, chap. 6, "That War May Be Waged Justly on Both Sides," 31–32.
16. Whitman 2012:3–5.
17. Whitman 2012:16.
18. Whitman 2012: 10. Furthermore, the eighteenth-century purpose of "taking calculated risks in the pursuit of territorial gain" was actually consistent with, not a departure from, classical thought, as medieval just war theory was concerned with the acquisition of property, and not moralistic in the way it is often assumed to be (Whitman 2012:16–19).

    Medieval jurist literature held that God revealed his judgments through "ordeals, trials by combat, and battle. All three were ways of inducing God to intervene in human affairs by putting possibly innocent persons at such risk that He would feel obliged to aid them miraculously. All three were ways of 'tempting' God into intervening, as the medieval analysis had it" (Whitman 2012:33–34). As barbaric as it was, this idea carried over to the pitched battle, which set the stage for God to act.
19. Whitman 2012:9–12, 16–17, 19. Although many have likened the pitched battle to the mass version of the duel, it is an inaccurate analogy, notes Whitman, because jurists at the time considered dueling to be "a shadowy, illegal activity, a last refuge of recalcitrant nobles who were still resisting the sovereign monopoly of legitimate violence," whereas wars were "princely trials by combat" and trial by combat was a "lawful procedure" (2012:17).
20. Whitman 2012:54.
21. Whitman 2012:20, 23. Wars were frequently described with "game" terminology, e.g., dice or sporting contests (Whitman 2012:185–86).

22. Whitman 2012:52, 272FN; Mauvillon 1747:2:1.
23. Can it really be said that "rules" existed for battle (both its structure and the fight itself), when everyone was ready to violate the rules as it suited them? Skepticism is understandable. Certainly the force of and adherence to the rules varied, and like every other ethic of cooperation in warfare, some of the rules contradicted each other, e.g., different rules could be utilized to determine who won, such as who retreated or who suffered the most casualties, although, generally, people adhered to the requirement of occupying the "killing field" in order to demonstrate one's victory and secure ensuing property rights. There was a general obedience to the "law of booty," under which soldiers were not supposed to plunder before they had achieved victory—they were to behave as warriors, not as brigands. The law of booty rested on some other law that determined victory, and generally, the retreat rule (gaining control of the battlefield) was used. While observance to the rules was not entirely strict, warfare during this period, Whitman and Ober claim, was a "rule-*oriented*" activity." Whitman 2012:180–89; Ober 1994:25.
24. Whitman 2012:20–22.
25. Whitman 2012:41–43.
26. Whitman 2012:45, 77–78.
27. Whitman 2012:51–52.
28. This equal subjection to chance is what makes the battle "fair." (See also chapter 2 on fair fights.)
29. Whitman 2012:52, 79–80.
30. Whitman 2012:70–71.
31. Whitman 2012:37.
32. Whitman 2012:71.
33. Whitman 2012:75.
34. Whitman 2012:73–75.
35. This raises separate theological concerns about *when* wagers could be used, and there is ample religious writing (e.g., Aquinas) arguing that it is wrong to summon *sors*/chance to solve problems that could be answered with human reason. Later thinkers wrestled with the role of human effort, and ultimately settled on battles being "mixed games of chance, not pure ones," per Grotius—part God, part human effort, the latter of which was required to make the battle as wager both militarily and theologically acceptable (Whitman 2012:85, 89–91). Whitman asks, however:

    > But if that was so, could it be theologically legitimate to use only limited human effort? In his unsettling conclusion, Grotius held that it was not. It was theologically necessary to use *all* of one's forces: unless the cause was completely hopeless, it was wrong to settle matters through the chance of battle. . . . There was an obvious paradox in this, and an uncomfortable one. Grotius held that if a war was justified because it could save the lives of innocents, then it must be conducted with maximum force—in such a way that is, as to kill as many as possible. (2012:89–90)

36. Whitman 2012:81–84.
37. Whitman 2012:52–55.
38. Whitman 2012:209–10, 215.
39. Whitman 2012:53.
40. Whitman 2012:22–23, 52–55, 234–35.
41. Whitman 2012:235, 251. Ideological commitments can shape one's views of the structure of warfare in pernicious ways, such as in the Vietnam War. For example, US

intelligence analyst Konrad Kellen argued in 1965, after reading extensive transcripts of interviews with captured Vietcong soldiers, that the United States could not win the Vietnam War (1955–72), contrary to the dominant view at the time that victory was imminent:

> Years later, [Kellen] would say that his rethinking began with one memorable interview with a senior Vietcong captain. [The captain] was asked very early in the interview if he thought the Vietcong could win the war, and he said no. But pages later, he was asked if he thought that the US could win the war, and he said no. The second answer profoundly changes the meaning of the first. (Gladwell 2013)

The Vietcong did not conceive of war in conventional terms: they thought that war could be open-ended, and were willing to simply outlast the United States in a grinding war of attrition. Said Kellen, both NVA and Vietcong soldiers were

> sustained in their firm belief that they cannot and will not lose this war. This does not mean that they expect to win it in the conventional sense, by driving out the Americans. Rather, they feel convinced that sooner or later, in some as yet indistinct form, the war will come to an end and the Americans will depart, leaving "the Vietnamese to settle their own differences." (Kellen, June 1971:12–14)

As a result, the American belief that they simply had to kill enough North Vietnamese (to damage their morale sufficiently to induce surrender) was tragically wrong, which was borne out by successive interviews with POWs over the long years of the war. See also Kellen 1970.

42. Whitman 2012:214.
43. See, e.g., Whitman 2012:5–6; Witt 2012; Neff 2008 on the development of modern law to ameliorate warfare with *jus ad bellum* and especially *jus in bello* constraints.
44. This will be revisited in the later discussion on pure and perfect procedural justice.
45. Holquist 2004.
46. This argument was also made during the Nuremberg Trials, that "to initiate a war of aggression . . . is the supreme international crime differing from other war crimes in that it contains within itself the accumulated evil of the whole" (September 30, 1946; Nuremberg Trial Proceedings 1946, 22:427).
47. Like the honor-driven duel, the glory-fueled war is now also forbidden. Whether for personal honor (e.g., the Trojan War in *The Iliad*), national splendor (e.g., the Marx Brothers' *Duck Soup*, the Spanish-American War [1898] according to William Graham Sumner, or any number of other military endeavors), or the glory of God (e.g., the Crusades), it is now prohibited to wage war for reasons of renown.
48. Where one has *jus ad bellum*, it is still constrained by proportionality considerations: only self-defense actions proportional to the attack are justified. (See, e.g., International Court of Justice 2003.)
49. This happens domestically, in civil wars, as well. The aforementioned Reconciliation Plaza and Wall at West Point (chapter 2n33) also exemplifies the abdication of *jus ad bellum* judgment in order to focus on fighting behavior. Given that the just side ultimately won, however, it may be prudent in the aftermath of an especially bloody and divisive civil conflict to promote national unity by ignoring the original cause of dispute.
50. Witt 2012:45. This move was consistent with seventeenth-century Law of Nations warfare (e.g., Grotius, Pufendorf, Vattel).

51. Dunant 1862.
52. Resolutions of the Geneva International Conference 1863.
53. For a wide-ranging list, see ICRC n.d.: "Practice Relating to Rule 25. Medical Personnel."
54. There is, however, ambiguity with respect to whether or not they have to be captured. Major international laws declare that "wounded or sick soldiers *shall be brought in*" or "*collected* and cared for" (The Oxford Manual, or, The Laws of War on Land 1880: Art. 10; Geneva Convention [III] relative to the Treatment of Prisoners of War, 1949; ICRC n.d.: "Practice Relating to Rule 110. Treatment and Care of the Wounded, Sick and Shipwrecked," emphasis added). The law is unspecific, however, regarding wounded soldiers on the battlefield who have not surrendered and who would probably die in short order without medical care. It may be that those fighters can be left for dead without committing any legal offense.

    In a recent case, an Israeli medic killed a wounded Palestinian assailant on the scene, as the latter lay immobilized on the ground, several minutes after the attack had ended and the threat had been neutralized. The killing was caught on video and the medic was later convicted of manslaughter and sentenced to eighteen months in prison (Kershner 2017; I. Fisher 2017). In this case, the attack occurred at a checkpoint and the intentional killing, which clearly violated national and international laws, was videotaped. Had an attack occurred in a more remote area where medical assistance is not proximate—as many do—and the perpetrator, once incapacitated, had simply been left to die—as many are—that would have been more ethically ambiguous.
55. Doane 2011; Frayer, Associated Press, 2011; Leonard 2010; Olson 2010 (photos); Wagner, Associated Press, 2007.
56. "In Enemy Care" 2013; Amichay and Ratner 2017.
57. Klay 2017.
58. "Blood and Dust" 2011:minutes 7:29–8:30. See also "Blood and Dust: What Happened to Tyrone Jordan?," Rewind 2016.
59. Carroll 2010.
60. Apel and Apel 1998:63, 64, 181.
61. Apel and Apel 1998:181.
62. Apel and Apel 1998:64. For an extensive history of medical care in the US Army during the Korean War, see Cowdrey 1987, which references the war's well-documented brutality, attacks on medics (e.g., p. 75), and treatment of enemy POWs (e.g., pp. 105, 106, 109, 111, 162, 306–21).
63. Simons 2017.
64. Winer 2015.
65. Simons 2017.
66. Cowdrey 1987:317.
67. Cowdrey 1987:311.
68. Hickley 2009.
69. Gross and Carrick 2013; Howe 2015.
70. For more on dilemmas in the ethics of military medical care, see, e.g., Gross 2004.
71. Gross 2004:4. There emerges a paradox of sorts, as soldiers, because of the possibility of salvage, are entitled to faster and better medical care—but also lose some rights, such as autonomy. When they are no longer salvageable, they regain those rights but lose their claim to the higher-quality medical treatment. For more on these and other issues facing military physicians, such as "dual loyalty," informed consent, and medical roles in military operations such as interrogations, see Gross 2004.

72. For wealthy countries without a military draft, the convention of medical immunity helps to recruit highly trained and well-paid doctors who would not otherwise be willing to put their lives at risk. Given the financial constraints on militaries, medical immunity is a nonpecuniary benefit they can offer, made possible by international cooperation between enemies.
73. Gross 2007.
74. Stinner et al. 2010. Classifications are, from most to least fit: fit for duty, continuation on active duty/reserve in a limited capacity (COAD/COAR), temporary disabled retirement list (TDRL), separated from service with severance and no long-term benefits, and permanently medically retired. The return-to-duty rate is highest among the special forces, with 58 percent of amputees from 2001 to 2011 retained (21 percent fit for duty, 37 percent COAD/COAR) (Belisle et al. 2013).
75. Rauch 2012; Hull 2004.
76. Mortality rates have dramatically decreased over the course the twentieth century through today. In World War I, 21 percent of all American casualties (injuries and fatalities, across the Army, Navy, and Marines) resulted in battle deaths (killed in action, died of wounds, missing, or captured and declared dead). In World War II, the figure rose to 30 percent, partly due to much more extensive American involvement, then dropped to 25 percent in the Korean War, 14 percent in the Vietnam War, 10 percent in Iraq since 2003, and 8 percent in Afghanistan since 2001. (Extrapolated from US Department of Veterans Affairs 2017; DeBruyne 2017; United States Department of Defense 2017.) The film also notes this side effect at 16:41–16:54.
77. There is a separate and important debate within the question of civilian immunity about whether it is acceptable to privilege the lives of one's co-nationals in some aspects of warfare but not in others, as well as ongoing controversy about how much risk a soldier should take on himself in order to protect the enemy's civilians. See, e.g., Margalit and Walzer 2009, Kasher and Yadlin 2009, Avineri and Sternhell 2009. These questions are relevant for medical military personnel as well.
78. Related to the question of the legitimacy of individual warfighters is that of *legitimate state participation* in war, and it has been traditional to try to apply the similarly exclusive standards to this as well. Said Gentili in the sixteenth century:

> War is a just and public contest of arms.... The strife must be public; for war is not a broil, a fight, the hostility of individuals. And the arms on both sides should be public, for bellum, "war," derives its name from the fact that there is a contest for victory between two equal parties, and for that reason it was at first called *duellem*, "a contest of two."... In the same way we have *perduellum*, "war," *duelles* and *perduelles*, "enemies," whom we call *hostes*. The term *hostis* was applied to a foreigner who had equal rights with the Romans. In fact, *hostire* means "to make equal."... Therefore *hostis* is a person with whom war is waged and is the [legal] equal of his opponent.... Therefore, that definition... "war is armed force against a foreign prince or people," is shown to be incorrect by the fact that it applies the term "war" to the violence of private individuals and brigands. (Gentili 1933 [1598]:bk. 1, chap. 2, "The Definition of War," 12)

> Related to legitimate state participation is the question of legitimate nonparticipation: the right of state neutrality is both significant and puzzling, and grounded entirely in cooperative convention. It has been officially recognized in international law since the Hague Conventions, although the earlier Lieber Code makes mention

of it. (Article 87 recommends but does not require safe passage for diplomatic agents of neutral powers.) Neutrality for countries in close proximity to the conflict, and increasingly for those further afield in a more interdependent world, is artificial: no country is ever truly neutral, but it is conventional to accept and respect that declaration, which accords certain rights (inviolability) and duties (impartiality, abstention). (See, e.g., Thomas and Duncan 1999:chap. 7, "The Law of Neutrality.")

Separately, the neutrality doctrine raises questions about the distinction between doing and allowing, and the place of duties of assistance and care in the international arena. Conventional norms and practice deem that these are not required, but they are also predicated on conventions about the (artificially) impermeable nature of national borders when it comes to international obligations.

There is additional ambiguity in cases of civil war, rebellions, or when any government seeks official international recognition, and the law is once again stacked in favor of the status quo, and against those who are not already considered to hold legitimate power. Lieber Code Article 152 says that neutral states may not extend recognition to a rebel group as an independent power on the basis of the territory's official government having decided to apply the rules of war to that group. This section is rooted in part in Lincoln's decision to impose a blockade (international action) instead of port closure (domestic action) on the South, upon which he was accused of mistakenly conceding the South's independence and quasi-governance; what Lincoln and Seward wanted, however, was to thread the needle and continue to regulate relations with maritime merchants from neutral foreign powers (Witt 2012:144–56).

79. Regulations concerning the Laws and Customs of War on Land, Annexed to Hague Convention (II) of 1899 and Hague Convention (IV) of 1907, esp. Articles I, II, and III.
80. This designation was later changed to "unprivileged enemy belligerents," in the Military Commissions Act of 2009 (H.R. 2647), which amended the Military Commissions Act of 2006 (H.R. 6166).
81. Yoo and Delahunty 2002:1–2, 7–10. This second point is reinforced a few weeks later by the White House counsel, who says that although the Geneva Conventions on POW treatment pertain "'whenever hostilities occur *with regular foreign armed forces*,' . . . the policy does not apply to a conflict with terrorists, or with irregular forces, like the Taliban, who are armed militants that oppressed and terrorized the people of Afghanistan" (Gonzalez 2002:3). Other reasons were given, including that customary international law is not binding on the US president as federal law. Yoo and Delahunty 2002:2.
82. The United States has used the Combatant Status Review Tribunal (est. 2004), Military Commissions Act of 2006, and Military Commissions Act of 2009—the latter two of which were legislated after various court challenges, including *Hamdan v. Rumsfeld*, 548 U.S. 557 (2006).
83. Yoo 2005:83–84, emphasis added.
84. Cicero 1991 (44 BCE):1.36–37.
85. See earlier in this chapter, and Geneva Conventions (III) (1949), Article 4(A).
86. Chiu 2010.
87. Yoo and Delahunty 2002:2.
88. See, e.g., Daoud 2015.
89. This collusion is no different from restrictions in other areas of geopolitics, e.g., not recognizing Taiwan as a legitimate nation-state, therefore barring it from crucial participation in international organizations and from receiving certain essential

international rights and privileges, the dangers of which were amply demonstrated during the SARS crisis in 2003.
90. The Commentary of 1987 is explicit that the Protocol "encourage[s] gestures of reconciliation which can contribute to reestablishing normal relations in the life of a nation which has been divided" (§4618).
91. Common Article 3 covers any noninternational conflict within the contracting party's territory, whereas Protocol II is more stringent in the conditions: it applies to government conflicts with "dissident armed forces or other organized armed groups which, under responsible command, exercise such control over a part of its territory as to enable them to carry out sustained and concerted military operations and to implement this Protocol" (II, Art. 1.1), thus imposing certain requirements for command structure and control of territory, e.g., civil war.
92. Consistent with the generous interpretation of Common Article 3, in 2009, ICRC issued the Interpretative Guidance on the Notion of Direct Participation in Hostilities (2009), which addresses individuals who enter the conflict but not as soldiers and without wearing uniforms. The document seeks to strengthen the distinction between civilians and combatants, in order to better protect civilians, but acknowledges the ambiguity in many situations:

> Treaty IHL governing non-international armed conflict uses the terms "civilian," "armed forces" and "organized armed group" without expressly defining them. These concepts must therefore be interpreted in good faith in accordance with the ordinary meaning to be given to them in their context and in the light of the object and purpose of IHL. (§II.1.a, p. 27)

> Such "good faith" is essential because international law, bilateral treaties, and state practices disagree on whether "members of organized armed groups" (e.g., nonstate political institutions such as revolutionary movements) qualify for the same treatment. If they are treated as "civilians who, owing to their continuous direct participation in hostilities, lose protection against direct attack," this would "seriously undermine the conceptual integrity" of the civilian/combatant distinction, "notably because it would create parties to noninternational armed conflicts whose entire armed forces remain part of the civilian population." These are meant to be "mutually exclusive categories" in all conflicts, international or noninternational (Melzer 2009:27–28).

93. Unfortunately, Department of Defense and White House counsel's interpretation of the international law that landed al Qaeda and Taliban in Guantánamo Bay was a *legally* reasonable—if imprudent and perhaps immoral—interpretation of the statute.
94. American soldiers captured during the Korean War endured far worse treatment than they were prepared for, including torture and summary executions, which resulted in a much higher death rate than in other modern wars: of the over seven thousand American POWs, about 40 percent died in captivity, compared to 14 percent of the nearly eight hundred POWs in the Vietnam War. Brutal prison conditions prompted much dissension and defection, including studying Communism, denouncing the United States, and otherwise abetting the enemy. After repatriation, the US military and FBI controversially investigated about five hundred POWs for misconduct, ultimately court-martialing fourteen and convicting eleven for criminal activities, mostly collaboration/treason (Lech 2000). Persisting concerns with troop discipline and the high rates of prisoner collaboration led to the implementation of a code of conduct meant to bolster morale, prevent treason, and impress upon POWs that they needed to withstand abuse and torture in order to safeguard their fellow

soldiers. The Code of Conduct for Members of the United States Armed Forces (Executive Order 10631 [1955], later amended) stipulates:

I. I am an American, fighting in the forces which guard my country and our way of life. I am prepared to give my life in their defense.

II. I will never surrender of my own free will. If in command, I will never surrender the members of my command while they still have the means to resist.

III. If I am captured I will continue to resist by all means available. I will make every effort to escape and aid others to escape. I will accept neither parole nor special favors from the enemy.

IV. If I become a prisoner of war, I will keep faith with my fellow prisoners. I will give no information or take part in any action which might be harmful to my comrades. If I am senior, I will take command. If not, I will obey the lawful orders of those appointed over me and will back them up in every way.

V. When questioned, should I become a prisoner of war, I am required to give name, rank, service number and date of birth. I will evade answering further questions to the utmost of my ability. I will make no oral or written statements disloyal to my country and its allies or harmful to their cause.

VI. I will never forget that I am an American, fighting for freedom, responsible for my actions, and dedicated to the principles which made my country free. I will trust in my God and in the United States of America.

In contrast, says military strategist and historian James Blaker, the French, who at the time were fighting to quell an independence movement in Algeria where both sides used torture extensively, did not have such a code of conduct, and "they didn't condemn their own soldiers who gave up information" as POWs under those circumstances (Blaker 2017). These different approaches reflect different conceptions of a soldier's status, specifically whether he retains full obligations to his country as its representative under extreme POW conditions such as torture. It reminds us that there are other models, e.g., parole, that reflect different ways of thinking about a soldier's function, role, and status in the interstices of war (e.g., when captured) that may be worth examination.

95. Whitman 2012:3, 83.
96. There is also something in between pure and perfect procedural justice: It is unclear how independent the desired outcome of perfect procedural justice must be, with respect to the procedure. (In Rawls's example of cutting the cake, the desired outcome is completely independent, but he does not specify whether this degree of independence is strictly necessary for perfect procedural justice or just an attribute of his example.) Even in sporting events, as discussed, people often desire the meritorious side to win, but in such competitions, the determination of merit is indexed to the procedure used, so the criteria for the outcome is not completely independent of the procedure. Would it still qualify as im/perfect procedural justice, if we have some nonindependent notion of what the "correct" outcome would be? (Yet, neither does it seem to be simply pure procedural justice, because there is a conception of what the correct answer would be, as abstract as that answer is.) Applied to warfare, this in-between category might best describe the ethic of cooperation for a fair fight.
97. A hymn thanking God for the victory (Whitman 2012:177).
98. Lincoln 1862.
99. Freedom House 2016; World Bank 2015.
100. Based on Correlates of War Project data (interstate military conflicts with at least one thousand battle casualties) for all wars from 1816 to 1990, when democracies initiated

wars during that period, they won 93 percent of the time. As targets of aggression, they still won 63 percent of wars, compared with dictatorships and oligarchies (Reiter and Stam 2002:28–29).
101. Choi 2004.
102. E.g., Tilly 1975.
103. In a way, this would be Kant's theory in *Perpetual Peace* in action.
104. Reiter and Stam 2002.
105. See the literature on political intervention and regime change, e.g., Immanuel Kant and J. S. Mill. This also relates to questions about the justice of humanitarian intervention.
106. Whitman (2012:80–81) notes that from the Middle Ages onward, trial by combat was discussed in two ways—as God's judgment and as a wager/game of change that participants agreed to—that are related.
107. McCarthy 1992 (1985):chap. 17, 260–61.
108. See Holquist 2004 on natural law versus international conventional law.
109. Walzer 2015:36–37, second emphasis added.
110. In a glaring moral gap—the Nuremberg Trials and some other criminal trials notwithstanding—political leaders are similarly not held to account and are considered largely off-limits, even though they are actually responsible for *jus ad bellum* decisions. See chapters 3 and 5.
111. Neff 2010:63–64.
112. See, e.g., McMahan 2009, 1994a, 1994b, 2004.
113. Chiu 2011.
114. McMahan 2009.
115. Thus, revisionists make *jus in bello* dependent on *jus ad bellum*, as one cannot claim the former without first having the latter, which harkens back to Augustine in some ways.
116. Michael Walzer discusses the special and "peculiar" circumstances of war, including its unique coerciveness, its collectivization, and its "radical and pervasive uncertainty" (2015:postscript, 339–46). "The moral equality of soldiers finds its parallel in the moral equality of civilians. Individuals are incorporated into both these collectives without regard to their personal moral standing," says Walzer. Being a combatant or a noncombatant is the most "radical" way of being collectivized, as belonging to one category or the other determines whether or not one can be legitimately targeted and killed. The nature of war requires a large degree of collectivization, and judgments to be made in broad strokes:

> Perhaps there are soldiers who, given the morality of everyday life, don't deserve to be targeted (they are against the war; they shoot their guns in the air), perhaps there are civilians who do deserve to be targeted (they are fierce and uncompromising hawks). In the circumstances of war, we cannot make these distinctions. . . . When the two armies are engaged, and civilians are radically at risk, individual attentiveness isn't possible. We fight with soldiers; we don't fight with civilians. (2015:342–43)

As a result, when fine distinctions cannot be made, it is perhaps wise to err on the side of overinclusiveness in extending protections.
117. See Geneva Convention (III) Relative to the Treatment of Prisoners of War 1949, and here chapter 3, "POW Treatment."

# 7. Abdication of Judgment, Noncooperative Fights

1. Cowdrey 1987:121.
2. I discuss alternatives models of warfare that are mostly less fatal and more ritualistic, but there are options at the other, more nihilistic end of the spectrum, such as the apocalyptic ambitions held by certain types of religious extremists. Malcolm Gladwell (2013) mistakenly says the following about the Vietcong—in fact, they were firmly attached to the outcome of the war, although they took a more Stoic view of the results of each individual battle—but it can and does apply to others: "He didn't think in terms of winning or losing at all, which is a very different proposition. An enemy who is indifferent to the outcome of a battle is the most dangerous enemy of all."
3. Whitman 2012:6.
4. The genealogy of the development of existing institutions of warfare recalls Schelling's scenario of audience members sitting only in the last two-thirds of the auditorium rows. It might appear after the fact that they were following a rule of some sort, but instead, it is more likely that the people were behaving in a "purposive" way based on their preferences and individually problem-solving given existing constraints, such that their behavior is "contingent . . . on what others are doing" (2006 [1978]:17). Schelling notes that this very likely results in a suboptimal arrangement:

    > The most interesting question is not how many people would like to change their seats after they see where everybody else is sitting; it is whether some altogether different seating arrangement might better serve the purposes of the many, or most, or all of them. How well each does for himself in adapting to his social environment is not the same thing as how satisfactory a social environment they collectively create for themselves. (20)

    This is much in the manner that the normative meanings of the structures and practices of warfare have developed—in purposive, contingent ways—yet result in a suboptimal arrangement that no one wants to change.
5. Whitman 2012:19.
6. The attempt to find value in or to salvage some humanity from war is frequently demonstrated, both on the battlefield and after the fact. For example, the few living recipients of the US Medal of Honor commonly reject the label of "hero" and derive meaning from their sacrifices by crediting their compatriots.

    There is a "feeling of freedom and power instilled in us by communal effort in combat," says J. Glenn Gray, and moreover a "sense of power and liberation" that comes from "the assurance of immortality that makes self-sacrifice at these moments so relatively easy." The unifying communal experience of warfighting cannot be replicated in peacetime. (See Gray 1998:39–51.)

    Searching for significance is also not limited to one's honorable actions or tests of virtue during war. It is also the reason why it is common for "a pitched battle [to be] remembered after the fact as a drama that exposed its contestants to the play of fate. . . . If we did not perceive it as a drama, pitched battle might well seem what it seems to a modern humanitarian: simply a senseless collective slaughter, a horror" (Whitman 2012: 46). Post-hoc justicial or teleological significance is often ascribed to a war's outcome.
7. Fanon 1963 (1961):37, 85–86, 93–95.
8. Speech, October 29, 1941, Harrow School.
9. Letter to Johann Caspar Bluntschli, December 11, 1880.

10. Wees 2000.
11. Gray 1998 (1959):28–31, 35.
12. Cowdrey 1987:211.
13. "Joseph Medicine Crow" 2016.
14. 5.263, emphasis added.
15. Kant 2000:§5:432.
16. J. Glenn Gray sits somewhere in between Kant and Churchill/Moltke, when he recognizes the uniqueness of humanity's ability to sacrifice for the sake of comradeship:

    > Are we not right in honoring the fighter's impulse to sacrifice himself for a comrade, even though it be done, as it so frequently is, in an evil cause? I think so. It is some kind of world pathos that the striving for union and for immortality must again and again be consummated while men are in the service of destruction. I do not doubt for a moment that wars are made many times more deadly because of this striving and this impulse. Yet I would not want to be without the assurance their existence gives me that our species has a different destiny than is granted to other animals. Though we often sink below them, we can at moments rise above them, too. (1998:50–51)

17. Ignatieff 1997:119–20, emphasis added.
18. States can terrorize not only other peoples but their own populations as well. (For an outstanding explication of terrorism, see Scheffler 2006.)
19. Hanson 2009 (1989):xxix.
20. Although he does not speak of the present-day transnational terrorist, Carl Schmitt's *Theory of the Partisan* (1962) is relevant here. Partisans—and terrorists—destroy the *jus publicum Europaeum*, the "classical" laws of war, says Schmitt, which make clear distinctions (e.g., combatant/noncombatant) and conceive of war as between states and regular state armies, who "in war respected each other as enemies, and did not discriminate against each other as criminals" (2007 [1962]:9, 11). Schmitt rightly notes that war remains "bracketed," that there is "no place for the partisan in the modern sense" because he is "*hors la loi*" (10). The partisan's political engagement distinguishes him from "ordinary" thieves or criminals, and "this conceptual criterion of the *political* character [of the partisan]" has "in exact inversion the same structure as does the pirate in the law of sea war" (14). Cf. Heller-Roazen 2009. Schmitt is correct to observe that the "power and significance of [the partisan's] irregularity has been dependent on the power and significance of the regularity that he challenges" (3), but not necessarily that, as Napoleon says, "in fighting the partisan,... one must fight like a partisan" (13), as discussed in chapter 3 and later in this chapter.
21. Gearan, Associated Press 2006.
22. Cicero: "Furthermore, we have laws regulating warfare, and fidelity to an oath must often be observed in dealings with an enemy: for an oath sworn with the clear understanding in one's own mind that it should be performed must be kept; but if there is no such understanding, it does not count as perjury if one does not perform the vow. For example, suppose that one does not deliver the amount agreed upon with pirates as the price of one's life, that would be accounted no deception—not even if one should fail to deliver the ransom after having sworn to do so; for a pirate is not included in the number of lawful enemies, but is the common foe of all the world; and with him there ought not to be any pledged word nor any oath mutually binding. For swearing to what is false is not necessarily perjury, but to take an oath 'upon your conscience,' as it is expressed in our legal formulas, and then fail to perform it, that is perjury" (Cicero 1913 [44 BCE]:3.107–8, LCL 30:384–87).

23. See, e.g., *American Journal of Bioethics* 9 (10), published October 2009, for several articles on various aspects of the ethics of medical care for terrorists.
24. This does not imply that nonstate groups using terrorist techniques are always in the wrong: *jus ad bellum* can belong to any type of claimant, and then it is a separate question of what can be done in pursuit of that righteous claim.
25. Witt 2012:330, 355.
26. This is not necessarily a statement about "supreme emergency" ethics, which many believe require distinct ethical reasoning and consideration. In those cases, the existential threats are so unique, horrifying, and irreversible, that the normal rules of war—which are already abnormal, as "every war is an emergency" (Walzer 2015:250)—should not apply and should be overridden. (See, e.g., Walzer, Rawls, and others on supreme emergency.)

    Instead, this may be the idea that all war, even short of "supreme emergency" situations, is a departure from everyday norms and moral scenarios. As Walzer notes, "wars and battles are not 'cases' to which the law and morality of everyday life can be applied; by definition, they don't take place in civil society. War is a long-standing human practice (however uncomfortable we are with it), which represents a radical break with our ordinary social activities" (2015:postscript, 337).

    And yet, as abnormal as the ethics of war are, there is still a tendency to apply peacetime norms to it, not just by proponents of revisionist just war theory who view military ethics largely through the lens of criminal and civil law and legal philosophy, but also (to a lesser or at least different extent) by the warriors who fight those wars.
27. Norms of warfare have been justified with different reasons at different times, as we have seen, and that is no different for the various cooperative moralities. They have been substantiated with both conventional/positivist and natural law arguments, and it is not practically necessary to champion one over the other. (Determining what grounds a particular norm matters more at the points at which different norms contradict one another in practical effect. Then understanding the precise basis of each norm can help determine which should take priority.)
28. Bernard 1856:116–18, emphasis added.
29. "Il est revenu cette semaine une mission sur trois. Il est donc une haute densité du danger de guerre. Cependant, si nous sommes de ceux qui reviennent, nous n'aurions rien à raconter. J'ai autrefois vécu des aventures: la création des lignes postales, la dissidence saharienne, l'Amérique du Sud . . . mais la guerre n'est point une aventure véritable, elle n'est qu'un ersatz d'aventure. L'aventure repose sur la richesse des liens qu'elle établit, des problèmes qu'elle pose, des créations qu'elle provoque. Il ne suffit pas, pour transformer en aventure le simple jeu de pile ou face, d'engager sur lui la vie et la mort. La guerre n'est pas une aventure. La guerre est une maladie. Comme le typhus." Saint-Exupéry 1942: chap. 10.

# References

"5 o'Clock Charlie." 1973. *M.A.S.H.* Season 2, episode 2. CBS, September 22.
Abbas, Hassan. 2013a. "Are Drone Strikes Killing Terrorists or Creating Them?" *Atlantic*, March 31.
———. 2013b. "How Drones Create More Terrorists." *Atlantic*, August 23.
Abbott, Chris, Steve Hathorn, and Scott Hickie. 2016. *The Remote Warfare Digest*. Remote Control Project—Oxford Research Group, November.
Abell, Francis. 1914. *Prisoners of War in Britain 1756 to 1815: A Record of Their Lives, Their Romance, and Their Suffering*. London: Oxford University Press.
Abu Sway, Mustafa. 2006. "The Concept of Hudna (Truce) in Islamic Sources." *Palestine-Israel Journal of Politics, Economics, and Culture* 13 (3): 20–27.
Addicott, Jeffrey F. 2004. *Terrorism Law: The Rule of Law and the War on Terror*. 2nd ed. Tucson: Lawyers and Judges.
Ahmad, Eqbal. 2006. "The Making of *The Battle of Algiers*" (1998). In *The Selected Writings of Eqbal Ahmad*, edited by Carollee Bengelsdorf, Margaret Cerullo, and Yogesh Chandrani, 85–93. New York: Columbia University Press.
"Al Houthis Deliberately Misused the Ceasefire to Rearm." 2017. *Gulf News*, March 8.
"American Cryptology: The Black Chamber." 2015. *Economist*, December 19.
*American Journal of Bioethics*. 2009. 9 (10).
Amichay, Rami, and Baz Ratner 2017. "Under Cover of Night, Syrian Wounded Seek Help from Enemy Israel." *Reuters*, January 24.
Angers, Trent. 1999. *The Forgotten Hero of My Lai: The Hugh Thompson Story*. Lafayette, LA: Acadian House.
Anonymous, United States Armed Forces. 2014. Personal interview. July 16.
Anonymous, United States Army. 2015. Personal interview. July 21.
Anonymous, United States Marines. 2014. Personal interview. June 24.
Anscombe, G. E. M. 1958. *Mr. Truman's Degree* (pamphlet). Oxford.
———. 1961. "War and Murder." In *Nuclear Weapons: A Catholic Response*, edited by Walter Stein, 44–52. London.

Apel, Otto F., Jr., MD, and Pat Apel. 1998. *MASH: An Army Surgeon in Korea*. Lexington: University Press of Kentucky.

*Apocalypse Now*. 1979. Directed by Francis Ford Coppola. United Artists.

Appian. 1912 (second century CE). *Roman History 8.1. The Punic Wars*. In *Roman History*, vol. 1, edited and translated by Brian McGing. Loeb Classical Library 2. Cambridge, MA: Harvard University Press.

Aquinas, St. Thomas. 2017 (c. 1265–73). *Summa Theologicæ*. Translated by Fathers of the English Dominican Province. 1911; Westminster, MD: Christian Classics, 1981. Reprinted by New Advent, edited by Kevin Knight.

Arendt, Hannah. 1987. "Collective Responsibility." In *Amor Mundi—Explorations in the Faith and Thought of Hannah Arendt*, edited by James Bernhauer, 43–50. Dordrecht: Martinus Nijhoff.

Aristotle. 1932 (fourth century BCE). *Politics*. Translated by H. Rackham. Loeb Classical Library 264. Cambridge, MA: Harvard University Press.

Arkush, Elizabeth, and Mark Allen, eds. 2008. *The Archaeology of Warfare: Prehistories of Raiding and Conquest*. Gainesville: University Press of Florida.

Arnold, Matthew. 1867. "Dover Beach." In *New Poems*, 112–14. London: Macmillan.

Aschmann, Rudolph. 1972. *Memoirs of a Swiss Officer in the American Civil War*. Edited by Hanz K. Meier. Translated by Hedwig D. Rappolt. Bern: Herbert Lang.

Ashworth, Tony. 2000 (1980). *Trench Warfare, 1914–1918: The Live-and-Let-Live System*. Pan Grand Strategy Series. London: Pan.

Augustine. 2017 (c. 400 CE). *Contra Faustum (Against Faustus)*. Translated by Richard Stothert. In *Nicene and Post-Nicene Fathers*, first series, vol. 4, edited by Philip Schaff. Buffalo, NY: Christian Literature, 1887. Reprinted by New Advent, edited by Kevin Knight.

Aussaresses, Paul. 2001. *Services Spéciaux: Algérie, 1955–1957: Mon témoignage sur la torture*. Perrin.

Avineri, Shlomo, and Zeev Sternhell. 2009. Letter to the Editor. With reply by Avishai Margalit and Michael Walzer. "'Israel: Civilians and Combatants:' An Exchange." *New York Review of Books* 56 (13).

Axelrod, Robert. 2006 (1984). *The Evolution of Cooperation*. Rev. ed. New York: Basic.

Axelrod, Robert, and William D. Hamilton. 1981. "The Evolution of Cooperation." *Science*, new series, 211 (4489): 1390–96.

Axelrod, Robert, and Robert O. Keohane. 1985. "Achieving Cooperation Under Anarchy: Strategies and Institutions." *World Politics* 38 (1): 226–54.

Bafana, Haykal هيكل بافنع (@BaFana3). 2012. "Dear Obama, when a US drone missile kills a child in Yemen, the father will go to war with you, guaranteed. Nothing to do with Al Qaeda." 5:50 AM, May 11. Tweet.

Bairnsfather, Bruce. 1917. *Bullets and Billets*. New York: G. P. Putnam's Sons.

Baker, Peter. 2013. "Obama Says 'World Set a Red Line' on Chemical Arms." *New York Times*, September 4.

———. 2014. "Obama Defends Swap of Taliban for American P.O.W." *New York Times*, June 3.

"The Balance of Terror." 1966. *Star Trek*. Season 1, episode 14. NBC, December 15.

Balzac, Honoré de. 1997 (1832). *Le colonel Chabert*. Translated by Carol Cosman. New York: New Directions.

Bamford, James. 2016. "Terrorists Have Drones Now. Thanks, Obama." *Foreign Policy*, April 28.

Barash, David P. 2013. "Are We Hard-Wired for War?" *New York Times*, September 29.

Barnett, Arnold. 1998. "Flying? No Point in Trying to Beat the Odds." *Wall Street Journal*, September 9.

"Baron von Richthofen: The Red Baron." n.d. *Australian War Memorial Online*, Australian War Memorial (Campbell, ACT).

Bassford, Christopher, and Edward J. Villacres. 1995. "Reclaiming the Clausewitzian Trinity." *Parameters* 25 (3): 9–19.

*The Battle of Algiers (La battaglia di Algeri)*. 1966. Directed by Gillo Pontecorvo. Magna.

Bauer, P. T. 1969. "Dissent on Development." *Scottish Journal of Political Economy* 16 (3): 75–94.

Beaugé, Florence. 2007. "Le général Aussaresses confirme que le chef du FLN à Alger, Larbi Ben M'Hidi, a été pendu." *Le Monde: Édition Afrique*, March 5.

Beckett, Ian F. W. 2017. "The Myth of Decisive Battle—Wars Are Defense and Attrition, Not the All-Out Clashes That So Often Tempt Generals." *Wall Street Journal Asia*, March 3.

Belisle, Jeffery G., MD, MBA, Joseph C. Wenke, PhD, and Chad A. Krueger, MD. 2013. "Return-to-Duty Rates Among US Military Combat-Related Amputees in the Global War on Terror: Job Description Matters." *Journal of Trauma and Acute Care Surgery* 75 (2): 279–86.

Ben-David, Calev. 2008. "Analyze This: The Danger of a Hamas 'Tahadiya' Becoming a Palestinian 'Hafuga.'" *Jerusalem Post*, April 28.

Berman, Eric. 1996. *Managing Arms in Peace Processes: Mozambique*. Disarmament and Conflict Resolution Project. United Nations.

Bernard, Mountague. 1856. "The Growth of Laws and Usages of War." In *Oxford Essays, Contributed by Members of the University*, 2:88–136. London: John W. Parker and Son.

Bernhardi, Wilhelm. 1883. "Lateranconcil des Jahres 1139" [Tenth Ecumenical Council: Lateran II, 1139]. In *Jahrbuecher der deutschen Geschichte under Konrad III, I (1138–1145)*, 153–59. Leipzig: Duncker und Humblot.

"Bertie Felstead: The Last Known Survivor of No-Man's-Land Football Died on July 22nd, Aged 106." 2001. *Economist*, August 2.

Bethea, Nathan Bradley. 2014. "We Lost Soldiers in the Hunt for Bergdahl, a Guy Who Walked Off in the Dead of Night." *Daily Beast*, June 2.

*The Bible*. n.d. Authorized King James Version. King James Bible Online.

Bin Laden, Usama. 2002a. "Full Text: bin Laden's 'Letter to America.'" *Guardian* (UK), November 24, 2002.

———. 2002b. "Statement From Shaykh Usama Bin Ladin, May God Protect Him, and Al Qaeda Organization." *Al Qal'ah* (website), October 14.

Biological Weapons Convention (BWC), or Convention on the Prohibition of the Development, Production and Stockpiling of Bacteriological (Biological) and Toxin Weapons and on their Destruction. April 10, 1972, entered into force March 26, 1975. London, Moscow, and Washington, DC.

Blaker, James. 2017. Personal interview. April 28.

Blanchard, Christopher M. 2004. "Al Qaeda: Statements and Evolving Ideology." CRS Report for Congress (Order Code RL3275), updated July 9, 2007, originally November 16.

"Blood and Dust." 2011. *People and Power*. Filmed by Vaughan Smith. Al Jazeera, June 19.

"Blood and Dust: What Happened to Tyrone Jordan?" 2016. Rewind. Al Jazeera, October 3.

Blum, Gabriella. 2007. *Islands of Agreement: Managing Enduring Armed Rivalries*. Cambridge, MA: Harvard University Press.

Boal, Mark. 2005. "The Man in the Bomb Suit." *Playboy*, September.

Boot, Max. 2010. "The Consummate Warrior: Marcel Bigeard, 1916–2010." *Weekly Standard* 15 (40): 20–22.

———. 2013. *Invisible Armies: An Epic History of Guerrilla Warfare from Ancient Times to the Present*. New York: Liveright.

———. 2014. "How Not to Handle a Prisoner Swap." *Commentary Magazine*, June 2.

Bowden, Mark. 2013. "The Killing Machines: How to Think About Drones." *Atlantic* 312 (2): 58–70.

Bowles, Samuel. 2009. "Did Warfare Among Ancestral Hunter-Gatherer Groups Affect the Evolution of Human Social Behaviors." *Science* 324:1293–98.

Brandenberg, Bert. 1987. "The Legality of Assassination as Foreign Policy, Note." *Virginia Journal of International Law* 27 (3): 655–97.

Brecht, Bertolt. 1973 (1941). *Mutter Courage und ihre Kinder: Eine Chronik aus dem Dreissigjährigen Krieg*. Frankfurt: Suhrkamp.

Breiding, Dirk H. 2014. *A Deadly Art: European Crossbows, 1250–1850*. New York: Metropolitan Museum of Art.

Bronner, Ethan, and Stephen Farrell. 2011. "Israeli Soldier Swapped for Hundreds of Palestinians." *New York Times*, October 18.

Brown, David. 2004. "Remembering a Victory for Human Kindness: WWI's Puzzling, Poignant Christmas Truce." *Washington Post*, December 25.

Brown, Jeffrey. 2012. "What Can 'Friends Of Syria' Do To Help Stop Killings?" *Newshour on PBS* (USA), February 24.

Brown, Malcolm, and Shirley Seaton. 1999. *Christmas Truce: The Western Front, December 1914*. Pan Grand Strategy Series. London: Pan.

Bruce, Robert, Iain Dickie, Kevin Kiley, Michael Pavkovic, and Frederick Schneid. 2008. *Fighting Techniques of the Napoleonic Age, 1792–1815: Equipment, Combat Skills, and Tactics*. New York: Thomas Dunne.

Brussels Declaration, or Project of an International Declaration Concerning the Laws and Customs of War. 1874. Brussels, August 27.

*Budōshoshinshū: The Warrior's Primer of Daidōji Yūzan*. 1984 (seventeenth century CE). Translated by William Scott Wilson. Burbank, CA: Black Belt, Ohara.

Burg, Steven L., and Paul S. Shoup. 1999. *The War in Bosnia-Herzegovina: Ethnic Conflict and International Intervention*. New York: M. E. Sharpe.

Callaway, Ewen. 2009. "Ancient Warfare: Fighting for the Greater Good." *New Scientist*, June 4, 2009.

Cambanis, Thanassis. 2014. "Could Aid to Syrians Be Prolonging the War?" *Boston Globe*, June 1.

Cao, Song (曹松). n.d. "Ji Hai Two Poems" 己亥歲(二首僖宗廣明元年), 曹夢徵詩集 [Tang dynasty, 年代:唐, 618–907 CE].

Card, Orson Scott. 1985. *Ender's Game*. New York: Tor.

Carroll, Aaron E. 2017. "Wearable Fitness Devices Don't Seem to Make Your Fitter." *New York Times*, February 20.

Carroll, Andrew. 2010. "A Jewish Medic Reflects on Treating Wounded Nazis." *HistoryNet.com* (World History Group), July 30.

Carter, Violet Bonham. 1965. *Winston Churchill As I Knew Him*. London: Eyre and Spottiswoode and Collins.

Chaliand, Gérard, ed. 1994. *The Art of War in World History: From Antiquity to the Nuclear Age*. Berkeley: University of California Press.

Chamberlain, General Joshua L. 1901. "Lenient Terms of General Grant." Reprinted in "The Last Salute Of The Army Of Northern Virginia: Details of the Surrender of General Lee at Appomattox Courthouse, April 9th, 1865." *Boston Journal*, May. Reprinted by Southern Historical Society Papers, vol. 32, Richmond, VA, January–December 1904.

Chambers, John Whiteclay, II. 2003. "S. L. A. Marshall's Men Against Fire: New Evidence Regarding Fire Ratios." *Parameters* 33 (3): 114–21.

Chang, Mina. 2016. "Does Providing Aid in War Zones Do More Harm Than Good?" *Foreign Policy in Focus*. Institute for Policy Studies (Washington, DC), March 7.

Charny, Israel W. 2007. *Fighting Suicide Bombing: A Worldwide Campaign for Life*. Praeger Security International.

Chaudhry, Shahzad. 2012. "The Military-Military Divide." *Express Tribune* (Karachi, Pakistan), October 31.

Chemical Weapons Convention (CWC), or Convention on the Prohibition of the Development, Production, Stockpiling and Use of Chemical Weapons and on Their Destruction. January 13, 1993, entered into force April 29, 1997. Paris.

Chiu, Yvonne. n.d. "Good Governance in Chinese Just War Theory as *Jus ad Bellum*." Working paper.

———. 2010. "Uniform Exceptions and Rights Violations." *Social Theory and Practice* 36 (1): 44–77.

———. 2011. "Liberal Lustration." *Journal of Political Philosophy* 19 (4): 440–64.

Choi, Ajin. 2004. "Democratic Synergy and Victory in War, 1816–1992." *International Studies Quarterly* 48 (3): 663–82.

Chu, Henry, and Borzou Daragahi. 2006. "Cease-Fire Begins After Fierce Battles." *Los Angeles Times*, August 14.

Churchill, Winston S. 1902 (1899). *The River War: An Historical Account of the Reconquest of the Soudan*. London: Longmans, Green, 1902.

———. 1941. Speech to the Harrow School. London, October 29. Transcript. National Churchill Museum (Fulton, Missouri, USA).

———. 1942. Prime Minister's Address to the Central Council of the Conservative Party, March 26, 1942, published in *The Times* (London), March 27.

"Churchill's Request to Accompany Invasion Force." 2004. Exhibit: Churchill and the Great Republic, February 5–July 10. United States Library of Congress.

Cicero, Marcus Tullius. 1913 (44 BCE). *De Officiis*. Translated by Walter Miller. Loeb Classical Library 30, Cicero Volume 21. Cambridge, MA: Harvard University Press.

———. 1991 (44 BCE). *On Duties (De Officiis)*. Edited by M. T. Griffin and E. M. Atkins. Cambridge Texts in the History of Political Thought. Cambridge: Cambridge University Press.

Clarke, O. W., J. Glasson, A. M. August, C. H. Epps, V. N. Ruff, C. H. Kliger, C. W. Plows, G. T. Wilkins, J. H. Cosgriff, K. B. Johnson, D. Orentlicher, and R. B. Conley. 1993. "Caring for the Poor." *JAMA* 269 (19): 2533–37.

Clausewitz, Carl von. 1873 (1832). *On War*. Translated by Colonel J. J. Graham. London: N. Trübner, 1873.

———. 2000. *On War*. Translated by O. J. Matthijs Jolles. In *The Book of War: Sun-Tzu's The Art of Warfare and Carl von Clausewitz's On War*. New York: Modern Library/Random House.

Clay, Henry. 1819. Speech to House of Representatives, January 20. *Annals of Congress of the United States*, Fifteenth Congress, Second Session, vol. 1 (November 16, 1818–February 17, 1819): 631–55.

Clinton, Hillary Rodham. 2014. *Hard Choices*. New York: Simon and Schuster.

"Clouds of Death." 2014. *WWI: The First Modern War*. Season 1, episode 3. History Channel, July 26.

Cobb, Humphrey. 2010 (1935). *Paths of Glory*. New York: Penguin.

Cobb, Thomas. 1819. Speech to House of Representatives, January 18. *Annals of Congress of the United States*, Fifteenth Congress, Second Session, vol. 1 (November 16, 1818–February 17, 1819): 583–97.

Code Duello, or Irish Code of Honor (Ireland, 1777). 1858 In *The Code of Honor, or, Rules for the Government of Principals and Seconds in Dueling*, by John Lyde Wilson, appendix, 35–44. Charleston, SC: James Phinney.

Cody, Edward. 2006. "Israel Strikes Deep in Lebanon." *Washington Post*, August 20.

Cohen, Guy. 2014. "Israel and Gaza: Just One More Ceasefire, 7 Hours, That's All." *Israel Defense*, April 8.

Cole, Matthew. 2017. "The Crimes of SEAL Team 6." *Intercept*, January 10.

Collins, Liat. 2008. "Calm Down, If You Can." *Jerusalem Post*, June 21.

Connor, W. R. 1988. "Early Greek Land Warfare as Symbolic Expression." *Past and Present* 119:3–29.

Convention on the Prevention and Punishment of Crimes Against Internationally Protected Persons, Including Diplomatic Agents. 1973. December 14, entered into force February 20, 1977. New York. Art. 1, para 1, 28 U.S.T. 1975, U.N.T.S. Vol. 1035, p. 167. Annexed to General Assembly Resolution 3166 (XVIII) of December 14, 1973.

Convention on the Prohibition of the Use, Stockpiling, Production and Transfer of Anti-Personnel Mines and on Their Destruction, aka "Ottawa Treaty." September 18, 1997, entered into force March 1, 1999. Oslo. UNTS, vol. 2056, p. 211.

Cordesman, Anthony H. 2009. *Saudi Arabia: National Security in a Troubled Region*. Center for Strategic and International Studies. Santa Barbara, CA: Prager Security International.

Cordesman, Anthony H., George Sullivan, and William D. Sullivan. 2007. *Lessons of the 2006 Israeli-Hezbollah War*. Washington, DC: CSIS.

Cowdrey, Albert E. 1987. *The Medics' War: United States Army in the Korean War*. Washington, DC: Center of Military History, United States Army.

Crane, Conrad. 2013. "The Lure of the Strike." Special Commentary. *Parameters* 43 (2): 5–12.

Crane, Robert D. 2008. "Hudna: A Long-Range Islamic Strategy for Conflict Resolution." Shalom Center (Philadelphia, PA), January 19.

Crawford, Neta. 2007. "Individual and Collective Moral Responsibility for Systematic Military Atrocity." *Journal of Political Philosophy* 15 (2): 187–212.

"Cricket," n. 3. *Oxford English Dictionary Online*. Oxford English Dictionary.

Curtius, Quintus. 1946 (c. 41 CE). *History of Alexander the Great of Macedon*. Vol. 1, Books 1–5, translated by J. C. Rolfe. Loeb Classical Library 368. Cambridge, MA: Harvard University Press.

Cushing, Harvey. 1936. *From A Surgeon's Journal, 1915–1918*. Boston: Little, Brown.

Daileda, Colin. 2014. "The Military History of 'Leave No Man Behind.'" *Mashable*, June 14.

Daoud, Kamel. 2015. "Saudi Arabia, an ISIS That Has Made It." *New York Times*, November 20.

Davenport, David. 2002–03. "The New Diplomacy." *Policy Review* 116:17–30. Stanford, CA: Hoover Institution, Stanford University.

David, Saul. 2009. *War: From Bronze-Age Battles to 21st-Century Conflict*. London: Dorling Kindersley.

David, Steven R. 2003. "Fatal Choices: Israel's Policy of Targeted Killing." In *Democracies and Small Wars*, edited by Efraim Inbar, 138–58. BESA Studies in International Security. London: Frank Cass.

Deaton, Angus. 2013. *The Great Escape: Health, Wealth, and the Origins of Inequality*. Princeton: Princeton University Press.

DeBruyne, Nese F. 2017. "American War and Military Operations Casualties: Lists and Statistics" (RL32492). Congressional Research Service, April 26.

Dickens, Charles. 1862. "Dead (and Gone) Shots." *All the Year Round* 7:212–16.

Dionysius of Halicarnassus. 2006. *The Roman Antiquities*, bk. 2, chap. 72 [ca. 60–65 BCE]. In *The Ethics of War: Classic and Contemporary Readings*, edited by Gregory M. Reichberg, Henrik Syse, and Endre Begby, §4: "Roman Law of War and Peace (Seventh Century BC–First Century AD): Ius Fetiale," 48–49. Malden, MA: Blackwell.

Dixon, David. 2005. *Never Come to Peace Again: Pontiac's Uprising and the Fate of the British Empire in North America*. Norman: University of Oklahoma Press.

Doane, Seth. 2011. "Medevac Team Saves Lives in Afghanistan." *CBS News*, August 11.

Donald, David Herbert. 1995. *Lincoln*. New York: Simon and Schuster.

"Do the Right Thing: HS Soccer Coach Refuses to Run Up Score, Even Though It Costs Team Trip to Playoffs." 2012. *NBC Sports*—Sports Talk, December 24.

"A Duel Involving Representative Sam Houston of Tennessee, September 22, 1826." 1826. History, Art and Archives, United States House of Representatives.

Dunant, Henri. 1862. *Un souvenir de Solférino (A Memory of Solferino)*. Genève.

Edmonds, James Edward. 1928. *History of the Great War: Military Operations, France and Belgium, 1915*. London: Macmillan.

Eisenhower, Dwight D. 1946. Address Before the Canadian Club, Ottawa, Canada, January 10. Dwight D. Eisenhower Presidential Library, Museum, and Boyhood Home (Abilene, Kansas, USA).

Eisenstadt, Michael, and Robert Satloff. 2014. "Toward an Enduring Ceasefire: Preventing the Rocket Rearmament of Gaza Terrorist Groups." Washington Institute for Near East Policy (Washington, DC), August 21.

Eisikovits, Nir. 2015. *A Theory of Truces*. Palgrave Studies in Ethics and Public Policy. New York: Palgrave MacMillan.

Ekstein, Modris. 2000. *Rites of Spring: The Great War and the Birth of the Modern Age*. Boston: First Mariner.

Engen, Robert. 2011. "S. L. A. Marshall and the Ratio of Fire: History, Interpretation, and the Canadian Experience." *Canadian Military History* 20 (4): 39–48.

Erlanger, Steven. 2013. "A Weapon Seen as Too Horrible, Even in War." *New York Times*, September 6.

Estlund, David. 2007. "On Following Orders in an Unjust War." *Journal of Political Philosophy* 15 (2): 213–34.

Evans, John L. W., III. 2013. Petition: Lower the Precedence of the New Distinguished Warfare Medal.

"The Evolution of Generosity: Welcome, Stranger." 2011. *Economist*, July 30.

*Eye in the Sky*. 2015. Directed by Gavin Hood. Entertainment One.

Fahim, Kareem. 2006. "He's Got One Word for You: Hudna." *New York Times*, January 22.

"Fair." *Oxford English Dictionary Online*. Oxford English Dictionary.

Fanon, Frantz. 1963 (1961). "Concerning Violence." In *The Wretched of the Earth*, translated by Constance Farrington, 35–106. New York: Grove.

Feaver, Peter, and Chris Gelpi. 2005. *Choosing Your Battles: American Civil-Military Relations and the Use of Force*. New ed. Princeton: Princeton University Press.

Fehr, Ernst, Urs Fischbacher, and Simon Gächter. 2002. "Strong Reciprocity, Human Cooperation and the Enforcement of Social Norms." *Human Nature* 13:1–25.

Fenn, Elizabeth A. 2000. "Biological Warfare in Eighteenth-Century North America: Beyond Jeffery Amherst." *Journal of American History* 86 (4): 1552–80.

Ferdinando, Lisa. 2016. "Pentagon Announces Changes to Military Awards Program." *DoD News*, Defense Media Activity, Department of Defense, January 7.

Ferguson, Maj. Patrick. 1780. "Original Letter of Major Patrick Ferguson" (Cambden, August 28), *The Gentleman's Magazine and Historical Review*, by Sylvanus Urban, Gent., vol. 40, New Series, August 1853. London: John Bowyer Nichols and Sons, 1853, 128. (Reprinted from Adam Ferguson, "Biographical Sketch or Memoir of Lieutenant-Colonel Patrick Ferguson: Originally Intended for the British Encyclopedia." Edinburgh: John Moir, Royal Bank Close, 1817.)

Ficarrotta, J. Carl. 2001. "A Higher Moral Standard for the Military." In *Ethics for Military Leaders*, edited by George R. Lucas, Paul E. Roush, Lawrence Beyer, Shannon E. French, and Douglas MacLean, 61–71. Boston: Pearson Custom.

Fink, Sheri, and Helene Cooper. 2017. "Inside Trump Defense Secretary Pick's Efforts to Halt Torture." *New York Times*, January 2.

Fisher, Ian. 2017. "Elor Azaria, Israeli Soldier Who Killed Wounded Assailant, Gets 18 Months in Prison." *New York Times*, February 21.

Fisher, Max. 2016. "Does Killing Terrorist Leaders Make Any Difference? Scholars Are Divided." *New York Times*, August 30.

———. 2017. "Why the Syrian Chemical Weapons Problem Is So Hard to Solve." *New York Times*, April 13.

Fisher, Richard. 2006. "Why Altruism Paid Off for Our Ancestors." *New Scientist*, December 7.

Ford, John C., SJ. 1944. "The Morality of Obliteration Bombing." *Theological Studies* 5 (3): 261–309.

Foucault, Michel. 1984. *The Foucault Reader*. Edited by Paul Rabinow. New York: Pantheon.

———. 1995 (1975). *Discipline and Punish: The Birth of the Prison*. New York: Vintage.

———. 2003. *Society Must Be Defended: Lectures at the Collège de France, 1975–1976*. Translated by David Macey. New York: Picador.

———. 2010. *The Birth of Biopolitics: Lectures at the Collège de France, 1978–1979*. Translated by Graham Burchell. New York: Picador.

Fountain, Charles. 1993. *Sportswriter: The Life and Times of Grantland Rice*. New York: Oxford University Press.

Frank, Steven A. 1995. "George Price's Contributions to Evolutionary Genetics." *Journal of Theoretical Biology* 175 (3): 373–88.

"Fraternization Between the Lines." 1914. Special Cable to *New York Times*, December 31 [*Daily News*, London, December 30, 1914].

Frayer, Kevin, Associated Press. 2011. "US Medics Brave Fire to Save Lives in Afghan War." *Boston Globe*, May 30.

Frederick II (Friedrich der Große). 1747. *Instruction militaire du Roi de Prusse pour ses généraux* (traduite de l'Allemand, par Monsier Faesch, Lieutenant-Colonel dans les Troupes Saxonnes, Frankfort, MDCCLXI). French; revised as *General Principles of War*; reprinted German, 1761; translated back into French, 1761.

"Freedom for Sgt. Bergdahl, at a Price." 2014. *New York Times*, June 3.

Freedom House. 2016. *Freedom in the World 2016: Anxious Dictators, Wavering Democracies: Global Freedom Under Pressure*. Washington, DC: Freedom House.

French, Shannon. 2017 (2003). *The Code of the Warrior*. 2nd ed. Lanham, MD: Rowman and Littlefield.

Fricker, John. 1979. *The Battle for Pakistan: The Air War of 1965*. London: Ian Allan.

Friedersdorf, Conor. 2016. "The Obama Administration's Drone-Strike Dissembling." *Atlantic*, March 14.

Frowe, Helen. 2014. *Defensive Killing*. Oxford: Oxford University Press.

Fry, Douglas P. 2009. *Beyond War: The Human Potential for Peace*. New York: Oxford University Press.

"Funeral of the Red Baron" (silent film). 1918. Australian War Memorial. Virtual Museum of Canada, Canadian Museum of History.

Gabriel, Richard A., and Karen S. Metz. 1992. *A Short History of War: The Evolution of Warfare and Weapons*. Professional Readings in Military Strategy 5. Carlisle, PA: Strategic Studies Institute, US Army War College.

Gallagher, Brendan. 2010. "Tour de France 2010: Alberto Contador apologises to Andy Schleck on YouTube." *Telegraph*, July 20.

Galliott, Jai. 2016. *Military Robots: Mapping the Moral Landscape*. Military and Defence Series. New York: Routledge.

*Gandhi*. 1982. Directed by Richard Attenborough. Columbia Pictures.

Ganguly, Sumit. 2014. Personal interview. July 1.

Garamone, Jim. 2016. "U.S. Troops Should Not Be Sent Into Fair Fights, Dunford Says." US Department of Defense, *DoD News*, April 27.

Gardner, Andy, Ashleigh Griffin, and Stuart West. 2016. "Theory of Cooperation." *eLS*.

Gardner, Robert, and Karl G. Heider. 1968. *Gardens of War: Life and Death in the New Guinea Stone Age*. New York: Random House.

Garner, James Wilford. 1920. *International Law and the World War*. London: Longmans.

Gat, Azar. 2006. *War in Human Civilization*. Oxford: Oxford University Press.

Gearan, Anne, Associated Press. 2006. "U.S. Opposed to Cease-Fire in Hezbollah." *Washington Post*, July 20.

Geneva Convention (III) Relative to the Treatment of Prisoners of War. 1949. 75 UNTS 135. August 12. Geneva. Supercedes: Convention Relative to the Treatment of Prisoners of War. Geneva, July 27, 1929.

Geneva Convention (IV) Relative to the Protection of Civilian Persons in Time of War. August 12, 1949. Geneva.

Geneva Convention. 1977. Protocol Additional to the Geneva Conventions of August 12, 1949, and Relating to the Protection of Victims of International Armed Conflicts (Protocol I). June 8.

Geneva Convention. 1977. Protocol Additional to the Geneva Conventions of August 12, 1949, and Relating to the Protection of Victims of Non-International Armed Conflicts (Protocol II). June 8.

Geneva Protocol 1925, or Protocol for the Prohibition of the Use of Asphyxiating, Poisonous or Other Gases, and of Bacteriological Methods of Warfare. June 17, 1925. Geneva.

Gentili, Alberico. 1933 (1598). *De iure belli libre tres* (*On the Law of War in Three Books*). Translation of the 1612 edition by John C. Rolfe. Oxford: Clarendon.

Gertz, Nolen. 2014. *The Philosophy of War and Exile*. Palgrave Studies in Ethics and Public Policy. New York: Palgrave MacMillan.

Gilbert, Adrian. 1996. *Sniper: Master of Terrain, Technology, and Timing*. New York: St. Martin's.

——. 1998. *Stalk and Kill: The Thrill and Danger of the Sniper Experience*. New York: St. Martin's.

Gilbert, Martin. 1971. *Winston S. Churchill, 1874–1965*. Vol. 3, *The Challenge of War, 1914–16*. London: Heinemann.

*Gilgamesh and Aga* (*Gilgameš and Aga, Bilgames and Akka*). 1999. In *The Epic of Gilgamesh: Babylonian Epic Poem and Texts in Akkadian and Sumerian*, translated by Andrew George, 143–48. London: Penguin.

Girardot, Frank C. 2015. "Sportsmanship a Matter of Common Sense, and Common Decency." *Pasadena Star-News* (Pasadena, California), January 19.

Gladwell, Malcolm. 2013. "Listening in Vietnam." BBC Radio 4.

Goldstein, Richard. 2006. "Hugh Thompson, 62, Who Saved Civilian Lives at My Lai, Dies." *New York Times*, January 7.
Gonzalez, Alberto R. (White House Counsel). 2002. Memorandum for the President: Decision re: Application of the Geneva Convention on Prisoners of War to the Conflict with al Qaeda and the Taliban, January 25, 2002.
Gouré, Leon. 1962. *The Siege of Leningrad*. Rand Corporation, Stanford University Press.
Goya, Francisco. 1810–20. *The Disasters of War*. Prints.
"The Gracious Mr. Walsh." n.d. *ESPN Cricinfo*: World Cup Timeline.
Graves, Robert. 1958 (1929). *Goodbye to All That*. New York: Anchor.
Gray, J. Glenn. 1998 (1959). *Warriors: Reflections on Men in Battle*, with a foreword (1970) by the author. Lincoln: University of Nebraska Press.
Gross, Michael L. 2004. "Bioethics and Armed Conflict: Mapping the Moral Dimensions of Medicine and War." *Hastings Center Report* 34 (6): 22–30.
———. 2007. "From Medical Neutrality to Medical Immunity." *AMA Journal of Ethics* 9 (10): 718–21.
Gross, Michael L., and Don Carrick, eds. 2013. *Military Medical Ethics for the 21st Century*. Military and Defence Ethics. Farnham, UK: Ashgate.
Grossman, Dave. 1995. *On Killing: The Psychological Cost of Learning to Kill in War and Society*. New York: Little, Brown.
Grossman, Dave, and Loren W. Christensen. 2008. *On Combat: The Psychology and Physiology of Deadly Conflict in War and Peace*. 3rd ed. Warrior Science.
Grotius, Hugo. 1901 (1625). *The Rights of War and Peace, Including the Law of Nature and of Nations*. Translated by A. C. Campbell. New York: M. Walter Dunne.
Hague Convention (III) relative to the Opening of Hostilities. October 18, 1907, entered into force January 26, 1910. Hague.
Hague Convention (IV) Respecting the Laws and Customs of War on Land and Its Annex: Regulations Concerning the Laws and Customs of War on Land. October 18, 1907, entered into force January 26, 1910. Hague.
Hague Convention (IV, 1) Declaration Prohibiting Launching of Projectiles and Explosives from Balloons. July 29, 1899. Hague.
Hague Convention (IV, 3) Declaration Concerning the Use of Bullets Which Expand or Flatten Easily in the Human Body. July 29, 1899. Hague.
Hague Convention (XIV) Declaration Prohibiting the Discharge of Projectiles and Explosives from Balloons. October 18, 1907, entered into force November 27, 1909. Hague.
Hahn, Robert W. 1996. "The Cost of Antiterrorist Rhetoric." *Regulation* 19 (4): 51–57.
Hallett, Brien. 1998. *The Lost Art of Declaring War*. Champaign: University of Illinois Press.
"Hamas Awaits Truce Offer Reply." 2008. *Al Jazeera*, April 28.
Hamilton, Joseph. 1829. *The Dueling Handbook, or, The Only Approved Guide Through All the Stages of a Quarrel*. London: Hatchard and Sons.
"Hanging Up the Boxing Gloves." 2015. *Economist*, January 15.
Hanson, Victor Davis. 1983. *Warfare and Agriculture in Classical Greece*. 1st ed. Pisa: Giardini.
———. 1991. "The Ideology of Hoplite Battle, Ancient and Modern." In *Hoplites: The Classical Greek Battle Experience*, edited by Victor Davis Hanson, 3–14. London: Routledge.
———. 1995. *The Other Greeks: The Family Farm and the Agrarian Roots of Western Civilization*. New York: Free.
———. 1996. "Hoplites Into Democrats: The Ideology of Athenian Infantry." In *Demokratia: A Conversation on Democracies, Ancient and Modern*, edited by Josiah Ober and Charles Hedrick, 289–312. Princeton: Princeton University Press.
———. 2005. *A War Like No Other: How the Athenians and Spartans Fought the Peloponnesian War*. New York: Random House.

———. 2009 (1989). *The Western Way of War: Infantry Battle in Classical Greece*. 2nd ed. Berkeley: University of California Press.

Hanstock, Bill. 2012. "The 8 Most Memorable Tour de France Crashes." *SBNation*, July 18.

Hart, Donna, and Robert Sussman. 2005. *Man the Hunted: Primates, Predators, and Human Evolution*. Cambridge, MA: Westview.

Hastings, Max. 1984. *Overlord: D-Day and the Battle for Normandy*. New York: Simon and Schuster.

———. 2004. *Armageddon: The Battle for Germany, 1944–45*. New York: Knopf.

Hayden, General Michael V. 2016. "To Keep America Safe, Embrace Drone Warfare." *New York Times*, February 19.

Headrick, Daniel R. 2010. *Power Over Peoples: Technology, Environments, and Western Imperialism*. Princeton: Princeton University Press.

Hedges, Chris. 2002. *War Is a Force That Gives Us Meaning*. New York: Public Affairs

Hefele, Karl Joseph von. 1912. *Histoire des conciles d'apres les documents originaux*. Translated and continued by Henri Leclerq, vol. 5, no. 1, pp. 721–22. Paris: Letouzey et Ané.

Heller-Roazen, Daniel. 2009. *The Enemy of All: Piracy and the Law of Nations*. Brooklyn, NY: Zone.

Hemingway, Ernest. 1952. *The Old Man and the Sea*. London: Jonathan Cape.

Herodotus. 1922 (c. 440 BCE). *The Persian Wars, Volume III: Books 5–7*. Translated by A. D. Godley. Loeb Classical Library 119. Cambridge, MA: Harvard University Press. Aka *The Histories*.

Hickley, Matthew. 2009. "British Troops on Same Ward as Taliban: Soldiers' Fury as Wounded Wake Up Next to the Enemy." *Daily Mail*, January 23.

Hippocratic Oath, classical and modern versions. 2001. "The Hippocratic Oath Today." *NOVA*. Public Broadcasting Service (USA), March 23.

Hitler, Adolf. 2016 (1925). *Mein Kampf*. CreateSpace Independent Publishing Platform.

Hobbes, Thomas. 1996 (1651). *Leviathan*. Edited by Richard Tuck. Cambridge Texts in the History of Political Thought. Cambridge: Cambridge University Press.

Holmes, Bob. 2008. "Born to Fight, Evolved for Peace." *New Scientist* 200 (2682): 8–9.

Holmes, Richard, ed. 2001. *The Oxford Companion to Military History*. New York: Oxford University Press.

Holquist, Peter. 2004. "The Russian Empire as a 'Civilized State': International Law as Principle and Practice in Imperial Russia, 1874–1878." Grant Proposal to the National Council for Eurasian and East European Research, July 14.

Homer. 1998 (c. 800 BCE). *The Iliad*. Translated by Robert Fagles. Introduction by Bernard Knox. New York: Penguin.

Housman, Laurence, ed. 1930. *War Letters of Fallen Englishmen*. New York: E. P. Dutton.

Howe, Edmund G. 2015. "When, If Ever, Should Military Physicians Violate a Military Order to Give Medical Obligations Higher Priority?" *Military Medicine* 180 (11): 1118–19.

"Hudna." 2005. The Reut Institute (Tel Aviv, Israel), April 20.

Hull, Anne. 2004. "Wounded or Disabled But Still on Active Duty." *Washington Post*, December 1.

"Human Behavior: Deviations from the Mean." 2002. *Economist*, March 21.

Humane Society of the United States. n.d. "Internet Hunting Fact Sheet." *Humane Society of the United States* Online (Washington, DC).

Humanitarian Policy Group at ODI. 2010. Opinion: "Aid and War: A Response to Linda Polman's Critique of Humanitarianism." Overseas Development Institute (London, UK), No. 144, May.

Human Rights Watch. 2011. "Q and A: US Targeted Killings and International Law." *Human Rights Watch* Online (New York, NY), December 19.

Hume, David. 1896 (1738–40). *A Treatise of Human Nature.* Edited by L. A. Selby-Bigge. Oxford: Clarendon.
*The Hurt Locker.* 2008. Directed by Kathryn Bigelow. Voltage Pictures.
Ignatieff, Michael. 1997. *The Warrior's Honor: Ethnic War and the Modern Conscience.* New York: Holt.
Imperial German Embassy. 1915. Notice to Travelers. Washington, DC, April 22. Posted in various American newspapers.
"In Enemy Care: Syrians Treated in Israeli Hospitals." 2013. *France24.com,* September 18.
International Committee of the Red Cross (ICRC). n.d. Customary IHL (International Humanitarian Law) Database.
———. 1958. Commentary of 1958 on Geneva Convention (IV) Relative to the Protection of Civilian Persons in Time of War of August 12, 1949.
———. 1987a. Commentary of 1987 on the Additional Protocols of June 8, 1977 (Protocol I) to the Geneva Conventions of August 12, 1949, edited by Yves Sandoz, Christophe Swinarski, Bruno Zimmermann. Geneva: Martinus Nijhoff.
———. 1987b. Commentary of 1987 on the Additional Protocols of June 8, 1977 (Protocol II) to the Geneva Conventions of August 12, 1949, edited by Yves Sandoz, Christophe Swinarski, Bruno Zimmermann. Geneva: Martinus Nijhoff.
———. 1995. "Vienna Diplomatic Conference Achieves Prohibition on Blinding Laser Weapons and Deadlock on Landmines." October 13.
———. 2007. "Overview of the Convention on the Prohibition of Anti-Personnel Mines." August 15.
———. 2009. *Interpretive Guidance on the Notion of Direct Participation in Hostilities Under International Humanitarian Law.* Geneva: ICRC.
———. 2011. "What Does the Law Say About Torture?" (FAQ). *International Committee of the Red Cross* online, June 24.
International Court of Justice. 2003. *Oil Platforms (Islamic Republic of Iran v. United States of America),* Judgment, ICJ GL No 90, [2003] ICJ Rep 161, ICGJ 74 (ICJ 2003).
Ip, Greg. 2015. *Foolproof: Why Safety Can Be Dangerous and How Danger Makes Us Safe.* Headline.
"The Iran-Contra Affair" (Article from Collection: The Presidents). n.d. *American Experience.* Public Broadcasting Service (USA).
Iran Human Rights Documentation Center. 2008. *Condemned by Law: Assassination of Political Dissidents Abroad.* New Haven, CT: Iran Human Rights Documentation Center, November.
Ismay, John, Eric Schmitt, and Thomas Gibbons-Neff. 2017. "Navy SEALs Investigated in Green Beret's Death Also Under Scrutiny in Theft." *New York Times,* November 13.
Israel Ministry of Foreign Affairs. 2004. "Background on Israeli POWs and MIAs (Communicated by the Israeli Security Sources)." January 26.
"It's Just Not Cricket." n.d. *BBC Learning English,* BBC.
Jaspers, Karl. 1961. *The Question of German Guilt.* Translated by E. B. Ashton. New York: Capricorn.
Jenkins, Mark. 2012. "The Healing Fields." *National Geographic Magazine,* January.
Jett, Dennis C. 1999. *Why Peacekeeping Fails.* New York: Palgrave.
Johnson, Dominic, and Bradley A. Thayer. 2013. "What Our Primate Relatives Say About War." *National Interest* (Washington, DC), January 29.
Jones, Simon. 2014. Interviewed in "Clouds of Death." *WWI: The First Modern War.* Season 1, episode 3. History Channel, July 26.
"Joseph Medicine Crow: War Songs of the Plains." 2016. *Economist,* April 16.

Jürgs, Michael. 2005. *Der kleine Frieden im Großen Krieg: Westfront 1914: Als Deutsche, Franzosen und Briten gemeinsam Weihnachten feierten*. Goldman.

Kaeuper, Richard W. 2000. "Chivalry and the 'Civilizing Process.'" In *Violence in Medieval Society*, edited by R. W. Kaeuper. Rochester, NY: Boydell and Brewer.

Kahn, Clea, and Elena Lucci. 2009. "Are Humanitarians Fueling Conflicts? Evidence from Eastern Chad and Darfur." *Humanitarian Practice Network* Online, Humanitarian Policy Group, Overseas Development Institute (London, UK), July.

Kahn, Paul. 2002. "The Paradox of Riskless Warfare." *Philosophy and Public Policy Quarterly* 22 (3): 2–8.

Kant, Immanuel. 1996. *Practical Philosophy*. Edited and translated by Mary Gregor. Cambridge: Cambridge University Press. *The Metaphysics of Morals* (1797), *Perpetual Peace* (1795).

———. 2000 (1790). *Critique of the Power of Judgment*. Edited by Paul Guyer. Translated by Paul Guyer and Eric Matthews. Cambridge: Cambridge University Press.

Kaplan, Fred. 2014. "Why the Deal to Free Bowe Bergdahl Could Lead to Bigger Things." *Slate*, June 2.

Karami, Arash. 2016. "Iran Wary Groups Might Use Syria Cease-Fire to Rearm." *Al-Monitor* (Washington, DC), September 12.

Kasher, Asa, and Maj. Gen. Amos Yadlin, with a reply by Avishai Margalit and Michael Walzer. 2009. "Israel and the Rules of War: An Exchange." *New York Review of Books* 56 (10).

Keating, Joshua E. 2012. "Please, Don't Send Food." *Foreign Policy*, June 18.

Keegan, John. 1988. *The Mask of Command: Alexander the Great, Wellington, Ulysses S. Grant, Hitler, and the Nature of Leadership*. New York: Penguin.

———. 1993. *A History of Warfare*. New York: Random House.

Kellen, Konrad. 1970. *Conversations with Enemy Soldiers in Late 1968/Early 1969: A Study of Motivation and Morale* (RM-6131-1-ISA/ARPA), Sept. Santa Monica, CA: Rand Corporation.

———. 1971. *1971 and Beyond: The View from Hanoi* (P-4634-1), June. Santa Monica, CA: Rand Corporation.

Kent, James. 1873 (1826). *Commentaries on American Law*. 12th ed. Edited by Oliver Wendell Holmes. 1826: Boston: Little, Brown.

Kershaw, Ian. 2008. *Hitler*. New York: Norton.

Kershner, Isabel. 2017. "Israeli Soldier Who Shot Wounded Palestinian Assailant is Convicted." *New York Times*, January 4.

Kesling, Ben. 2017. "World News: Islamic State Drones Terrorize Iraqi Forces." *Wall Street Journal Asia*, February 27.

Kierman, Frank A., Jr. 1974. "Phases and Modes of Combat in Early China." In *Chinese Ways in Warfare*, edited by Frank A. Kierman, Jr., and John K. Fairbank, 27–66. Cambridge, MA: Harvard University Press.

Kinsella, Helen. 2005. "Discourses of Difference: Combatants, Civilians, and Compliance with the Laws of War." *Review of International Studies* 31, special issue, "Force and Legitimacy in World Politics," December, 163–85.

Kipling, Rudyard. 1990 (1889). *The Ballad of East and West*. New York: M. F. Mansfield and A. Wessels.

Klay, Phil. 2017. "What We're Fighting For." *New York Times*, February 10.

Krammer, Arnold P. 1996. *Nazi Prisoners of War in America*. Lanham, MD: Scarborough House.

Krentz, Peter. 2002. "Fighting by the Rules: The Invention of the Hoplite Agôn." *Hesperia* 71 (1): 23–39.

Kulish, Nicholas, Christopher Drew, and Matthew Rosenberg. 2015. "Navy SEALs, a Beating Death and Claims of a Cover-Up." *New York Times*, December 17.

Kutz, Christopher. 2000. *Complicity: Ethics and Law for a Collective Age*. Cambridge Studies in Philosophy and Law. Cambridge: Cambridge University Press.

Lamb, Dean Ivan. 1934. *The Incurable Filibuster: Adventures of Colonel Dean Ivan Lamb*. New York: Farrar and Rinehart.

Landau, Ian. 2013. "Tour Scandals." *Outside*, July 15.

Lanni, Adriaan. 2008. "The Laws of War in Ancient Greece." *Law and History Review* 26 (3): 469–89.

LaVaque-Manty, Mika. 2006. "Dueling for Equality: Masculine Honor and the Modern Politics of Dignity." *Political Theory* 34 (6): 715–40.

Lawrence, T. E. 1973 (1926). *Seven Pillars of Wisdom: A Triumph*. London: Cape.

Lawson, Eric, and Jane Lawson. 1996. *The First Air Campaign: August 1914–November 1918*. Cambridge, MA: Da Capo.

Lech, Raymond B. 2000. *Broken Soldiers*. Urbana: University of Illinois Press.

Lee, Gen. Robert E. 2006. Spoken comments, Fredericksburg, December 1962. Quoted in *Robert E. Lee, A Life*, edited by Roy Blount, Jr., 1, 108. New York: Penguin.

Le Guin, Ursula. 1969. *The Left Hand of Darkness*. New York: Ace.

Leonard, Tom. 2010. "Get Us Outta Here! Explained, How Medic Battles to Save the Life of a Captured Taliban on Board a Black Hawk Helicopter." *Daily Mail*, October 7.

LeRiche, Matthew. 2004. "Unintended Alliance: The Co-Option of Humanitarian Aid in Conflicts." *Parameters* 34 (1): 104–20.

Levinson, Sanford. 1974. "Responsibility for Crimes of War." In *War and Moral Responsibility: A "Philosophy & Public Affairs" Reader*, edited by Marshall Cohen, Thomas Nagel, and Thomas Scanlon, 104–33. Princeton: Princeton University Press.

Lewis, David. 1969. *Convention: A Philosophical Study*. Cambridge, MA: Harvard University Press.

Lewis, Mark. 1990. *Sanctioned Violence in Early China*. Albany: State University of New York.

Lieber, Francis. 1898. Instructions for the Government of Armies of the United States in the Field. Originally Issued as General Orders No. 100, Adjutant General's Office, Apr. 24, 1863. Washington, DC: Government Printing Office. Aka the Lieber Code.

Lincoln, Abraham. 1862. "Meditation on the Divine Will [September 2, 1862?]." In *Collected Works of Abraham Lincoln*, edited by Roy Basler, 5:403–4. New Brunswick, NJ: Rutgers University Press, 1953.

———. 1863. Letter to James C. Conkling, August 26, in *The Collected Works of Abraham Lincoln*, edited by Roy Basler, 6:408. New Brunswick, NJ: Rutgers University Press, 1953.

Livy, Titus. 1919 (27–9 BCE). *Ab Urbe Condita (History of Rome)*. Vol. 1, Books 1–2. Translated by B. O. Foster. Loeb Classical Library 114. Cambridge, MA: Harvard University Press.

Londoño, Ernesto. 2011. "Prisoner Swap with Israel Emboldens Hamas." *Washington Post*, October 18.

———. 2013. "Pentagon Cancels Divisive Distinguished Warfare Medal for Cyber Ops, Drone Strikes." *Washington Post*, April 15.

Luban, David. 2014. "Risk Taking and Force Protection." In *Reading Walzer*, edited by Itzhak Benbaji and Naomi Sussman, 277–301. London: Routledge.

Lubold, Gordon, and John Hudson. 2014. "The Bergdahl Bargain Was Just the Beginning." *Foreign Policy*, June 2.

Lussu, Emilio. 2014 (1939). *A Soldier on the Southern Front (Un Anno Sull'Altipiano)*. Translated by Gregory Conti. New York: Rizzoli Ex Libris.

Luttwak, Edward N. 1999. "Give War a Chance." *Foreign Affairs* 78 (4): 36–44.
Luvass, Jay, ed. 1966. *Frederick the Great on the Art of War*. New York: Free.
MacArthur, Gen. Douglas. 1946. Review of the Trial of General Yamashita, February. MacArthur Memorial Online, MacArthur Memorial (Norfolk, Virginia).
MacEoin, Denis. 2008. "Tactical Hudna and Islamist Intolerance." *Middle East Quarterly* 15 (3): 39–48.
Machiavelli, Niccolò. 1997 (1531). *Discourses on Livy*. Translated by P. E. Bondanella and J. C. Bondanella. New York: Oxford University Press.
———. 1998 (1513). *The Prince*. Translated by Harvey C. Mansfield. 2nd ed. Chicago: University of Chicago Press.
Madrigal, Alexis C. 2017. "The Computer That Predicted the U.S. Would Win the Vietnam War." *Atlantic*, October 5.
*The Mahābhārata of Krishna-Dwaipayana Vyasa*. 1883–96 (c. 400 BCE). Translated by Kisari Mohan Ganguli. Internet Sacred Text Archive, Evinity Publishing, www.sacred-texts.com/hin/maha/index.htm.
Makos, Adam, with Larry Alexander. 2012. *A Higher Call: An Incredible True Story of Combat and Chivalry in the War-Torn Skies of World War II*. New York: Berkley Caliber.
Mallett, Michael. 1974. *Mercenaries and Their Masters: Warfare in Renaissance Italy*. London: Bodley Head.
Malory, Sir Thomas. 2003 (1485). *Le Morte Darthur*. Edited by Stephen H. A. Shepherd. Norton Critical Edition. New York: Norton.
*Manu's Code of Law: A Critical Edition and Translation of the Mānava-Dharmásāstra*. 2004 (c. 200 CE). Translated by Patrick Olivelle. Oxford: Oxford University Press. Aka *Manusmrti*.
Mao, Tse-tung (毛泽东). 1938. "On Protracted War" (论持久战). Marxists Internet Archive.
Margalit, Avishai. 2004. *The Ethics of Memory*. Cambridge, MA: Harvard University Press.
Margalit, Avishai, and Michael Walzer. 2009. "Israel: Civilians and Combatants." *New York Review of Books* 56 (8).
Marshall, S. L. A. 1951. "Commentary on Infantry Operations and Weapons Usage in Korea, Winter of 1950–51." Report Completed Under Department of the Army Contract by Operations Research Office. Johns Hopkins University, October 27.
———. 2000 (1947) *Men Against Fire: The Problem of Battle Command*. Norman: University of Oklahoma Press.
Martini, Fausto Maria. 2008. "Why I Didn't Kill You." Quoted in *The White War: Life and Death on the Italian Front, 1915–1919*, by Mark Thompson, 184. New York: Basic.
Mauvillon, Éléazar de. 1747. *Histoire de la dernière guerre de Bohème*. Francfort: Paul Lenclums.
Maxwell, Mark David. 2012. "Targeted Killing, the Law, and Terrorists: Feeling Safe?" *Joint Force Quarterly* 64 (1): 123–30.
May, Andrew. 2017. Personal interview, May 18.
May, Larry. 2005. "Killing Naked Soldiers: Distinguishing Between Combatants and Noncombatants." *Ethics and International Affairs* 19 (3): 39–53.
McCarthy, Cormac. 1992 (1985). *Blood Meridian, or, The Evening Redness in the West*. New York: Vintage.
McCullough, David. 2005a. *1776*. New York: Simon and Schuster.
———. 2005b. Lecture to the Union League Club, Chicago, Illinois, June 13. Illinois Channel archive.
McMahan, Jeff. 1994a. "Innocence, Self-Defense, and Killing in War." *Journal of Political Philosophy* 2 (3): 193–221.
———. 1994b. "Self-Defense and the Problem of the Innocent Attacker." *Ethics* 104 (2): 252–90.
———. 2004. "The Ethics of Killing in War." *Ethics* 114 (4): 693–733.

———. 2009. *Killing in War*. Uehiro Series in Practical Ethics. Oxford: Oxford University Press.
———. 2012. "Rethinking the Just War." Parts 1 and 2, *New York Times*, November 11 and 12.
Mehendale, M. A. 1995. *Reflections on the Mahābhārata War*. Shimla: Indian Institute for Advanced Study.
Melzer, Nils. 2008. *Targeted Killing in International Law*. Oxford Monographs in International Law. Oxford: Oxford University Press.
———. 2009. *Interpretive Guidance on the Notion of Direct Participation in Hostilities Under International Humanitarian Law*. International Committee of the Red Cross.
Metz, Thaddeus. 2017. "*Jus Interruptus Bellum*: The Ethics of Truce-Making." *Journal of Global Ethics* 13 (1): 6–13.
Michaels, Jim. 2015. "*American Sniper* as Viewed by Real American Snipers." *USA Today*, January 22.
*Mifune: The Last Samurai* (documentary). 2015. Directed by Steven Okazaki. Creative Associates Limited (CAL).
Mill, John Stuart. 1984 (1859). "A Few Words on Non-Intervention." In *The Collected Works of John Stuart Mill*, vol. 21, *Essays on Equality, Law, and Education*, edited by John M. Robson, 109–24. Toronto: University of Toronto.
———. 1991 (1859). *On Liberty*. London: Routledge.
Minnich, J. W. 1922. "That Affair at Dandridge, Tenn." In *Confederate Veteran*, vol. 30, 294–97. Nashville, TN: S. A. Cunningham, Founder.
Mir, Hamid. 2001. Interview. "Osama Claims He Has Nukes: If US Uses N-Arms It Will Get Same Response." *Dawn* (Karachi, Pakistan), November 10.
Moltke, Helmut Graf von. 1880. Letter to Johann Caspar Bluntschli, December 11, in *The Law Magazine and Review: For Both Branches of the Legal Profession at Home and Abroad*, edited by G. Sherston Baker, vol. 22, Fourth Series, 1896–97, pp. 15–18. London: Stevens and Haynes, Law Publishers, 1897. (Original text: Helmuth Graf von Moltke. 1922. *Aufzeichnungen, Briefe, Schriften, Reden mit Zeichnungen aus Moltkes Skizzenbuch*. Auswahl und Verbindungen von Peter Kurz. München: W. Langewiesche-Brandt.)
———. 1893. *Field-Marshall Count Helmuth Von Moltke as a Correspondent*. Translated by Mary Herms. New York: Harper and Brothers, Franklin Square.
Moore, Harold G., and Joseph L. Galloway. 2008. *We Are Soldiers Still: A Journey Back to the Battlefields of Vietnam*. New York: Harper.
Moore, Michael (@MMFlint). 2015. "My uncle killed by sniper in WW2. We were taught snipers were cowards. Will shoot u in the back. Snipers aren't heroes. And invaders r worse." 12:40 PM, January 18. Tweet.
Moore, Norman, et al. 1918. "The Abolition of Gas Warfare." *British Medical Journal*, July–December, 611.
More, Thomas. 1965 (1516). *Utopia*. Translated by Paul Turner. London: Penguin.
Moreno, Sylvia. 2005. "Mouse Click Brings Home Thrill of the Hunt." *Washington Post*, May 8.
Mothana, Ibrahim. 2012. "How Drones Help Al Qaeda." *New York Times*, June 13.
*My Enemy, My Brother*. 2015. Directed by Ann Shin. Fathom Film Group.
"My Lai." 2010. *The American Experience*. Season 22, episode 6. Public Broadcasting Service (USA), April 26.
Nagel, Thomas. 1972. "War and Massacre." *Philosophy and Public Affairs* 1 (2): 123–44.
Narang, Neil. 2015. "Assisting Uncertainty: How Post–Cold War Humanitarian Aid Inadvertently Prolongs Civil Wars." *International Studies Quarterly* 59 (1): 184–95. doi: 10.1111/isqu.12151.
"A Nation at War: A Historical View." 2003. *New York Times*, April 20.

Neely, Mark E., Jr. 1991. *The Fate of Liberty: Abraham Lincoln and Civil Liberties.* New York: Oxford University Press.
Neff, Stephen C. 2008. *War and the Law of Nations: A General History.* New York: Cambridge University Press.
———. 2010. "Prisoners of War in International Law: The Nineteenth Century." In *Prisoners in War,* edited Sibylle Scheipers, 57–73. Oxford: Oxford University Press.
Newman, David, and Tyll Van Geel. 1989. "Executive Order 12,333: A Clear Declaration of Intent." *Harvard Journal of Law and Public Policy* 12 (2): 433–48.
Nolan, Cathal J. 2017. *The Allure of Battle: A History of How Wars Have Been Won and Lost.* New York: Oxford University Press.
Nunn, Nathan, and Nancy Qian. 2014. "US Food Aid and Civil Conflict." *American Economic Review* 104 (6): 1630–66.
Nuremberg Trial Proceedings. 1946. *Trial of the Major War Criminals Before the International Military Tribunal, Nuremberg, 14 November 1945–01 October 1946.* Nuremberg, Germany (1947): Vol. 1; Vol. 22: Two Hundred and Seventeenth Day, Monday, September 30.
Nyon Arrangement. 1937. Nyon, Switzerland: September 14.
"Obama Was Right to Strike a Deal with the Taliban." 2014. *Bloomberg View,* June 2.
Ober, Josiah. 1994. "Classical Greek Times." In *The Laws of War: Constraints on Warfare in the Western World,* edited by Michael Howard, George J. Andreopoulos, and Mark R. Shulman, 12–26. New Haven, CT: Yale University Press.
———. 1996. "Rules of War in Classical Greece." In *The Athenian Revolution: Essays on Ancient Greek Democracy and Political Theory,* 53–71. Princeton: Princeton University Press.
Oikonomides, Nicolas. 1991. "Prisoners, Exchanges of." In *The Oxford Dictionary of Byzantium,* edited by Alexander Kazhdan, 1722. New York: Oxford University Press.
Olson, Scott. 2010. "Army Medevac Unit Tends to the War Wounded Near Marja, Afghanistan" (photos). Getty Images, September 25.
Onishi, Norimitsu, and Selam Gebrekidan. 2018. "Hit Men and Power: South African Leaders Are Killing One Another." *New York Times,* September 30.
Onuah, Felix, and Ahmed Kingimi. 2017. "Nigeria Exchanges 82 Chibok Girls Kidnapped by Boko Haram for Prisoners." *Reuters,* May 6.
Oppel, Richard A., Jr. 2017. "Sgt. Bowe Bergdahl's Odd Journey from Victim to Criminal." *New York Times,* October 23.
Orbinski, James. 1999. Médecins Sans Frontières—Nobel Lecture, Oslo, December 10.
Ordeshook, Peter C. 1986. *Game Theory and Political Theory: An Introduction.* Cambridge: Cambridge University Press.
Orend, Brian. 2006. *The Morality of War.* Ontario: Broadview.
Orwell, George. 1970. "Looking Back on the Spanish War." In *The Collected Essays, Journalism and Letters of George Orwell,* vol. 2, edited by Sonia Orwell and Ian Angus. London.
Overy, Richard. 1996. *Why the Allies Won.* New York: Norton.
The Oxford Manual, or, The Laws of War on Land. 1880. Oxford, September 9.
Paret, Peter, Gordon A. Craig, and Felix Gilbert, eds. 1986. *Makers of Modern Strategy: From Machiavelli to the Nuclear Age.* Princeton: Princeton University Press.
Parker, Geoffrey, ed. 1988. *The Military Revolution: Military Innovation and the Rise of the West, 1500–1800.* New York: Cambridge University Press.
———. 2005. *The Cambridge History of Warfare.* New York: Cambridge University Press.
*Paths of Glory.* 1957. Directed by Stanley Kubrick. United Artists.
*Patton.* 1970. Directed by Franklin J. Schaffner. Twentieth Century Fox.

Paxman, Jeremy. 2014. *Great Britain's Great War*. New York: Viking.

Payne-Gallwey, Ralph. 2007. *The Crossbow: Its Military and Sporting History, Construction and Use*. New York: Skyhorse.

Peace of Westphalia. October 24, 1648. Comprising: Peace Treaty of Münster (*Instrumentum Pacis Monasteriensis*) between the HRE (Emperor Ferdinand III) and France (King Louis XIV), and their respective allies, October 24, 1648. Peace Treaty of Osnabrück (*Instrumentum Pacis Osnabrugensis*) between the Holy Roman Empire of the German Nation (HRE) (Emperor Ferdinand III) and Sweden (Queen Christina), and their respective allies, October 24, 1648.

Peckham, Howard H. 1974. *Pontiac and the Indian Uprising*. Princeton: Princeton University Press.

Pegler, Martin. 2004. *Out of Nowhere: A History of the Military Sniper*. Oxford: Osprey.

Perrin, Pierre. 1998. "The Impact of Humanitarian Aid on Conflict Development." *International Review of the Red Cross* 323.

Pfanner, Toni. 2004. "Military Uniforms and the Law of War." *International Review of the Red Cross* 853:93–130.

Pickard, Daniel B. 2001. "Legalizing Assassination? Terrorism, the Central Intelligence Agency, and International Law." *Georgia Journal of International and Comparative Law* 30 (1): 3–35.

Pinker, Steven. 2012. *The Better Angels of Our Nature: Why Violence Has Declined*. New York: Penguin.

Plato. 2013 (c. 380 BCE). *Republic*. Edited and translated by Christopher Emlyn-Jones and William Preddy. Loeb Classical Library 237 and 276. Cambridge, MA: Harvard University Press.

Plutarch. 1931 (c. 100 CE). "Various Sayings of Spartans to Fame Unknown." In *Moralia*, vol. 3, *Sayings of Kings and Commanders; Sayings of Romans; Sayings of Spartans; The Ancient Customs of the Spartans; Sayings of Spartan Women; Bravery of Women*, translated by Frank Cole Babbitt. Loeb Classical Library 245, 394–421, §234: E5, E46. Cambridge, MA: Harvard University Press.

Polman, Linda. 2010. *The Crisis Caravan: What's Wrong with Humanitarian Aid*. New York: Metropolitan.

———. 2011. *War Games: The Story of Aid and War in Modern Times*. New York: Viking.

Polybius. 2010 (second century BCE). *The Histories*, vol. 1, *Books 1–2*. Translated by W. R. Paton. Revised by F. W. Walbank and Christian Habicht. Loeb Classical Library 128. Cambridge, MA: Harvard University Press.

———. 2012 (second century BCE). *The Histories*, vol. 6, *Books 28–39. Fragments*. Edited and translated by S. Douglas Olson. Translated by W. R. Paton. Revised by F. W. Walbank and Christian Habicht. Loeb Classical Library 161. Cambridge, MA: Harvard University Press.

Primoratz, Igor. 2002. "Michael Walzer's Just War Theory: Some Issues of Responsibility." *Ethical Theory and Moral Practice* 5 (2): 221–43.

*The Princess Bride*. 1987. Directed by Rob Reiner. Act III Communications.

Pritchett, W. Kendrick. 1974. *The Greek State at War*. Part 2. Berkeley: University of California Press.

———. 1985. *The Greek State at War*. Part 4. Berkeley: University of California Press.

Prothero, Mitchell. 2007. "Hezbollah Rearms and Bides Its Time." *U.S. News and World Report*, December 6.

Pruszewicz, Marek. 2015. "How Deadly Was the Poison Gas of WWI?" *BBC News–Magazine*, January 30.

Pucin, Diane. 2003. "In Cycling, Winning with Honor Means Everything." *Los Angeles Times*, July 23.
Pufendorf, Samuel von. 1729 (1672). *Of the Law of Nature and Nations (De jure naturae et gentium)*. Eight books, 4th ed. (Carefully Corrected). Translated by Basil Kennett. London: J. Walthoe, R. Wilkin, J. and J. Bonwicke, S. Birt, T. Ward, and T. Osborne.
Pyle, Ernie. 2001 (1944). *Brave Men*. Lincoln: University of Nebraska Press.
"Qatar Allowing Freed Taliban Men to Move Freely in Country: Gulf Official." 2014. *Reuters*, June 3.
Rauch, Laura. 2012. "Growing Number of Troops Return to Battle After Suffering Severe Wounds." *Stars and Stripes* (Washington, DC), March 4.
Rawls, John. 1993. *Political Liberalism*. New York: Columbia University Press.
Reichberg, Gregory M. 2015. "Historiography of Just War Theory." In *The Oxford Handbook of Ethics of War*, edited by Seth Lazar and Helen Frowe. New York: Oxford University Press.
Reichberg, Gregory M., Henrik Syse, and Endre Begby, eds. 2006. *The Ethics of War: Classic and Contemporary Readings*. Malden, MA: Blackwell.
Reisman, W. Michael. 1998. "Stopping Wars and Making Peace." *Tulane Journal of International and Comparative Law* 6:5–56.
Reiter, Dan, and Allan C. Stam. 2002. *Democracies at War*. Princeton: Princeton University Press.
Remarque, Erich Maria. 1975 (1928). *All Quiet on the Western Front (Im Westen nichts Neues)*. Translated by A. W. Wheen. Boston: Little, Brown.
*Report of the Permanent Advisory Commission for Military, Naval and Air Questions to the Council of the League of Nations*. 1920. Brussels: League of Nations, October 22.
Resolutions of the Geneva International Conference. 1863. Regarding the founding of the ICRC. Geneva, October 26–29.
Reuters. 2011. "A History of Israel's Prisoner Swaps." *Jerusalem Post*, October 27.
Reynolds, Gretchen. 2016. "Activity Trackers May Undermine Weight Loss Efforts." *New York Times*, September 20.
Richthofen, Capt. Manfred von Freiherr. 1918. *The Red Battle Flyer (Der Rote Kampfflieger)*. Translated by T. Ellis Barker. New York: Robert M. McBride.
Roberts, Andrew. 2011. *The Storm of War: A New History of the Second World War*. New York: HarperCollins.
Roberts, Sam. 2016. "Larry Colburn, Who Helped Stop My Lai Massacre, Dies at 67." *New York Times*, December 16.
———. 2017. "Lt. Gen. Harold Moore, Whose Vietnam Heroism Was Depicted in Film, Dies at 94." *New York Times*, February 13.
Robson, Eric. 1957. "The Armed Forces and the Art of War." In *The New Cambridge Modern History*, vol. 7, *The Old Regime 1713–63*, edited by J. O. Lindsay, 163–89. Cambridge: Cambridge University Press.
Rosenberg, Jonathan. 1999. "Before the Bomb and After: Winston Churchill and the Use of Force." In *Cold War Statesmen Confront the Bomb: Nuclear Diplomacy Since 1945*, edited by John Lewis Gaddis, Philip H. Gordon, Ernest R. May, and Jonathan Rosenberg, 171–93. Oxford: Oxford University Press.
Rosenberg, Matthew, and Carlotta Gall. 2014. "Prisoner Trade Yields Rare View Into the Taliban." *New York Times*, June 2.
Roy, Kaushik. 2012. *Hinduism and the Ethics of Warfare in South Asia: From Antiquity to the Present*. New York: Cambridge University Press.
"The Rules of Dueling." n.d. *The American Experience*. Public Broadcasting Service (USA).

Sagan, Scott D., and Benjamin A. Valentino. 2017. "Revisiting Hiroshima: What Americans Really Think About Using Nuclear Weapons and Killing Noncombatants." *International Security* 42 (1): 41–79.

Saint-Exupéry, Antoine de. 1942. *Pilote de guerre (Flight to Arras)*. Paris: Gallimard.

Saint Petersburg Declaration 1868, or, Declaration Renouncing the Use, in Time of War, of Explosive Projectiles Under 400 Grammes Weight. Saint Petersburg, November 29, 1868, entered into force December 11, 1868.

Sanger, David E., and Ashley Parker. 2014. "Strategy and Objectives for Gaining Soldier's Release Shifted Over Time." *New York Times*, June 3.

Savage, Charlie, and Eric Schmitt. 2014. "Bergdahl Is Said to Have History of Leaving Post." *New York Times*, June 6.

Scham, Paul, and Osama Abu-Irshaid. 2009. "Hamas: Ideological Rigidity and Political Flexibility." Special Report no. 224, United States Institute of Peace (Washington, DC).

Scheffler, Samuel. 2006. "Is Terrorism Morally Distinctive?" *Journal of Political Philosophy* 14 (1): 1–17.

Schelling, Thomas. 1960. *The Strategy of Conflict*. Cambridge, MA: Harvard University Press.

———. 2006 (1978). *Micromotives and Macrobehavior*. New York: Norton.

Schindler, Dietrich, and Jiri Toman, eds. 1988. *The Laws of Armed Conflicts: A Collection of Conventions, Resolutions, and Other Documents*. 3rd ed. Dordrecht: Martinus Nijhoff.

"Schleck Loses Chain, Contador Pounces." 2010. *ESPN.com*, July 19.

Schmitt, Carl. 2007 (1962). *Theory of the Partisan: Intermediate Commentary on the Concept of the Political*. Translated by G. L. Ulmen. New York: Telos.

Schmitt, Eric, and Charlie Savage. 2014. "American Soldier Freed by Taliban in Prisoner Trade." *New York Times*, June 1.

Schmitt, Eric, Helene Cooper, and Charlie Savage. 2014. "G.I.'s Vanishing Before Capture Angered His Unit." *New York Times*, June 3.

Schmitt, Michael N. 1992. "State-Sponsored Assassination in International and Domestic Law." *Yale Journal of International Law* 17 (2): 610–85.

Scott, Gen. Winfield. 1847. General Orders No. 20, General Headquarters of the U.S. Army. Tampico, Mexico, February 19.

Seck, Hope Hodge. 2016. "Pentagon Debuts 'R' Award Device for Drone Warfare to Mixed Reviews." *Military.com* (Monster Worldwide, Randstad Holding), January 9.

"Selflessness of Strangers: The Search for an Evolutionary Theory." 2010. *Economist*, May 20.

*The Seven Military Classics of Ancient China* 武經七書. 2007. Translated by Ralph D. Sawyer. New York: Basic.

*The Seven Samurai* 七人の侍. 1954. Directed by Akira Kurosawa (黒沢明). Toho Company.

Shakespeare, William. 2004 (1599). *Henry V*. Folger Shakespeare Library. New York: Washington Square Press.

Shane, Scott. 2015. "Drone Strikes Reveal Uncomfortable Truth: U.S. Is Often Unsure About Who Will Die." *New York Times*, April 23.

Shannon, Elaine, and Tim McGirk. 2006. "Iran and Syria Helping Hizballah Rearm." *Time Magazine*, November 24.

Shay, Jonathan. 2003 (1994). *Achilles in Vietnam: Combat Trauma and the Undoing of Character*. New York: Scribner.

Shi, Nai An 施耐菴. 2001 (fourteenth century). *Outlaws of the Marsh* (*Water Margin* 水滸傳). Translated by Sidney Shapiro. Foreign Languages Press.

Sigal, Leon. 2006. *Negotiating Minefields: The Landmines Ban in American Politics*. New York: Routledge.

Simons, Jake Wallis. 2017. "Saving Their Sworn Enemy: Heartstopping Footage Shows Israeli Commandos Rescuing Wounded Men from Syrian Warzone—but WHY Are They Risking Their Lives for Islamic Militants?" *Daily Mail*, February 7.

Simpson, Robert, and Robert Sparrow. 2014. "Nanotechnologically Enhanced Combat Systems: The Downside of Invulnerability." In *The Pursuit of Nanoethics*, 2014 ed., edited by Bert Gordijn and Anthony Cutter, International Library of Ethics, Law and Technology, 10:89–91. Dordrecht: Springer.

Singer, Peter. 2009. *The Life You Can Save: Acting Now to End World Poverty*. New York: Random House.

Singh, Arjan. 2006. "Flying in the Face of the Facts." *Indian Express* (Mumbai, India), August 6.

Sinha, Manoj Kumar. 2005. "Hinduism and International Humanitarian Law." *International Review of the Red Cross* 87 (858): 285–94.

Slim, Hugo. 2015. "Wonderful Work: Globalizing the Ethics of Humanitarian Action." In *The Routledge Companion to Humanitarian Action*, edited by Roger MacGinty and Jenny H. Peterson, 13–25. New York: Routledge.

Smith, Adam. 1982. *The Theory of Moral Sentiments*. Edited by D. D. Raphael and A. L. Macfie. Indianapolis: Liberty Fund. 1759 first edition, 1790 sixth edition.

Smith, J. Maynard, and G. R. Price. 1973. "The Logic of Animal Conflict." *Nature* 246 (5427): 15–18.

Smoler, Fredric. 1989. "The Secret of the Soldiers Who Didn't Shoot." *American Heritage* 40 (2): 36–45.

Smyth, Rob. 2010. *The Spirit of Cricket: What Makes Cricket the Greatest Game on Earth*. London: Elliott and Thompson.

Solomon, Norman. 2009. "The Ethics of War in Judaism." In *The Ethics of War in Asian Civilizations: A Comparative Perspective*, edited by Torkel Brekke, 39–80. Abingdon: Routledge.

Sorley, Charles. 1919. *The Letters of Charles Sorley, with a Chapter of Biography*. Cambridge: Cambridge University Press.

Spiller, Roger J. 1988. "S. L. A. Marshall and the Ratio of Fire." *RUSI Journal* 133 (4): 63–71. Royal United Services Institute for Defence and Security Studies (London).

*Spring and Autumn Annals/Chunqiu* 春秋. 1960 (722–481 BCE). In *The Chinese Classics*, vol. 5, *The Ch'un Ts'ew with The Tso Chuen*, translated by James Legge. Hong Kong: Hong Kong University Press.

Srivastava, C. P. 2006. *Lal Bahadur Shastri, Prime Minister of India, 1964–1966: A Life of Truth in Politics*. Oxford: Oxford University Press.

Stedman, Stephen J. 1997. "Spoiler Problems in Peace Processes." *International Security* 22 (2): 5–53.

Stedman, Stephen J., and Fred Tanner, eds. 2003. *Refugee Manipulation: War, Politics, and the Abuse of Human Suffering*. Washington, DC: Brookings Institution Press.

Stendhal. *The Charterhouse of Parma* (*La Chartreuse de Parme*). 1997 (1839). Translated by Margaret Mauldon. New York: Oxford University Press.

Stewart, Frances. 2013. "The Causes of Civil War and Genocide: A Comparison." In *Responding to Genocide: The Politics of International Action*, edited by Adam Lupel and Ernesto Verdeja, 47–84. Boulder, CO: Lynne Rienner.

Stilz, Anna. 2011. "Collective Responsibility and the State." *Journal of Political Philosophy* 19 (2): 190–208.

Stinner, CPT Daniel J., MD, MAJ Travis C. Burns, MD, LTC Kevin L. Kirk, DO, and COL James R. Ficke, MD. 2010. "Return to Duty Rate of Amputee Soldiers in the

Current Conflicts in Afghanistan and Iraq." *Journal of Trauma, Injury, Infection, and Critical Care* 68 (6): 1476–79.

Summers, Harry G., Jr. 1995 (1982). *On Strategy: A Critical Analysis of the Vietnam War.* Novato, CA: Presidio.

Sumner, Charles. 1846. *The True Grandeur of Nations, an Oration Delivered Before the Authorities of the City of Boston, July 4, 1845.* London: William Smith.

Sun Tzu 孫子. 1993 (fifth century BCE). *The Art of Warfare* (孫子兵法). Translated by Roger T. Ames. New York: Ballantine.

Tacitus. 1931 (c. 115 CE). *Histories: Books 4–5. Annals: Books 1–3.* Translated by Clifford H. Moore and John Jackson. Loeb Classical Library 249. Cambridge, MA: Harvard University Press.

Tanguy, Joelle (US Executive Director, MSF). 2000. Speech: "Foreign and Humanitarian Aid: Paradox and Perspectives." March 7, Institute for International Liberal Education, Bard College (Annandale-on-Hudson, NY).

Tap, Bruce. 1998. *Over Lincoln's Shoulder: The Committee on the Conduct of the War.* Lawrence: University Press of Kansas.

"A Taste of Armageddon." 1967. *Star Trek.* Season 1, episode 23. NBC, February 23.

Taustad, Dag. 2010. "The Hudna: Hamas's Concept of a Long-Term Ceasefire." PRIO Policy Brief, No. 9. Oslo: Peace Research Institute Oslo.

Taylor, Robert S. 2011. *Reconstructing Rawls.* University Park: Pennsylvania State University Press.

"Tenth Ecumenical Council: Lateran II 1139." 1996. In Internet Medieval Source Book, edited by Paul Halsall, Fordham University Center for Medieval Studies (New York), November.

Teplitz, Robert F. 1995. "Taking Assassination Attempts Seriously: Did the United States Violate International Law in Forcefully Responding to the Iraq Plot to Kill George Bush." *Cornell International Law Journal* 28 (3): 569–617.

Terkel, Amanda. 2013. "Distinguished Warfare Medal Honoring Drone Pilots Canceled by Chuck Hagel." *Huffington Post*, April 15.

Teslik, Lee Hudson. 2006. "Is Hezbollah Rearming?" *Council on Foreign Relations* (New York), October 19.

Thapliyal, U. P. 2002. "Military Organization in the Ancient Period." In *Historical Perspectives of Warfare in India: Some Morale and Matériel Determinants*, edited by S. N. Prasad, 68–103. Project of History of Indian Science, Philosophy and Culture: Centre for Studies in Civilizations. New Delhi: Motilal Banarasidass.

Thomas, A. R., and James C. Duncan, eds. 1999. *International Law Studies* 73, Annotated Supplement to the Commander's Handbook on the Law of Naval Operations: Chapter 7, "The Law of Neutrality," 365–400. Newport, Rhode Island: US Naval War College.

Thompson, Mark. 2013. "Medal of Dishonor?" *Time*, February 13.

Thucydides. 1998 (431–400 BCE). *The Peloponnesian War.* Translated by Walter Blanco. Edited by Walter Blanco and Jennifer Tolbert Roberts. A Norton Critical Edition. New York: Norton.

Tilghman, Andrew. 2013. "Petition Asks for Change to New Drone Medal." *USA Today*, February 18.

———. 2016. "DoD Rejects 'Nintendo Medal' for Drone Pilots and Cyber Warriors." *Military Times* (Sightline Media Group), January 6.

Tilly, Charles. 1975. *The Formation of National States in Western Europe.* Princeton: Princeton University Press.

Toynbee, Arnold. 1973. *Constantine Porphyrogenitus and His World.* London: Oxford University Press.

A Traveler. 1836. *The Art of Duelling, Containing Much Information Useful to Young Continental Tourists*. London: Joseph Thomas.

Treaty of Peace with Germany (Treaty of Versailles). 1919. June 28 (Paris Peace Conference). United States Library of Congress.

United Nations. 1945. Charter. San Francisco, June 26, 1945, entered into force October 24, 1945.

———. 1980a. Convention on Prohibitions or Restrictions on the Use of Certain Conventional Weapons Which May Be Deemed to Be Excessively Injurious or to Have Indiscriminate Effects (Geneva, October 10), aka Convention on Certain Conventional Weapons (CCW). In *The Laws of Armed Conflicts*, edited by D. Schindler and J. Toman, 179–84. Dordrecht: Martinus Nijhoff, 1988.

———. 1980b. Convention on Prohibitions or Restrictions on the Use of Certain Conventional Weapons Which May Be Deemed to Be Excessively Injurious or to Have Indiscriminate Effects—Protocol (II) on Prohibitions or Restrictions on the Use of Mines, Booby-Traps and Other Devices. Geneva, October 10, 1980; amended May 3, 1996. Dordrecht: Martinus Nijhoff, 185–89.

———. 1995. Convention on Prohibitions or Restrictions on the Use of Certain Conventional Weapons Which May Be Deemed to Be Excessively Injurious or to Have Indiscriminate Effects—Protocol (IV) on Blinding Laser Weapons. Vienna, October 13.

———. 2003a. Convention on Prohibitions or Restrictions on the Use of Certain Conventional Weapons Which May Be Deemed to Be Excessively Injurious or to Have Indiscriminate Effects—Protocol (V) on Explosive Remnants of War. November 28.

———. 2003b. "United Nations Operation in Somalia II—UNOSOM II (Mar 1993—Mar 1995): Background." Information Technology Section/ Department of Public Information (DPI).

United States Air Force. 2007. The Non-Commissioned Officer's Creed. Quoted in Staff Sgt. Glenn Mitchell, "NCO Reviews Creed and Charge, Develops Answers." Anderson Air Force Base online, US Air Force, September 12.

United States Army. n.d. The Non-Commissioned Officer's Creed.

———. 2006. Field Manual 3–24 *Counterinsurgency* (MCWP 3–33.5). Headquarters, Department of the Army. Revised May 13, 2014. Original December 15, 2006. Department of Homeland Security Digital Library.

———. 2007. Commissioned Officer's Creed. Quoted in *Walking Away from Nuremberg: Just War and the Doctrine of Command Responsibility*, by Lawrence P. Rockwood, 135. Amherst: University of Massachusetts Press.

———. 2012. Field Manual 6–22 *Army Leadership* ADRP 6–22, C1, FM 6–22. Headquarters, Department of the Army, August.

———. 2013. The Soldier's Creed. US Army Training Circular TC 3–21.75. *The Warrior Ethos and Soldier Combat Skills*, August 13.

———. 2014. Field Manual 3–50 *Army Personnel Recovery*, September 2.

United States Continental Congress (Second). 1905. Articles of War, September 20, 1776. Journals of the Continental Congress 1774–79, Edited from the original records in the Library of Congress by Worthington Chauncey Ford, Chief, Division of Manuscripts. Washington, DC: Government Printing Office.

United States Department of Defense. 2015. *Law of War Manual*, June 12. Office of General Counsel, Department of Defense. Updated December 2016.

———. 2017. "Casualty Status (PDF)." October 13.

United States Department of State. 2004. "Frequently Asked Questions on the New United States Landmine Policy." February 27. Washington, DC: Bureau of Political-Military Affairs.

———. 2014. "U.S. Landmine Policy." Office of Website Management, Bureau of Public Affairs, Department of State.

United States Department of Veterans Affairs. 2017. "America's Wars Fact Sheet." May. Office of Public Affairs, Department of Veterans Affairs.

United States Detainee Treatment Act of 2005 (H.R. 2863). 2005. Pub. L. No. 109–148, Div. A, Title X, §§1001–6, 119 Stat. 2680, 2739–44. December 30. (See also Title XIV of the National Defense Authorization Act for Fiscal Year 2006 [Pub. L. No. 109–163, div. A, Title XIV §§1401–6, 119 Stat. 3136, 3474–80. January 06, 2006. H.R. 1815].)

United States Executive Order No. 10631: Code of Conduct for Members of the United States Armed Forces. 1955. August 17, 1955. 20 FR 6057, August 20, 1955. Amended by: EO 11382, November 28, 1967; EO 12017, November 3, 1977; EO 13286, February 28, 2003.

United States Executive Order No. 11905: United States Foreign Intelligence Activities. 1976. February 18, 1976. 41 FR 7703; February 19, 1976. Amended by: EO 11985, May 13, 1977; EO 11994, June 1, 1977; EO 12038, February 3, 1978. Superseded by: EO 12036, January 24, 1978.

United States Executive Order No. 12036: United States Intelligence Activities. 1978. January 24, 1978. 43 FR 3674; January 26, 1978. Supersedes: EO 11905, February 18, 1976; EO 11985, May 13, 1977; EO 11994, June 1, 1977. Amended by: EO 12139, May 23, 1979. Revoked by: EO 12333, December 4, 1981. See: EO 12333, December 4, 1981; EO 13470, July 30, 2008.

United States Executive Order No. 12333: United States Intelligence Activities. 1981. December 04, 1981. 46 FR 59941; December 8, 1981. Amends: EO 12139, May 23, 1979. Amended by: EO 13284, January 23, 2003; EO 13355, August 27, 2004; EO 13470, July 30, 2008. Revokes: EO 12036, January 24, 1978.

United States Marines. 2013. The Non-Commissioned Officer's Creed. Quoted in *Marine Corps Magic*, by Ret. Sgt. Gary Haun (USMC), 53. Bloomington, IN: AuthorHouse.

United States Military Commissions Act of 2006 (H.R. 6166 / S. 3930) Pub. L. No. 109–366, 120 Stat. 2600. 2006. October 17. Amended by United States Military Commissions Act of 2009 (H.R. 2647).

United States Military Commissions Act of 2009 (H.R. 2647). Title XVIII of the National Defense Authorization Act for Fiscal Year 2010. Pub. L. No. 111–84, H.R. 2647, 123 Stat. 2190, enacted October 28, 2009. Amended the United States Military Commissions Act of 2006 (H.R. 6166).

United States Supreme Court. 1814. *Brown v. United States* 12 U.S. 110.

———. 1946. *In re Yamashita* 327 U.S. 1 (1946), February 4, pp. 327 U.S. 13–15.

———. 2006. *Hamdan v. Rumsfeld* 548 U.S. 557.

Valdez, Inés. 2017. "It's Not About Race: Good Wars, Bad Wars, and the Origins of Kant's Anti-Colonialism." *American Political Science Review* 111 (4): 819–34.

Van Emden, Richard. 2013. *Meeting The Enemy: The Human Face Of The Great War*. London: Bloomsbury.

Vattel, Emer de. 2008 (1758). *The Law of Nations, or, Principles of the Law of Nature, Applied to the Conduct and Affairs of Nations and Sovereigns, with Three Early Essays on the Origin and Nature of Natural Law and on Luxury*. Edited by B. Kapossy and R. Whitmore. Natural Law and Enlightenment Classics. Indianapolis: Liberty Fund. Reprint of the edition published by Robinson in London in 1797.

*The Vietnam War* (documentary series, 10 episodes). 2017. Directed by Ken Burns and Lynn Novick. Public Broadcasting Service (USA).

Vinciguerra, Thomas. 2005. "The Truce of Christmas, 1914." *New York Times: Week in Review*, December 25.

Vlasic, Mark V. 2012. "Assassination and Targeted Killing—a Historical and Post-Bin Laden Legal Analysis." *Georgetown Journal of International Law* 43:259–333.
Voltaire. 1994 (1764). *Dictionnaire philosophique. Œuvres Complètes de Voltaire* 35 and 36. Edited by Christiane Mervaud. Voltaire Foundation, University of Oxford.
Wagner, Thomas, Associated Press. 2007. "US Medical Flights Take Iraqi Insurgents." *Washington Post*, May 11.
Wallace, Kelly. 2002. "W. H. Rejects Bush-Saddam Duel Offer." *CNN*, October 3.
Walzer, Michael. 1973. "Political Action: The Problem of Dirty Hands." *Philosophy and Public Affairs* 2 (2): 160–80.
———. 2015 (1977). *Just and Unjust Wars*. 5th ed. New York: Basic.
"Warfare, Culture and Human Evolution: Blood and Treasure." 2004. *Economist*, June 4.
Warrick, Joby. 2017. "Use of Weaponized Drones by ISIS Spurs Terrorism Fears." *Washington Post*, February 21.
Washington, George. 1775a. Footnote No. 5 to General Orders, August 9. United States National Archives.
———. 1775b. Letter to John Hancock, September 21. United States National Archives.
Wasserstrom, Richard. 1971. "The Relevance of Nuremberg." *Philosophy and Public Affairs* 1 (1): 22–46.
Weaver, Lt. Col. Michael (United States Air Force). 2015. Personal interview. July 16.
Weber, Max. 1922. "Bürokratie." In *Grundriss der Sozialökonomik*, vol. 3, Abteilung, *Wirtschaft und Gesellschaft*, 650–78. Tübingen: J. C. B. Mohr (Paul Siebeck).
———. 1946 (1922). "Bureaucracy." In *From Max Weber: Essays in Sociology*, translated and edited by H. H. Gerth and C. Wright Mills, 196–244. New York: Oxford University Press.
Wees, Hans van, ed. 2000. *War and Violence in Ancient Greece*. London: Duckworth and the Classical Press of Wales.
———. 2004. *Greek Warfare: Myth and Realities*. London: Bristol Classical.
Weintraub, Stanley. 2001. *Silent Night: The Story of the World War I Christmas Truce*. New York: Free Press.
Wheaton, Henry. 1836. *Elements of International Law*. Philadelphia, PA: Carey, Lea, and Blanchard.
Wheeler, William. 1993 (1951). *The Letters of Private Wheeler, 1809–1828*. Edited by Captain B. H. Liddell Hart. Adlestrop, UK: Windrush.
Whitman, James Q. 2012. *The Verdict of Battle: The Law of Victory and the Making of Modern War*. Cambridge, MA: Harvard University Press.
Wiebe, Matthew C. 2003. "Assassination in Domestic and International Law: The Central Intelligence Agency, State-Sponsored Terrorism, and the Right of Self-Defense." *Tulsa Journal of Comparative and International Law* 11 (1): 363–406.
Williams, John. 2015. "Distant Intimacy: Space, Drones, and Just War." *Ethics and International Affairs* 29 (1): 93–110.
Williams, Roger. 1988. Quoted in Adam J. Hirsch, "The Collision of Military Cultures in Seventeenth-Century New England." *Journal of American History* 74 (4): 1187–212.
Wilson, John Lyde. 1858. *The Code of Honor or, Rules for the Government of Principals and Seconds in Dueling*. Charleston, SC: James Phinney.
Winer, Stuart. 2015. "Israeli Medics Told to Treat Terrorists the Same as Victims." *Times of Israel* (Jerusalem), December 16.
Wingfield, Thomas C. 1998. "Taking Aim at Regime Elites: Assassination, Tyrannicide, and the Clancy Doctrine." *Maryland Journal of International Law and Trade* 22 (2): 287–317.
Witt, John Fabian. 2012. *Lincoln's Code: The Laws of War in American History*. New York: Free.

———. 2013. "A Response to David Luban." *Just Security*, October 3.
Wood, Graeme. 2015. "Why We Fear and Admire the Military Sniper." *Boston Globe*, January 16.
World Bank. 2015. Data: GDP per capita (current US$).
"World Cup 1987: Courtney Walsh's Sporting Gesture Costs West Indies a Semifinal Berth." 2012. *CricketCountry.com* (India), October 16.
Xenophon of Athens. 1918, 1921. *Hellenica* [fifth–fourth centuries BCE]. In *Xenophon in Seven Volumes*, vols. 1 and 2, edited by Carleton L. Brownson. Cambridge, MA: Harvard University Press.
Yoo, John. 2005. "Enemy Combatants and the Problem of Judicial Competence." In *Terrorism, the Laws of War, and the Constitution: Debating the Enemy Combatant Cases*, edited by Peter Berkowitz, 69–100. Stanford: Hoover Institution Press.
Yoo, John (Deputy Assistant Attorney General), and Robert J. Delahunty (Special Counsel). 2002. Memorandum for William J. Haynes II (General Counsel, Department of Defense), US Department of Justice, January 9.
Zengal, Lt. Commander Patricia, JAGC, USN. 1991. "Assassination and the Law of Armed Conflict." Thesis for the Judge Advocate General's School, US Army.
Zenko, Micah, and Amelia Mae Wolf. 2016. "Drones Kill More Civilians Than Pilots Do." *Foreign Policy*, April 25.
"Zeppelin Terror Attack." 2014. *NOVA*. Season 41, episode 2. Public Broadcasting Service (USA), January 14.
*Zuo Zhuan* 左傳. 1960 (fourth century BCE). In *The Chinese Classics*, vol. 5, *The Ch'un Ts'ew with the Tso Chuen*, translated by James Legge. Hong Kong: Hong Kong University Press. Aka *Commentary of Zuo* or *Tso Chuen*.

# Index

Absolute war, Clausewitz on, 90
Accountability gap, assassination and, 176–77. *See also* Assassination; Responsibility for war
Adverse effects of Lieber Code, 172–73, 178
Aemilianus, Scipio, 92
Aesthetics of war, 237, 239–40
Afghanistan, war in, 30, 218; cooperation to minimize damage and, 99–100, 105; medical neutrality and, 207–8, 210; mortality rates in, 293*n*76; uniforms and, 105
Aggressiveness as evolutionary advantage, 8–9, 253*n*8
Aggressive wars, international law against, 205, 291*n*46. *See also* Self-defense
Alexander of Macedon, 56
Algerian War, 67
*All Quiet on the Western Front* (Remarque), 4–5, 14–15, 126

Altruism: animals and, 253*n*22; as evolutionary advantage, 8–9, 253*n*23; Iran-Iraq War and, 9–10; warfare making possible, 9; World War I and, 10; World War II and, 9
Ambushes, 123; cooperation for a fair fight and, 55–57
Animals, 258*n*18; altruism in, 253*n*22
Anscombe, G. E. M., 258*n*10
Antiterrorism security measures, 133. *See also* Unintended consequences
Apel, Otto F., 15–16, 184, 208–9, 286*n*63
Aquinas, Thomas, 55, 125, 228, 262*n*71
Arab Caliphate, prisoner exchanges and, 27
Areas of conflict, drones and, 269*n*163. *See also* Battlefield
Aristotle, 39–40, 200
Armstrong, Lance, 46, 259*n*26. *See also* Misfortune
Army, US: Commissioned Officer's Creed of, 74–75; empathy and, 76–77; Soldier's Creed of, 73–74,

Army, US (*continued*)
    266*n*125; virtue ethics and,
    74–77
*Army Leadership* manual, US, 76
Articles of War, Revolutionary War,
    252*n*14
Artillery, 13, 81, 86
*Art of War, The* (Sun Tzu), 53, 267*n*146
Aschmann, Rudolph, 254*n*43
Assassination, 276*n*86, 277*n*93, 277*n*95;
    accountability gap and, 176–77;
    cooperation for a fair fight and, 71,
    166, 268*n*148; cooperation to
    minimize damage and, 123–27;
    Hague Conventions and, 124,
    276*n*84; Kant on, 125–26; of
    King, Jr., 277*n*96; Lieber Code and,
    124, 176; moral injury and, 79–80;
    political elites as targets of, 125–27;
    targeting and, 124–26; treacherous
    methods of, 123–24; United Nations
    Charter and, 124
Atlanta, Civil War siege of, 90–91, 148,
    172–73
Augustine, 55, 78, 262*n*71
Automatic weapons, 82, 86
Axelrod, Robert, 14; cooperation
    and, 19
Axworthy, Lloyd, 112

Bad luck. *See* Misfortune
*Ballad of East and West, The* (Kipling),
    65–66
Barbarians, 220; cooperation for a fair
    fight excluding, 87–88, 130–31,
    269*n*172, 270*n*173, 270*n*178, 278*n*110.
    *See also* Laws of war
*Bataille rangée. See* Linear battle
Battlefield: boundaries of, 165, 269*n*163;
    physical presence on, 85. *See also*
    Areas of conflict

Battle function, 71–72; virtue ethics
    and, 77; war function and, 88,
    182–84
Battle of Agincourt, 81, 268*n*152
Ben M'hidi, Mohammed Larbi, 67
Bergdahl, Bowe, 25–27, 256*n*64. *See also*
    Prisoner exchanges
Bernard, Mountague, 147, 198, 248–49,
    300*n*29
Bible, 262*n*71; cooperation for a fair
    fight and, 56, 58; cooperation to end
    war quickly in, 141
Bigeard, Marcel, 67
Bin Laden, Osama, 96
Biological weapons, 62–63, 130,
    278*n*111; as indiscriminate weapons,
    113
Biological Weapons Convention, 62
Blaker, James, 295*n*94
*Blood Meridian* (McCarthy), 226
Blum, Gabriella, 143, 154
Body armor in Korean War, 238
Boko Haram, 28
Bolton, John, 243
Boot, Max, 252*n*7
Bosnian War, 246
Bowles, Samuel, 253*n*23
Brecht, Bertolt, 126
Brown v. United States, 174
Brussels Declaration, 124
Burr-Hamilton duel, 187
Bushido, 53; virtue ethics and, 75
Byzantine Empire, prisoner exchanges
    in, 27

Cambodia, war in, 111
Casualty rates, in modern wars, 279*n*5;
    classical Greek hoplite pitched battle,
    low in, 137
CCW. *See* UN Convention on Certain
    Conventional Weapons

Ceasefires: cooperation to end war quickly and, 143–44; cooperation to minimize damage and, 168–71; *hudna* as, 169–70, 284*n*14, 284*nn*16–17; *tahadiya* as, 169–70; terrorism and, 243; unintended consequences of, 168–71

Champions, soldiers as, 227, 233. *See also* Trial by combat

Chemical weapons, 264*n*101; as indiscriminate weapons, 113; League of Nations and, 85; weapons bans and, 62–63, 85–86

Chemical Weapons Convention, 62, 113

China, Chou period, 52–53, 262*nn*56–57, 262*nn*63–64

Chivalry, 51, 203–4, 261*nn*47–48; cooperation to minimize damage and, 122–23; professionalism and, 248–49

Christmas truces, World War I, 10. *See also* Live and let live

Churchill, Winston S., 63, 236, 240, 251*n*4

Cicero, 122, 176, 244, 299*n*22; declarations of war and, 58; legitimate soldiering and, 217; promises and, 75–76

Citizen, 80, *106*; citizen-soldier, 159–60, 288*n*5; democratic, 96, 271*n*19

Civilians, 295*n*92; cooperation for a fair fight and, 39, 258*n*10; cooperation to minimize damage and, 90–105, *106*, 162–66, 185, 195–96, 271*n*13, 271*nn*19–21, 272*n*22; democracies and, 96; drones and, 164–65, 269*n*161; economic and military involvement of, 95; guerrilla warfare and, 98; human rights and, 97, 288*n*4; just war theory and, 97; medical neutrality and, 293*n*77; political responsibility of, 96–97, 271*n*19; Taliban and, 99–100

Civil-military relations, *106*, 231, 273*n*39, 278*n*100; cooperation to end war quickly and, 159; democracies and, vii–viii

Civil War, American, x, 260*n*33, 275*n*64; cooperation to end war quickly and, 148; linear battle and, 167; live and let live and, 15, 254*n*43; LOAC, exclusion from, in, 129–32; military courts and, 277*n*97; mutual respect and, 67, 265*n*111; parole and, 276*n*73; pitched battle and, 203–4; prisoner exchanges and, 131, 148; procedural justice, perfect, and, 224–25; siege warfare and, 90–91, 148, 172–73; snipers and, 180–82

Clausewitz, Carl von, 273*n*39, 281*n*39; absolute war and, 90; cooperation to end war quickly and, 146; emotion, rationality, and interests and, 20–21; international law and, 128, 278*n*104; *jus ad bellum* and, 202; political tool, warfare as, and, 183–84, 199–200, 286*n*61; will, war as imposition of, and, 19

Clay, Henry, 59, 88, 270*n*178, 278*n*110

Clinton, Hillary, 25–26

Cobb, Thomas, 59

Code of Conduct for Members of the United States Armed Forces, 295*n*94

COIN. *See* Counterinsurgency

Collective agency, 255*n*58; jointness and, 22

Combatants, viii–ix; lawful versus unlawful, 215–18, 220–22; relationship between state and, *106*, 220; terrorism and "illegal enemy combatants," 242–45

Commissioned Officer's Creed of US Army, 74–75
Compensating behavior, 279n117, 285n39, 285n43; cooperation to minimize damage and, 132–34, 178; POWs and, 178; sports and, 177
Competition, 24; between businesses, 29. See also Sports
Comprehensive doctrines, 257n87; international law nonreliance on, 32, 241
Conflict resolution, war as tool of, ix–x, 197, 201–3; political purpose, 199–200; war's function for, 182–83
Contador, Alberto, 47. See also Misfortune
Convention, normative force of, 241–42
Conventional warfare: narrative biases towards, 6; origins of, 5–6
Cooperation. See specific topics
Cooperation (types of), 34–35; collective agency in, 22, 255n58; institutionalization and, 28–33; for same, but not shared, goals, 24; for shared goals, 23–24; strong versus weak, 21–23; for variety of goals, 24
Cooperation for a fair fight, 34, 161, 283n1, 285n26, 286n59; ambushes and, 55–57; areas of conflict and, 269n163; assassination and, 71, 166, 268n148; barbarians excluded by, 87, 269n172, 270n173; Bible and, 56, 58; chivalry and, 51, 261nn47–48; Chou period, China, and, 52–53, 262nn56–57, 262nn63–64; civilians and, 39, 258n10; cooperation to minimize damage and, 162–65, 185–86; deception and, 53–57, 162; declarations of war and, 57–58, 258n17, 263n84, 263nn87–88; dogfights, aerial, and, 50–51, 260n44;

drones and, 83–84, 164–65, 269nn163–64; duels and, 50–51, 77, 260nn41–42; empathy and, 76–77; false flags and, 58–60, 87–88; Geneva Conventions and, 54–55, 59–61, 262n67; hoplite warfare, classical Greek, and, 55–56, 263n76; *The Iliad* and, 40–41, 264n110; indiscriminate weapons and, 163; Indo-Pakistani War and, 49–50; Lieber Code and, 58–59, 71–72, 79–80, 263n76, 264n92, 265n120; LOAC and, 264n93; *Mahābhārata* and, 261n51; making it harder to win and, 88; Marshall on, 37–38; Mexican-American War and, 63–64, 264n107; misfortune and, 47–49; moral injury and, 78–81, 267n146; perfidy and, 58–61, 264n92; politicization of, 87–89; professionalism and, 65–74, 265n121; reciprocity and, 63–64; as search for significance, 184–85; sentries and, 56–57; snipers and, 36–37, 39–42, 68, 84, 163–65, 167–68, 179–82, 270n174; sports and, 42–49, 258n17, 258n19, 259n20, 259n24, 259nn30–32, 261n46, 268n156; torture and, 71; trench warfare and, 36–37, 69–71; uniforms and, 43, 54–55, 60, 77, 102, 262n67; unintended consequences of, 166–68, 191; virtue ethics and, 74–78, 266nn132–33; Walzer on, 36–37, 39–40, 56; weapons bans and, 61–63, 85–86, 162, 264n94, 269n169; World War I and, 69–71; World War II and, 37–38. See also Parity
Cooperation to end war quickly, 34, 135, 161; Bible and, 141; ceasefires and, 143–44; civil-military relations and, 159; Civil War, American, and, 148; Clausewitz on, 146; definitive

outcomes and, 139–41, 150, *152*, 153–57, 160; duels and, 141, 186–89; Frederick the Great on, 146, 149, 280*n*35, 280*n*37; Greek hoplite warfare, 136–41; human rights and, 158–59; *jus in bello* and, 159–60; Lieber Code and, 147; Machiavelli on, 145–46, 149, 155, 280*n*36; nation-states and, 159; nuclear warfare and, 150; pitched battle and, 136–41, 144–51, *152*, 153–60; pursuit of fleeing enemies and, 139–40; ritual warfare and, 141–43, 153–54, 282*n*60, 282*n*63; spectacle, war as, and, 159–60; sports and, 143; truces and, 143–44; weapons bans and, 189–90
Cooperation to minimize damage, 34, 161; Afghanistan, war in, and, 99–100, 105; assassination and, 123–27; ceasefires and, 168–71; chivalry and, 122–23; civilians and, 90–105, *106*, 162–66, 185, 195–96, 271*n*13, 271*nn*19–21, 272*n*22; compensating behavior and, 132–34, 178; cooperation for a fair fight and, 162–65, 185–86; deception and, 162; drones and, 164–65; Geneva Conventions and, 94–97, 104, 271*n*13, 273*n*36; ICRC and, 94, 273*n*42; indiscriminate weapons and, 109–13, 163; international law and, 93; limits of, 165–66; LOAC, exclusion from, and, 129–32; LOAC and, 185; making it harder to win and, 129, 168–71, 185–86; POWs and, 113–20, 131; responsibilities of soldiers and, 97–100; responsibility for war and, 126–27; siege warfare and, 90–94; snipers and, 163–65, 167–68; torture and, 107–9; uniforms and, 93, 100–105; unintended consequences of, 127–35, 168–71, 191; virtue ethics and, 122–23; Walzer and, 95; war on terror, US, and, 273*n*36; weapons bans and, 105, 107, 162

Counterinsurgency (COIN), 274*n*45; torture and, 107–8
Cromwell, Oliver, 101
Crow, Joseph Medicine, 238–39
Cuban Missile Crisis, 281*n*52
Cycling. *See* Misfortune; Tour de France

Dani of New Guinea, 153–54, 282*n*60
Deception: cooperation for a fair fight and, 53–57, 162; cooperation to minimize damage and, 162; Sun Tzu on, 55. *See also* Perfidy
Declarations of war, 258*n*17, 263*n*84; Cicero on, 58; *fetiales*, Roman, as, 57–58, 263*n*87; Hague Conventions on, 58; sports and, 263*n*88
Decolonization, necessity of violence in, 235–36
Definitive outcomes, 203; cooperation to end war quickly and, 139–41, 150, *152*, 153–57, 160; international law and, 204; ritual warfare and, 153–54
Delayed surrender, siege warfare and, 17
Democracies, 203, 231; civilians and, 96; civil-military relations and, vii–viii; Greek, 288*n*5, 289*n*12; military achievements of, 204, 224–25, 296*n*100; universal consistency and, 245–46; wealth and, 224–25
Detainee Treatment Act, US, 107
Deterrence, 13–14, 199, 281*n*52. *See also* Nuclear warfare
*Dharmaśāstra*, 51–52
Discrimination, 93–94, 273*n*36; international law and, 97; limits of, 165–66, 176. *See also* Cooperation to minimize damage

Distance of weapons, parity and, 82
Dogfights, aerial, 50–51, 67, 260n44
Double effect, 195–96, 288n2
Drones, 183; areas of conflict and, 269n163; civilians and, 164–65, 269n161; moral injury and, 268n158, 269n164; reciprocal risk and, 83–84, 269n164
Duels, 77, 234, 260n42; Burr-Hamilton duel as, 187; cooperation to end war quickly and, 141, 186–89; equal opportunity and, 50–51, 260n41; fencing and, 261n46; *The Iliad* and, 50, 187–88, 287n67; *monomachia* (duel warfare), 135, 141, 186–87, 234, 288n75; pitched battle and, 289n19; political, 186–89
Dunford, Joe, 269n164

Effective right, 193, 228; procedural justice and, 225–27
Eisenhower, Dwight D., 5
Empathy, 253n36; Army, US, and, 76–77; cooperation for a fair fight and, 76–77; sympathy as, 266n130; truces and, 12
Equal opportunity: duels and, 50–51, 260n41, 261n51; parity as, 50–55
Ethic of cooperation. *See specific topics*
Evolution, human, 35, 254n53; aggressiveness in, 8–9, 253n18; altruism in, 8–9, 253n23
Exile, 188, 287n70

Fairness, 42; automation and, 82; distance and, 81–83; procedural justice and, 43; risk and, 83–85; technology and, 166–68. *See also* Cooperation for a fair fight
False flags, 58–60, 87–88
Fanon, Frantz, 235–36

Feaver, Peter, 253n36
Ferguson, Patrick, 68
*Fetiales*, Roman, 57–58, 263n87
Fire suppression, unintended consequences of, 133–34
Flamethrowers, 86
Force multiplier, medical treatment as, 213
Foucault, Michel, 199–200, 273n33
Franklin, Benjamin, 173–74, 206
Frederick the Great, 101; cooperation to end war quickly and, 146, 149, 280n35, 280n37
French-Indian War, 7–8

Game theory, 240, 254n53; limits of, 20–21, 255n54; Vietnam War and, 255n54
Gandhi, Mahatma, 253n25
Gardner, Robert, 153
Gas. *See* Chemical weapons
Gelpi, Chris, 253n36
General Orders No. 100. *See* Lieber Code
Geneva Conventions, 149, 241, 276n74; Additional Protocol I of, 60–61, 94–95, 109–10, 215–16, 271n13; Additional Protocol II of, 221, 295n90–91; Common Article 3 of, 216, 221, 295n92; cooperation for a fair fight and, 54–55, 59–61, 262n67; cooperation to minimize damage and, 94–97, 104, 271n13, 273n36; First Protocol of, 101–2; Fourth, 94; *jus in bello* and, 215; on lawful combatants, 217–18; moral injury and, 80; perfidy and, 59–61, 80; POWs and, 115–16, 120, 215–16, 275n62, 275n64, 275nn70; torture and, 107; uniforms and, 101–2, 216; virtue ethics and, 266n132; weapons bans, 62, 85, 109

[332] INDEX

Geneva Protocol, 1925, 62, 85
Gentili, Alberico, 173, 200–1, 293n78
Gertz, Nolen, 38
*Gilgamesh and Aga*, 57
Gladwell, Malcolm, 298n2
Gouré, Leon, 92
Graves, Robert, 36
Gray, J. Glenn, 11, 237, 251n3, 253n36, 298n6, 299n16
Greeks, classical. *See* Hoplite warfare
Gross, Michael, 212
Grossman, Dave, 258n6
Grotius, Hugo, 97, 114, 125, 290n35
Group agency. *See* Collective agency
Guantánamo Bay, 216–17, 221–22, 295n93
Guerrilla warfare, 281n50; civilians and, 98; French-Indian War and, 7–8; as historical norm, 5, 252n7; Mexican-American War and, 64; Peloponnesian War and, 7; Revolutionary War, American, and, 7
Gulf War, 151, 282n53
Guter, Donald J., 107, 109

Habits, 167, 284n9
Haftlang, Zahed, 9–10, 253n25
Hagel, Chuck, 84
Hague Conventions: assassination and, 124, 276n84; declarations of war and, 58; indiscriminate weapons and, 274n49; neutrality doctrine and, 293n78; POWs and, 115; weapons bans and, 33, 62, 107, 109–10
Hallett, Brien, 263n88
*Hamdan v. Rumsfeld*, 221
Hamilton, Alexander, 175–76, 187
Hamilton, W. D., 14
Hansen, Chester B., 180
Hanson, Victor Davis, 242; democracies, Greek, and, 288n5; political elites and, 277n92; shock battle and, 136, 139–40, 152, 156, 277n92, 279n13, 280n27, 281n49, 288n5
Hastings, Max, 167, 181, 286n51
Hedges, Chris, 4, 78, 251n3
Heider, Karl G., 153
Hemingway, Ernest, 66
Hezbollah, 243
Hippocratic Oath, 72
Hitchcock, Ethan Allen, 130–31
Hitler, Adolf, 63
Hobbes, Thomas, 8
Holquist, Peter, 205
Homer. *See Iliad, The*
Honor, 268n150; moral injury and, 77–81. *See also* Virtue ethics
Hoplite warfare, classical Greek, 55–56, 87, 136–41, 152, 263n76, 289n12; farmers as soldiers in, 138; resources, limited, and, 138, 154–55; structural cooperation and, 197; trade-offs in, 151–52. *See also* Shock battle, classical Greek
*Hudna*, 284n14, 284nn16–17; *tahadiya* versus, 169–70
Humanitarian aid, 285n24
Humanitarianism, 35, 112, 150; expectations for, 164, 249; humanitarian aid, "pauses," and corridors, 129, 133, 168–71, 285n24; international humanitarian law, 124, 273n42, 274n55; making it harder to win the war, 178–79; motive of, 146–49, 172, 188–89, 232, 235, 241, 248; paradox of, 173–76, 249; POWs and, 119–20; unintended consequences, 130–32, 133, 172–73. *See also* Medical immunity; Medical treatment
Human rights, 235, 241, 248–49; civilians and, 97, 288n4; cooperation

Human rights (*continued*)
to end war quickly and, 158–59; just war theory, secular, and, xii; limits of, 248–49; POWs and, 119–20; Universal Declaration of Human Rights and, 107
Hume, David, 21–22
Hunting, 258*n*17, 286*n*59; war as, 39–40

ICBL. *See* International Campaign to Ban Landmines
ICRC. *See* International Committee of the Red Cross
ICRC Commentary, 109–11
Ignatieff, Michael, 241
*Iliad, The* (Homer), 2–4; ceasefires in, 169; cooperation for a fair fight and, 40–41, 264*n*110; duels in, 50, 187–88, 287*n*67; sports in, 44
Immunity: civilian, 93–100, 101–2, 106; medical personnel and, 206, 212–14; political elites and, 123–27. *See also* Civilians, political responsibility of; Moral equality of combatants; Moral inequality of combatants; Responsibility for war
Indian Wars, 246
Indirect communication, 21–22
Indiscriminate weapons: artillery as, 86; biological weapons as, 113; chemical weapons as, 113; cooperation for a fair fight and, 163; cooperation to minimize damage and, 109–13, 163; Hague Conventions and, 274*n*49; ICRC Commentary on, 109–11; mines as, 110–13, 163, 274*n*52, 274*n*55, 275*n*58; nuclear weapons as, 111, 113, 150; weapons bans and, 109–13, 274*n*55, 275*n*58; World War I and, 109–10; World War II and, 109, 274*n*48

Indo-Pakistani War, 49–50. *See also* Rann of Kutch
Injury, sports and, 46. *See also* Moral injury
Institutionalization, cooperation (types of) and, 28–33. *See also* International law; Structural cooperation
Institutional stability, perfidy and, 60–61
International Campaign to Ban Landmines (ICBL), 111–12
International Committee of the Red Cross (ICRC), 188; cooperation to minimize damage and, 94, 273*n*42; ICRC Commentary by, 109–11; Interpretative Guidance on the Notion of Direct Participation in Hostilities by, 295*n*92; medical neutrality and, 206
International Covenant on Civil and Political Rights, 107
International law, 28–30, *194*, 278*n*105; aggressive wars and, 205, 291*n*46; Clausewitz on, 128, 278*n*104; comprehensive doctrines, nonreliance on, 32, 241; as cooperation for variety of goals, 24; cooperation to minimize damage and, 93; customary, 94, 124; definitive outcomes and, 204; discrimination and, 97; efficacy and inefficacy of, 128, 147, 198; *jus ad bellum* and, 35, 204–6, 222, 227–29, 235, 248; *jus in bello* and, 34, 205–6, 227–29, 235, 248; legal specificity of, 32, 241; legitimacy and, 215–22; LOAC and, 32; making it harder to win and, ix, 33; medical immunity and, 206; medical neutrality and, 206; self-defense and, 222, 227, 229–31; terrorism rejecting, 243–44;

unintended consequences of, 127–34, 157–58; universalizability of, 31–32, 241. *See also* Geneva Conventions; Hague Conventions

International Society of Military Law and the Law of War, 274*n*52

Interpretative Guidance on the Notion of Direct Participation in Hostilities, 295*n*92

Intramilitary conflicts, 254*n*50; live and let live and, 12–13, 17–19, 30, 257*n*84

Iran-Iraq War, 9–10

Iraq War: medical neutrality and, 207; mortality rates in, 293*n*76

Iroquoia, 142–43

ISIS, 219

Israeli military: medical neutrality and, 206, 209–10, 292*n*54; prisoner exchanges and, 28

Iterated games, trench warfare and, 13

Jackson, Andrew, 58–59, 87–88, 278*n*110

Jointness, 21; collective agency and, 22; parametric action and, 22, 255*n*57, 256*n*61; strategic action and, 22, 256*n*61

Jones, Simon, 264*n*101

Judicial duel. *See* Trial by combat

*Jus ad bellum*, 55, 157, 172, 192–93, 215, 291*n*49, 297*n*110; Clausewitz and, 202; international law and, 35, 204–6, 222, 227–29, 235, 248; moral inequality of combatants and, 232, 244, 300*n*24; proportionality and, 291*n*48; revisionism on, 231, 297*n*115

*Jus in bello*, 81, 182, 192–93, 222; cooperation to end war quickly and, 159–60; Geneva Conventions and, 215; international law and, 34, 205–6, 227–29, 235, 248

*Just and Unjust Wars* (Walzer), vii, 36–37

Justice. *See Jus ad bellum*; *Jus in bello*; *Jus victoriae*; Procedural justice

Just war theory, 192, *194*, 228, 240, 289*n*18; civilians and, 97; double effect in, 195–96, 288*n*3; military necessity and, 195–96, 288*n*3; proportionality in, 195–96; revisionism in, 231, 297*n*115; right intention, principle of, and, xi–xii, 195–96; secularization of, xi–xiii, 33–34, 97

*Jus victoriae*, 201–3

Kant, Immanuel, 158, 267*n*144; aesthetics of war and, 239–40; assassination and, 125–26; moral injury and, 79–80; virtue ethics and, 267*n*138

Karachi Agreement, 144

Keegan, John, 156

Kellen, Konrad, 290*n*41

Kent, James, 174

Khalidi, Rashid, 170

Kierman, Frank A., Jr., 258*n*17, 267*n*146

King, Martin Luther, Jr., 277*n*96

Kipling, Rudyard, 65–66

Klay, Phil, 207

Korean DMZ, 144, 155

Korean War, 184, 258*n*8, 286*n*63; body armor and, 238; live and let live and, 15–17, 254*n*44; medical neutrality and, 208–10; mortality rates in, 293*n*76; POWs and, 238, 295*n*94; purpose, loss of, in, 238

Krentz, Peter, 139

Lamb, Dean Ivan, 260*n*42

Lawful combatants: Geneva Conventions on, 217–18. *See also* Unlawful enemy combatants

Law of Armed Conflict (LOAC), 32, 185, 264n93; exclusion from, 129–32
*Law of Nations, The* (Vattel), 59, 116
Law of War Manual, US Department of Defense, 80–81, 268n150
Lawrence, T. E., 118–19
Laws of war, exclusion from, 87–88, 129–32
League of Nations, chemical weapons and, 85
Legal proceeding, pitched battle as, 200–3, 289nn18–19, 290n23, 290n35
Legal specificity of international law, 32, 241
Legitimacy, 273n35; Cicero on, 217; cooperation providing, 25–28; international law and, 215–22; of nation-states, 295n89; nation-states defining, 35, 193, 196, 218–22, 247; nonstate actors, marginalization of, and, 220–22; qualifications for, 215–16; of state participation in war, 293n78; territorial sovereignty and, 221; trial by combat and, 222–29; unlawful enemy combatants excluded from, 216–22, 294nn81–82, 295n93
Leningrad, World War II siege of, 90–91
Liberal democracies. *See* Democracies
Lieber, Francis, 147–48
Lieber Code, 195, 246; adverse effects of, 172–73; assassination and, 124, 176; cooperation for a fair fight and, 58–59, 71–72, 79–80, 263n76, 264n92, 265n120; cooperation to end war quickly and, 147; medical immunity and, 206; moral equality of combatants and, 121; neutrality doctrine and, 293n78; POWs and, 114–15, 117, 278n114; private property protections and, 174; race and, 130–31; responsibility for war and, 127
Liggett, Phil, 47
Lincoln, Abraham, 129–31, 175–76, 187, 224–25, 275n64, 278n114
Linear battle (*bataille rangée*), 55, 103, 166–67, 191, 263n74, 283n8
Live and let live: Civil War, American, and, 15, 254n43; intramilitary conflicts and, 12–13, 17–19, 30, 257n84; Korean War and, 15–17, 254n44; rule-following versus, 30; self-interest and, 18–19, 24–25; soldiers motivations to, 17–18; trench warfare and, 10, 13–15, 18, 24–25, 157, 254n42; World War I and, 15–16, 18–19, 24–25, 157, 247, 254n42, 257n84; World War II and, 10–13
LOAC. *See* Law of Armed Conflict
*Lusitania*, RMS, sinking of, 271n21
Lussu, Emilio, 254n50; snipers and, 39–41; trench warfare and, 18, 36, 69–70, 254n42
Luttwak, Edward, 170–71

MacArthur, Douglas, 98–99
Machiavelli, Niccolò, 32–33; cooperation to end war quickly and, 145–46, 149, 155, 280n36
MAD. *See* Mutually assured destruction
*Mahābhārata*, 261n51
Making it harder to win, 23, 191; cooperation for a fair fight and, 88; cooperation to minimize damage and, 129, 168–71, 185–86; international law and, ix, 33; resources, limited, and, 178–79; uniforms and, 102–4
Malory, Thomas, 51, 261nn47–48, 267n133
Mao Tse-tung, 53

Mardonios, 145
Marines, US, NCO's Creed of, 73
Marshall, S. L. A., 37–38, 69, 258n6, 258n8
M.A.S.H., 254n44
Mattis, James N., 108
Mauvillon, Éléazar de, 202
May, Andrew, 247
McCarthy, Cormac, 226
McClellan, George B., 49
McCullough, David, 7
McMahan, Jeff, 231, 233
McRaven, William, 79
Medical immunity, 293n72; international law and, 206; Lieber Code and, 206; normative questions regarding, 211–15; structural implications of, 214–16
Medical neutrality, 291n50, 292n71; Afghanistan, war in, and, 207–8, 210; civilians and, 293n77; ICRC and, 206; international law and, 206; Iraq War and, 207; Israeli military and, 206, 209–10, 292n54; Korean War and, 208–10; normative questions regarding, 211–15; political tool, warfare as, and, 209; POWs and, 207–11, 214, 244; structural implications of, 214–16; World War II and, 208; wounded soldiers and, 116, 206–11, 292n54
Medical personnel as military targets, x, 211–15
Medical treatment, effectiveness of: force multiplier, 213; morale and, 213; soldiers returned to field by, 212–14, 293n74, 293n76
Meshaal, Khaled, 170
Mexican-American War: cooperation for a fair fight and, 63–64, 264n107; guerrilla warfare and, 64

Mexican Revolution, 260n44
Military courts, Civil War, American, and, 277n97
Military necessity, 195–96, 288n3; POWs and, 116–17. See also Battle function
Mill, John Stuart, 200
Mines, 163, 274n52, 275n58; weapons bans and, 110–13, 274n55
Misfortune, 46, 259nn31–32; types of, 47–49
Moltke, Helmuth Karl Bernhard Graf von, 188–89, 236–37, 240, 288n72
Monomachia (duel warfare). See Duels
Moore, Harold G., 184
Moore, Michael, 180
Morale, medical treatment, effectiveness of, and, 213
Moral equality of combatants, viii–ix, 97, 166, 285n26; Lieber Code and, 121; nation-states and, 120–22, 230; POWs and, 229–33; trial by combat and, 227; Walzer on, 230–31, 297n116
Moral inequality of combatants, 231; costs of, 231–33; *jus ad bellum* and, 232, 244, 300n24; POWs and, 232–33. See also Revisionism
Moral injury, 267n142, 267n146; assassination and, 79–80; drones and, 268n158, 269n164; Geneva Conventions and, 80; honor and, 79–81; Kant on, 79–80; torture and, 108–9; virtue ethics and, 78
Mortality rates, list of, 293n76. See also Casualty rates
*Morte d'Arthur, Le* (Malory), 51, 261nn47–48, 267n133
Murder, 40, 56; soldiering versus, 69–72
Mutually assured destruction (MAD), 281n52. See also Nuclear warfare
Mutual respect, 65–69, 265n111
My Lai massacre, Vietnam War, 98

Nakajima, Sadao, 276n80
Napoleonic Wars, 17–18, 31, 101, 146, 166–67, 283n8
National Security Agency, US (NSA), 76
Nation-states, 31, 97, 190–91; cooperation to end war quickly and, 159; legitimacy defined by, 35, 193, 196, 218–22, 247, 294n89; legitimacy of, 295n89; moral equality of combatants and, 120–22, 230; terrorism committed by, 242; uniforms and, 101; Westphalian (nation-state) system, 221, 242
Natural disasters, compensating behavior and, 132–33, 279n117
Natural law conception of war, 228–29, 300n27
NCO's Creed of US Marines, 73
Neff, Stephen, 119–21
Neutrality doctrine, 293n78
Nietzsche, Friedrich, 237
9/11 attacks, 96
Noncooperative warfare, 240–41; terrorism as, 242–45
Nonlethal weapons, 288n75
Nonpenal killing and detention of POWs, 117–19
Nonstate actors, marginalization of, 220–22
Normative obligations for future cooperation, 245
Norms, 167, 284n9, 298n4, 300n27
Norms of war, contemporary, 167, 193, 194, 195
NSA. *See* National Security Agency
Nuclear warfare, 111, 113; casualties in, 272n22; Cuban Missile Crisis and, 281n52; Mutually assured destruction (MAD) and, 281n52; World War II and, 150

Nuremberg Trials, 291n46
Nyon Arrangement, 110, 264n51

Obama, Barack, 27, 256n66
Ober, Josiah, 139, 279n13, 288n5
*Old Man and the Sea, The* (Hemingway), 66
Olympics, ancient, 44
*Omertà*, 10
*On Duties* (Cicero), 122
Orwell, George, 36–37
Ottawa Treaty, 111–12, 274n55
Overy, Richard, 271n14
Oxford Manual, 124

Panetta, Leon, 83
Parametric action, jointness and, 22, 255n57, 256n61
Paris Declaration Respecting Maritime Law, 278n105
Parity, 161; distance of weapons and, 82; as equal opportunity, 50–55, 261n51; inconsistencies in, 81–89; of randomness, 179–82; reciprocal risk and, 83–85; of risk and opportunity, 49–50; sports and, 44–49, 182; technological disparities and, 81–85, 268n153
Parole of POWs, 114–16, 276n73
Partisans, 299n20
*Patton*, 66–67
Patton, George S., 179
Peace of Westphalia, 114, 275n59
Pegler, Martin, 181, 270n174
Peloponnesian War, 7, 57
Pequot War, 142
Perfidy: cooperation for a fair fight and institutional stability, 58–61, 264n92; Geneva Conventions and, 59–61, 80; institutional stability and, 60–61. *See also* Assassination; False flags; Poison

Pinker, Steven, 35
Pirates, 244, 299n20, 299n22
Pitched battle, 281n50, 282n54, 284n10; aesthetic appeal of, 136, 145; brevity of, 137–39, 150; casualty rates low in, 137; Civil War, American, and, 203–4; cooperation to end war quickly and, 136–41, 144–51, 152, 153–60; decisiveness of, 139–41, 150, 160; duels and, 289n19; Gulf War as, 151, 282n53; influence of, 144–53; as legal proceeding, 200–3, 289nn18–19, 290n23, 290n35; pursuit of fleeing enemies and, 139–40; simplicity of, 137; as spectacle, 159–60; structural cooperation and, 197; Vietnam War and, 151
Plato, 32
Poison, 79–80
Political elites, 277n92; assassination, as targets of, 125–27; duels between, 186–89; Hanson on, 277n92; responsibility and accountability of, 126–27, 176–77, 186–89, 278n100, 297n110
Political responsibility of civilians, 96–97, 271n19
Political tool, warfare as, 183–84, 199–200, 286n61; medical neutrality and, 209; structural cooperation and, 197–204
Polybius, 56
Positivist conception of war, 228–29, 300n27
POWs. See Prisoners of war
*Princess Bride, The*, 65
Prisoner exchanges, 25–28, 115, 121; Civil War, American, and, 131, 148; Taliban and, 25–27, 243, 256nn64–66
Prisoners of war (POWs), 191, 275n59, 275n69; Civil War and, 129–32; Code of Conduct for Members of the United States Armed Forces on, 295n94; compensating behavior and, 178; cooperation to minimize damage and, 113–20, 131; disincentives to capture, 119; exclusion from protections of, 129–32; Geneva Conventions and, 115–16, 120, 215–16, 275n62, 275n64, 275nn70; Hague Conventions and, 115; home rulers paying for maintenance of, 275n68; humane treatment of, arguments for, 116–20; human rights and, 119–20; Korean War and, 238, 295n94; Lieber Code and, 114–15, 117, 278n114; medical neutrality and, 207–11, 214, 244; military necessity and, 116–17; moral equality of combatants and, 229–33; moral inequality of combatants and, 232–33; nonpenal killing and detention and, 117–19; parole and, 114–16, 276n73; resources consumed by, 114–19, 178–79, 191, 210–11, 232, 276n73; Vietnam War and, 295n94; World War II and, 178–79
Pritchett, W. Kendrick, 57, 141
Privacy, respect for, 76
Private property protections: Lieber Code and, 174; Revolutionary War, American, and, 172–73; slavery and, 174–76; unintended consequences of, 173–76
Procedural justice: effective right and, 225–27; fairness and, 43; pure versus perfect, 223–25, 296n96; trial by combat and, 223–25
Professional ethics, 72, 265n121, 266n122; Army, US, and, 73–74; Marines, US, and, 73

Professionalism: battle function and, 71–72; chivalry and, 248–49; mutual respect and, 65–69, 265n111; professional ethics and, 72–74, 265n121, 266n122; soldiering, murdering versus, and, 69–71; uniforms and, 101–3
Promises, 75–76
Proportionality, 195–96; *jus ad bellum* and, 291n48
Pursuit of fleeing enemies, 139–40

al Qaeda, 216–19

Race, Lieber Code and, 130–31
Ramadan, Taha Yassin, 186
Randomness, parity of, 179–82
Rann of Kutch, 49–50
Rationality, Clausewitz on, 21–22
Rawls, John, 257n87
Reciprocal risk: drones and, 83–84, 269n164; parity and, 83–85; snipers and, 84
Reciprocity: cooperation for a fair fight and, 63–64; torture and, 107
Reisman, W. Michael, 171
Remarque, Erich Maria, 4–5, 14–15, 126
Remotely piloted aircraft (RPA). *See* Drones
Renaissance Italy, siege warfare and, 17
Resources, limited: aggressiveness and, 8–9; hoplite warfare, classical Greek, and, 138, 154–55; making it harder to win and, 178–79; POWs consuming, 114–18, 178–79, 191, 210–11, 232, 276n73
Respect. *See* Mutual respect
Responsibilities of soldiers: cooperation to minimize damage and, 97–100; privileges to kill in exchange for, 97–100

Responsibility for war: civilian and democratic responsibility, 96–97; Lieber Code and, 127; political elites and, 126–27, 176–77, 186–89, 278n100, 297n110
Restraint. *See* Duels; Snipers
Revisionism, 230, 297n115; costs of, 231–33. *See also* Moral inequality of combatants
Revolutionary War, American, 270n174; Articles of War for, 252n14; guerrilla warfare and, 7; private property protections and, 172–73
Rheault, Robert, xii–xiii
Rice, Grantland, 258n19
Richthofen, Manfred von, 51, 67
Right intention, principle of, xi–xii, 195–96
Risk and opportunity, parity of, 49–50
Ritual warfare, 141, 238–39, 280n20, 282n63; Dani of New Guinea and, 153–54, 282n60; definitive outcomes and, 153–54; Iroquoia and, 142–43
Roy, Kaushik, 261n51
RPA. *See* Drones
Rule-following, 29, 290n23, 298n4; live and let live versus, 30; as a signal, 64, 105, 244
Russo-Japanese War, 58

Saint Petersburg Declaration, 189–90, 288n74
Samurai, code for, 75; films, 53, 83, 122–23
Schelling, Thomas, 20, 22, 298n4
Schleck, Andy, 47–48. *See also* Misfortune
Schmitt, Carl, 299n20
Schofield, John M., 148–49
Scott, Winfield, 64
SEALs, US Navy, 79

Second Lateran Council, 264n94
Self-defense, 291n48; domestic, ix; international law and, 205, 222, 227, 229–31
Self-interest, 23; live and let live and, 18–19, 24–25
Self-sacrifice. *See* Altruism
Seminoles, 1818 campaign against, 58–59, 87–88, 270n178
Seminole Wars, 1840s, 131
Sentries, cooperation for a fair fight and, 56–57
*Seven Military Classics*, 267n146, 273n35
*Seven Samurai, The*, 53, 83
Seven Years War, 275n68
Shay, Jonathan, 78
Sherman, William T., 90–91, 148, 172–73
Shock battle, classical Greek, 137–38, 144–45, 149–50, 152, 154–55, 157–60, 234; Hanson on, 136, 139–40, 152, 156, 277n92, 279n13, 280n27, 281n49, 288n5; structural cooperation and, 197. *See also* Pitched battle
Shogunates, Japanese, 101
*Siege of Leningrad, The* (Gouré), 92
Siege warfare, 278n116, 284n10; Civil War, American, and, 90–91, 148, 172–73; cooperation to minimize damage and, 90–94; delayed surrender and, 17; Renaissance Italy and, 17; Trojan War and, 2–3; World War II and Siege of Leningrad, 91–92
Sino-Vietnamese war, 144
Slavery, 130–31, 278n114; private property protections and, 174–76. *See also* Prisoners of war, exclusion from protections of
Smith, Adam, 266n130
Smith, Jacob, 246
Smith, Vaughan, 207–8, 213–14

Snipers: cooperation for a fair fight and, 36–37, 39–42, 68, 84, 163–65, 167–68, 179–82, 270n174; cooperation to minimize damage and, 163–65, 167–68; Lussu on, 39–41; reciprocal risk and, 84; reputation of and animosity toward, 180–82; World War II and, 286n51
Soldier-civilian-state relationship, 106, 273n39
Soldiering, murdering versus, 69–72
Solomon, Norman, 278n116
Sovereignty, 205, 219–21, 256n74; legitimacy of, 218–19; territory and, 221. *See also* Nation-states
Spectacle, war as, 159–60
Sporting behavior, 44–47, 50, 259n20. *See also* Fairness
Sports, 42–43, 258n17, 258n19, 259n20, 259n30, 268n156, 290n21; compensating behavior in, 177; cooperation to end war quickly and, 143; declarations of war and, 263n88; fencing as, 261n46; *The Iliad* and, 44; injury and, 46; misfortune and, 47–49, 259nn31–32; parity and, 44–49, 182; rule violations in, 259n24; Tour de France and, 46–48, 259nn25–26
Stanton, Edwin, 275n64
*Star Trek*, 65, 287n69
Stendhal, 283n8
Stigler, Franz, 9
Stimson, Henry, 76
Strasser, Peter, 271n20
Strategic action, jointness and, 22, 256n61
Structural cooperation: conflict resolution, war as tool of, and, 200; pitched battle as, 197; political tool, warfare as, and, 197–204

Submarines, 109–10, 271n21, 274n51
Summers, Harry G., Jr., 151
Sumner, Charles, 72
Sun Tzu, 53; deception and, 55
Supreme emergency ethics, 247, 300n26
Surprise. *See* Ambushes; Declarations of war; Perfidy
Sympathy, 266n130
Syria, civil war in, 63, 94, 219

Tacitus, 265n121
*Tahadiya*, hudna versus, 169–70
Taliban, 207–8, 210, 256n67; civilians and, 99–100; prisoner exchanges and, 25–27, 243, 256nn64–66; as unlawful enemy combatants, 216, 218–19
Targeting, 163–65, 283n3; assassination and, 124–26; fairness versus, 166–68
Technology, effects of, 63, 147, 166–68; accuracy versus fairness, 163–68; interaction between habits, norms, and, 167, 284n9; parity and, 81–85, 268n53
Terrorism, 196; antiterrorism security measures and, 133; ceasefires and, 243; Hezbollah and, 243; international law rejected by, 243–44; nation-states committing, 242; 9/11 attacks and, 96; as noncooperative warfare, 242–45; partisans and, 299n20; al Qaeda and, 216–19; unlawful enemy combatants and, 216–17; war on terror, US, and, 273n36. *See also* Taliban
Thompson, Hugh, Jr., 98–99
Thucydides, 7
Torture, 295n94; COIN and, 107–8; cooperation for a fair fight and, 71; cooperation to minimize damage and, 107–9; Detainee Treatment Act and, 107; Geneva Conventions and, 107; moral injury and, 108–9; reciprocity and, 107
Tour de France, 46–48, 259nn25–26. *See also* Misfortune
Trade-offs, 136, 140, 142, 151–53, 188, 220
Treacherous methods of assassination, 123–24
Treaty of Hudaybiyyah, 284n14
Treaty of Versailles, 62
Trench warfare: cooperation for a fair fight and, 36–37, 69–71; iterated games and, 13; live and let live and, 10, 13–14, 18, 24–25, 157, 254n42; Lussu on, 18, 36, 69–70, 254n42; truces and, 10–13
Trial by combat, 297n106; champions, soldiers as, and, 227, 233; legitimacy and, 222–29; modern warfare as, 193, 222–29; moral equality of combatants and, 227; procedural justice and, 223–25
Trial by ordeal, 227–28
Trinquier, Roger, 67
Trojan War, 4; siege warfare and, 2–3; women, 2–3
Truce flags, 58–60. *See also* False flags
Truces: cooperation to end war quickly and, 143–44; empathy and, 12; trench warfare and, 10–13; War of 1812 and, 256n62; World War I and, 10; World War II and, 10–13. *See also* Hudna; *Tahadiya*
Truman, Harry, 272n24

UAV. *See* Drones
Ullrich, Jan, 46–48, 259n26. *See also* Misfortune
UN Charter, 205
UN Convention Against Torture and Other Cruel, Inhuman, or

Degrading Treatment or Punishment, 107
Unconventional warfare. *See* Guerrilla warfare; Terrorism
UN Convention on Certain Conventional Weapons (CCW), 110
Uniforms, 30; Afghanistan, war in, and, 105; cooperation for a fair fight and, 43, 54–55, 60, 77, 102, 262*n*67; cooperation to minimize damage and, 93, 100–5; enforcing use of, 104–5; Geneva Conventions and, 101–2, 216; historical evolution of, 100–1; making it harder to win and, 102–4; nation-states and, 101; professionalism and, 101–3; shogunates, Japanese, and, 101; virtue ethics and, 77
Unintended consequences, 287*n*69; adverse effects as, 172–73; of ceasefires, 168–71; of cooperation for a fair fight, 166–68, 191; of cooperation to minimize damage, 127–35, 168–71, 191; of international law, 127–34, 157–58; of private property protections, 173–76. *See also* Compensating behavior
United Nations Charter, 124
Universal consistency, democracies and, 245–46
Universal Declaration of Human Rights, 107
Universalizability of international law, 31–32, 241
Unlawful enemy combatants: legitimate warfare excluded from, 216–22, 294*nn*81–82, 295*n*93; terrorism and, 216–17
Unmanned aerial vehicles (UAV). *See* Drones
US-Iraq War, first. *See* Gulf War

Vattel, Emerich de, 59, 80, 116, 123, 173
Vietnam War, xii–xiii, 184, 258*n*8, 277*n*92, 290*n*41, 298*n*2; game theory and, 255*n*54; mortality rates in, 293*n*76; My Lai massacre in, 98; pitched battle and, 151; POWs and, 295*n*94
Virtue ethics, 267*n*133; Army, US, and, 74–77; battle function and "function argument" and, 77–78; Bushido as, 75; cooperation to minimize damage and, 122–23; Geneva Conventions and, 266*n*132; Kant on, 267*n*138; moral injury and, 78; privacy, respect for, and, 76; promises and, 75–76; uniforms and, 77
Vitoria, Francisco de, 97

Wager of battle. *See* Trial by combat
Walsh, Courtney, 45
Walzer, Michael, 288*n*3, 300*n*26; cooperation for a fair fight and, 36–37, 39–40, 56; cooperation to minimize damage and, 95; moral equality of combatants and, 230–31, 297*n*116; practical import of, vii
War: aesthetics of, 136, 145, 237, 239; collectivization in, 297*n*116; search for significance in, 184–85, 235–40, 251*n*3, 298*n*6, 299*n*16; types and outcomes of, 152; veneration of, 235–37, 239–40, 298*n*6, 299*n*16. *See also* Conflict resolution; Legal proceeding; Structural cooperation
War function, battle function and, 88, 182–84, 189–90
War of 1812, 256*n*62
War on terror, US, 273*n*36
Washington, George, 7–8, 68, 252*n*14
Wealth of democracies, 224–25

Weapons. *See* Indiscriminate weapons; Nonlethal weapons; Weapons bans
Weapons bans, 61, 269*n*169; biological weapons and, 62–63; Biological Weapons Convention and, 62; CCW and, 110; chemical weapons and, 62–63, 85–86; Chemical Weapons Convention and, 62, 113; cooperation to end war quickly and, 189–90; cooperation to minimize damage and, 105, 107, 162; Geneva Conventions and, 62, 85, 109; Geneva Protocol, 1925, and, 62, 85; Hague Conventions and, 62, 107, 109–10; indiscriminate weapons and, 109–13, 274*n*55, 275*n*58; mines and, 110–13, 274*n*55; Ottawa Treaty as, 111–12, 274*n*55; Saint Petersburg Declaration as, 189–90; Second Lateran Council as, 264*n*94; World War I and, 62–63, 86; World War II and, 63
Weber, Max, 265*n*121
Wees, Hans van, 139
Westphalia, Treaty of. *See* Nation-states; Sovereignty
Wheaton, Henry, 174
Wheeler, William, 17–18, 146, 283*n*8
Whitman, James Q., 201–4, 234–35, 289*nn*18–19, 297*n*106
WikiLeaks, 76
Will, war as imposition of, 19
Willbanks, James, 255*n*54
Williams, Roger, 142
Witt, John Fabian, 90–91, 130, 172–74, 278*n*105, 280*n*20

Women in Trojan War, 2–3
World War I, ix, 254*n*50, 271*nn*20–21; altruism in, 10; Churchill and, 251*n*4; cooperation for a fair fight and, 69–71; indiscriminate weapons and, 109–10; live and let live and, 15–16, 18–19, 24–25, 157, 247, 254*n*42, 257*n*84; mortality rates in, 293*n*76; truces and, 10; weapons bans inspired by, 62–63, 86
World War II, 238–39, 268*n*153, 271*nn*13–14; altruism in, 9; Churchill and, 251*n*4; cooperation for a fair fight and, 37–38; indiscriminate weapons and, 109, 274*n*48; live and let live and, 10–13; medical neutrality and, 208; mortality rates in, 293*n*76; nuclear warfare and, 150; POWs and, 178–79; siege warfare and, 90–92; snipers and, 286*n*51; truces and, 10–13; weapons bans and, 63
Wounded soldiers, 119; Chou period, China, and, 52–53; killing of, 276*n*74; medical neutrality and, 116, 206–11, 292*n*54; medical treatment, effectiveness of, and, 212–14, 293*n*74, 293*n*76

Yakusho, Koji, 122–23
Yamashita, Tomoyuki, 272*n*24
Yoo, John, 217
Yousef, Hassan, 170

Zone of combat. *See* Battlefield
*Zuo-zhuan*, 52–53, 262*nn*56–57, 262*nn*63–64